DEAR MR BIGELOW

Bournemouth.

March 21st 1953.

Dear Mr.Bigelow,

If ever you get a nice warm fire burning in Casa
Bigelow - one that is not authorised, I mean - just let me
know and I'll come over right away with my little stirrup
pump, and my even littler hatchet, and put it out for you.
Me, thoroughly experienced putter-out-of-fires. Since last
Saturday. About which I will now proceed to tell you.

Eleven years ago, or thereabouts, I reluctantly
bought myself a pair of slacks for fire-watching and air-
raids in general. I dislike women in trousers, and myself
especially, but they have their uses in such troublesome
times. Since 1945, however, mine have reposed with moth
balls in the rag-box. Two weeks ago I fished them out,
cleaned and pressed them, and to my joy discovered they still
fit! I think they must fit a little more closely than
when they were new, for I know my weight is up fifteen
pounds or more over war-time years; but they fitted well
enough.

So I clad myself in them on Saturday and rushed
headlong after luncheon, full of good food and peppermint,
to the place where the local Corporation people burn out
refuse, and where a shed is placed at the disposal of the
Civil Defence crowd for training such as me. I was the
only one (apart from two men) to arrive wearing trousers,
but we all finished up wearing navy blue boiler suits (men
for the use of) so I was practically the only comfortable
woman present. Especially as I have such large feet they
almost fitted the rubber gum-boots we were also made to wear.
Two of the women have tiny little feet, and in spite of stuffing
the toes of the gum-boots with their gloves, they could only
proceed by shuffling along. When it was their turn to be
No.4 in the team (the water fetcher) we had to hold up the
fire until they had shuffled the fifty yards or more to the
water faucet and back.

Being silly-like, and nobody else showing any signs of
volunteering, I went first. There was a small tin shed,
with a corridor at the back and a door opening from this into
the main room. This latter was fitted up with a furnishing
scheme I don't think Park Avenue would approve of. There was
a large armchair, sort of greeny-black in colour and circa 1900
in years; there was a sofa of completely indeterminate shade
and no pedigree whatsoever; there was a little sort of table,
and there was a pile of wood shavings. All the furniture was
covered with wood shavings too, I would mention. In one corner
was a small incendiary bomb which the instructors lit, as they
did also the piles of wood shavings. When they thought it
was nice and warm and smokey one of them yelled"Fire", and this
was my cue. I dashed(at least two yards) to the door in the
corridor. Opened this a trifle, reeled a bit, recollected myself
and shouted "Water on." Remembered I was English, and hastily
added "please".

This is the opening scene. If you would like time out
now for a drink or a smoke, please do so. The three-piece
orchestra will play (probably "In a Monastery Garden")during
the interval. If your appetite is now sufficiently
wetted, we will return to the scene of the conflagation.

Dear Mr Bigelow

A TRANSATLANTIC FRIENDSHIP

Frances Woodsford

CHATTO & WINDUS

LONDON

Published by Chatto & Windus 2009

2 4 6 8 10 9 7 5 3

Copyright © Frances Norah Woodsford 2009

Frances Norah Woodsford has asserted her right under the Copyright, Designs
and Patents Act 1988 to be identified as the author of this work.

First published in Great Britain in 2009 by
Chatto & Windus
Random House, 20 Vauxhall Bridge Road,
London SW1V 2SA

www.rbooks.co.uk

Addresses for companies within The Random House Group Limited can
be found at: www.randomhouse.co.uk/offices.htm

The Random House Group Limited Reg. No. 954009

A CIP catalogue record for this book
is available from the British Library

Hardback ISBN 9780701184803

The Random House Group Limited makes every effort to ensure that
the papers used in its books are made from trees that have been legally sourced
from well-managed and credibly certified forests. Our paper procurement
policy can be found at: www.rbooks.co.uk/environment

Mixed Sources
Product group from well-managed
forests and other controlled sources
www.fsc.org Cert no. TT-COC-2139
© 1996 Forest Stewardship Council
FSC

Text design by Peter Ward
Printed in Great Britain by
Clays Ltd, St Ives plc

Contents

Frances Norah Woodsford

Commodore Paul Bigelow

Cast of characters

FRANCES NORAH WOODSFORD: known as Norah (or Nori) to family and friends, Frances to Mr Bigelow. Born on November 11th 1913. She was exceptionally bright at school, excelling at Mathematics but her father's death in 1926 interrupted the prospects of an academic career. Edwin Frank Woodsford was the inventor of the Goray skirt; he left his dress-designing business to his son and daughters and not to his wife. Without his creative input his business partner went into liquidation; when the children were old enough to inherit there was nothing left. Frances left school and earned money to keep the family together. In 1930, Frances's elder sister, Peggy, died of meningitis, aged 19, and later, her younger brother 'Mac' was made a prisoner of war in Germany. When the Second World War ended Frances took a job as secretary in the Public Baths Department of Bournemouth Town Council, where she worked for the duration of her correspondence with Mr Bigelow.

In Britain:

Amy Woodsford (née Mould): widowed mother of Frances and Mac, living with Frances in the family flat in Bournemouth

Frank MacPherson Woodsford: Frances's younger brother, known as Mac also living at home with Frances

Mould relatives: Frances's mother Amy was one of ten children: seven brothers and three sisters. Mould uncles and aunts who appear in this selection of the letters include: Syd (Lyme Regis), father to Frances's cousin Arthur; Ethel (Somerset); Ronald (Sussex) and his wife, Phyllis; and Herbert (Wirral).

Dr Keith Russell: Frances's suitor, a medical doctor from Canada, nicknamed **Sir Bertrand** by Mr Bigelow

Audrey Fagan: Mac's wife-to-be

Wendy Fagan: Audrey's younger sister

Mrs Fagan: Audrey's mother

Mr Bond: Manager of Bournemouth Baths Department, Frances's boss

Mr Samson: Frances's dentist
Mr Watts, Mr Peet: Frances's French teachers
Mrs Bendle, Mrs Hedges, Mrs Noble: fellow students in French class
Dorothy Smith: friend of Frances, another Council secretary
Phyllis Murray: married friend
Sammie, Freckleface, Willie Jackson: cats

In America:

Commodore Paul Bigelow, widower: Frances's correspondent and mentor. Born in Brooklyn, New York, in 1863, he was a civil engineer by profession, and spent time with a firm building cottonseed oil mills in the Southern states. Later, he returned to New York and, until his retirement in 1924, was the Eastern sales representative for the Buckeye Engine Company, a firm that produced steam engines used for operating electric generating plants. During the First World War he was commissioned as a Major in the U.S. Army Ordnance Service. Paul Bigelow's great passion was sailing and he was Commodore of the Bellport Bay Yacht Club for seven years, and a keen yachtsman all his life, although he retired from racing aged 70. His wife, Pauline, died in 1942. They had two children, Rosalind and Perry.

Rosalind Akin (née Bigelow): daughter of Mr Bigelow, pen-friend to Frances, nickname **Roady**. Married to Bill Akin, steel magnate, of Alton, Missouri. They had three children: Bill (who died at sea as a teenager), Paul and Tommy.

Mrs Gudrun Arnfast: the Commodore's housekeeper, nicknamed **The Tin-Opener** (also **The Can-Opener**) by Frances

The Dalls: Mr Bigelow's neighbours in Bellport, Long Island

Mrs Harriet Beall, Mrs Lucia Watson: American friends of Rosalind Bigelow in Alton

Mrs Florence Olsen: American friend of Rosalind Bigelow in New England

Angel Face: Mr Bigelow's cat
Missie: Mr Bigelow's dog

A letter to the reader

How I came to write these letters is a rather extraordinary story in itself. I first got to know Mr Bigelow through his daughter, Rosalind, who was a wonderful friend. She and I grew to know one another through a funny misunderstanding; one of the many coincidences that have feathered my life and made it much happier.

During the Second World War I used to visit overseas servicemen in hospital in Bournemouth. By 1947 I had saved up the fare to sail the Atlantic in order to visit the Americans and Canadians who had become friends. On my way home, I met three ladies from St Louis and we got talking. The women were amazed to learn that England still had rationing of food, petrol and clothing. I told them that the dress I was wearing was made out of a tent and that I had another made from strips of air balloons. They promised to send me a parcel of clothes and a parcel of food to keep or distribute as I chose.

I waited excitedly for these gifts, and eventually a gigantic parcel did arrive, stuffed with silk blouses, nylons and the most beautiful brand-new gabardine suit. There was nothing to say who these riches came from but the box was inside another box and that had a label on it from a tailor in St Louis addressed to a Mrs Rosalind Akin.

I wrote to Mrs Akin thinking she must have been one of the three ladies I'd met but whose name I'd forgotten. She wrote back and said no, but she'd heard about me, and the weird clothes I was wearing on my trip. And so a pen-friendship grew between us, ending only with Rosalind's death in 1984. Although Rosalind was extremely wealthy and I was poor, we had the same take on life.

In one letter Roady said that she hoped I didn't mind but that she'd taken to the habit of cutting pieces out of my letters to send on to her father, Commodore Paul Bigelow who was, she wrote, very old and lonely, living in a big house with only a housekeeper and a dog for company. She did not say *why* he was lonely, and thereafter I think there was a conspiracy to prevent me knowing that he was deaf, as he would not have invited pity.

Roady was not only a wonderful friend, she was also very generous: she overwhelmed us with parcels of food and clothes. Because I'm independent and I don't like being on the receiving end all the time – and because I couldn't send Roady presents that were anything like the ones she sent me – I thought that if I wrote to her lonely father might not that be a kind of present for her? On January 24th 1949 I started writing to him. And so began my marathon.

I didn't have a typewriter at home so I wrote the letters in the week during my lunch hour at the Baths. It would have been wrong to use Council property for personal correspondence so I would switch to using old typewriter ribbons. The letters didn't take me long because I was a very fast typist, and provided I had my little list of notes of what I wanted to say next, I could do one in ten or fifteen minutes. I called them my 'Saturday Specials' but I actually mailed them on Friday when I went to the post office with the office post.

I only once ran over into office time. Life at the Baths was either all or nothing: nothing happened for forty minutes, and then you were rushed off your feet for twenty, and then back to nothing. In one of those empty stretches, my boss, Mr Bond, caught me drawing something: Mr Bigelow used to make the most wonderful rag rugs, and he would send sketches, and I would transfer them onto graph paper so that it was easier for him to follow.

My boss wrote very bad letters but liked very quick dictation. He made me sit on a chair but not at a desk, and I had to write resting on my knee taking down 125 words a minute. I had to change the sentences as I went along so that his letters made sense; it taught me how to write a letter the hard way, I suppose.

Mr Bigelow did not reply to my first few letters, but when he did I believe his notes were aimed at cajoling, annoying, or pricking me into writing an extra mid-week letter. His letters were indecipherable scrawls on scrap paper with no date and no 'Dear Miss Woodsford' or 'Dear Frances'. (My family and friends call me Norah, but when writing to Mr Bigelow I chose to call myself by my first name, Frances, because I preferred it.) I am terribly sorry now not to have kept his notes to me, but they weren't consecutive – word-games, jokes, that sort of thing. Mr

Bigelow wasn't a pen-pal; he was a sparring partner. Still, I got him tamed, and he looked forward to hearing from me I think. He kept the letters in a special wooden box, so they weren't loose about the place.

Writing to Mr Bigelow was very important – it lightened my life. Without the weekly letters I would have been enclosed in the to-and-fro of home and work. I was sharing a small flat with my mother and my brother, Mac, and I didn't have any social life because I couldn't afford it. Mac had the social life; he was out to find a wife! He was a committee clerk at the town hall, and during the time I was writing to Mr Bigelow, he was headhunted to be Deputy Children's Officer at the Council.

I didn't like my job. My office window looked over the pier, the one nice thing about it. We had such appalling staff – they stayed a day and a half if I was lucky – and I was always the Muggins who had to take over their job. My boss didn't mind! I was called secretary but I really ran the Baths except for the engineering side and estimates and stock-taking (although I ended up doing that too). And I had to deal with all the complaints because my office door was labelled Superintendent Enquiries and Mr Bond's was labelled Private! He wasn't silly.

I would patrol the Baths once an hour to find out what crisis had erupted. I organised the staff timetables, the wages and tax returns and the correspondence – and did the flower arranging and helped with the washing-up in the café when needed. I organised the Police Gala, and all the other galas, and in summer we had a water show, and I had to be Front of House Manager, and receive honoured guests. I would wear Roady's beautiful silk dresses – it was wonderful because if somebody came to complain and the person they were complaining to was better dressed than their wife then they couldn't bully me quite so much!

The Baths was a very closed circuit but the letters gave me broader horizons. Mr Bigelow and I had common interests in books, films, theatre and music and common fears in hospitals and dentists. I would keep him informed of local events and British news, and we would often discuss international politics. He sent me copies of *Holiday* magazine and I would always clip out 'Giles' cartoons to send on to him. When

Roady came to visit, I sent Mr Bigelow reports from our jaunts in the invariably wet English countryside.

I regularly attended Civil Defence and First Aid Classes and these were good subjects for my letters, full of satirical potential. I had always been good with my hands, and signed up for Pottery and Painting at evening school, but with varying success; Mr Bigelow got to hear about the scrapes I got into, and I would send him the fruits of my labours. I also learnt to drive in the early years of writing to Mr Bigelow and Mac and I bought a car together. My share of the car used to be on Sundays between two and four o'clock when Mac was having his nap. He would also drive me to work and pick me up at the end of the day, but he was always late. I didn't stay at the Baths one moment more than I had to, and I would wait for him outside on the steps. That was why I started learning French, to occupy the time.

I never met Mr Bigelow and, recently, I was very upset to see a photograph of him as he was when I wrote to him, with a pale, haggard, thin face – a sad old man – and not the virile yachtsman with a cap on his head and a grin on his face that I had imagined. I didn't intend to write to him for twelve years; I didn't expect him to live that long. 97 and a half is a very good age to reach – after all, I'm only 95 and a half!

I was told that my last letter written on February 11th 1961 arrived at 'Casa Bigelow' on the day he died. My brother had got married and left home in August the previous year. I had lost the two most important men in my life within the space of six months.

After the funeral I wrote to Rosalind to ask if she would keep my letters and I would pick them up if I ever got back to America. She wrote back, most upset, to say that she was very sorry but they had been disposed of when the house was cleared, and that was sadly that. Some time later I disposed of his letters to me.

Then, in 2006, I received a 'phone call. The letters had turned up!

In 2005, George Mitchell of Long Island, New York, was accompanying a friend, Bob Sheppard, with the travel delivery of a new yacht from the South. Over the four-day voyage, they got talking about their early lives. The name of a Long Island yachtsman, Paul Bigelow, came up, and Bob said that his brother had been married to Mr Bigelow's granddaughter,

Clare, and that her daughter, Cindy Leadbeater, had been researching the family.

George recalled that his mother-in-law had been Housekeeper to a Commodore Bigelow of Bellport and when the old man died the Housekeeper, Gudrun Arnfast ('The Tin-Opener' in my letters) was asked by the family to dispose of various effects. When Gudrun died, her daughter was clearing the house and came upon a decorated wooden box full of letters to Mr Bigelow written by an Englishwoman. She showed them to her husband, George, who was about to ditch them, but then he read a few and decided they were far too good to throw away. He wanted to read more and put them in his basement. And there they had sat for over forty years.

It transpired that Bob's brother was still alive, although gravely ill, and Bob went to visit, and brought with him the box of letters that George Mitchell felt a good deed to return to the family. Cindy's cousin, Nancy Akin (and Roady's daughter-in-law), was still in occasional touch with me and knew just how thrilled I would be to hear of the rediscovery of the letters. She called to say the letters had come to light. My cousin Barbara came to visit, and shared my delight. She suggested we try to get them published.

This book is the result of happy chance and teamwork. I wrote the letters all those years ago, but the book would not have happened if my cousin, Barbara Bass, had not had the idea of publishing the letters, and been enabled to make it happen with the technical support and patience of her husband, Colin, and the encouragement and expertise of her agent, Andrew Lownie. Barbara reduced twelve years of letters to two books. Clara Farmer, my editor at Chatto & Windus, reduced the two to one. To all of them I am very grateful and to Cindy Leadbeater in America for returning the letters to me in 2006, and to George Mitchell for returning them to Cindy's family. I am thrilled that this chain of goodwill has resulted in *Dear Mr Bigelow*.

Frances Woodsford
Bournemouth
June 2009

Editor's note

Frances Woodsford wrote over seven hundred letters to Mr Bigelow – some six hundred 'Saturday Specials' and a hundred other letters – and this book contains a selection. The letters were closely typed (to save paper and weight) although occasionally, when Frances was away from the office, she sent handwritten Air Mail letters. For ease of reading, numbers, dates and times have been standardised, French accents added and obvious typing errors corrected. At times, and most reluctantly, the editors have been obliged to cut material within the letters, indicated by a three-point ellipsis. The author's own ellipses are reproduced as in the original letters, as six-point ellipses.

1949

Pier Approach Baths
(*reproduced by permission of Bournemouth Libraries*);
Miss Frances Woodsford

BOURNEMOUTH
March 23rd 1949

Dear Mr Bigelow,

I am pretending that your eyesight, whilst not exactly poor, isn't quite good enough to interpret my handwriting. There's no doubt at all about that – it *certainly* is poor – so I am seizing upon it as an excuse for typing this letter. Let us just say that it is kinder to both of us. If bad mannered on my part!

In a letter from Roady last week she remarked that you had asked when she was going to send you another of my letters. So here is one especially for you. A sort of prize for having such a nice daughter.

Some weeks ago I referred to a large-scale map of Long Island, to see where your cottage was located. Now maps are a weakness of mine, and when coupled with a vivid imagination, I can picture a place nearly as well as a physical visit. So, to my reading of the map, I have added my view of the Jersey shore (which at the time I thought to be the north side of Long Island) as I sailed up Hudson last winter, and the composite picture gives me some idea of your home. Long Island looked rather drab when I saw it on a cold day in December, but my mind's eye has painted it more vividly and even given you a few flowers in the spring and fall! See how kind I am to you!

Even though it is nearly eighteen months since I saw New York for the first wonderful time, it is painted like a primitive watercolour for me. Especially Staten Island with an inflamed red sun suspended a yard or so above it in a uniformly grey sky. And even more especially the Statue of Liberty etched in grey on hundreds of other shades of the same grey. Something only the Chinese would do justice to in putting on paper; certainly I cannot.

Long before I visited America I knew what it looked like, and had quite made up my mind that the only place to live, if living in New York, was a houseboat on the river so that the famous skyline would be your backyard fence. And on actual sight, I was right again. A *tiny*, hardly-to-be-mentioned obstacle to this ideal domicile, I thought, was the scent of the rubbish barges as they sailed heavily downstream with their redolent, smouldering burdens. You are very quiet about them and very noisy about your skyline, and you are quite, quite right in both instances!

I loved the gay highway connecting the city with Long Island, with its beautiful riverside houses and apartments, and as I have always been a fervid reader of American thrillers (they intersperse my heavy reading, like bicarbonate between courses of a banquet) I can easily imagine the various towns and villages of Long Island itself. Most of the best types of thrillers are located either in a city (New York, Boston, or sometimes San Francisco) or in Long Island. One would think nobody lived any-where else at all, and that nobody could possibly be other than one of the 400! They make good escapist reading, and are very slick and polished and I enjoy them for that and not for the picture they paint, so please don't worry that I think Hollywood depicts America accurately because I don't.

What else struck me about New York? The squirrels in Central Park – one of whom carried a large brown paper bag right up to the top of a tall tree and stuffed it there into a little wooden box-nest. You can imagine my feelings as I noticed this brown paper bag walking along the path by itself, for it wasn't until it had gone some dozen yards that the squirrel underneath came up for air and a rest. Harlem, that struck me all of a heap. I went there all alone on my first day in New York, when I had money enough only for coffee and cereal for breakfast and a long, long wait until I could embark on the *Queen Mary* at midnight. So I decided that the cheapest way of keeping out of the cold was the longest bus ride I could find, and it turned out to be Harlem and I was so upset and scared that I got straight back on the bus and returned to Central Park, where I wandered around and around the lovely Museum until the attendants began looking *very oddly* at me and fingering their weapons, just in case. Another thing I noticed particularly was the strange beauty of some of the negresses. When well dressed in colours toning with their skins I thought them exquisite. In fact, the loveliest woman I saw in the whole of America was an (I'm not sure of the word) octoroon in New Orleans. For me she conjured up at once a picture of the old city with two gay young blades fighting a duel over her.

The ankles and silly little shoes of the New York women; the equally silly, but by no means so attractive, coats flapping in the breeze with hoods hanging down between the shoulder blades – for two days I thought every woman was about to become a mother and had my lips pursed to whistle for an ambulance, until I discovered it was merely fashion, and not nature, at work.

The dirty sidewalks (I live in a seaside town where there is no industry, and therefore no smoky dirt, though I must say that New York was far dirtier than I remember seeing London) and the garishness of Broadway. The dignity and beauty of the buildings surrounding Central Park, and of course, Grand Central Station. The infuriating slowness of the Customs (it took me six hours to get off the boat and through them!) and the wonderful hospitality of the girl who waited all that time on the dock to welcome me. I stayed the first night at a horrible hotel in West 49th Street and the noise was another thing that struck me there. On my way home, being at the end of the trip and also the end – or beyond it – of my exchequer – I stayed at a YMCA hostel down on the East side, quite near the river, and the noise was much less there.

My other impressions are mostly of the West. The Rockies, the funny little round hills, pimple-like and sometimes quilted with vines, in California. The warmth, oh the heavenly warmth of that state. And the scorn my Scottish friends there had for the heather, growing in that warmth to a mere ten feet instead of the scrubby 15 inches it normally does in Scotland. The arty-crafty air of Carmel; the unpleasantness of Los Angeles's Mexican-cum-Negro quarter, in which I got lost. And of course, the food. Being quite mad I believe in having the best when possible, and going without everything when it is not. So I spent six dollars having gumbo creole and chicken baked in a bag, at Antoine's in New Orleans, even though it meant three days in New York on break-fast only. I had a very bad cold when I reached S.F., and remembering the ironic laughter with which the public here in England had greeted a newspaper article just before I sailed, in which it said that the best cure for a cold was 24 oranges (since oranges arrive about three times a year and then we get a pound a head) . . . remembering this, I went out and bought 24 oranges and set to eat them. If I remember rightly, I stuck on the ninth, but it was wonderful going up to then.

Another joy was to go down into Union Square in San Francisco in the mornings, and watch what I think must have been the most elegant collection of women in the *world*, going, presumably, to a lecture in one of the theatres.

I loved also going into small stores and interrupting all business by getting into arguments! Once when I had (as usual) been asked if I were Australian I answered, 'No, I'm English.' 'Well, are you going to Australia?' 'No, I'm going home to England.' 'Whatever for?' Up came my fists, I gave my best impersonation of Mr Churchill looking fierce, and bellowed, 'Why ever not! It's a *nice* place!' And of course all the other customers came over to see what the fight was about, and we had the loveliest time.

The casual way in which people take public graft for granted shook me to the core. Even more, has the recent exposure of Socialist Members of our Parliament for taking bribes, shaken me, so it seems nobody's hands are very clean nowadays. Mine least of all, for I was always ready to try for an extra pint of milk, or a pair of stockings going without any annoying questions of 'coupons' for them. We are in a sorry mess all round, aren't we?

Roady, in her letter, mentioned a friend of yours, a Mr Dahl, saying to his wife, 'Now, why don't you write to somebody in England and get letters like that?' Well, you may tell Mr Dahl that 999 English people out of 1,000 are just as bad correspondents as the same number of Americans. At least, that is my own experience. I correspond with upwards of eighty people (not regularly, or frequently) and at the moment 76 of them owe *me* a letter. That is partly why I was so delighted to meet Roady, if only so far by means of correspondence. She writes the loveliest letters, full of humour and picture-painting. Such a pleasant change from the other 79, who mostly send me a Christmas card on which they have scribbled, 'Thanks for letters – Drop me a line some time.' Bah! to them!

Roady told me some time ago that your two hobbies (apart from the dogs) are clocks and yachts. I know nothing of the one, and my experience of the other has mostly been confined to my sitting up in the bows pretending to be a Viking Figurehead, in spite of my figure, which isn't sufficiently robust for that role. Anyway, next time I write, I will discourse on yachts I have known, and if that doesn't last the course, then I can always go on for a long time about Mr Jackson, a cat who has a passion for me and spends all day long in my office or following me around the building like a dog. He stops sometimes to nip customers neatly in the ankle, but for the most part he cannot tear himself away from me long enough to do so. Why isn't he a man!!!

I feel very grateful to you for having a daughter; she seems so extremely fond of you and so close to you, that I feel a little the same, at third hand twice removed as it were. So please don't think it an impertinence if I wish you well and hope that the spring has come to Long Island as it has to this island and brought you the happiness it always brings me.

Yours sincerely,

Frances Woodsford

PS On *no* account are you to feel this calls for an answer, because it doesn't, so there!

PPS On rereading. Nothing like being vain, is there? Fancy taking it for granted a letter from me would count as a prize!

ENGLAND
On a glorious August day
August 11th 1949

Dear Mr Bigelow,

Come, come – have you no shame? Throwing Latin tags around like that! You might hit somebody. In any case, your initial paragraph reads to me like a mixture of Greek, Dutch-Dutch and the Harvard College Yell. I was delighted with your last bit of dog-Latin – I quote you *exactly* – 'compost mentis and all that sort of thing'. I always thought it was comp*os*, but possibly I misunderstand you, and you were merely being extraordinarily frank in suggesting you have a mind like a manure heap. Do I get an A+ for that?

. . . To my utter astonishment, my boss has decided I am in need of a break and told me I may have a week's holiday before the end of the summer. Normally I get three or four weeks (three weeks plus any national holidays I have worked) any time between November and March! So I am going, all alone, since I have so little prior notice and all my friends fixed their holidays long ago, to Exmoor and the Lorna Doone country. I am to stay at a hotel open only during summer so that the owner can make enough money to do nothing but hunt all winter. It's very huntin' shootin' fishin', and as I do none of those, I shall probably spend a week twiddling my fingers. Maybe, though, they'll trust me with an air rifle to shoot rooks. I am a very good shot (I think) but as that opinion is based on three shots at a fair, and three at a Home Guard target during the war, when I upset everybody by getting bullseyes all the time and making them look much worse than they were, possibly the hotelier will not feel me trustworthy. So it's a piece of string, a worm and a bent pin for me. Will you cross your fingers for luck over weather, Mr B.? In the middle of nowhere I shall need fine weather. Not, please, quite as hot as you are having just now – I'd hate that. Wish for something around the 65–70 degree mark, if you will.

I hope you are well, and that Rosalind managed to visit you on her hectic-sounding holiday. And that no more neighbours have fallen in the Atlantic.

Yours sincerely,

Frances Woodsford

BOURNEMOUTH
November 14th 1949

Dear Mr Bigelow,

Thank you for your long letter, and also for the 'epic' on your experience of hospital hospitality. I'm downright surprised at you, Mr B., making a play on words that way. Thought only decadent English punned these days.

Oh and by the way – I would hate to tell you you're wrong . . . . . . Well, would hate to now and then, that is . . . . . . but over here we spell willy-nilly that way, and not 'Will I nill I'. Since you seem, from other evidence, to be a well-informed gentleman you will probably know that the expression comes from the word 'nill', 3rd sing.pres. condit. (Oxford Dictionary) 'Will he, nill he – whether he likes it or not (now usually willy-nilly) – from the obsolete *ne* (not) plus *will*'. End of lecture, which I couldn't resist as a return gesture after your own little admonition over my spelling of 'inured'. Do you remember? You told me the fulsome use of 'n's was unnecessary in the States. Now we are quits.

But, nonetheless, grammar and syntax notwithstanding, I enjoyed your account and chuckled lustily as I read it. You seem to have a good eye for nurses.

And talking of your eye for anatomy, I wasn't suggesting you went to the ballet to study that. You've a nasty mind, that you have; and in any case, by now you should know what anatomy is all about. After all, you will have had *Esquire* for years and years. My suggestion you visit the Sadler's Wells ballet company was more of an invitation to partake of a lovely experience. Anatomy is one part of it, admittedly, but not the main part. Most ballet-dancers have ugly legs, anyway (not Margot Fonteyn, nor Moira Shearer but most of the others have) and hide them in long net skirts. A memento of the days of Dhiagelif (spelled wrongly, I know) who disliked women in general and their legs in particular and always insisted on the dancers in his company wearing long skirts. No, ballet is not the answer to a tired business- man's prayer. It is a mixture of sound, sight and movement, welded together.

However, it is too late now, as the company has moved on, but I hope Rosalind has been able to see it and I know she would love it.

. . . On Friday I went in my lunch hour, to our little art gallery and museum.* This was gathered together by one of the families originally settling in Bournemouth, and then, when the cat left in disgust because he couldn't turn round any longer, they departed this life and left the house and contents to the town, only stipulating certain items *must* always be on show. This makes it rather awkward for the Museum Committee who, when planning exhibitions of, say, modern art, have to sandwich Picasso between two permanent pictures of Victorian Misses. Complete with birds, dear little cheeldren and the odd pussy cat or two.

I love visiting this museum, which is perched on the edge of the cliffs with a really magnificent view over the bay, embracing a sight of the Isle of Wight to the east, and the Dorset hills sweeping out to sea on the western side. My first reaction is always to slip down the first half-dozen steps, just inside the main entrance, as I gaze entranced at the marble statue one sees on entering. This statue is of a mother with baby on her shoulder, just stepping off a rock into the sea. It is entitled *The Bathers*, in case you didn't guess . . .

My second choice in statues is one of a young girl sending off a dove with a message. This dates it as being pre-telephonic. This lass is throwing the poor bird into the air with one chubby hand, while the other is coyly pressed across the Victorian bosom. She quite obviously hasn't the first idea of throwing, and would be hopeless at cricket or baseball. The lass is wearing a smirk and a shift (or chemise) that has slipped.

Possibly the Victorian shape of the girl explains why the chemise didn't slip all the way down, but I still don't know how it got off arms and shoulders in the first place, unless she was the original film star and was sewn into it each day? I can't begin to think why she would have been out for a walk in her chemise, or with a dove for sending messages on the spur of inspiration. So I leave this mystery to you to solve during the long winter evenings.

Now come to think of it, fashions don't seem to change as often as

* *Editor's note*: The Russell-Cotes Art Gallery and Museum, on East Cliff Promenade.

we think. For outside the museum is a small bronze statue of Pan, in the act of throwing something (if it was a football, the ball is missing) out to sea. Pan is dressed in a smart-alec sort of smile, for the most part, but during the war he was frequently dressed in undergarments looking very like those issued to the little English Air Force girls. He lives next door to the main Canadian Air Force Officers' mess on one side, and opposite two large hotels used as leave-centres for the U.S. other ranks, and I think it was once more a case of the American Forces, both sides of the 49th Parallel, sending clothing parcels to Britain. What I often wanted to know was, were his warm wearings given voluntarily or not?

. . . Enough of all this: I do hope you are better now, and continuing to disappoint your doctor by refusing to have pneumonia. I understand the medicine for pneumonia is *horrible*. It's much better to stick to colds, which carry with them much less drastic doses of physic. Anyway, by now you will be better, I'm sure, and are probably overseeing the tying of your rose bushes against the winter. Two of mine are still blooming, yah, yah! I think they are crazy, but that may be the company they keep.

I've not heard from Rosalind since she wrote on her visit to Vancouver Island, and do hope this doesn't mean she's been ill. Probably just busy; and in any case, there's no real reason why she should write.

Last Saturday I went to Salisbury, a cathedral town with a market place about 30 miles from Bournemouth, in the hope of finding some antique bargains for Christmas gifts. As it rained very heavily in the morning I decided not to go. And then just as I was about to leave the office, it stopped raining, so I dashed off to the bus station and caught the bus, only stopping to think when halfway there that I'd had no lunch and made no arrangements about taking sandwiches. So I thought I'd have something when we reached Salisbury at 2.30. At 2.30 we did reach Salisbury, and I was frozen to the marrow, sitting in a cold bus with wet feet. So I tore round to the market square looking for a cup of something hot. Only to turn my nose up at the cheap, nasty, snack-bars which surround the market place along with the public houses. All the good restaurants were filled with lunches, and not started with teas. So I went at the double round the stalls looking for bargains. Only bargain I saw was on the part of the stall holder I discovered selling Bristol Blue glass at fabulous prices to two American ladies shopping there! So I came away, unable to bear the sight, and merely stopped to purchase a small silver brooch for a young girl who'll probably hate it anyway, and dashed back to the bus station to find a bus waiting. Popped on, and decided I'd wait to eat until we got back to Bournemouth when I could have a tea-snack before going to friends where I was due for dinner. Of course, on arriving back in Bournemouth I was once more frozen to the marrow, and finding a bus to the friends' district ready and waiting (and not another for an hour) I popped in and arrived at their house cold and hungry, about 5.30 p.m., having eaten breakfast at 7 a.m. and nothing since. AND WE HAD DINNER AT EIGHT O'CLOCK! Before dinner I was given two sherries, and oh Mr Bigelow I've never felt so giddy in my life! It wasn't much fun (I've never yet got drunk or near-drunk and can't imagine it being a happy condition, judging by my misery after a couple of cocktails) and it was very, very hard work being polite and applauding the firework display in the garden, when all I wanted was a good beefsteak. Not that I was likely to get a good beefsteak, or even a steak, but these friends are well in with the blackmarket and their tables always groan (their guests too, but afterwards, with overeating) and to have to wait all that time nearly killed me.

And that is why I say it's the company my rose bushes keep that turns them crazy.

I *do* hope you are well again.

Yours sincerely,

Frances Woodsford

1950

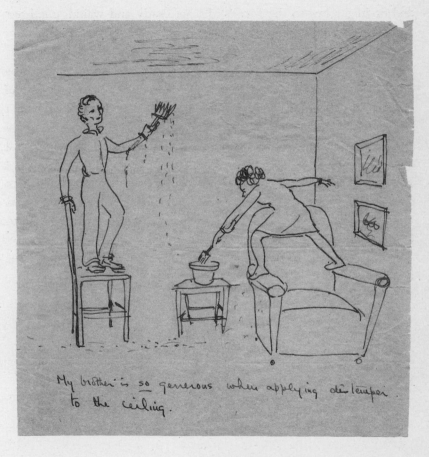

My brother is so generous when applying distemper to the ceiling.

April 29th (p. 26), 'I am going to distemper and paint the bathroom, spring clean the kitchen and repaint it, and do Mother's bedroom as well if I get time.'

January 17th 1950

Dear Mr Bigelow,

It's a glorious day today; a rich apricot-coloured sunshine is wrapped round everything, and I have just come in from a walk in a short- sleeved wool frock and bolero only. Privately, I was a fool to let the sun tempt me, because it wasn't until I got outside that I discovered it was tempered by a nice little breeze from your part of the world.

I was delighted with your letter, Mr B., and even more delighted with all the trouble Mr Dahl obviously took to make the package seem so much more important than it was. I have written him a short note of thanks, which he well deserves. He won't be overwhelmed this time! My earlier letter to him was, I will admit, very, very carefully written with two rough drafts first, as I had no intention of giving him any loophole at all through which he could get out of doing my behest. Incidentally thank you for a new word for my vocabulary – I'd never heard of 'whelmed' as a separate word before, but it's there in the Concise Oxford and scores you a point . . .

I'm afraid 'you've had it', so far as your new kitten is concerned. That was a phrase much in use in the Forces during the war, and indicated that, whatever it was you wanted, it was just as though you'd already had it, so far as any likelihood of future having was concerned. Dogs and cats who 'find' people do it on purpose, and are not to be got rid of by wily advertisements or other means. Your cat has obviously taken over the house, as I can see from his behaviour towards your dogs already. What are you going to call her? Cara? Autocat!! Orphan Annie? I had a Mr Perkins once who turned out to be a Dorothy Perkins instead. Perky made quite a good name for a cat; it was easy for her to hear. Of course, no cat hears itself called unless it wants to, but just the same it's a good thing to find a name they can easily understand. Mine are called Sammie, Fatty Freckleface (Frecks, or Fatty, or Culls when we call him) and the office one is Willie Jackson, as you know.

Rereading your letter: I cannot help thinking Mr Dahl's guests were the ultra-polite type. The suit and shoes in the snapshot are both about seven years old! The ring is an heirloom and I don't wear an engagement ring, never having got that far! I had intended sending my prize-snapshot to you, but as several friends to whom I showed it remarked 'Oh, what a pretty girl! *Who is it?*' I decided it couldn't be a good likeness, so plumped for this one instead. I am usually smiling except when I am not. Many, many years ago I was born with gastritis, a hernia, and so weak my eyes had to be bathed open every morning for six months. I am told that between turning blue with the pain of my various sicknesses, I blew the happiest bubbles in London. Thus proving at an early age that there's one born every minute, and reflecting no credit on me for my happy disposition. There's so much horror and sorrow in the world about which we can do absolutely nothing at all, it seems stupid to go around with a long face just because it is there. As reasonable to go around laughing for joy because there are buttercups and sunshine and light on water.

The *Radio Times* was not marked with *all* the best programmes. I remember being rather annoyed with myself for not having listened to the type of programme I would feel proud to acknowledge having heard! It (the B.B.C.) is not exactly a government enterprise, although it is run by a Board of Governors appointed by Parliament, and it is thought at the moment to err rather in showing left-wing bias, but that might be explained by the fact that so many scientists are that way inclined. They never were in touch with the facts of life, were they?

So now I have a warped mentality, have I? Because I enjoy an occasional crossword puzzle! Let me tell you Mr B., that the one I do – in the *Daily Telegraph* – is a very good exercise in clear thinking. An exercise I am always in need of. The clues (usually there are two or three hints rather hidden in the one clue) say exactly what the compiler means. Only, they say it in such a way that the solver automatically thinks it means something else. Careless reading – just as we have so much careless listening – we hear what we expect to hear, and not always what is being actually spoken. As for those crosswords which are full of unknown words, there is no fun or interest in them at all, I'll grant you that. One day I will solve one of the *Telegraph* items, and send it to you to see for yourself . . .

Thank you for your letter from Mr Meserole. Is he like our own J. B. Priestley? Woolly minded? I love the idea of world-planning so that nobody wants for anything, nobody suffers, nobody is unhappy. How many murders were there in the world last year? How many divorces? How many arguments between the U.S. Navy Department and the U.S. Army big-shots? How many between Foreign Ministers? How many between Dictators? Perhaps if we start with the family rows and work up from there we may yet have a world-plan, but personally I don't expect to see it. If, say, we had a sudden, overwhelming revival of the Christian spirit that wouldn't be big enough to solve world problems, because it wouldn't take in the Jews, the Mohammedans, the Buddhists, the Hindus, the sun-worshippers or the Hottentots. It wouldn't even affect the Mormons or the Seventh-Day Adventists. I think it's too big a problem for Mr Meserole to tackle, even with your help.

Incidentally, I'd love to know where he got his $400,000,000,000 from. Did he go round all the firms in the U.S.A. asking how much they lost in the depression, then add it all up. Personally, I stop counting, or being affected by any figure above the ten thousand mark. I earn £350 a year and I know, to the penny, just how far that stretches. What I don't know, and can't visualise, is how far forty-million-times-£350 would stretch. I can't take in our National Debt; the amount of Marshall Aid now rising up in a mountain round our necks (makes a change from the National Debt, which was only called a millstone) or how many light hours it would take to reach the moon. So now you know my Achilles tendon!

. . . Having been rather busy lately, I haven't proceeded very far with your life history, but here are a couple of chapters for you to be getting on with. I think, in the next chapter, I will bring in one or two of the relatives I found for you under the 'Bigelow' group in the American *Who's Who* I studied at the library the other week. You'd be surprised to know who you picked up as brothers. I was always told my father's family were related to the Woodsford-Strangeways (the 17th, or something, Earl of Ilminster), but when I came back from the States somebody wrote to me and said she was an Elizabeth Woodsford before her marriage, and were we related – her mother had been maid to Mrs So-and-so and her only brother was a farm labourer. I was *livid*. Served us right for being snobs, yes? Of course we indignantly denied any such relationship, which is actually, about as likely as the earldom one . . .

I hope the dentist didn't wreak too much of his will on you. Sadists all, and only one step better than wife beaters. If I were Dictator of Mr Meserole's nicely planned world I'd forbid toothache, that I would. With about as much possibility of global co-operation as any other edict, rule or law would have, were it sent around the entire globe to apply to everybody. Still I expect Mr M. is quite happy pottering around in his life-work, and who are we cynics to make him cry?

Very sincerely yours,

Frances Woodsford

BOURNEMOUTH
January 27th 1950

Dear Mr Bigelow,

Imagine me, if you can, with a cheese sandwich in one hand and a swatch of letters in the other, trying to get the one digested and the other answered, before tearing off to London for a week's holiday. Excuse, beforehand, expected low standard of epistle, that is.

Thank you for your latest letter, with the enclosure regarding different governments and their effects on cows. I must confess I had seen it many years ago, and in retaliation all I can think of is to send you another hoary chestnut – the one about who's doing the work. Here it is, therefore.

Also enclosed is a cutting from a magazine, in case you've never met the dear girls of that super super school, St Trinian's. Mostly, they appear in sketches only (like the one of the small girl kept back in class to write out a hundred times, 'I must not smoke cigars in chapel') but in this instance the artist and Arthur Marshall have co-operated. Arthur

Marshall, himself an ex-schoolmaster, is well known for his extremely funny impersonations of a schoolmistress in just such a school as St Trinian's. You may chuckle; you may not.

I have just finished reading my Christmas book of the comedies of William Congreve. I can imagine a whole lot of hearty friends in whose company I would *not* like to see one of these plays enacted! Apart from the juicy bits, though, they are beautifully written and confirm my old love of Millamant. What a gorgeous role to play!

Also finished, for the third time since Christmas, *Pride and Prejudice*. Did I tell you, or was it before our time? How I went especially to the National Portrait Gallery in London one day, just to see their newly acquired portrait of Jane Austen by her sister Cassandra? And how amazed I was to find she had, apart from such things as large brown eyes, frizzy hair, a long straight nose, and pink cheeks, a mouth shut tight like a small button cemented over. I was astounded that such a mouth could go with such a wide sense of humour – wide enough to embrace humanity as a whole, and not merely the falling-on-banana-skin type.

Rereading *P. & P.* I was struck by the exceedingly bad manners of the majority of the characters. Although we always say that today our manners are appalling, I think their roughness hurts less than the sheer brutality of so many of J.A.'s characters. And today we in ourselves are more independent, less influenced by others' opinions and behaviour, so that we do not so readily blush for our friends. If manners are there to make one at ease, and to make others at ease as well, then I think we are an improvement over the Regency grade. True, Elizabeth and Jane Bennet later are exquisitely mannered in the best way, but they do stand out as a pair of little candles in a very uncouth world. Quite a change to hear anybody say, 'Ah, the younger generation isn't what it was. Thank goodness,' isn't it?

And now I must get on with the other letters. I do hope you had a lovely visit from Rosalind, and the weather was good to you both. I wonder why you called her Rosalind? It's such a lovely name as are most in Shakespeare, but so few people make use of them. Did you hear of the white woman who called her fifth son Ling-Hi because she'd heard that every fifth child born is Chinese?

I will tell you what the Thames looks like on fire after I have set it.
And if.

Till then, au revoir, and a bonne santé,

Sincerely,

Frances Woodsford

BOURNEMOUTH
March 28th 1950

Dear Mr Bigelow,

If you have a blackboard knocking around the place, chalk up one point
to you over this business of coffee. I will go halfway to meet you over it
– coffee in England, in public restaurants and cafés (where they ought to
know better) is *awful*. The coffee you get in private homes is usually a
good deal better. Whereas in my opinion, and judging by my slight
experience, coffee in the States is drinkable anywhere, at worst, and very
good, at best.

I was forcibly reminded of this vileness of English coffee on Sunday,
when I went to Southampton to meet two American ladies off their
ship, and took them to the best hotel in Southampton for lunch. A
horrible meal, too, of which I was heartily ashamed. The soup was just
warm brown thickness; the Yorkshire pudding (I didn't have any) looked
soggy and rubber-like, and the coffee was awful.

It was great fun, playing hostess to somebody who had reversed the
roles in America. It was also great fun putting on one of my No. 1 beam-
ing smiles to get me through forbidden territory! Having no official
permit, I should not have gone into the docks at all, but the policeman
on duty took pity on my blank look of disappointment and let me
through upon signing some paper or other. Nobody lower than a
Cabinet minister is allowed on board while ships are in the docks, but I
looked helpless and appealing at three very tall men, one of whom
looked down and remarked, 'Oh dear, no, you can't go on board.

Besides, this man is the doctor and he has to go on board first of all, to give the ship a clean bill of health. Then this man goes on – he is the Immigration Officer – and then *I* go aboard. I'm the Customs Officer. You just follow us.' So I did.

Coming out, we had a taxi and went another way. Then the police stopped our car for the production of passports, and upon saying I hadn't one, but had come in by the other gate, the bobby remarked, 'Oh yes, I know all about *you*.' See how the Gestapo keep us under their watchful eye! The police apparently passed me from one to the other, for they didn't argue when we came back later and I accompanied my friends on board and stayed to dinner. Nor did the gatekeeper object when I arrived back at his post, completely, utterly and absolutely breathless, too breathless even to speak. Even to object to the fact that the clock in the distance I had been running by, was twenty-five minutes *fast* and I was in no danger of losing my train, by the clock over the dock gates. But then, I always manage to catch my trains in plenty of time. This day, just as I was walking (yes, walking by then) down the steps leading to the station yard, I saw a train in the platform and heard the loudspeaker voice announcing . . . . . . 'stopping at Boscombe, Bournemouth Central, Bournemouth West, and Weymouth'. So I went back to my normal twelve miles per hour rush and promptly got clutched by the ticket-collector who wanted to know, reasonably enough, where I was going to. 'Don't stop me – I want to catch the Bournemouth train!' I retorted, struggling. 'Well, you'll do it. It's not due in for ten minutes', was the nasty answer. The train I had seen was going the other way, anyway. I know quite well that when I die I shall pop out of my coffin and run all the way to the cemetery so as to be there in plenty of time for the arrival of the cortège.

. . . Disappointed woman all round, I am today. From a friend I borrowed a pair of silver-fox furs last weekend. I wanted the two American ladies to think I was affluent – as though I wasn't a bit worried whether my money'd be enough to pay the lunch bill! – and so I dressed up in my Sunday best. Unfortunately, my family decided I looked common in the furs. I didn't agree, but I did think they made me look old – look my age, anyway! – and as it was actually too cold to go without a coat, I had the furs returned without showing them off. I suppose I must stick to mutation mink (the pale stuff, like captured moonlight) or nothing. Or perhaps chinchilla would suit my particular beauty. I *knew* I should have persuaded Mrs Watson, a friend of Rosalind's from Fairmount, to return to the docks in time to see the *Caronia* come in with its 22 millionaire passengers aboard. Might have found one to suit me, I might.

I am going up to London again in a few weeks, to spend a couple of days showing Mrs Watson around. What I lack in information as to our famous sights, I more than make up in imagination. And who cares about dates anyway! I am using the task as practice for next year, by which time surely I should have worn down Rosalind enough to get her to come over, when my ability as a guide will have increased with use.

That's all for now,

Very sincerely,

Frances Woodsford

BOURNEMOUTH
April 27th 1950

Dear Mr Bigelow,

It is raining; it is cold; I have been, all the morning, interviewing applicants for one or two staff vacancies, and that's a job I loathe because I either feel so sorry for obvious misfits that I want to give them the position whether they could fill it successfully or not; or else I get cross with them for being bumptious and self-opinionated with little reason. In any case I'm bound to choose the wrong people, so the whole morning has been generally depressing, and I am venting my spleen on you.

I am sorry not to have answered your lovely long letter before. My reason is that Easter is a headache for me and has resulted in a bout of sleepless nights, which in turn mean irritability which I do not like trans-ferring to my friends by way of letters. So you've been postponed, but don't think it was because I didn't wish to write off at once and thank you for taking all that trouble, because I did.

Now, Mr Bigelow, you really mustn't take me to task for referring to a 'road connecting New York with Long Island'. When I say a thing happened in 1535 I mean it happened in 1535 or thereabouts – say fifty years either way. I cannot be held down to finicky details, see? I'm one of the large gesture type; the world planners, as opposed to the scientists with their noses to the retort. Not that I'm often at a loss for a retort. Ah me, I'm in fine form today. Did you notice that pun just gone past? And heave a sigh of relief that it had gone past, perhaps? Anyway, to get back to the road. *With the help of a bridge* it connects the city of New York with the outlying towns on Long Island, and looking at your map (for which many thanks: I love maps) it seems to be called Shore Parkway, and a very fine Parkway it looked from my ship too.

You say in your letter, 'What is it that makes English people so?' You politely don't say what it is they are so, but I will give you an explanation anyway. We are a homogeneous race, as contrasted with the American, which is a mixed race. I am talking, again, in large gestures, of the majority, not the minority, in both instances. I have a Dutch great-grandfather on my mother's side, and a Scottish great-grandfather. Apart from that, on both sides of the family my ancestors came from the west part of England – Dorset and Devon – from back so far they got lost with William the Conqueror. That means that the amount of non-English blood in me must be very small, and it is so with most English people as well. That again means that my characteristics are those which are in English people for twenty or thirty generations back. And as climate and environment play such a large part in our natures, it means that any deviation from the norm has to be caused by an exceptionally strong characteristic, different from the usual ones. Now I am a genius, say (I'm not, but we'll just pretend. It's one of my favourite daydreams) and that genius, being such a hard taskmaster, forces me into being different from everybody else not a genius. But an English non-genius differs only in nice particulars from all the other non-geniuses – not outstandingly. Whereas in America your mother might be French, your father German, your grandparents Red Indian, English, Polish and Greek, and your great-grandparents eight other nationalities. These characteristics are going a'warring in you, and the strongest will come out. But it will be the strongest from each separate nationality, and as a result you, the offspring, may have (for an example) the volatile nature of a Frenchman with the painstaking plodding of a German and the sun-loving habits of the Greek and the poetry of an Englishman. No wonder you have so many neurotics, you poor things, with that private war going on in so many of you!

Anyway, ancestry aside, I believe the climate is what 'makes English people so'. We never know what tomorrow will bring. We say, 'Yes, I see' when we mean – 'I understand'. We are so used to thinking in terms of seeing through the mists that we really do see around them, through them, and as though they do not exist. Our climate is equable, though often deplorable. It is possible to be very uncomfortable – and our houses make it easy! – but it is never too hot or too cold to work and go about our ordinary business. Our twilights and our springs are things of exquisite loveliness, and have resulted in Shakespeare and a whole lot of little Shakespeares. I bet you what you like (anything up to a $) that you could stop ten people in an English street, and at least five of them, if honest, would admit that they had written poetry at some time or another. Even our love of our little gardens is a way of expressing our appreciation of beauty.

The characteristic about English people which hits other people, I believe, is snobbishness. It must be awful, to be so glaring, and I don't know the root of it unless the early nineteenth century was to blame. Why, in my job this morning, did I automatically say to myself, 'Oh, he's much too good a type for the job' about some of the men, if not for snobbish reasons? – they were 'too good' to scrub floors. But why do so many American women belong, by hook or by crook, to the Daughters of the Revolution? It's the same thing, different country. And you know, Mr Bigelow, most prime ministers of England have come from the lower strata of society (Lloyd George was a miner's son, McDonald a post-man's son etc., etc., I could name half a dozen) than U.S. Presidents have. So that snobbishness does not keep everybody in the station in life to which they were born, as the Victorians expressed it, and as most Americans believe it does.

Enough of England . . . . . .

I am glad you did manage to agree with me about women's shoes. And the sketch you enclosed was, horrors, exactly like my house slippers, though my heels are lower than that you drew. Still, you wouldn't like women to be plain sensible creatures, now would you? It'd take all the fun out of life. I remember one evening during the war, when I did hospital visiting in my spare time, wearing a plain sensible hat with a plain sensible suit, and a plain sensible American from San Francisco (bronchitis, hospitalised three weeks) leaned towards me, perching on the end of the bed, and said, 'Excuse me, ma'am, but I *do* like your bloody hat.' I wasn't at all sure whether that was a bit of flattery or sarcasm, so to obviate any repetition I went home and straight away cut the hat into bits, added a bow here and a ribbon there, popped it back over one eye, and thereafter wore it like that. And nobody thought it was bl—dy, or likeable any more. They laughed at it, which was just what I wanted them to do, as they had little else to laugh at in the hospital. Besides, we females get fun out of being silly, so why should we forgo that just to oblige a lot of spoil-sports like you men?????? My biggest hat-success of my career as a Florence Nightingale was a hat I made out of the cellophane wrappers of cigarette packets. For weeks and weeks everybody in hospital saved these wrappers, and I wound them round and round like pipe spills, until I had made a little cellophane boater. To this was added white and pink flowers, and a white ribbon to keep the concoction on. I never dared wear it in the street, but it used to be popped on outside the ward doors (and out of view of the orderly on duty in the hall, whenever possible) and then paraded up and down between the beds, to the loud (and possibly sarcastic) admiration of the sick men and women. It was so darn heavy I got a headache after two minutes, but it was certainly pretty and a change from nurses' starched handkerchiefs.

I have just finished reading a book about the Brontës. Too finicky and detailed, it was yet interesting and enlightening. What queer people they were, weren't they? I prefer Emily, both as a writer and as a person, but alas have more in common (except genius) with Charlotte. And here I have the nerve to try and explain to you 'what makes the English so', when nobody knows what makes that particular English family so, however hard they delve and analyse and interpret. With tight-lacing and women being 'interesting invalids' every time they had an annual baby, I cannot imagine how any family of women managed to be so outstandingly stoic, Emily and Anne both dying out of bed after illnesses of months' duration. The last time I was in bed was back in 1943, when I had flu and stayed in bed one day; running red nose, shining skin, lank straight hair and an 'ackin' corf. That was the day my number one beau came up to say goodbye before going overseas, and the shock of seeing me as I was, nipped in the bud what might have been the love affair of the century! So I haven't stayed in bed since, but that is only because I've not been ill, for I am no Brontë stoic, not by a million miles, and the least pain would put me down on the pillow wailing for my mummy. You should have heard the moaning I've been doing this last couple of months because I have developed neuritis in one arm. You probably did hear it, and thought it was the ghosts of the drowned dead marching up the Hudson and wailing as they went!

. . . thank you again for writing me and don't ever feel you *have* to, because you haven't . . .

Very sincerely,

Frances Woodsford

BOURNEMOUTH
April 29th 1950

Dear Mr Bigelow,

. . . Mother has gone gallivanting off to London for a couple of weeks today, leaving me to cope with the flat, the cats, the shopping, the job, and the BROTHER. He is the biggest cope of all, announcing calmly to Mother this morning that he is confident he will not be called upon to do more than his usual share of domestic work during the next two weeks. Yes, that really *is* the way he speaks. If I want to annoy him, I call him Pompous Pete. I overheard this, and merely called out that his confidence was misplaced! I am going to distemper and paint the bathroom, spring clean the kitchen and repaint it, and do Mother's bed-room as well if I get time. If we eat at all, the brother will do the cook-ing. I will merely do the burping! I know his cooking of old – he makes lovely cakes (he says) but only if he is given crumpled biscuits instead of flour, for that is the only flour they were able to get when he learnt cooking as a prisoner of war. Except for the time when they swapped tea (used tea, dried off and repackaged with the addition of a little soda bicarbonate to make it draw when reused) with the German guards, and the Huns got wind of what they had done with the tea, and mixed cement with the flour they bartered in exchange.

And so I must rush off and start ruining my lilywhite hands (see ads) peeling spuds, and shredding fish for two starving cats whose plumpness is due to dropsy, but never, never, to overfeeding.

So, till the next letter, I hope you enjoy the books and a laugh or two to go with them,

Very sincerely,

Frances Woodsford

BOURNEMOUTH
May 20th 1950

Dear Mr Bigelow,

. . . Today all 'points' are cancelled for food-stuffs. That means we can get treacle, and syrup, dried fruits and biscuits, tinned milk or condensed milk, tinned meats and fishes, without having to balance our need for the one against our need for the others, and adjust the answer against the number of points allowed us. Always an inadequate number, I may say. We are still rationed (and terribly meanly) on sugar, fresh meat, tea, and confectionery. But the relaxation, long overdue, of this points business will mean such a weight off the housewife, and she has been carrying more than Atlas these past nine years and deserves it if anybody does. There will, of course, remain a certain amount of rationing, because the shopkeepers only get a certain amount of goods in short supply, but it will mean that if Mrs Jones doesn't want any syrup, but could do with an extra pound of dried apricots, and Mrs Brown doesn't want the apricots but would like some syrup, they won't both be penalised because they can only have their ration and if they don't want it, they can't take something else in its place. Now if we can't get one commodity, the chances are we'll be able to get something in its place.

I see from the papers that two bodies of experts had been to America (at the expense of the taxpayers, of course) to study production methods in the steel industry and in the building industry. And do you know, they have come back and published papers showing that the reason you have higher productivity in these industries is because your workers have more incentive in the way of wages, and more incentive to work in the way of the sack if they don't! For which wonderful discovery we have probably paid through the nose in our scant dollars. I am at once setting up as an expert in the rotundity of the globe, in the hope that in a week or two I can persuade the British Government to send me on a world cruise so that, on my return to England, I can publish a paper setting out my discovery that the World Is Round. Not only are we having Jobs For the Boys now that everything is nation-alised, on a scale never before imagined, let alone known, in England. We are, apparently, having Holidays For the Boys in Dollar Areas, so that they can come back and tell us what the Conservatives have known for two hundred years.

On which note of indignation I think I will stop. There has been no letter from you, Sir, for about three weeks now, and It's Not Good Enough. I shall, in desperation, probably write to Russ next Saturday instead of to you, and that will be fatal for the only way I ever get an answer out of that difficult gentleman is by being so nasty he writes back to tell me I'm unkind, unsympathetic, un-understanding and generally doing him wrong. Incidentally, you asked once if he was English. How Dare You! No Englishman I know (I know two, as a matter of fact, Bournemouth being exclusively female) was ever as difficult, moody, soul-searing, wolfish and altogether over-dramatic as W.K.R. And he does it on his head, so I think he must have practised a long, long time, and knowing me hasn't been the cause, hard though he tries to pretend it is.

Sincerely,

Frances Woodsford

BOURNEMOUTH
July 22nd 1950

Dear Mr Bigelow,

. . . My brother is very fond of telling the story of Dr Johnson, who was said to have spat out a mouthful of too-hot soup with the remark, 'Some dam' fool would have swallowed that.' Not that my brother does more than copy the remark, I would have you know. My brother does seem sometimes to be ashamed to be seen in public with me. One fine day, when I am out with the scion of the Woodsford family, I will do everything I know, and a few things I imagine, to give him really something to be shamed for – I shall scratch, hitch my skirts, smooth my girdle, pick my ear, run my nails through my hair for dandruff; stare at people; laugh like a noisy hyena, and belch whenever we come within hearing distance of any and everybody. That'll larn 'im.

The peculiar thing is that I really know my one and only brother isn't ashamed of me. At least, I am always clean and tidy in public, and fairly quiet. I wore gloves (as I always do) and a hat, *and* my fur cape, a decent, quiet dress and stockings. *He* wore a tennis shirt (he did have a tie, I will grant you) but no hat (never does) and no gloves. So why he should act as though I were a leprous barmaid, heaven knows! In the street, we alternately crawled along to avoid catching up with somebody he knew, or raced along side streets to ensure meeting as few people as possible. It brings out the nasty, catty side of my nature, and I dream of becoming the Hampshire Lady Tennis Champion (much chance!) and then joining his club after they begged me to do so on bended knee, just for the pleasure of refusing to associate with Mac. See what a horrid nature I have at bottom, but you won't tell anybody, I know.

I can, to an extent, sympathise with his agonies if he really is embarrassed by my presence. When Dr Russell was in England last summer, and stayed with us for a week or two, I loathed going out with him, as I had to do each evening. But in that case there was some reason – his behaviour in public is far too affectionate for my liking, and at the least suggestion that I disliked it, it became more so than ever, just to tease. Not very pleasant, when there are about sixty town Councillors here there and everywhere in Town, all keeping a watchful eye on the council officers, to see that they do not Let The Place Down. Where my brother is concerned, of course, there is no such worry for him, and the only explanation I can think of is that he has spread the tale at his club so hard, that he is a lonely bachelor living in rooms, that the presence of a real live sister might bring his house of cards to the ground any moment, and show him up for the romancer he seems to be. Mind you, that is surmise on my part: I've only heard of this 'living in digs,' family lives miles away' story once and it may not be generally accepted.

Enough of difficult men. A small boy came to my office yesterday to know if we had found his false tooth (on a tiny plate) which he had lost in the Baths. 'I shouldn't have lost it,' he explained, 'because I put it for safe-keeping in my shoe!'

. . . And now it's time to get back to work again. I am on late duty three nights this week and four next week, and shall be dead by Saturday. No flowers, please. Ah, my vanished youth, when four 14-hour days and two nine-hour ones wouldn't have caused the bat of an eyelash!! However every time I think of my pay cheque at the end of the month, with all this extra time, I hug myself for glee. So I must off, to earn all that pay.

Sincerely,

Frances Woodsford

BOURNEMOUTH
September 7th 1950

Dear Mr Bigelow,

. . . The other day, just as the water show was beginning, a nice clean
grey little mouse ran down the steps and swam right across the pool, to
be picked out, poor fellow, the other side and removed in ignominy by
his tail. The audience was delighted, thinking it was part of the show.
The next night, when the compère announced 'Bournemouth's twelve
Beautiful Aquabelles', out walked thirteen, the thirteenth having four
legs! A stray dog got through to the dressing rooms and, being an
exhibitionist, had taken the best possible way of drawing applause. Oh
we do see life, we do . . .

Reading through your two letters: no, the Dr Russell to whom I refer
sometimes is not Bertrand R. He is a Canadian from Toronto who has a
rather pathological love of England. Mind you, I don't suggest that anybody who loves England and the English must of necessity be pathological about it, but this particular man is inclined to weep because his
health won't permit of his living in England, and I detest men who weep
because they can't have their own way. I dislike, disapprove, or detest a
great deal about Dr R., and it is one of the Seven Wonders of the World
why I am still, in a remote sort of way, fond of him. Possibly because he
is sophisticated, terribly experienced with women, and the very fact that
he was attracted to me seemed the highest form of flattery. And goodness knows I needed a bit of flattery, to offset his other insults – for it is
really an insult to want to marry somebody merely because they won't
be your mistress, and to make it quite obvious, whilst in the very midst
of proposing for the umpteenth time, that you loathe and dread the idea
of being 'tied' in marriage.

Anyway, you notice I am not married; nor do I ever intend to be so
merely to be able to put a handle to my name. My Dr R. is, at the
moment, way down in my bad books, with all his letters torn up in a
huff and thrown away. Most dull letters too, so he deserves to live in the
rubbish basket.

This is a shorter letter than usual, and probably when I reread it I shall be ashamed of its scrappy style and lack of interest.

Sincerely,

Frances Woodsford

BOURNEMOUTH
November 4th 1950

Dear Mr Bigelow,

. . . What a to-do this attempt on Mr Truman's life is! I cannot help feeling sorry for the two assassins (would-be) for they so obviously are mentally deficient, and therefore pitiable. They *must* be, for no sane person would imagine he could walk into a very large, many-roomed house, and search through all the rooms until he found one man (the victim) without meeting some other person who would want to know what was afoot.

I imagine, probably wrongly, that the attempt must have been a terrific shock to Americans (perhaps not to you personally, but to the rank and file) who fondly imagine they are beloved wherever they are. We in England are well used to being regarded as bloated beasts, and so our unpopularity, which grieves us with our so-clean consciences (!) does not come as a rude shock. One of the things which so exasperated my friends in Canada was the impossibility of convincing visiting neighbours from the States, that Canada was not dying – nay, did not have the slightest wish – to become another State. The Canucks used to wail that the Yankees wouldn't even *start* to believe them.

. . . Enough of politics. I have been reading, with delight, *The Silverado Mine*, and *Travels with a Donkey*, by R.L.S.

I have been today to a new antique shop – new, that is, to me. I'm always looking for new antique shops, but the result is all the same. I'm done, diddled and bedevilled. One of the things I bought today is intended for a Christmas gift for somebody (probably poor Rosalind will get it slung at her!) and I bought it mostly because I loved its rich dark blue colour. It wasn't until I was busily washing it that I realised a) it had no containers for the ink it was supposed to hold, and b) even if it did, most people use fountain pens these days and not eighteenth-century (I hope) ink stands. So I sat down and thought and thought and thought, and now I shall claim that immediately (note that – *immediately*) my eyes lit on it I said to myself, I said, 'Now, that could make a delightful holder for pencils – in the pen-holes – and cigarettes, in the centre hole, for somebody to hand around a bridge table. Or they could put flowers in it, a clump in the middle and a small flower in the individual holes.' See how I trim my inspiration to my sucker-nature!

. . . I am sorry to learn you feel this is your last season as Chairman of the Regatta Committee. I hope by the time this reaches you, you and Rosalind will have had a lovely drive up through New England in the fall, to visit your sister. Isn't she the Mrs Crocker you said hardly went anywhere even though she was only eighty?

Now my lunch hour is finished and I must tackle the week's most unpleasant task – wage sheets. I hope you are enjoying something more felicitous, like yachting, or dozing, or a good book, or just sitting playing with the kittens. Wage sheets, indeed – we should have a big copper bowl full of money, and everybody dip in once or twice a week. Bags I first dip!

Sincerely,

Frances Woodsford

BOURNEMOUTH
November 11th 1950

Dear Mr Bigelow,

. . . Tonight we are all out to dinner and the theatre (it's my birthday today) and tomorrow I start on the kitchen painting and distempering. By January 17th, or thereabouts, I should be finished. And I probably *will* be finished, washed up, wore out, and knocking at the knees by that time. It's hard work, interior decorating, you know.

My brother, discovering that in my cleaning out I had thrown away about an inch of after-shave lotion which has been on the bathroom shelf for over two years, raised Cain about it yesterday morning, and not even the offer of my eau-de-cologne would soothe him. So I said alright, *he* could darn well do the kitchen, and last night I solemnly presented him with a supply of typed labels to put on the bottles I knew he would find about that room. Each label is marked 'Unknown Muck' and I suggested he should put them on before replacing the bottles where he finds 'em. Mother *will not* throw things away, and there's always a battle royal when I do. Me, I have fits, during which I throw out everything in sight except those pieces of furniture I can't lift. It's drastic, but I claim it is essential if we are to get through the front door into our tiny flat.

To my enormous surprise and gratification, I find that the Council are in the process of regrading me WITHOUT ASKING! When I came to work for them, four years ago, the job was advertised as being in the General Division. That's the lowest officer division. I was in that for two years, then asked to be regraded, and got transferred halfway up to the next grade. Like jumping a couple of grades at school. I haven't reached the top salary in that second grade yet, and here they are putting me halfway up the next grade still. I am most satisfied about it . . . It's not finally agreed to, yet, but I have an idea it will go through satisfactorily, and it gives me the notion that my boss thinks my work better than he will admit personally. The other day he was grumbling to somebody, when I chipped him about something or other, that I never gave him 'any encouragement'. When I retorted acidly that what you never give you never get given, he looked a bit nonplussed for an answer and then sheepishly grinned! I am the only person around here who gives praise to the staff for individual bits of work, and I firmly believe in it. It sweetens life, and pays good dividends as well. It's really very silly of him from a psychological point of view, for after four years he should know that I thrive on encouragement (not to say blossom on praise) and that I go right down in the dumps if the job becomes especially unpleasant – as it sometimes does, as do all jobs I imagine – and there is no sunshine to offset the gloom . . .

And now I will leave you to contemplate just what you would do, and if it gives you indigestion, I recommend soda bicarbonate.

Sincerely yours,

Frances Woodsford

BOURNEMOUTH
December 16th 1950

Dear Mr Bigelow,

We have had snow! And it's no use your turning up your no-doubt aristocratic nose at that statement. I know full well you've had snow yourself, and that you always get snow. But not here in Bournemouth – that is why I say 'We have had snow' and put an indignant exclamation mark after it.

. . . I woke yesterday morning to hear Mother laughing in the kitchen and saying, 'No! You can't go in, you poor little pussy, you' and then the rattle of newspaper. I knew from that sound, that Freckleface was being wiped dry, and went out to see how he had become wet enough to make Mother laugh. And getting in the kitchen, Mother said sharply, 'Don't let Frecks through to your bedroom – his paws are all snowed over.' But his paws weren't – he was walking around with about forty snowballs pendant from his underfur. Talk about de-icing a cat! If I tried combing them out, the fur came with the ice and hurt him. When I picked them off by hand, it apparently tickled him; and when I held him up in front of the fire, his tender tummy got scorched long before the snow had melted. Later in the day, after we had turned him out for a duty-walk, he came back with his tail frozen solid. It's no use your writing back by return and suggesting a dish of cinders or sand, a) because by then the snow will have gone, and b) Freckleface always refuses to use a dish of cinders, preferring the floor just outside the dish. Hence the forcible ejection from time to time, to his utter *fury*.

Well, anyway, having defrosted cat, and tucked him warmly on my

bed as a treat, I dashed out and swept snow in all directions. Off our
back steps – being an upstairs flat, we have a flight of concrete steps
which come up outside the building, then turn inside and finish up
under cover, outside our kitchen door. These were sifted and drifted into
a plane. Then the path from the bottom, to the main path we share with
the downstairs tenants – the man downstairs had swept his bit of path
from his kitchen door to his coal bin, and no farther. I swept from his
kitchen door to the roadway, for the sake of tradespeople calling, then
went round and swept the other path which comes to our front door,
downstairs front door, and the two back doors of the block of flats next
to ours. The tenants next door had swept nothing; one is too lazy, and
the others are only given to sweeping past with haughty looks – they
wouldn't know what a broom was. Well, having done all this, and got up
some coal for Mother (to the accompaniment of 'Oh – I'll get *that*', from
my brother, still in bed) I simply glowed with warmth and smugness.
Said to Mother, 'It's too deep for you to go out today, dear, so will you
please stay home and I'll use the Wellington boots.' Marched smugly
and proudly down my little pathway through the snow, stepped from

No room for sparrows.

Who'd be a cat?

Oh, this is much better.
(Flecks favourite position, bang in front of the
fire, but usually on the Chesterfield)

the pathway into virgin snow on the roadway, and went right over the top of my boots and way up under my skirt! There's probably a moral in there somewhere, but, wet and frozen, I failed to see it at the time.

. . . I don't suppose this letter will reach you much before the New Year, so will wish you well in that Year, and hope your Christmas was a happy one. We always drink a toast at lunchtime on December 25th, to our friends who are not with us, and so if your ears burned and wakened you about eight o'clock on Christmas morning, you'll know who it was thinking about you.

Very sincerely,

Frances Woodsford

1951

Uncles Mould, Marine Parade, Lyme Regis;
Frank 'Mac' Woodsford

BOURNEMOUTH
February 3rd 1951

Dear Mr Bigelow,

How strange, sometimes, comparisons work. The February copy of
Holiday arrived this morning, many thanks, just as I was leaving for the
office, so I took it with me to look at on the bus. While I was working,
I gave it to the cashier to look at (she's hardly anything to do this week,
as the premises are closed except for hot baths, and the poor cashier on
duty just sits and thinks and wishes for something to occupy her) and, as
they passed her desk, most of the staff stopped and had a good horse-
laugh at the Holiday Diet page.

I was intending to send you back one of the meals illustrated – either
the breakfast of two pork chops and orange, apple and banana slices,
or the dinner of two roast potatoes and roast beef, with a sarcastic
question, 'Is this one meal or two *weeks* meat ration?' (which, over here,
either meal would be!). But, suddenly, in came a customer as I passed
across the hall and *he* looked at it, the cashier obligingly holding the
book round for him to see it better, and he turned to me and said, 'Well,
it looks very nice, but you don't do too badly here in England – you *do*
get meat now and then.' I said, 'Yes, we do, but what I object to is that
we got more meat "then" than we do "now".' He shook his head at such
stubborn greed and said, 'Well, when I was a prisoner in Russia, I didn't
have any bread for seven months. *Bread*, mind you.' 'You mean you
didn't even have cake instead of bread, like Marie Antoinette? Well, I can
understand that, but surely you're not going to say it was *healthy* for
you?'

So, you see, a diet that seems inadequate to English housewives (and
their husbands) seems wonderful to an ex-Russian prisoner of war from
(I imagine) Czechoslovakia. And both would seem inadequate to an
American. It's mostly a matter of point of view. You moan (just a little
bit, not much!) because you only have toast and coffee and an egg and

Quaker Oats for your breakfast. I have never had an egg and coffee and Quaker Oats for *mine*. Partly because I loathe and detest that boiled woollen underwear which is called Porridge, and partly because I have always had orange juice, toast, and cornflakes with milk since I was about ten years old . . .

I was amused to see in the newspapers that this week the London butchers are going into mourning for meat! Their shops are being draped with black, and they are having black-edged cards printed for distribution to their customers with their ration of meat, the cards reading, 'We regret to announce the all-but passing away of Meat from this Country', or words to that effect. According to the papers, people are getting really angry about this dilly-dallying with the Argentine. After all, we are charging them two or three times pre-war prices for the coal and machinery they buy from us, so why all this hypocritical screaming because they are charging us the same increase on their meat? And people are saying they'd rather pay the extra few pence a pound for meat, than pay eight or nine times the price for rabbits or ham or tinned Spam-stuff. It's all this dam' Gov. planning. To keep down the official cost of living, they refuse import licences for firms to bring dried fruit into the country. Then they grant licences to Eire and Holland to import what is called 'Dried mincemeat', which is ordinary dried fruit stuck in bottles and covered with a slight sprinkling of sugar. Ordinary dried fruit costs (when we are allowed to buy it) about 2s. a pound. This so called 'mincemeat' costs about five times that – and what makes us so mad is that it is the fruit sent over for us, and bought by the Government in bulk, and then sold by the Government in bulk (to Eire and Holland etc.) and then sold back to us at enormously inflated prices. You see, dried fruit could be classed as an ordinary item of diet, to count in any cost of living index. But nobody can say 'mincemeat' is an essential, so we don't count that. It's like saying, 'we'll take all the shoes off the market, and then nobody'll have to pay money for shoes and then they'll all save that much money and it will cut down the cost of living.' Then they'd put, say, Chinese wooden clogs on the market at umpteen dollars a pair, and we'd *have* to buy them when our ordinary shoes gave out, and we'd then get told off for such extravagance – fancy buying Chinese wooden clogs! What an idea, indeed! Bah! and likewise Pah!

. . . And now for home, and four days at home next week, with a type-writer and a big fire – the coal-man having called when we were down to burning twigs and yesterday's ashes!

Very sincerely,

Frances Woodsford

PS Remember March 22nd's the date.

BOURNEMOUTH
Saturday, March 31st 1951

Dear Mr Bigelow,

. . . Looking over my old wartime hospital visiting reports the other day, I came across a report in which I had said, '. . . . . . I met this patient out in the street last week, when I was hungry and tired and rushed, what with going without my midday meal to do shopping for the patients, and running, or jog-trotting, nearly two miles in order to deliver their requirements to the hospital. Mark Garven was surprised, therefore, instead of getting a beaming hospital-visitor sort of smile, to get the full blast of my tiredness and exasperation with Canadians who wanted impossible things and weren't even grateful when I got 'em. He listened to me in silence, and when I stopped for breath said meekly, 'Well, you know you only do it because you like doing it – you wouldn't do it at all, otherwise.' And he was right. Whatever the trouble, I do my visiting because the joy it gives me is worth more than all the worry and disappointment and work.

Well, then, I write to you because I like writing to you, and because I like hearing from you and taking part, third hand, in your life in Bellport. If I didn't like doing it – or if I were doing it only out of gratitude for Rosalind's kindnesses, my letters would long ago have dried up or become stilted, dull 'bread-and-butter' affairs. So there is one chore less you can give yourself – that final paragraph in your letters thanking me for mine! Don't, for Heaven's sake, feel grateful for these

Saturday Specials; our indebtedness is well balanced in that respect, so our thanks can cancel each other's out, see?

. . . It is raining again, and I'm all dolled up in my best suit and my silliest hat, as my brother and I are invited out to lunch today. Serves me right for not wearing a heavy coat – I came out in my suit and my fur titfer and I refuse to carry an umbrella since they don't match my suit. Expect next week's epistle to be even less coherent than yesterday's, as I shall by then probably be delirious with triple pneumonia.

In the meantime of course, I remain strong and healthy and

Very sincerely yours,

Frances Woodsford

BOURNEMOUTH
June 15th 1951

Dear Mr Bigelow,

Yes, I know it's only Friday, but the way I feel today, tomorrow the family will be ordering wreaths, and I should hate to break the sequence of letters by not sending you one every Saturday until the last possible Saturday.

In other words, I am suffering; and oh, Mr B., I don't often suffer, but when I do, I make the most of it! Either I have

tonsillitis,
neuralgia down the r.hand side of my face,
fibrositis down the left of my head and neck,
abscesses in both ears,
insomnia,
and a hangover without benefit of spree

or I have a nice case of something or other not yet diagnosed. My boss is due back today, and I dragged myself down about ten o'clock hoping he'd catch the early train and be back so that I could go home immediately after lunch. Alas, it is only twenty minutes to five o'clock now and there's no sign of him so I don't know quite what to do – for to do another 14-hour day is quite out of the question. I do think four 14-hour days in a row is enough. I get home about 10.45, have supper in bed; toss and turn and count money, check tickets, deal with complaining customers, count some more money, check some more millions of tickets, add up and subtract, and generally have a very busy night until about three o'clock in the morning when I sleep. Breakfast is at quarter to seven, and after that is over and I am washed and dressed (not, I will admit, quite in my right mind this week) I go off to work and repeat the whole thing again.

Do you think I could be overworked, Mr B.? I certainly intend to hint so, when and if my boss turns up. Trouble with that man is that when the summer ends and we sink back exhausted he's full of plans for extra staff here there and everywhere to help us in the summer. When the spring comes along, he's forgotten last year and cheesepares as merrily as ever.

I finished *South Wind* one day over the weekend, I think. As I don't (yet) know Capri I can't compare the picture Norman Douglas paints of the island with the reality, but I should imagine it was a brilliant portrait if you take out the volcanic soil stuff and the smelly fountains. The characters were brilliantly drawn; and the arguments were brilliantly thought out, and I loathed the whole lot of 'em.

. . . This is a depressing and depressed letter, and I'm going to stop it this instant. Don't feel too sorry for me when you get it, for I shall probably be jumping the moon again by then. I hope you are well and busy with the yachts and the sunshine and the gay breeze.

Very sincerely,

Frances Woodsford

BOURNEMOUTH
June 30th 1951

Dear Mr Bigelow,

Work, work, nothing but work. And last week I was miserable because there was nothing to do but read with one eye (the other being buried in pillows and hot-water bottles) or feel miserable. So this week I have been miserable at work, for a change – one of the deepest down depressions, in which only two things prevented me throwing myself off the end of the pier. One, I can swim. And two, I think four pence is too much to pay to go on our trumpery pier, still in bits where they blew it up to stop the Germans using it in 1941.

My doctor allowed me to go back to work on Monday, at my earnest request, but forbade long hours or hard work for a bit. Today, therefore, is the first time this week I am doing evening duty, so my absence last week did somehow or other frighten my dear boss, since he is being so careful of my health this week! Needless to say, he didn't say it was nice to see me back. Nor, in fact, did he say anything except blow me up for writing what he thought was too friendly a note to thank the cashiers for the flowers they sent me. Apparently he can have a bit of slap and tickle with them when the mood takes him, but I must always stand aloof, Olympian and Awful (in the original sense of that word) and, in short, give a good impersonation of a mid-Victorian Overlord. I was so mad I nearly burst into tears and went straight home to my doctor to ask him to take back his permission!!

Instead, I went to my own office and had a small weep. Just as I was blowing the old nose (my head being wrapped in a white wool scarf to keep out possible draughts) a woman I know walked in to ask if she might have a Turkish Bath and send her ticket in by post, as she had left her book of tickets at home. She looked a bit oddly at me, so I murmured something about an abscess . . . . . . hurting . . . . bit run down . . . . . . and so on, and, to turn the subject, remarked on how very nautical she looked. 'Oh, my dear, yes,' she replied. 'I was all ready to go out on the yacht, when I stepped on the scales – and my *dear*, the most awful thing – I'd put on two pounds!! So I said to myself, "It's no good

– I must give up the yacht today. I *must* get rid of that weight."' So, at
great self-sacrifice, there she was to get that weight taken off by hot air
and other people's efforts. Apparently she has taken up the canasta craze,
and my dear, we sit and play on each other's terraces, in the sun, from
about three o'clock until seven every day. My dear, it is simply
lovely – you've no idea – and then you go home and are all ready for your
dinner. But you see, all her friends supply tea and little fancy cakes to eat,
and this dear lady isn't used to taking anything to eat with her afternoon
tea (I suspect the effort of having to order them from the cake-shop
would be too much for her frail strength) hence the extra two pounds.

. . . What a horrible mess the Socialists are making of this Persia
affair! People of all kinds here are feeling disgusted. I daresay it's right in
a way to say we have no rights in another's country; and that we exploit
them for a profit; that they are entitled to nationalise their own
resources. But are we right in letting them when so obviously they are
doing it for the benefit of a few (or possibly for the benefit of a
country they dislike as heartily as we do) and not for the many? As far as
I can make out, the only people who will do well out of the Persian
oil are a) the Sheiks etc., on whose land oil was found, and who get
royalties, b) the Government and their friends, and c) the Persians who
happen to work for the Oil Company and get housed, fed, and given
hospital treatment as part of the company's universal methods. One
paper, quoting a Persian employee of Anglo-Iranian the other day, said
that he remarked he wouldn't believe in nationalisation of oil until his
wages were two weeks overdue.

And today, when we have sent a cruiser to the spot, and Morrison has
at last said the refinery would shortly have to close because of lack of
storage space, the Persians seem to be getting a bit of sense. But why
wait until now? It may well be too late.

. On the other hand, the news from Korea seems to be a little brighter.
I wonder if the Russians have other trouble-making elsewhere in mind,
and wish to clear Korea off their plate before stirring up mud
somewhere else. I also cannot help wondering what General MacArthur
would think if the war in Korea comes to an end without the bombing
of Manchuria etc. I hope he will be big enough to be glad not to have
any more bloodshed.

Rereading up to here, I think possibly I should have added

d) the Oil Company

to my list of people who get benefit from the Persian oil-wells! I have an uncle who is an executive in the Anglo-Iranian, with fingers in a lot of other oil pies, and I gather from things he says that the oil companies (though he considers they are sitting birds for whoever likes to hold them up for a bit more in royalties) don't have to raid the petty-cash box for odd pennies.

Oh – news. I'm afraid General Jackson has been demoted, and renamed. In the local newspaper this week was an article about the cat at the Winter Gardens, who was being called upon to take part in an opera which was being presented there this week. The cat had to sit on a brick wall at the back of the stage, for how long I do not know. Well, on Wednesday I got a message from the Pavilion to say that I needn't expect Jackson over to see me this week, because he was far too busy. The Winter Gardens cat got stage-fright, so they sent Willie (Irving) Jackson and he was such a success in the part he was given two dinners each night he performed, with the Pavilion Supervisor waiting in the wings to escort him to No. 2 dinner. He turned up on Thursday morning (Thursday night being the concert night, his presence would not be wanted) and told me all about it, and how very simple it was to act on the stage when, like him, you had been brought up in the theatrical atmosphere of a large theatre!

And now I *must* do some work.

Very sincerely,

Frances Woodsford

BOURNEMOUTH
July 7th 1951

Dear Mr Bigelow,

To show you the old ego is back to normal, here is an anecdote culled from the latest autobiography. Written by the head of Cassells, the publishers, the book is crammed full of memories of Victorian figures in literature, and extremely good reading.

The author writes of a friend, a doctor, who, when he was a student, used to ride to hospital on a horse-drawn bus, and paid the driver a shilling a week for the privilege of riding up in front with him. One day, as they were jogging down Holborn, the driver suddenly thrust the reins at this student and told him to carry on. The driver took a bit of string out of his pocket, and as the westbound bus came up to them, dangled it in front of the other driver's face. The second driver thereupon burst into a scream of abuse and obscenity.

The westbound bus passed, and the eastbound driver put his length of string back into his pocket, and took back the reins. Of course, the medical student couldn't bear it, so he asked why the string had such an effect on the other man.

'Ah,' retorted the driver, "e ain't got no sense of 'umour. They 'anged 'is old man at Newgate this mornin'.'

Having got that horrific tale off my chest (I thought it would appeal to you, since the protagonists are all well and truly dead and therefore do not call, quite so much, for our sympathy!) thank you for your letter which came this morning, and for the snapshot of Victoria Regina of Bellport and her betrothed, the Rev. Eros. As to both looking as though they'd swallowed the canary, I can't say, but they did look a bit pleased, as though to say, 'Ah – got him!' or her, as the case may be. Betty Dall doesn't, in appearance, at all resemble the 'average' American girl; she has far too adult a set of features – so many Americans have snub noses all their lives, which are all right in extreme youth but a bit out of place as one grows older. I speak from experience. I can't pass comment on the Rev. Godfrey because I just can't see his face for his grin!

. . . My brother went to Wimbledon last Saturday. He is a very unimpressed young man, my brother, but he came back raving – not about Beverley Baker's legs; not about Miss Chaffee's chic outfit; not even about the tennis – but about Queen Mary!! Her complexion; her hair; the colours she wore; the beauty of her turnout (even if it is a bit out of date!); the exquisite care with which she timed her entrances and exits, so as not to interfere with the players in the least. She is a remarkable lady, held partly in awe, partly in affection by the English people. Rather more in affection now, as she gets older.

You'll have to hurry with your boat if you want to get in with the first swing of yachting. Or is the bottom-scraping, caulking and painting already done, and only the rigging to be put right? When we lived at Westcliff – a very pleasant residential suburb of the seaside town of Southend, right where the Thames joins the North Sea – the seafront (about six miles in length) was always edged during the winter with beached yachts. Around Easter, the smell of paint and tar and oil was terrific, and we all used loyally to pretend it was attar of roses and oh, ever so good for us.

. . . My brother (I am reminded above) put a pair of tennis shorts across the back of a chair about three weeks ago, and asked loudly if somebody would mend them – the edges were torn and ravelled [sic] and had already been adjusted once, to hide the first lot of torn edge. Mother and I eventually went into Committee and decided they were beyond help, and Mac would just have to belie his name and buy a new pair. We conveyed this decision to him. Sunday afternoon I heard him ask plaintively where was the key to my sewing-machine. I said sweetly, 'In the tray of my needlework box', and produced it for him. Next I heard him asking how you worked the machine, so I went in, looked at it, and said, 'Well, first of all you take off the lid and then you lift the machine off the floor onto the table and you find it much easier that way.' I gave him cotton, just to be co-operative, and he settled down quite happily to lift up the machine, look at it, put it back, put the lid on backwards and mend the shorts by hand!!! Since then he has told Mother twice, and me three times, how nice his shorts look. I can imagine they must be as short as those minute things little French boys wear! All because he won't spend about two dollars on a pair of ex-Naval shorts – he only wants them to wear when his others are being washed. And, do you know, Mr B., it isn't until you go back to his great-grandmother that you come to the Scots blood in my brother! Shows how strong the wretched stuff is, doesn't it? Like Scots whisky and their accent. I bought him a new blanket (badly needed) for his bed, and a pair of hand-knitted socks this week. I think he thought the package was, at least, a winter overcoat!! Yes, you're *quite* right, we do! Spoil him, I mean. I have promised to make him a shirt some time, when I get through with making Mother two jumper-dresses, two short jackets, altering three blouses for her, and making a skirt myself. Shall we say, 1955 for Mac's shirt?

Oh dear, I meant this to be such a superlative letter, to make up for the last two (which have been poor indeed) but it is being written during my third evening spell of duty this week – in patches, between running upstairs to see how the show is progressing, pushing the usherettes along with their preparations for the interval; finding lost people their seats, helping the cashiers cash up, taking peculiar telephone calls nobody else is free to handle . . . I must admit that by now (9.25 p.m.) I am more than ready for home, supper and bed. This year I staged a one-man revolt, and told my boss outright I refused to do evening work unless I could take at least two hours for lunch, so that I could get home and eat in peace and leisure. So I catch the bus about half past twelve, and get back to work on the 2.15 or 2.30 bus (2.30 if I know my boss is going to be late!). And it makes all the difference in the world.

Have a good sail today, and don't tear your spinnaker!

Very sincerely,

Frances Woodsford

PS I have opened this letter to put on two postscripts. One, to tell you that I have a visit today from General Willie Irving Jackson, Esquire, and a message from the Pavilion Supervisor that since his stage triumphs he has become very vain, and when it is sunny, goes out and sits in a pose on a large rock in the Pavilion Rockery where he waits for holidaymakers to admire and photograph him! Secondly, it has only just occurred to me that, instead of being virtuous in writing you on that

Friday I felt so ill, I was really being extremely selfish in spreading any germs I might have had – how awful if I really had had polio! I might have infected everybody through the postal services to you and the rest of Bellport. My humble apologies. I am glad I didn't.

BOURNEMOUTH

July 21st 1951

Dear Mr Bigelow,

. . . On Sunday my fond momma departed for a week's stay with friends, and left Jemima Muggins to look after No. —, brother, and two cats. Yesterday, for example (all the days have been about the same, some a bit worse but none any better) I woke at 4.30 a.m. in order to make certain I was awake at 6.30 to get breakfast. That's the awkward way my sub-conscious has of seeing that I keep my reputation for punctuality. Well, I got up at 6.30, produced breakfast for the cats and for ourselves by five to seven. Lay back in bed and ate my toast and drank my tea, and then up again for good about 7.25 a.m. to wash the dishes, clean up the kitchen (lick and promise) rush around dining room with a duster moving dust from here to there, put up cake in bag for brother's lunch; out at 8.20 to catch the bus to work. Left office at 5 p.m., ran all the way to the square to catch the bus, arrived home at 5.32 p.m., cooked new potatoes and green peas and laid the table, dished up dinner at 5.55 p.m. (special request, as Mac was due to play tennis at six and really wanted his meal about eight only he couldn't get me to co-operate). After dinner, wash dishes, feed cats, scald milk (no ice-box) wash milk saucepans, cool milk; wash milk bottles; replenish dining-room flowers, turn down beds, catch bus to get back to the square by 7.05 p.m. for the Symphony Concert.

I was so exhausted and hot by the time the half-time interval came along I just wilted and went home, where I lay panting for three minutes flat, and then set to work putting the breakfast things ready to hand, and doing some more flowers and tidying. Fell into bed about 11 p.m. and woke up again at four ack emma.

And that, Mr Bigelow, is why there just isn't any meat, or other substance, to this letter. There just isn't any to me any more. Today I left a little picture pinned to the front door, looking rather like this, for nobody could be more pleased to see Mother back than her two horrors. Freckles in particular has been firmly turned out of the flat at 8.20 a.m. every morning, and not allowed back

HURRAH!

until late evening – oh, way past his dinner time and way past his boiling point in temper. The half-cat on the right is Uncle Sam, afraid to come right out in the open . . .

Oh dear, my poor boss! He keeps saying, 'Thank you' this morning – a thing he doesn't normally do once in a blue moon. It's all because I'm cross with him, and he knows I am right to be so – we had a rip-roaring row yesterday. One of the male staff accused one of the women of lying over some trivial matter, and Mr B. and the man came into my office and we all set to. It occurred to me to ask a) why the woman should have lied, since there was no logical reason for a lie (the man had asked when a particular bath was filled with hot water, and didn't believe the woman when she had said 'nine o'clock') or b) why she should be condemned as a liar by both this man and my boss without so much as a hearing.

I, stuck mid-way between staff and boss, get ground into very small pieces at very frequent intervals! It must be quite the same thing as being a bit of coffee bean . . . . . . you get ground up small, and then you still get into hot water.

This is a very poor letter, and the only thing I can do is to see that it doesn't go on being poor any longer.

I'll try to do better next week . . .

Very sincerely,

Frances Woodsford

BOURNEMOUTH
August 31st 1951

Dear Mr Bigelow,

. . . On the way back to Bournemouth on Monday I had coffee on the train, and a tall man came along and said, 'May I?' as he sat opposite me. Now there isn't much opportunity for an accent in the words 'May I?' so I couldn't tell from whence he came. Two other glum people came and sat at the other seats, and we all sat there glum and silent as English people so often do in a train. The waiter came up and asked, 'Tea or coffee?' We all mumbled, 'Coffee.' I longed to say to the man opposite me (who looked so interesting) 'Excuse me, but I see from the cleanness of your shirt you are an American – would you care to have the recipe for British Railway's coffee? You never know – the Metropolitan Museum of Art might like it. For art it surely must be, it cannot be made this way by accident – not every day, every week, every month of every year.' But I was so shy I didn't say anything and we all finished our mouthwash in the same glum silence we started. The fluid was hot and faintly brown in colour, but other relationship to coffee it had none.

When we had all finished, the waiter came round and demanded a king's ransom, and the man opposite me asked 'What time does this train get to Southampton?' in a broad American accent! So I was right, though very unkind to my fellow English for judging a man to be an American merely because his white shirt was so pristine. It is a fact, though – your shirts always seem so clean and new and freshly laundered. Perhaps ours are so expensive our menfolk have to wear them when they get shabby, or keep them on one day longer than they should (our laundries are another thing we don't boast about). I noticed in Canada the brilliant whiteness of shirts, though at that time I thought I was being unfair to Englishmen, who were severely rationed with theirs. Perhaps they still are, financially, when you compare them with Americans visiting this country. After all, you wouldn't wear your oldest clothes if you wanted to impress foreigners, would you?

Did you hear of the three little French cats, called Un, Deux and

Trois? They went skating in the winter, but unfortunately the ice cracked, and Un Deux Trois Quatre Cinq!

Awful isn't it? I'll leave before you hurl that book at me,

Very sincerely,

Frances Woodsford

BOURNEMOUTH
October 20th 1951

Dear Mr Bigelow,

Thank you for your letter of October 10th, which came this week, and which delighted me with your tales of young Master Toddy and his ways. And writing of Toddy brings me to the Subject For Today – 'The Tragedy of The Bellport Riders'.

Now I can take any hint weighing over half a ton, and it was not through obtuseness that I did not react to yours and send you a second illustration of this famous ride. No, my reason was that I had had a brainwave, I thought. Why, said I to myself, do another silly water colour? Why not perpetuate the thing in clay?

So when term finished at the art school I begged a piece of clay and took it home with me. This I rolled and kneaded into a flat slab, on which I painstakingly built up bit by bit, in relief, a horse being ridden by Messrs T. Akin and P. Bigelow. I scratched (literally) in a background of trees and children.

This was so much fun I asked myself once again whether it was good enough, and conscience (and inclination) said No. So I went across the town and bought 7lbs of modelling clay powder. It was horribly difficult turning this powder into usable clay, with no equipment whatsoever, but eventually I managed. And with the clay I modelled the whole thing in a group of figures measuring about 7 inches high by 8 inches long. This was very charming and I was so excited about it as I proceeded that I did it rather quickly, with the result that when the clay dried off, a couple of legs fell off here and there.

But did this daunt me? No! Indeed, No, Sir! I started all over again, this time taking extreme care. Finding, with this third attempt, that there was a space on the horse's back (behind you) measuring about 1½ x 1 inches, I modelled Missie and stood her behind you, barking wildly at something or other. For why should she be left alone and moping at home, while you two were having all the fun?

This third statue was, I flattered myself, delightful. I treated it as though it were an atomic bomb likely to go off if touched. How I got it to the pottery class, goodness only knows, but get it there I did, unharmed; and it sat on the bench and charmed all the other students and the two teachers as well. My head by now was reaching astronomical dimensions.

Everybody coddled that little group. It was given a tin biscuit-box to itself, where it rested in a bed of straw. It was labelled (the box) all over with DO NOT TOUCH notices, and placed high out of reach on a shelf. I used to stand on a chair each time I went to classes, and gently lift the box. Last Wednesday the box felt light and empty, so I hugged myself in anticipation.

And on Monday of this week, as I walked along the corridor, I suddenly saw on a chest further along, a little pile of 'biscuited' pottery . . . . . . the Bellport Riders. In ten separate pieces. In ten pieces, Mr Bigelow (and even so, two other bits were missing when I fitted them together, jigsaw like). I walked into the pottery room too miserable to say anything, and as soon as I was seated Peter (our new teacher) came up and started asking about the way I made the group, in an endeavour to find out the cause of its explosion in the great heat of the kiln. We decided in the end it was probably my fault – that I had, somehow or other, got an air bubble in the clay of the horse's body, and, in exploding, the body had taken with it all the other parts of the group which had been broken.

I said at length, 'Ah well, it can't be helped, but thank you for all the trouble you have taken. Now I shall just have to be content with the relief-tile.' 'Oh, but that one blew up too,' said Peter. 'There were only two failures in the whole kinful, and they were both yours.' 'Oh no, there weren't only two,' I said miserably, 'for I've just looked in the cupboard and my biscuit barrel has had its handle broken off.' Only three failures, and *all* of them mine. Why?

So I took my ten little pieces home, and I stuck them carefully together with glue, and I made a false left leg for you and a false left leg for Dogsbody (the horse) and a new tail for Missie. And then I painted it all with ordinary watercolours – a white horse dappled with grey. A red, red blanket. Toddy in red trousers (short ones) and a white shirt with red band around his neck and arms. You in grey-green trousers and a shirt striped in green and white, with a gay yellow kerchief, around your neck, dotted with black. Your 14-gallon Stetson (a 10-gallon was too small!) was in grey-green to match your trousers, and Missie, whose colouring I did not know, is white with black and brown patches. The horse has two feathers (red) between his ears, and a very naughty look in his eyes. The whole thing was then varnished with colourless nail-varnish, and reposes in state on the sideboard in my living room, with a large antique brass tray at its back.

It is the most charming thing I have ever done, and it was going to be *such* a pleasant gift for you. And now it is all in pieces. It's all very well for my family to say that misfortune, if well taken, is good for character. But my character, as you know, is too near perfection for it to need any improvement, by misfortune or any other means. Besides, most of the pleasant things that happen to me seem to happen without any deserts on my part; this makes it all the harder to bear hard luck when I feel I do deserve good – as though I need never bother or take trouble, because it will all come to naught, whereas if I just sit back, the only fortunes that come to me will be good ones, undeserved and unexpected. This, I realise, is a very lazy and bad philosophy to get around the place, and I don't really expect to adopt it. But it *is* disappointing, especially when I have gone to such pains (and believe me, for such as me, pains is the word) to keep it a secret from you.

However, when I got home last night from the cinema, I peeped in the living room to look at the group, and I suddenly said, 'I will *not* be beaten by a bit of clay. I *will* do it again. I *will* get it right!' and suddenly, as I thought all those intense thoughts, there popped into my head a method of getting the body of the horse without any possibility of it containing air bubbles. So next week I shall jut out my chin and confront the pottery teachers with my determination to try, try again. It will, of course, take many weeks, for the clay is so thick in diameter for the horse that it takes many many weeks for the stuff to dry sufficiently for it to be baked . . . I should imagine, with luck, I might do it by next Easter! It shall be my New Year Resolution. This setback is all the more annoying since my delight with my first attempt (prior to baking and blowing-up) led me to plan all sorts of other little figures – a caricature of my brother playing tennis; a sailor and his girl sitting on a bank under a tall tree – the tree trunk to be the column of the table-lamp, the shade to be the tree's greenery – a burlesque, in clay, of my fat cat asleep on his back. And so on. Full of ideas but inadequate to carry them out. You've no idea how exasperating it is, Mr Bigelow, to be fairly bright in the head but not capable of carrying through the ideas that arrive . . .

Very sincerely,

Frances (Brokenhearted) Woodsford

BOURNEMOUTH
December 22nd 1951

Dear Mr Bigelow,

. . . I had a letter from my Canadian doctor, Keith Russell, last week to tell me he was in hospital having one lung out. That poor man can't do anything without annoying me! Even when he writes for sympathy he annoys me because that's all he's writing for. Says he somehow feels he's never to hear from my sweet self (that's me in case you wondered) unless he gets down to it and writes to me again. He had seen a play in New York and wrote 'yours truly witnessed the same in New York' . . . . . . Talk about English as it is tortured . . . . . . Oh dear, maybe I'm too particular, too fussy for this imperfect world, but I'd rather stay single *and* fussy.

The other day my brother was out of the Town Hall on Council business when, presumably, eleven o'clock came around and he'd finished what he had to do. So instead of going straight back to the Town Hall and having a cup of coffee when he got there, he went to one of the big stores in town for his elevenses. In the restaurant he noticed a girl he knew, who was sitting near a pillar, with a body just visible to the main part of the room. Mac walked over and said hallo, and found to his horror, when he got around the pillar, that she was accompanied by seven female friends! They were delighted!! Mac joined them for coffee, and three of them decided to have another cup with him. When the waitress brought the bill she handed it to my brother automatically (she must have thought he kept a harem, or was a stage producer) and he was horrified to find it was for 17 cups of coffee! Apparently the girls had been there some time. The girls said but oh Mac wasn't to pay for them all, it was ridiculous. Mac quite agreed, privately, but made a pooh-pooh fuss just for the record I imagine, and the eventual upshot was that all the gals pushed their contributions into a pile on the tablecloth and refused to take it back. So Mac gathered it up and paid the bill and left a tip and had sixpence left over for himself! He was as pleased with himself as though he'd just made a thousand pounds on the Stock Exchange . . .

Oh – pottery. I have compromised. I will not go back to Ballantine's decoration muddle class, but I have allowed myself to be persuaded to stay in Miss Gilham's throwing class. That means that I shall have to leave my pots at the college to be biscuited, but Miss Gilham has promised to get them glazed for me elsewhere . . . When Mr Ballantine came up to me on Monday he said, 'I am sorry about those two side dishes, Miss Woodsford' (those were the two intended for you, which were ruined by being put in too hot a kiln) and I said it really didn't matter because I had no intention of continuing with pottery in such frustrating circumstances. 'Isn't there anything you can suggest we do to make you feel happier?' I ask you – could I have said, 'Yes, get yourself a new character'? So I just waved my hand around the filthy studio and left it at that . . .

Somebody on the radio said the other day the reason Americans make their tea with little bags and hot water is because they never keep the same wife long enough to get a kettle boiled! And with that calumny I will leave you for now!

Sincerely,

Frances Woodsford

BOURNEMOUTH
December 29th 1951

Dear Mr Bigelow,

A special treat for you, this letter was to be. All in my own handwriting. But on trying out this new paper (I have thousands of aunts, whose minds run comfortably in the twin grooves of notepaper and hand-kerchiefs) I am not sure whether it is paper or blotting paper, so the letter must be typed to be legible.

Well, I don't know about you, but I'm very glad Christmas is over. I think Christmas should be a time for children, and having none of my own and none handy for borrowing in times of emergency, there was just Mother and I at home, and occasionally my brother to mope and gloom (he's always miserable in between parties and nobody knows what he's like at them because he sees to it that none of his family go to them) so we just moped too. And overate a bit, of course, though the Ministry of Food do what they can to discourage such a thing. Buying all our food as they do, we eat what they buy, and if we don't like it, then we're just too fussy for this world. So our 'roasting' fowl was definitely a boiling fowl; our potatoes were earthy; our Christmas pudding was nearly minus fruit (Ministry of Food forgot to import any!) and our nuts looked and tasted as though they'd been left over from the year before last. However, there is peace on earth and for that I am grateful. And for many other things – the rudest health possible, a clean airy town, a wonderful mother, a job, and a sense of humour. And, of course, you to tilt at from time to time . . .

On Boxing Day Mother and I walked along the promenade on the sea-edge, and oh dear, people just dripped with diamonds and minks and new fur-backed gloves and new silk scarves and yellow pullovers and bright socks. I dripped a new wool scarf and a new handkerchief! . . .

Did you listen to the King's speech? I thought it one of the best Christmas talks he has given, and there was almost no hesitation at all, and none of those awful moments when the whole nation was holding its breath *wishing* him the next word, and quickly . . .

I went, for the first time for months and months, to the cinema last night. A British film, rather light and flimsy, it was nonetheless good holiday fun. 'Coming next week' was a trailer of an American film apeing (the right word, but probably the wrong spelling) *King Kong*, and the audience just rocked. With laughter, which I don't think was intended. I roared too, particularly when the trailer came to the bit where the enormous ape wrecked a Hollywood nightclub (breaking the lions' backs across a convenient window frame as one might snap firewood) and pulled down the orchestra on their platform, knocked out the ceiling, the walls, and, it appeared, 90% of the people there at the time. In the midst of all this carnage and earthquake destruction, walks the Heroine (yes, she's the type to deserve a capital H). She trots up to the great beast, and stamps her foot at him in annoyance, plainly saying, 'Oh! Joe Young, you *bad* thing, you!' I hadn't expected understatement from Hollywood . . . . . .

If this is to catch the mail, I must stop now. I remember now I wanted *this* letter to be more controversial than the last. And now that I've written the letter, it isn't very, though no doubt you will find plenty of bones to pick over.

So till next time, with more controversy,

Sincerely,

Frances Woodsford

1952

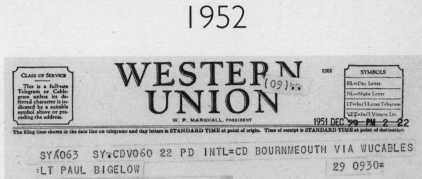

WESTERN UNION

(09)

W. P. MARSHALL, PRESIDENT

1201

1951 DEC 29 PM 2 22

The filing time shown in the date line on telegrams and day letters is STANDARD TIME at point of origin. Time of receipt is STANDARD TIME at point of destination

SYA063   SY CDV060 22 PD INTL=CD BOURNMEOUTH VIA WUCABLES

:LT PAUL BIGELOW   29 0930=

THORNHEDGE RAD BELLPORT

WISHING YOU THE VERY HAPPY NEWYEAR YOU DESERVE FROM

THE WELL FILLED WASSAILING WHELMED WOODSFORDS=

BOURNEMOUTH
January 5th 1952

Dear Mr Bigelow,

I knew it! In last week's letter I said the post office would undoubtedly maltreat my cablegram to you, and how right I was; it must be characteristic of all post offices all the world over. Here was the cable, pre-post-office version, as we composed it the day your scrumptious food parcel arrived:

WISHING YOU THE VERY HAPPY NEW YEAR YOU
DESERVE, FROM THE WELL-FILLED, WASSAILING,
WHELMED
WOODSFORDS.

And if you have to look up wassailing in your dictionary I shall claim two points to me!

Today also, as well as your letter, I had one from Rosalind, practically incoherent with delight at the idea of actually, positively, really, going to Jamaica. By now I hope she is warmly lying on the sands of Montego Bay surrounded by interesting high society, from both sides of the Atlantic . . .

Oh dear, Mr B., you do sometimes make me laugh; and sometimes you make me blush with shame. You write . . . . . . 'There are a lot of New Year's Eve parties for this evening – but I won't go to many – about three is my limit.' And all I could manage to do was go to the theatre, and on to bed about 11.30 p.m.! Perhaps, when I arrive at your age, I shall have more energy.

Talking of age – I see you are once more harping on it, for you say Rosalind started her holiday on the 4th January 1952, the date you never thought you would see . . . Our oldest customer at the Baths is Mr Russell (the name haunts me) and it is only these last two months that I've insisted somebody should take him downstairs in the lift, when he comes in for his weekly Turkish Bath. Normally, Mr Russell trots down and upstairs all by himself. Mr Russell is 93, and this week he bought himself a new book of tickets, with enough in it to last him another six months. Fie on you Mr B., you've a long way to go yet, and I shall continue to rely on you for nagging and nattering for many years to come . . .

The theatre I went to on New Year's Eve was presenting a Christmas Pantomime; very spectacular, lots of girls with long legs, little children with lisps, and scenery all over the place. The only thing I thought would really appeal to the children – though, actually, there are so few in Bournemouth no pantomime would dream of appealing only to children, for it wouldn't pay – was a scene in which somebody gave the principal comic a Wooffum-puff. The principal comic was, as is usual in pantomimes, the Dame – that is, he was dressed as an old woman. The Wooffum-puff was a long pale blue furry caterpillar, and on being let out of its cage it promptly escaped down a hole in the stage-floor. The Dame walked to the footlights and appealed to all the children in the audience to look around while he was getting tea, and call out 'Wooffum-puff' if they saw it. Of course, the children loved this. The Wooffum-puff kept appearing here and there, and the kids screamed their little heads off trying to attract the Dame's attention, but every time she (or he) saw the blue thing, the blue thing would promptly run off on the end of a piece of string or climb up a wall out of reach and disappear around a picture. Unfortunately, they only had this one scene which was of interest to the children. And I must admit that quite a few of the adults were making sounds suspiciously like 'Wooffum-puff' at the same time.

What a couple of heart-lifting events we have had in the newspapers during this last week: first we had the award of the Victoria Cross to a young lad in Korea, and now we have Captain Carlsen and his mad, foolhardy, glorious vigil in the Atlantic. Needless to say, as a seafaring race our newspapers are full of the *Flying Enterprise**, and the first item to be read on the radio at news time is, yesterday and today, of current progress there . . .

* *Editor's note*: On 25th December, the ship encountered a storm in the western approaches to the English Channel, and eventually sank thirteen days later, just off the coast of Cornwall. Captain Carlsen was declared a hero for refusing to leave his ship until all hope was lost.

Now I must stop: it's gone nine o'clock and there is much work to be done. On top of having a cashier away (she isn't coming back, there's a letter in the post this morning telling us so, oh so sweetly, after she's left us in the lurch for two whole weeks) I now have the Engineer ill (passed out on us yesterday, and frightened us all to bits, poor man) and his assistant on holiday and my boss away ill. I suppose I could now be said to be earning my salary, eh?

And so, au revoir until next week . . .

Very sincerely,

Frances Woodsford

BOURNEMOUTH
January 13th 1952

Dear Mr Bigelow,

Thank you for your letter, with the home-made envelope and the *ghastly* striped pink paper! It makes one go cross-eyed in reading it, doesn't it? . . . . . . Reading your letter, I thought I detected a note of chagrin when you wrote . . . . . . 'tomorrow there is to be a midnight booze party at the Ewitt's and someone asked me to *tea* in the afternoon. Wish I could think who it was.' I took it you were mad at being asked to tea instead of to the midnight booze party. On reading it again, though, I changed my mind and decided that you were merely boasting of your cramped calendar of appointments in the social whirl of Bellport! I am sending you the report of my dip in the social whirl, at my brother's cocktail party last week, which I enjoyed much more than I expected to – possibly something to do with my peculiarly nervous digestive system. Couldn't eat lunch through nervousness; couldn't eat anything at tea through ditto. Consequently, two cocktails, an orange juice and a sherry made me feel much better than they would have done on a full stomach. The sherry was *awful*, and I should have known better than to have it, knowing it was cheap stuff! I gave my brother a

copy of this 'epic' and have an idea he is using it for a bit of blackmail
. . . . . . to wit . . . . . . 'Let me take your blonde girlfriend to the
dance Saturday, or I'll read what my sister says about you, to the Club
members . . .' sort of thing.

On the reverse of that newspaper cutting I see a whole flock of real
estate advertisements: no wonder you thought cottages and houses
expensive, looking at the 'for sale' advertisements in *Country Life*. Your
rents seem to be high, but certainly some of the prices against the houses
seem to be most reasonable. I always divide your dollar prices by three,
to bring it roughly into pound sterling. Then I halve it on the under-
standing that salaries and wages are about twice as high in the States as
they are here, and the final answer gives me something to compare with
our own prices.

Now that's the article itself: I am returning this with comments (you
won't be able to read my shorthand notes, so here they are translated
and enlarged). I don't know much about Mr Herbert Hoover, but I'm
darned if I'd ever take any notice of anything Mr Joseph P. Kennedy says
on this subject, remembering that he sent home urgent and frequent
dispatches from London saying that Britain would not, and could not,
stand up to Hitler if France capitulated. And then when France did
capitulate, he urged the immediate withdrawal of all American aid into
the European continent, because obviously the British were finished,
caput, wiped out, nodamgood, ready to let Hitler walk all over them. So
I'm prejudiced against Mr Kennedy's ideas from the start . . .

As to all that blah-blah about demanding positive assurance,
declarations, ironclad commitments by the Western European
countries, what good would they be in the event? Scraps of paper?
France had an ironclad declaration and commitment she and Britain
would stand firm against Germany, but in the event, it didn't affect her
behaviour. We had an ironclad declaration and commitment she and
Britain would stand against Hitler. Mr Kennedy didn't believe we would
keep it, but we did. Now whom are we to believe? The governments
who make these declarations, or the people themselves who have to do
the fighting? And then again, might not the countries of Western
Europe turn round and ask the United States for an ironclad commitment not to wait for the *Lusitania* or Pearl Harbor? We can all throw

bricks. Trouble is, you're making so many more bricks than anybody else, these days!

. . . No, it seems to me that Britain and America are both dependent on each other. It's not all give on one side, and all take on the other. If *we* are defeated and lose the important points of the Empire, then *you're* in for a very nasty time indeed. And if *you* don't help us with your immense possibilities for the production of the weapons of war, then *we're* defeated. Squirrels in a cage, eh?

. . . And now for home and lunch. If Mother produces sausages or corned beef again, I shall not wait until *after* lunch to be sick. This week my main daily meal has been, Mon. chilli, Tues. stewed ewe (our week's ration!), Wed. chilli, Thurs. one slice Spam. Fri. one sausage. All with potatoes and greens and the everlasting 'trifle' (stale cake with custard and jelly thrown over it!) because my brother won't eat anything else for dessert. Poor Mother, it must be horrible for her to cope with two offspring who don't like the same things and who eat at different times anyway.

Finally: March 22nd is the date!

Very truly,

Frances Woodsford

BOURNEMOUTH
January 30th 1952

Dear Mr Bigelow,

A small extra letter because the sun is warm and shining on me as I sit at my typing desk, and because I feel pleased with the world, and because I wanted to rush off and congratulate you on attaining the fame of a bronze plaque on the Yacht Club premises. Nearly 50 years of yachting there is a proud record.

. . . We are enjoying here at the moment a spell of the most beautiful sunshine. Sunday there was a dusting of snow on the ground, absolutely sparkling with sun. The snow melted overnight, but we have had such heavy frosts overnight that everything has been white in the morning until the sun came up to melt it. The radio says England has been more or less covered by fog, but if so we have escaped it – we usually do – and wallow in wonder at the continuing warmth.

This morning we are glad there's something to make us feel cheerful, for the cuts in everything to make the country solvent (or have a shot at doing so) are enough to make us all pour into the Channel like suicidal lemmings. It is now 1952, and we have been controlled, rationed, impoverished, drained and depressed since war started for us in 1939. Deduct 1939 from 1952 and you get a horribly long time in comparison with one's normal expectation of life.

Quite by accident last week I discovered why the Bellport Riders blew up in the kiln! I had used modelling clay – obviously that was, I thought, a thing to use for modelling. *But*, you have to find a very special brand of modelling clay if you wish to fire it, otherwise it disintegrates (and how!) in the great heat of the kiln. I am once more fired with enthusiasm, and if the new clay has arrived when I go to pottery-throwing class tonight, I shall 'borrow' a little and get to work once more on the Masterpiece.

And now I have finished my lunch of one apple, one toasted cheese sandwich, and four nuts, and feel I should walk it off in a bit of exercise along the seafront; for who knows, when the sun disappears we may not see it again until Easter, this being England.

And so, au revoir 'til Saturday.

Frances W.

BOURNEMOUTH
February 9th 1952

Dear Mr Bigelow,

Twice during this sad half week I have been severely shocked by my fellow creatures. Shocked, and worried. On Wednesday afternoon, it being his half day, one of our attendants came back to the Baths for some tea in the café, and I heard in a roundabout way that he was really, actually, furious. Apparently it was inconsiderate of the King to die on a Wednesday. And even more inconsiderate of all the cinemas and theatres to close immediately the news was heard.

'Where'm I expected to go until 10 o'clock tonight?' asked Mr Smith indignantly. 'Am I supposed to go home and cry?'

That was one man's reaction. The other shock came today, when another male member of the staff (in fairness to him I must say his feelings have been echoed rather more faintly by several others) complained bitterly about the continuing misery of the radio programmes. I must tell you that we have music (classical and mostly depressing – things like roundelays and fourteenth-century part-songs and music for the harpsichord) then we have talks to farmers, *Children's Hour*, the Morning Service (and several others) and the News Bulletins. We are to continue in this strain until after the funeral, when programmes will gradually, very gradually, go back to including plays and light music and comedy.

Now what shook me this time was not so much the man's biting remarks – he is a red-hot Socialist, anti-Monarchist, anti-authority, and a thoroughly quarrelsome type – but the picture he unconsciously painted of many thousands of people, who are so utterly conditioned to the present fashion of being entertained artificially every spare moment of their time, that they cannot contemplate life without the comic turns on the radio. Not for two nights (which is all we've had so far). To think that people cannot live with themselves for so long as two evenings of, say, four hours each, is a horrifying thought . . .

I am sad, too, for Queen Mary. She has had more sorrow than any one person should have to bear, and in spite of it all, at the age of 85 and in sorrow at the loss of a favourite son, she did not do what the rest of us would do – keep herself shut away in privacy. She came out and passed the 2,000 or so people staring at Clarence House, so that Princess Elizabeth should have somebody there to welcome her when she returned to her home. Everybody I have listened to has felt most sorry for our grand old Queen. And most people have felt glad that the King's end was so peaceful after his recent painful storms. Now we are feeling sorry for Elizabeth. She has a long, hard job ahead of her with no half days, no complete holidays, no retiring. It is as if, Mr Akin died tomorrow, Rosalind was immediately told to go to the steel works and run them in his place. Immediately, with no space for grief or pause for preparation before she faced the work people. And today Royalty don't even get the panache and the panoply of the Kings and Queens of old. Can you imagine Elizabeth II being allowed to send some modern Drake off on an expedition – or to order somebody's head off because she felt bad-tempered?

. . . I'm off for a long weekend with friends who live on the edge of the New Forest. Then, Tuesday afternoon, I shall come home and repack and go off Wednesday morning to London and Surrey for the rest of the week. When I get my weekly washing and mending done I do not know . . .

Very sincerely,

Frances Woodsford

On holiday: London
Friday, February 15th 1952

Dear Mr Bigelow,

Today we are, after a long-drawn out agony of ten days, burying a very kind King. It has been sunny in spells, but for the most part a day of yellow-pearl texture, and icy cold.

I have just come back from a neighbour's house where my aunt and I watched the televised funeral procession in all its pomp, dignity and silence. Also watching was a young American, the wife of a medical man, who came in a little after us. She was much impressed, especially by the Guards Officers, be-plumed and mounted on glorious horses: I remarked that the silent crowds lining the route, edged by servicemen with bowed heads over reversed arms, looked through the cameras like banks of massed flowers, probably frozen flowers, for many had waited all night. The American girl said yes, it was better to watch it as we were doing, and as they were probably doing back home. 'Where's back home?' I asked. 'Oh, I'm from Illinois,' she said. And, of course – since coincidence and I go together – she had been at school at Duncan Grant or something, just about four miles from Alton!

At the top of my letter I mentioned the long agony of the last week. It seems to me that we are, in our insistence on ritual, imposing intolerable misery and strain on the King's family. In ordinary life when some husband and father dies there is privacy for his family, broken only by friends, and the funeral follows hard on the death. It does not make their sorrow any less, but it is less of a strain on them. But our late King's family have had strain upon strain: none of the church services they have attended have been private, but Monday they had to follow the coffin from Sandringham to the railway station; then the three Queens had to – or chose to – receive the cortège at the London terminus, the poor Queen Mother making at one moment a piteously 'lost' little motion. They then went to Westminster to receive the dead King there: twice they have been since to Westminster Hall to watch silently the silent lying-in-state, and the silent stream of people passing through – 300,000 of them in three days. And today there was the two-hour ceremonious march from Westminster to the station, and this afternoon there is, at long, long last the Windsor funeral. All in pomp, and *so* public . . .

Now I *must* go upstairs and take off my coat: it's so rude to go around dressed in everything I have with me, but I am once more sleeping with a Persian prayer-rug as an extra, unofficial blanket, and the only time I am warm is under it or in the bath. And no guests can stay in either place indefinitely!

Au revoir till next week,

Very sincerely,

Frances Woodsford

BOURNEMOUTH
March 8th 1952

Dear Mr Bigelow,

On Tuesday this week, members of the staff were horrified to see Smithy (an attendant) cook for his lunch some crumpets, covered with toasted cheese, covered in turn with TREACLE! On Wednesday, to their horror, he came up with fried bread, two fried eggs, and more TREACLE. On being twitted about this, he remarked blandly, 'The trouble with English people is that they've no imagination where cooking is concerned.' I have suggested, via the staff grapevine system of telegraphy, that Smithy should try kippers and strawberry jam, but so far all the other members of staff have refused point-blank to make such a suggestion out of kindness to their own olfactory sense.

On Tuesday this week I was not doing anything so plebeian as to dine in my office (I never use the staff room, believing that the staff should be able to get *somewhere* where they know I shan't appear on a tour of inspection!) because my cousin Arthur Mould called me up and took me out to luncheon at the Royal Bath. The Royal Bath is a hotel which used to cater for Edward VII, and also for the Prince of Wales in his heyday.

It remains static; the corridors are still covered with highly polished Prussian blue linoleum, that in turn being laid with bright red Turkey carpeting. The walls are dark brown up to waist-height, when they turn into a cream colour between enormous picture frames showing the Battle of Inkerman and so on. The lights are, for the most part, made of broken bottles fitted into a mosaic – at least, that is my opinion; when they were new they were probably the latest thing in stained-glass household what-nots. The hotel period extends not so far as the plumbing or the beds, but it faintly flavours the cooking, for the chef does tend to run to thick puddings. Arthur and I arrived in due course at the sweets, and I made myself very unpopular by asking the waiter if the mousse was still disguised blancmange. The waiter was properly horrified, so I chose coffee mousse, and it *was* disguised blancmange and still the same texture as foam-rubber.

It is very pleasant having Arthur as a cousin, even though I believe the superior luncheon to which he stands treat is put down to business expenses and even though it entailed listening to Arthur's small stock of personal anecdotes, which vary only in detail from year to year. There is one about Arthur in the desert during the war, playing tennis, unknowingly, against an ex-Wimbledon champion. And playing, what is more, as a favour to her because he disdained playing against weak and feeble women as a rule . . .

Now, in the garden, I have dark purple iris out, the snowdrops and the crocus buds, dark and pale mauve primroses and the ever-flowering veronica. Even the cats have gone gay, so I'm positive that it is spring and the itch to buy a new hat grows excessive!

. . . Thank you for your letters. I know I don't say 'ta ever so' as often as I should, but I appreciate them just the same, more than I say.

Very sincerely,

Frances Woodsford

BOURNEMOUTH
March 22nd 1952

Dear Mr Bigelow,

. . . I wonder *why* it is that families are so unable to speak of their inner thoughts to each other – or is it just my family are so afflicted? For some time now I have wanted to ask Mother to calculate just how much it costs, having my brother living at home. Then, if I knew that, I would know just how much more I would have to contribute to the exchequer if he were to leave; and if that amount were within my power, then I could telephone him at the office one day (I'd never be able to say it to his face) and tell him if Mother's financial dependence were the only stumbling block to his marriage, to hop over it, for Mother and I could manage quite well on our own. But so far I haven't been able to pluck up enough courage to ask Mother, let alone say anything to Mac.

Perhaps I shall have to soon, though, for both Mother and I feel desperately sorry for Mac's girlfriend, Betty, who returned home two days ago after spending six months in California. I sent a bunch of flowers to welcome her home; Mac, nothing – didn't even telephone her. She 'phoned him next day at his office. We expected he'd go out to her home next evening, but instead he took some other girl to the Fireman's Ball; and last night he said coolly that he had promised Desmond to play billiards with him at the Club, and off he went there. Mother and I were aghast at such cavalier treatment, if it shouldn't be described more strongly. And, of course, we neither of us can ask Mac what's happened; our imaginations however are running riot.

Tell me, does everybody indulge in voting at your Primaries, or only the people working in and for the two parties? I personally am torn between a wish to see General Eisenhower, whom I believe to be a very great man as well as a very good soldier, the United States President; and a wish to see him still in charge of the Armies over here, which need just such a good man to keep the difficult and temperamental bigwigs of the different countries working amicably together. Well, working together, anyway. I definitely don't want Taft, who seems to me to be a man making politics his living, with all that that implies in the States. He seems to be merely the Republican equivalent of Truman, another Party man. Both countries, both yours and mine, need at their head a man who can see higher than the top of his party programme; who can see a wider horizon, which may embrace both parties, so long as it is wide enough to embrace the whole country. And do we get such men? Not often, alas, but probably more often than we deserve.

Now I must get back to work – I have interrupted the affairs of the town to get this letter written, which is a highly antisocial thing to do, but friendly, perhaps. It is, I notice, the anniversary of our letter-exchanging, and may we both enjoy many more of them.*

Very sincerely,

Frances Woodsford

BOURNEMOUTH
April 1st 1952

Dear Mr Bigelow,

Trying very hard to keep an objective point of view about pain, I was quite delighted this morning to discover that under great stress (i.e. the drill of the dentist) I say 'Aah!' and not 'Ouch!'

. . . Did I tell you a neighbour of ours is to be our next Mayor? And that people up and down the road are saying 'he'll have to pull his socks up' because he has been in the habit of dashing down the road in his car – for cigarettes or something – dressed in pyjamas, rubber boots and a woollen pullover. A little bird must have whispered in the Mayor-elect's select ear, for now he goes up and down the road fully dressed in hat and gloves, a sight we have not seen for many years, coming from him. His wife, who has been waiting for this Great Occasion for upwards of a

* *Editor's note*: In fact, Frances first wrote to Mr Bigelow on January 24th 1949 but her first substantial letter is dated March 23rd 1949 (p. 3). In a letter dated March 17th 1956 (p. 214) she notes that she recorded the event in her 1949 diary on March 22nd.

quarter-century, is as deaf as could be and not in the least inclined to view it as a handicap, so we are all agog to see what happens. Will the guests at receptions be politely asked, as they enter, to shout? Or will the Mayor's Secretary tactfully give the Mayoress an ear-trumpet for Christmas? Time alone will tell.

We had the most exciting boat race last Saturday for many years. It was rowed in a howling gale with both coxes wearing eye goggles to enable them to see, faintly, through the driving snow! I'm Oxford, and Cambridge have been winning non-stop since I can remember, but on Saturday neither boat got more than half a length ahead of the other, and what with the weather and the Cambridge commentators being so darn fair all round – 'but Cambridge has a better pace . . . . . .' and what with the B.B.C. launch suddenly stopping in the middle of the commentary, we all had great fun. The next morning the newspapers reported that the owner of the launch had asked for a policeinvestigation, since he thought somebody had siphoned petrol out of his boat during the night before the race, while the launch was moored midstream. Sabotage the B.B.C., what sacrilege! As the television viewers were taking sound from the radio-launch (the snow having messed the microphones up on the television launch) I imagine there was a really beautiful panic at headquarters for a few moments.

Last night I went to the cinema to see a new Italian film called *Never take No for an Answer*. It was a simple little story about a small child whose donkey falls ill. The child, who lives in Assisi, believes if he takes his donkey to the crypt of the cathedral, where St Francis lies buried, his donkey will get better. But of course the Church officials are horrified. The little boy asks his friend, the Father. Then he asks the Father Superior. Then he goes to Rome to ask the Pope. Finally, the Pope writes a letter instructing the Assisi church people to knock down the entrance to the crypt from the cloisters, which has been bricked up for 400 years, so that the donkey can get through and not have to negotiate all the stairs. When they do this, a box containing the Treasure of St Francis, for which they have been digging for years, falls out of the archway, and the film finishes with the Fathers looking lovingly at the tiny box (all it contains is a piece of rope, a wild flower, an ear of wheat and a feather) while the donkey and the little boy pass over the rubble. You don't know whether the child's faith is sufficient, or whether the donkey dies; the film just ends without preaching to you; and it was all most charming and delightful, and the little boy, ugly and passionately alive and natural, is a sheer joy to watch.

I do hope you have a good time with Rosalind: you have both waited long enough for this visit, goodness knows; it should be all the pleasanter in consequence. Don't forget to be very kind and gentle with Rosalind, whose nerves will take some time to recover from seeing your latest rug!

Very sincerely,

Frances Woodsford

BOURNEMOUTH
April 6th 1952
Raining again

Dear Mr Bigelow,

Here we go on the merry-go-round again! About ten days ago I bought small gifts for the two women who have taught me pottery as a parting gift now that the classes have been cancelled. When I got home that evening there was a parcel from Rosalind! Tit-for-tat, so to speak.

And then yesterday I sent off a very small 'surprise' to you, together with my usual Saturday letter (though most uncharacteristically morbid letter). After lunch and when we were sitting by the fire having coffee there was a knock at the front door, and on going it was not somebody selling something, nor yet the Government Clerk with the form to be filled up. It was an Easter egg from you. Yet again, great big TIT for my little tat. I never seem to be able to keep up with you two, let alone get ahead of your twin brains, both of which seem always to forest my own ideas, and forestall them in a wholesale manner that leaves me and my family just gasping for breath, and grasping at words adequate to say 'thank you'.

One of Mother's sisters is spending Easter with us, and I will admit we have been thinking of queueing with the holiday crowds in order to eat out several times over the period, as rations just won't run to entertaining in one's home except occasionally and by sticking severely to fish! I like fish, myself, but I suppose it is rather restricting to the hostess. Today Mother is jubilantly arranging what she will do with your parcel, mainly, I think, the bacon for luncheon and the beef for evening meals, and the butter for voluptuous delight all around the clock. The ham and tongue we are going to hide for the present and it looks as though we *should* do the same to the sugar, which is going like candy at a children's party (our sugar is mainly beet, rather worse and not as sweet as the cane stuff). Altogether we are hugging ourselves for delight, and you too (metaphorically) for being so kind and generous as to send it. We all hope you have the pleasant Easter you fully deserve.

Very sincerely,

Frances Woodsford

SOMERSET
May 3rd 1952

Dear Mr Bigelow,

From being in a seaside town of ex-smugglers, I am now bang in the middle of a very damp bog, slightly drained here and there, in which (before my day) King Alfred spent a short time daydreaming in a farmhouse kitchen and thus burnt the cake and made history. Some time later, Cromwell knocked the stuffing out of the Duke of Monmouth in the same bog, and so made history again. Now I am here and you can follow through to the logical conclusion yourself.

The cottage is built on a high bank dividing the road from a man-made river which was dug to drain the bog. The disadvantages are obvious: the bank is no more than 20 feet across, and on the riverside there is a narrow towpath. So my friend's cottage is long and very narrow – one-room narrow, actually. Hall, lounge, dining room, kitchen, bathroom (miles from the two tiny bedrooms upstairs!) and, finally, work-shed, all strung along in a row. You can fish out of the kitchen window, or pick hats of passers-by through the lounge window, as the whim takes you.

It is all very peaceful after Lyme Regis, where you nearly lost your correspondent in a litter of boxer pups trying out their teeth and newly discovered aggressiveness on the strange female in their midst. You try disengaging yourself intact from eleven pups at once, and you will appreciate my current condition!

. . . Then here is my old friend Jem, who is ordinary, and her husband who is quite extraordinary. A brilliant engineer but terribly smug about his brain and, at a guess, a bit smug about his appearance. Why, otherwise, adorn your plain face with this sort of moustache?

We argued about education last night until midnight and I got off a lot of long words, most of them in the right place!

Today it is raining heavily. The fields across the road are full of withy, which is a small willow tree grown merely for the long twigs which are cut and used for basket-making. I hope to see the workshop near here before going home on Sunday.

And now that is quite enough of my handwriting for you, so I will promise you an extra Special Saturday Special next week. I am bursting to write a grim short story about the dog breeder's peculiar domestic staff, straight out of Chekhov!

For now, I hope your weather is better than mine, but your countryside *couldn't* look better than my flower-bedecked one as I saw it yesterday and on Monday.

Very sincerely,

Frances Woodsford

BOURNEMOUTH
May 10th 1952

Dear Mr Bigelow,

The postman was early on Thursday, and so I met him as my brother and I were turning out of our road on our way to the Polling Station where we were entombed from 7.45 a.m. until 10.35 p.m. He handed over *Holiday* and a bill, both of which I took with me, and the former of which was greatly enjoyed by sundry Poll Clerks and Supervising Officers up and down the Station.

Also to be answered is a letter from you written at the end of April, and disclosing the fact that, once again, you have been 'discovered' by a cat in need of a home. Do you have arrows all over Bellport pointing to Casa Bigelow and reading, 'This way for strays. Good chow and catnip supplied'?

. . . You wrote 'since starting this I have had breakfast and broken off a front tooth – that shows'. I can't tell whether it shows you eat rock-salmon with the salmon missing for your meal, or whether your house-keeper forgot to use the tin-opener and served it up complete. I hope the grimace is nicely repaired by now, and without too much dentist trouble.

I have been expecting daily to hear from Mr Dall that you cannot write because you are quite prostrate with ecstasy over the Bellport Star, but perhaps it has been delayed in transit, or perhaps it didn't have quite that effect . . . . . .

When I was in Lyme Regis I sent you a postcard of the dear little place . . . Lyme was first mentioned in the Domesday Book as being a place where a monastery was built, and the monks of which were allowed to distil salt and sell it for the benefit of the Monastery.* It was turned 'Regis' by, I believe, a very early Edward, in about 1400 or so. It is such a quaint and delightful little place that one of the Cadbury family (the chocolate manufacturers and extremely wealthy) who lives

* *Editor's note*: In fact, these were monks from Sherborne Abbey with land in Lyme.

there, when he found he could not easily manoeuvre his yacht in and
out of the Cobb, sold the yacht rather than move to a town with a
larger harbour.

. . . G. K. Chesterton always used to stay at the Three Cups Hotel . . .
He used to park his wife (who bullied him) on a chair on the steps, then
stroll down the hill, oh ever so nonchalantly, and if she was
looking the other way at the crucial moment, he'd dive into the bar of
the Royal Lion Hotel opposite, where the company was greatly to his
liking, and the beer likewise. On either side of the little place cliffs rush
up and down in great headlands, golden on one side and grey-white on
the other, and at the back the countryside is hilly and lush, not quite so
much so as deep into Devon (here you are right on the border of Devon
and Dorset, sometimes in one county and sometimes in the other as you
walk about) but quite lush and hilly enough for anybody with consideration for their legs or their cars.

My uncle and aunt and one unmarried cousin live in the fishing end of
the village, opposite the Cobb (so called, I understand, because it was
built of Cobb stones stuck between great wooden posts pushed into the
sand) and another cousin and his wife live at the back of the town in
an old manor house with thousands of boxer dogs, half a dozen
dachshunds, and a cow called Pam. Pam was produced and introduced
to me when I went there to tea one day, and it was comical to see the
expression of disgust on her face when she discovered she hadn't been
called up to the barn either for her meal or her milking! I have never seen
a cow look disgusted before, but she did it perfectly. It was probably a
joyous sight to see me endeavouring escape from the attentions of eleven
boxer pups which had just discovered they were aggressive! My cousin's
wife called out 'Just walk through them!' but, with two biting my shoe-
buckles, two more cutting off my feet at my ankles, one swinging on the
hem of my skirt at the back, two at each hand and a couple jumping up
in an endeavour to catch my nose as I stooped down to brush them aside,
'just walking through' was not as easy as it sounded. They came out all
in one piece, but only just. They *were* nice little things, all chubby and
firm but not puppy-fat. Rather, they are like dachshunds, miniature
copies of adults while they are still babies.

Jessamy, my cousin's wife, is six foot two and built to scale. She is the most unfeminine person I know as to character, although she has a very pretty face and curly fair hair. She dresses always in tweed slacks and woollen blouses and cardigans and swears better than (at a guess) General Patton! Apparently she deigned to marry Arthur on her own terms, amongst which were that she should not be asked to do housework, entertain guests, do gardening or, in fact, anything but keep dogs. Nonetheless she is most kind-hearted, and (though she tries to hide it) sincerely touched by kindness in others. She suffers from a series of unsuitable 'home helps' who, because of her refusal or inability to be a housewife, she has to employ to stop the roof falling in. When I was there she had a woman who had run a café of her own for years, but she wanted the lighter job because her husband was 'just getting over a nervous breakdown' and they thought country life would suit him.

They didn't tell Jessamy that 'just' meant eleven years ago; she found that out gradually! The husband never speaks except, occasionally, in a whisper to his wife. He is reputed to be stone deaf and wears a hearing aid, but about his complete deafness there is a certain amount of doubt. We were called in to tea, which was served in the enormous farmhouse kitchen. There was a gigantic sofa in one corner on which four equally gigantic boxers lolled. This sofa had been bought for about a dollar, especially for the dogs. Next to the sofa and near the large black kitchen range was a round dog-basket with an army blanket in it. Under the blanket was the most ancient dachshund, retired. He lived permanently under the blanket in the basket, coming out for a second for a biscuit, after which he snuggled out of sight again. On the other side of the kitchen range was an armchair upholstered in sacking; this belonged to another dog. Down the middle of the room was a giant-size kitchen table, the top covered in yellow-checked American cloth. A white-painted sideboard contained odds and ends and a few dog trophies and cups. An electric kettle boiled its heart out on top of a radio which, I was told, didn't work. The table was laid with thick brown pottery, lined with yellow and most in keeping with the size of everything, for the cups held a pint of tea!

Jessamy waved me to a chair halfway down one side. Uncle took a chair opposite me. Jessamy and Arthur sat across from each other higher up the table. Right down at the window end were the home helps, husband and wife, huddled together around the teapot and a large dog. Mrs Home Help wore a slightly worried, ingratiating expression and a gash of lipstick right across her face. Mr H.H. looked ten minutes off death from starvation, a darkly tense man. They both stared at me, but said nothing, and nobody introduced us.

Mrs H.H. it turned out eventually (I spoke to her next day when she came out and played with the puppies) speaks only in clichés, which come from her in a non-stop stream. At tea she merely said, 'Now, you'd like a nice cup of tea wouldn't you, Mrs Mould?' with a fond smile which was nearer a grimace than was comfortable. Then, later, she remarked, 'Another little drop won't do you any harm, Mrs Mould.' Maybe it wouldn't, but Jessamy took the second cup, tasted it, poured it straight-way into a gigantic basin standing near her and said loudly, 'God! Too hot and not sweet enough.' Arthur murmured something about getting cooler if she left it a moment, whereupon Jessamy looked at him in surprise and said coldly, 'I don't happen to want to leave it a moment; I want to drink it now and the dam' stuff's too hot and not sweet enough.' She held out the cup indignantly, and Mrs H.H. rushed up with the teapot and other bits and pieces, and clucked and tushed and dear-deared for some minutes. Jessamy turned back to her dog magazine, and the rest of the tea party returned to what was apparently 'normal' for this household. I was thoroughly enjoying myself, you can imagine!

They told me at my uncle's afterwards, that the home helps were the most helpless creatures who were so terrified of losing their jobs that Jessamy literally had to drive them out of the house for an afternoon's walk now and then. Jessamy did try once to give a dinner party. They were playing canasta when Mrs H.H. puts her head around the door, leered, and said coyly, 'Five minutes!' They said good, and finished the game. Mrs H.H. put her head in the room again, and said 'Oh dear, I *am* silly! I forgot the bread sauce. Won't be long now, folks!' They politely said that would be all right and went on with the canasta. Twenty minutes later Arthur went out to the kitchen to see what was happening, and came back and said, 'I think you'd better come, Jessamy, Mrs H.H. is in tears on the kitchen floor.' She had forgotten to switch on the electricity on the oven! So Jessamy now invites people to tea, which she says can't really go so terribly wrong because her guests have enough sense to bring their own cakes, and she merely puts a loaf, a knife and some butter on the table so that they help themselves. They sound like something out of a book or a Russian play, don't they?

And now I must take this to the post office for mailing. Thank you again for *Holiday*, which I read thoroughly last night (this was started Friday) and for all your very pleasant letters.

Most sincerely,

Frances Woodsford

Pam the cow with (*left to right*) Aunt Elsie, cousins Arthur and Barbara, and Uncle Herbert

BOURNEMOUTH
Black Monday, May 19th 1952

Oh no! Mr Bigelow,

Not broken, my little group, surely it can't be broken! It was wrapped in
paper and put in a cardboard box, wrapped in corrugated cardboard and
placed in a second box; then surrounded with straw and placed in a
wooden box. It *couldn't* get broken unless somebody dropped an
elephant on it, or unless somebody was criminally careless in unpacking
it.

I count this little group as an extension, or continuation, of the
Bellport Riders which, as you know, had so tragic a history. I made the
Bellport Riders three times only to have it smashed in firing each time.
The little dinghy in the Bellport Star group was made three times, and
the figures in the boat twice. Oh, it just couldn't be broken. Maybe when
they unpacked it in New York, to see why the sender would have taken
such care over an article only declared at a few pence, they noticed
the oars weren't attached to the rower's hands, and perhaps that is the
'damage' they notified to you. It's not much good saying 'I hope so' for
I have now given up hope altogether, and expect that, in reality, the thing
is in a hundred little bits.

What makes it all the worse is that I sent Rosalind a teapot and
pitcher a week after the Bellport Star group was posted to you. I hadn't
any boxes left except two very old cardboard ones, one just slightly
larger than the other. So I just stuffed the china in the smaller one,
packed in bits of straw in the spaces, pushed the small box into the large
one, and then pushed odd bits of corrugated cardboard down between
the two sides. I never expected, the day after I had mailed it, that they
would arrive in any sort of shape at all, for it was the roughest, most
miserable bit of packing I'd ever done. And yet Rosalind's parcel arrived
perfectly – and two weeks *before* yours, which was posted a week earlier
– and yours has been damaged. What have they been doing with yours
all that time? Dropping it off the Empire State Building to test it for
bounce, or something? Sages say it's no good crying over spilt milk, and
I'm not crying over this breakage. I just feel like throwing things through

the largest glass panes I can find. It's no good saying write to the post office and make a claim – how can I claim? And what? Eighteen pence in money and six months in time?

I do hope your mouth is feeling better now; you have had more than your fair share of bad luck with your teeth this last year. Somebody said the other day that you went regularly to your dentist to have your teeth attended to so that they would be so well-kept and healthy you wouldn't need to go regularly to your dentist to have your teeth attended to. A vicious circle if ever there was, and either way the patient suffers. My mother, who had terrible teeth, had them all out during the 1914–18 war when Daddy was away (and couldn't see her going around with bare gums, poor dear!) because, she tells us, she just got fed up with eternally undergoing painful treatments, paying painful bills, and still having toothache and more painful treatments and bills. I must say there is quite a lot to say in favour of false teeth.

I hope you enjoy your week yacht-racing at the end of this month. While you will be sitting in elegant comfort in the crow's nest or on the Judges' Launch or the terrace of the Yacht Club, I shall be stifling in the swimming-pool hall coping with non-existent staff.

Sorry about the smashed masterpiece.

Very sincerely,

Frances W.

BOURNEMOUTH
June 14th 1952

Dear Mr Bigelow,

Have you ever studied the intricacies of the sleepless mind? I have of late, to my misery, and it could prove quite a fascinating study were you not, at one and the same time, both the investigator *and* the unfortunate guinea pig.

Do you remember Jerome K. Jerome's book *Three Men in a Boat*? They got hold of a medical dictionary and discovered that between them they had every complaint listed except housemaid's knee. Well, I was reading an article last weekend on present-day stresses and strains, and came at once to the conclusion that that was me, stress and strain. Definitely. So I read on, thinking to find the cure. The writer ended his article by saying '. . . . . . the very best stress diet of the lot is caviar and champagne . . . . . .' But he did have a few more useful hints to pass on, amongst them the need for peaceful sleep and serene minds.

Now, due to the inability of most of my staff to count accurately beyond four, *I* go to bed prepared to rest but my *mind* thinks to its little self, 'Ah! Now is a good opportunity to think over all the things that have gone wrong today, and to work out ways of preventing them going wrong tomorrow and Tuesday and Wednesday and Thursday and next Christmas . . . . . . Now, where shall we start?' And so I spend half my nights, as well as half my days, coping with other people's problems. Sometimes in the night I'm busy counting pink tickets, mountains of them, all counted wrongly by the cashiers; only to stop myself with a jerk when my brain is calculating the value of the mountain at three shillings a ticket, with the realisation that this year pink tickets are four shillings each. By now my little mind has forgotten how many stubs there were in the mountain, so we go back to the beginning again.

Then I decide firmly that this won't do at all. I will think placid and serene thoughts, and none else. I conjure up a mental picture of a windswept headland, with the sea around it and a skylark overhead, and the faint mew of seagulls in my ears and the scent of wild thyme in my nostrils. I work on the picture quite hard, willing my mind to concentrate, and even manage to imagine how warmly the sun strikes my throat as I look up at the skylark. I decide to add to the serenity by reciting poetry to myself in a small, silent voice – and pick on my favourite: 'Ode to Autumn'.

I get happily to the line about 'filling all fruit with ripeness to the core', where I stick. What comes next? I start again, a little worried; and stick in exactly the same place. I am cross with myself. I lecture myself; telling me this won't do and where's my serenity. Out the window along with my memory, my alter ego replies. I get crosser and crosser, and more and more wakeful, until at last, in desperation, I get up and go to the living room and shut the door quietly (so as not to awaken the family) and put on the light and look for the poem.

Back to bed, with the book of poems, in case I get stuck again, and back to my serene thoughts once more. This time the windswept head-land seems a trifle lonely, so I change it for my current serial-story in which (but naturally) I am the glamorous and fascinating heroine. This story usually occupies about ten minutes, and if it proves particularly interesting I go back and use it all over again with extra details. The current tale involves a drug-taking wife, a frantic husband who blames himself; one or two awe-inspired friends and ME. I sort everything out most beautifully, far, far better than Adler would have done. But you can imagine that this is not quite the serene and peaceful sort of story suitable for putting me to sleep. So I allow myself to run over it once lightly, up to where I left off the night before, and then go firmly back to poetry. It has to be poetry, for I have a loathing for silly sheep, and mine only stroll through gates anyway so no help at all in my troubles.

This time I chose Gray's 'Elegy' because I fondly hope I shall remem-ber rather more of it. True, I get – more or less, ad-libbing here and there – as far as the verse about jewels lying undiscovered in deep sea-caves and many a flower being born to blush unseen and waste its sweetness on the desert air. I am about to weep myself to sleep in the mood of self-pity this brings flooding over me when it occurs to me to wonder whether the word *is* flower, or rose. And if it's rose, which seems to scan better, what rose ever grew in a desert? And come to think of it, I never heard of jewels being found lying around loose in sea-caves before. The man is crazy. Trust me to get a crazy poet around my neck! Flower? Rose? Rose? Oh well, it doesn't matter. Not really matter. Not a matter of life or death. No concern of mine. Go to sleep, mind. Stop larking about – I'm *tired*. Flower? I'm *sure* it's rose. But best put on the lights and make certain.

The poem is in the *other* anthology, of course – the one still in the living-room bookcase. I go out and look (It's flower all this time. It would be) and while I'm up, take a couple of aspirins and half a glass of cold water. I debate whether to drink the water cold, which will give me indigestion, or hot from the tap, which will probably give me chronic rust-poisoning. I decide that perhaps the aspirins will start work before the digesting of them gives me indigestion. But of course, they don't – the cause-and-effect follow in that order, and the hot pains start shuddering across from rib to rib. I get up (It's three o'clock now, and the dawn looks like breaking before my insomnia does) and go out and eat a peppermint. My bed looks a mite crumpled when I crawl back into it, and I match it.

I try a new idea – taking deep breaths. Guaranteed, so the article said, to send you to sleep before the first dozen are inhaled and exhaled. Before I arrive at No. 6 my heart is pounding like a road-drill and *both* ears are buzzing in time with the heartbeat. This is an increase of one ear over my usual left ear bedtime buzz and I decide I dislike it more than twice as much as usual, so I stop deep breathing. This is a help, but my heart goes on puffing for some time, and I make tentative plans for being an interesting invalid with serious heart-trouble for the rest of my life, but this involves having a gracious, spacious room in which to lie, and as mine is a large-size cupboard, it doesn't seem much good being an interesting invalid. I punch my pillow for the 47th time, and throw my head at it, slightly fracturing my skull on a hair-curler. The curtains billow out as my heavy sighs race across the room, but I can't help being miserable as I think of my poor self during the coming day, carrying that awful load of responsibility with no sleep, no rest, no respite at all . . . . . . and in comes Mother to waken me.

. . . Now I will stop before this letter weighs too much. I do hope your jaw is champing away right merrily again, and that the yachting week was successful and exciting and you didn't have to disqualify more than, say, two-thirds of the competitors.

Very sincerely,

Frances Woodsford

BOURNEMOUTH
June 21st 1952

Dear Mr Bigelow,

. . . On Monday I take out a provisional driving licence, and in July I am to take the course of lessons, hoping to pass the Government's Test some time in August, ready for my driving holiday the month after. I bought a book from the British School of Motoring, and enquired of them for fees. As I have no car in which to practise, they suggested I would need extra lessons, and quoted me £16 for 16 lessons (or it might have been £17 for 16, I forget now). This is the equivalent, to you, of about $100 for 16 lessons of an hour each! As I earned the equivalent of about $50 a week, the shock put me back quite a little, as you can imagine. However, I find other smaller schools charge far less so I'm hoping that a deep study of the book, plus a certain amount of common sense, will get me through at less than the cost of the Moon. I must admit that the book seems very perplexing, and I come to work each morning with a piece of paper on which I have scribbled notes about my queries, which I thereupon throw at my boss. You would enjoy, as I do, the sight of him sitting on my typewriting chair waggling his legs about because you can't describe the art of double declutching without working it out physically first! I'm glad it becomes so automatic your mind doesn't bother to record what your feet are up to, for at the moment I feel the pedal work must be as difficult as footwork on an organ . . . Altogether my peace of mind is going for good, but as I never had much perhaps I shan't miss it.

I do hope by the time this reaches you the hospital-and-bed-session will be far behind you in the past . . .

Very sincerely,

Frances W.

BOURNEMOUTH
June 26th 1952

Dear Mr Bigelow,

Yes, Mr Bigelow, I quite agree with you that the English make far too much use of the silly expression, 'I'm afraid'. I'm afraid we use it all the time.

Your 'recommendation' that I should adopt three children as a method of keeping myself busy and thus ensuring good sleep at night is an excellent one. I was, however, disappointed to see that you couldn't think of a child to match the eight-month-old red-haired Scot, or the two-year-old Sicilian girl. What about a four-year-old Fillum Star? She (or he) should be quite a match for the others, and would nicely round off the awful triangle, to mix my metaphors . . . And, just think of it, if I adopted three, a grateful Government would pay me 12s.6d. a week to keep them on. All of $75 . . .

One day this week I took Mac's ex-girlfriend out to lunch. Got myself up like yesterday's ham-bone to keep up the Good Name of the family (somebody on the Bath's steps said to an attendant as I passed, 'Place is full of glamour-girls this year, isn't it?' but I think he must have been short-sighted) and reserved a table at the best place in town. I am very fond of good food, well cooked, beautifully served, and don't mind paying for it on the rare occasions when I do go out to lunch. But we were confronted with the alternatives of

Kidney soup,
or
Consommé de tapioca!!!!!!!!!! (my exclamation marks)

on a boiling hot day. We decided to skip the soup, and ordered chicken and ham pie, salad and new potatoes. The pie was more like a galantine, very jelly-ish and spotted with little bits of chicken and ham skin. The salad was two half-leaves of lettuce, one slice of beetroot and a quarter of a tomato. The new potatoes were adequate. The sweets offered were (Heavens!) bread and butter pudding, treacle tart, ice-cream or mixed entremets. We chose the last-named, and it turned out to be custard with decoration on top (called 'trifle') or coffee mousse encased in sponge and topped with jelly . . . It was, taken all round, a grave disappointment and I was LIVID! My cider was iced and perfect, and I believe Betty's beer was also cold and good, but that, surely, isn't enough to make a feast.

It turns out that it was *Betty* who finished with my brother, and not any awful faux pas he made which caused a split. I suppose he felt it was a blow to his pride to have the girl break off their association, so he wouldn't tell us, but I must say I wish he had, for he might have saved us much heart-burning and the embarrassment. After all, we none of us can be loved by everybody, and it's no disparagement of our own personality if one particular person decides that, after all, it isn't love they (he, or she) feels for us. Silly boy, my brother . . .

My first driving lesson is at two o'clock next Tuesday. I have read *How to Drive a Car* twice right through, and some parts four or five times; the Highway Code I know more or less by heart, and I have gone deeply into the table which gives the braking distances at different speeds, so deeply that I have discovered the basic 'rhythm' of the table and can work out thinking- and braking-distances at any speed up to 10,874½ miles per hour. I love mathematics, they are so shapely, if you know what I mean . . .

I was glad to gather from the tone of your last letter that you are once more your normally spry and dander self. A letter from Rosalind earlier this week told me of her trip east to look after you: you sound a terrible hospital-patient: what sort of a home-patient do you make? The doctors seem to have done everything to their Bellport guinea pig except pick it up by its tail and shake it, but then I understand that is the thing they do only as a last resort, especially as the tail is so hard to find. Next time you feel a hiccup coming along, you try a mouthful of peppermints. Anyway, I am glad it is all over and done with, but don't do it again . . .

Very sincerely,

Frances W.

BOURNEMOUTH
July 3rd 1952

Dear Mr Bigelow,

Temperature 92°F; . . . and a rush to keep the two o'clock appointment
of my first driving lesson. I rushed to such an effect that my arrival was
greeted with 'Oh, you're early; well, I suppose it doesn't matter, we
might as well start.'

Truly an auspicious opening, and I don't think it was surprising that I
took an instant dislike to the man. Do you think that means I'm not
likely to learn quickly, since I have consciously to force myself to do
what he says, out of sheer dislike? I must admit, though, that I don't
think he's such a good driver as he imagines – or good teacher, perhaps
I should say. He showed me how to start the car, giving the sketches of
the engine, motivation of car, gears, clutch etc. (which I knew about
beforehand but that didn't stop him!) but he never told me how to stop.

Then, after demonstrating gear changes and saying blithely that most
cars have the gears marked on the top of the lever but his were worn off
we changed places. I was then lectured for *eight* minutes on the importance of making sure the doors are closed, and we set off. Now Mr
Bigelow *is* it good teaching to let somebody start driving immediately in
a fairly busy road? My first turn came after about 200 yards, and was at
a junction and across the traffic. We then turned again, sharply left (I
still didn't know how to slow down to a stop without stopping the car
altogether, and I still don't know whether I'm supposed to declutch,
brake, and start moving the gear into first ready to start when the road
is clear) into a road with buses, trolley-buses, cars, bikes, an estate of
Council Houses with attendant children running in the road, and a
gypsy encampment with horse-drawn carts up and down and across and
back. Good for the nerves?

Then another crossroads, another main road, and finally, the main
London–Exeter road for three miles, just in case the other traffic
hadn't quite finished me off. 'Blow your horn at him!' said the man at
one stage. 'Just where is the horn, please?' said I. That is an example.
Aren't you lucky to be getting this letter this week instead of a black-

edged card from my sorrowing mum? He also told me to pass a horse and cart when we were on a slight bend, and when I obediently pulled out it was to discover a fast-moving car (anything going over 30 was fast to me!) approaching around the bend. The man shouted something; I accelerated, thinking he wanted me to pass while there was time; he, of course, jammed the clutch and handbrake and then said it was all the horse-driver's fault for pulling out just as I did too. No, I have not that full confidence in him that I could wish for, and the worst thing is, I've paid for the course! He was once (about the time you were in rompers) a flying instructor, and spoke airily of teaching men to loop the loop without the benefit of parachutes. Possibly he feels that by putting the car-pupil on the road from the absolute word 'go' he gets a slight echo of that earlier thrill. Personally, I would prefer to bore him to tears. When I reached home late at night, I looked at the leaflet he had given me. It described his methods and suggested he was the world's best teacher of driving, and finished up with:

'Please be at the collecting-point punctually. When you see the car, come up and introduce yourself to me. You will not be disappointed.'

I am the exception.

. . . I hope you have a nice long visit from Rosalind, and that the weather is cooler, as it is here today. My garden looks like the Sahara, and simply glows with dust!

Very sincerely,

Frances W.

BOURNEMOUTH
July 19th 1952

Dear Mr Bigelow,

. . . Do you know that I start writing your Saturday letter on Wednesdays these weeks, in order to make sure it's ready by Saturday? And don't suggest I should send it off as soon as it is finished, because I know full well you would still expect your Saturday Special, and you mustn't be greedy. Of course, I *never* am (greedy) so I can lecture you from a smug pedestal.

Well, I've finished the full course of driving lessons, leaving a flummoxed instructor with his appointment book poised ready in his hands, while I got out of the car and walked off with a saccharine smile and a cheery wave of the fist. On my last hour's lesson I was taught how to start on a hill, which I did quite well. In fact, I did it excellently the first time, and thinking it easy, not nearly so well the next time, almost suffocating a passing cyclist when I revved the engine without letting the clutch up. No idea so much thick black smoke existed outside the steel towns . . . . . . Now all I need to learn is how to go backwards; but perhaps the instructor realised that my motto is 'Ever onwards!' and taught me accordingly. My own view is that, wearing one or two of Rosalind's delightful dresses, the impression was given that I was a Lady of Means and Good for at Least Two More Payments. So you see, Rosalind has a lot to answer for. I have written her this week to warn her she's going to have seven splendid corpses on her conscience on Saturday, when I wear the latest creation she sent me and the seven divers all miss the pool and hit the surrounds when they get an eyeful of me in brown silk, all a'shimmering in the light. On second thoughts, possibly only four of the seven will hit the deck, for out of consideration for the youth of the other three I put, last night, an extra two inches of material in the neck of the dress. Before that was done I could see if my shoe-laces were tied, without bending over, and the effect on passers-by was problematical but exciting . . .

My poor mother! Yesterday evening, while she was doing something or other in her room, she came rushing out to me crying, 'Oh! Jack Stockwell's had an accident on his motorbike and the ambulance is there!!' Now Jack Stockwell has only had his bike about a week, and everybody has been expecting the worst, in their usual ghoulish way. I went to the front of the flat and said, 'But Mother, Jack's bike is still there in the garden, and I saw him only half an hour ago. And there's Mr Stockwell – and there's Mrs, so it can't be anybody we know.' Mother was forced to stay in her room, ostensibly to powder her nose (she knocked the lid of her powder bowl against the bowl several times in the next ten minutes so that I, in the living room, would know by the sound that she *was* powdering her nose and not just nosing) until the ambulance men came out. And even then, she didn't recognise the body and had to report merely that 'it's a very short person' and conjecture from there as best she could. I suspect the minute I was out of the flat this morning she dashed across to admire Mr Stockwell's geraniums and find out All About It.

Now it's time to finish; a lovely motor launch has just sailed across the sea outside my office window. Although I think I would prefer sail to motor any day, a motor launch would be a very pleasant means of locomotion on a day such as this, still and heavy and flat and overcast. We want rain; we need rain; we are longing for rain. But do we get it? You know the answer to that one.

I hope your Timber Point meeting went off well, or goes off well if I am too previous. Don't get angry and start gnashing your teeth again – you know what happened last time. Be like me, placid and only given to hysterics now and then.

Very sincerely,

Frances W.

BOURNEMOUTH
August 23rd 1952

Dear Mr Bigelow,

Do you remember, some time ago, one of our submarines sank in the Channel, and all England followed with caught breath the frenzied race against time that was the search for it? Do you also remember that we were criticised in your newspapers for keeping our minds and hearts on a few square miles of grey sea instead of what was then happening in Korea? Well, another similar occasion has just occurred; and as I was thinking about it, the explanation of our previous narrow interest came to my mind: we are one family, the whole little Island, in a way that your own enormous continent can never be one family; and a family is always anxious when one member of it is in trouble, even if the whole of the next street is being flattened by some awful plague; the family's first thought is for its own sick.

This week we are all sorrowing, as one family, for the tiny village of Lynmouth, in North Devonshire. I believe when I spent three days at Lynton, 400 foot up the precipitous hill above Lynmouth, three years ago, I described the place to you and possibly also sent you postcards of it. Lynmouth is one of the English beauty spots we are so fond of – it is one of those 'cosy and charming' spots of which you wrote in your last letter. Architecturally it is not particularly beautiful . . . But nothing can spoil Lynmouth basically, because nothing – or so we thought – could destroy the beauty of its situation. It is built, huddled together, at the mouth of a tiny valley. Tiny but deep, with the hills rising sheer out of it to 500 and 600 feet, and two tiny streams rushing burbling along down from the heights of Exmoor in the hinterland, over miniature waterfalls formed of great brown round boulders; over flat grey slabs green with weed, and past luxurious growth of bush and flower scented and almost gross in its richness, in this tiny sheltered valley. At the mouth, Lynmouth. Perhaps a hundred houses, all jumbled together; a row of shops and hotels pressed close against Lyn Hill (the fourth floor of the hotels is one floor lower than the ground floor of the rare house built on the hillside, so steep is the incline) then a road, twelve foot in width; next to this is another row of small cottages and cafés, then comes the Lyn river (the two streams join in the village at one of the bridges, and then run together the hundred yards or so that remain before the harbour is reached). On the far side of the river is a pedestrian's walk, flower-edged. And beyond that a wide strip of grassland with the beautiful Manor House set in its centre. This meadow is, more or less, built out to sea, for that is the only place there's room for a meadow. Otherwise, you are no sooner slipped down Lyn Hill than you have to go vertically up Countisbury, on the other side. The place is crowded during August and September with honeymooners, and the native pirates make enough money then to live on in peace and quiet throughout the rest of the year. Except this year.

This year we had a day of heavy rain. Three months' rainfall fell last Friday on nine square miles of Exmoor. The bogs filled up and tipped over, the streams became rivers, the rivers torrents, the torrents lethal weapons bludgeoning ten-ton boulders, and the little town of Lynmouth is nearly wiped out and fifty people are either dead, or missing and believed dead. The little burn scorning its normal path, now rages down the main street, and through a corner group of buildings to the sea. It was no flood such as one gets, I imagine, in the great central plains of America; there, there is room for the water, although I realise that the damage old Mississippi does is not to be compared with Lynmouth. Here there was no room. Four cottages, built 20 feet above the river, were just swept away with most of the people in them; a boy, alone with two small brothers in one cottage, was sweeping the water coming in the front door, out of the back door, when the back door and the kitchen around it disappeared. He was lucky, he got his two brothers out of the house.

Well, that was Lynmouth. On Saturday morning we heard on the radio that only people with business in Lynmouth would be allowed there; by Saturday night the place was being evacuated as unliveable. By Sunday morning appeals were being launched all over the country for help. By Monday they were able to announce that they had enough clothes to go on with. The family had rallied round, you see. For the moment we can't be bothered with what is happening in the Volga valley or the Philippines; we only want to know how people are in Devon. It is, perhaps, parochialism, or narrow nationalism, but it is understandable, and I wish it were more realised.

It has always puzzled me that so many (I exclude you and other intelligent Americans, if there are any such!!) Americans love their own country and think it wonderful, as they have right and are right in think-ing, and yet they cannot conceive of other people loving their country in the same way. We shouldn't love England, they seem to feel; we should only feel sorry we aren't Americans. But love of one's country is nearly always born in one, and cannot be changed except at great trou-ble. And in great trouble, it comes swamping up smothering differences and making Britons of us all, English, Scots, Welsh and Irish. Just now we are all people who have seen the beauty of Lynmouth, or people who have heard of that beauty and wish they had seen it . . .

So au revoir until next week; and don't be too depressed about Lynmouth – it has brought out more strongly than before our eternal brotherhood, and it has even made Civil Servants human and Government Departments kindly, for postage has been waived on all parcels going to North Devon, a thing I can never remember happening before.

Till next week, then,

Very sincerely,

Frances Woodsford

PS My boss and I have been making collections for the Flood Fund and in two days we have got £80!!

BOURNEMOUTH
November 15th 1952

Dear Mr Bigelow,

. . . I went to the cinema this week and saw the pictures of the Queen at the opening of Parliament. She looked very lovely, with a long and slender neck rising out of a cloud of white fur, and topped by a small head and a diamond crown. The camera showed you the family on Buck. Palace balcony afterwards, with Princess Anne standing on a chair (to make her tall enough to look over the balcony) next to her brother. The Queen turned and went in, and the Duke lifted down the little girl and shooed her, with Prince Charles, back into the room. The two children were then put out of sight, being too small to be seen over the balcony, but the camera showed the Duke immediately turning around and coming back with his arms outstretched. I thought, 'Surely he hasn't come back to take the chair in!' and as I thought that, over the edge of the chair suddenly popped a little princess's head, as she started waving delightedly again. Prince Charles was there, too, but this time their father took both of them firmly by the hand and shoved them ahead of him into the room at the back. It was so human and so very sweet, the two little things dashing back for another wave, and so plainly enjoying themselves immensely. It must be very exciting to tiny children; all those lovely big soldiers, and their glittering uniforms, and horses, and people waving, and staying up late and so on. I heard the other day that the Queen will not allow them to be addressed by anyone except as Charles, and Anne. That will make a more normal childhood for both of them. We all love the little boy, but whenever I have seen the whole family on the screen, the Duke of Edinburgh is invariably look-ing after his daughter, and leaving Charles severely alone. I can imagine he doesn't allow his son to get spoiled, but perhaps he thinks a father should spoil his daughter a bit. At least, he appears to do so . . .

I'm off to London on Thursday for five days; pray for warm weather, please – today it is foggy, cold and raining, all at the same time, and I'm just sick and tired of having cold, horrid, rainy weather for my holidays. Do you know it is four years since I had a thoroughly fine week's holiday!

. . . Au revoir until next week,

Very sincerely,

Frances Woodsford

BOURNEMOUTH
November 17th 1952

Dear Mr Bigelow,

. . . Will you please do me a favour, Mr Bigelow? I don't often ask favours of you (only the favour of an occasional letter, as you know) but this time I am, and I am serious. Will you please omit any form of gift this Christmas and just send me a card? I mean that in all seriousness; I am not jumping to the conclusion that you're bankrupt because your house needs painting, but I know from hard experience how Christmas is apt to become a snowball unless you're very strict and hard with yourself, and I have myself cut out all gifts to the staff this year for the same reason. I can't promise not to send you anything because it is already bought and no earthly use to anybody else (nor to you!) but it is of no value whatsoever and doesn't count as a gift, merely as something to tickle your sense of humour, I hope. So please, leave me out except for good wishes and I will regard it as proof of my complete mastery in our friendship, in that I can get you to do what I want, when I want it badly enough. Please, now.

I hope Rosalind and Mr Akin are having a good time in Alabama, or wherever it is you say St Louis people have their hide-out. I suppose, poor souls, if they live in a cold place like St Louis they must have somewhere to get warm. It's freezing over here today; why don't you *keep* your cold winters, I don't like them. And in particular, I don't like them when I'm about to go on holiday to a very cold house on top of a very chilly hill.

Remember – a Christmas card only, to show proof of sincerity and friendship, Mr Bigelow.

Very sincerely,

Frances Woodsford

PS How dare you, Sir, be so rude about my driving! I would have you know, that like Lady Catherine de Bourgh's daughter (who would have been a wonderful pianist if only she had learned) I would be a wonderful driver if only I had continued my lessons. As it is, I am waiting a) for the car Frank and I plan to buy in the New Year, b) to be taught to drive an Ambulance in the Civil Defence Corps which I have joined with that end in view.

BOURNEMOUTH
December 6th 1952

Dear Mr Bigelow,

Do you think it is because I have had, of late years, so much experience in writing them that my 'thank you' letters are beginning to sound slick and professional? Frankly, it appals me. I like a letter of gratitude to be gracious, faintly surprised, sincere and appreciative; . . . You and Rosalind, between the two of you, have had ELEVEN thank you letters since the beginning of March. No wonder I find it so hard to think of something different to say to you both. But, of course, do not think from that last remark that I – and my family – am not extremely grateful for the latest pair of parcels, the chocolates and the well-chosen tinned goods. We are; we are also at a loss for exactly the right words to use in saying so.

Well, now to return to London, about which I was telling you when all these 'thank you' letters intervened. It was icy cold, as it always seems to be when I visit Uncle Ronald, but this time I was luckier than usual, for under the spread on the second bed in my room I found a folded collection of blankets and sheets. My aunt explained them later by saying that Peter, the son, was now at a new school where they did not expect parents to provide bedlinen (the stuff that the school provided went on the bill!). So she had more blankets and sheets than usual and would I like another blanket on my bed? I said oh no, thank you, I was as warm as toast. And only omitted to mention that I already had five blankets (including my own travel rug) and made quite certain I had remade my bed before anybody else got upstairs to find me out!! Even so, a glass of water left in my room froze both Saturday and Sunday night, so you can understand if I was warm in bed, it was sheer willpower and no help from nature.

Uncle took us to the theatre one evening, and Phyl and I went early up to town because she wanted some gloves. Uncle is the only man I have met who complains that his wife isn't extravagant enough! I will admit he has cause: he spent pounds bringing a length of fine silk home from Brunei for Phyllis to have made up for a dress to wear at a wedding they were going to, and then Phyl gets the little dressmaker in the village to make it! After Uncle had brought it safely through no less than seven Customs!! He gave her a lovely black fur coat, which she wore the day we went out. Underneath she had a nice thick silk cocktail suit, topped with a red and grey striped wool cardigan which had probably cost her about seven dollars. She had pleasant shoes on, but never pays more than (roughly) 50 cents for her stockings and as she has piano legs with elephantiasis cheap stockings are not, repeat not, for her. So, there was the beautiful fur coat and the stockings and the nice shoes, and a grey felt hat she'd bought somewhere in a sale and grey artificial wool-fur gloves. Just things to make black more exciting and chic! Admittedly black on a dull, cold day can and does look the same way, and I, too, was in black. But I had added a white fur felt hat with black and white pearls strung around a little knob on top, and both black and white pearl earrings, and fastened my pearl necklace after dark with a glittering diamond brooch. It isn't exactly *real*, but it sparkles just as nicely as anything Barbara Hutton possesses, and pleases me more than her gems do her, I'm sure.

Well, we had to eat very early (the theatre we were going to started at the ghastly hour of 7.15 p.m.) so we couldn't go to one of the smarter places. While we were waiting, keeping a table for the tardy man, Phyl and I had a martini, and when Uncle arrived he looked aghast we hadn't one waiting for him, so ordered a large one and two more small ones, to level things out. Now two dry martinis on an empty tummy is really one more than I need, so I started dinner in a nice state, and the fact that we shared a bottle of white wine with lamb cutlets helped no end. But by the time we arrived, in a flurry, at the theatre – Theatre Royal, Haymarket, and an exquisite little gem of a place it is, too, with lovely Corinthian pillars edging the pavement outside – we were all quite ready to enjoy the show. And as the play was good – a sort of modern *Month in the Country* – and the actresses in it included Dame Edith Evans, Dame Sybil Thorndike, Wendy Hiller and Kathleen Harrison, it could not possibly be anything but beautifully acted . . . We dashed to the station, caught a train for Chipstead and, when we arrived there and tore up the station steps in greatly deteriorated weather – it was now pelting with icy hail and rain – right at the end of a queue of theatre-going residents all aiming for the one and only taxi, we were absolutely delighted when the taxi-driver, perched high in his office window, saw Uncle over the heads of the other people and promptly pretended we'd ordered the taxi and bundled us in while the other people had to stand around and wait until he got back. Arrived at 'Oakhurst' Uncle told the driver to turn the car around and rushed into the hall, which he did, arriving coincident with a large whisky Uncle had promptly poured for him. Possibly this explains why it is that Uncle never has any trouble getting a taxi at the station, but it also makes it very pleasant to go out with the dear man, for you are wafted along all the time on a flood of good wishes from whatever staff you come in contact with.

. . . All the time, whenever we met anybody, Uncle kept moaning 'I've got to go to Paris' very much the same way my brother says on Sunday, 'Oh, Mother, I've got to go to the Club.' The operative word, of course, nobody believes in the slightest. Uncle was rather annoyed, though. He has been trying, for some time, to get a trip to New York fixed up, but at the weekend his firm (an oil firm, you know what they're like) told him they had arranged instead for three men to come from New York to England to see Uncle. In a way it was very flattering, but Uncle was *livid*, because he wanted that trip, and as he is retiring (five years later than anybody normally is allowed to stay) next July, it was his last chance of a free trip to the States. So, perhaps as a sop, they sent him to Paris just to oversee the experts who were going with him . . . I think he'll find life awfully dull after July, when he'll have nothing to do but concentrate on his wife's faults!

. . . Now I must get this mailed; I shall buy stamps so that you can see the new ones with the Queen's head on them. I think the green 1½d stamp is a little frilly – all those emblems around her head look a trifle unconnected, but the red 2½d stamp I think is quite charming. If you want one or two for your stamp collection (unfranked, I mean) just let me know and I'll pop them in another letter . . .

Very sincerely,

Frances Woodsford

1953

BY AIR MAIL
PAR AVION
AIR LETTER
AEROGRAMME

POSTAGE   POSTAGE
E II R
6ᴰ   2 JUNE 1953   6ᴰ

1953
CORONATION

Mr. Paul Bigelow,
Thorn Hedge Road,
Bellport,
Long Island, N.Y.
U.S.A.

BOURNEMOUTH
January 10th 1953

Dear Mr Bigelow,

. . . Mr Bigelow, I don't know if I occasionally give you the impression I am a very clever young woman. Just in case that is so, allow me to disillusion you this week: I am absolutely, utterly, entirely, completely, and wholeheartedly a washout as an upholsterer!

Mother gave my brother and me gift tokens for Christmas, which are exchangeable at certain stores for purchases to the value of the token. My brother didn't really want to have to spend his at a big store (he doesn't, as a rule, use women's clothes and knick-knacks! and the stores have only the smallest of men's departments) so I paid him cash for his voucher, and used both that one and my own and some more cash to buy remnants of green rep material with which to recover the sofa, Chesterfield or settee (whichever you prefer), and our large armchair. Also involved were millions of tacks, upholsterer's large-headed nails, webbing cord and what have you. I should have included iodine, bandages, nail oil (for growing new nails) and a spare hammer. As it was, on two evenings my brother just sat and watched me struggling because, as he pointed out, there weren't two hammers in the house so only one person could bang away at a time.

The sofa and chair are now recovered, *I* have not yet followed suit and am covered with torn flesh, broken nails, and dirt all over me, and the springs tied down to within an inch of themselves.

Mac 'helped' for a while by pulling out nails and dropping them into the mess on the spread-out newspapers on which I was kneeling, then he suddenly remembered an engagement – and brought out for me to see the actual invitation card, so he must have thought I'd view the engagement with a bit of jaundice – and departed in a hurry. After that, I was on my own, usually upside down in order to get the hammer to the nail. Next day, the dear man remarked icily that he thought I had not pulled the webbing nearly tight enough. So I made the sort of remark you can imagine, and he stayed at home an hour or so that evening, the better to instruct me in the art of webbing-pulling. I held down two of the coiled springs; he held down the third one, picked up the hammer in his right hand, and glared at me as I said brightly, 'Yes, dear, that's how Mother and I did it last evening. Now all you have to do is to pick up the nail in your teeth, place it where you want it to go, and give yourself a smart tap on the back of the head with the hammer. Or else grow a third hand in a hurry.'

Eventually he decided the webbing was quite tight enough, and went out. Eventually, too, I got the darn job done (more or less) and this included covering the easy chair. Mac suggested that instead of taking the bottom stuff off and working from under the piece of furniture, I should take the top off and work down. Unfortunately I was halfway through before I realised that this entailed cutting a line right through the present covering, in order to reach the stuffing. And then the stuffing had to be taken out and piled in dirty little mountains on newspaper all over the room. When the springs were disentangled, tied, and set firmly where they belonged, I put back most of the stuffing, and then the food parcels you sent me for Christmas came in useful again, for I had kept the boxes and the wood shavings, and these latter went in to implement the stuffing already in place. The seat now looks rather like that shapely Japanese mountain, but a few nights of Mother's weight plomped firmly in the centre will soon put that right.

And now the carpet looks unbearably worn and ragged! And, to be frank, I quite miss the untidy, homely appearance of our furniture, covered as it has been these last few years with a motley collection of travelling rugs, bits of old curtains, and the cats. Now Mother smacks the animals if they climb up, and it takes all the comfort out of home-life. Though, to be sure, it does give the human beings more chance at sitting on the sofa and chair than normal . . . . . .

I read your last letter, at first sight, as '. . . . . . I have a bird free lunch.' I too have a lunch table (non-stop) for sparrows at the office, and I have a poor little sparrow now feeding there with an injured foot. He holds his little leg close up against his body and hops on one foot and uses his wing as a sort of crutch. Trouble is the other birds in their greed are apt to push into old Hoppity, who overbalances and falls off the sill. Then he is too sorry for himself to fight his way back, so he gets a good feed only when the others are elsewhere, and that is rarely. If I could only catch him, I could take this bird to the Sick Animals' Dispensary (branches all over the country) where they could, perhaps, splint it and look after the little thing until the bone sets. Perhaps, though, if the bird keeps this bad foot off the ground long enough, the bone will set naturally and the foot will be of use again later. I watch for him every day (he gets out of bed late) but have no way of telling which bird he is except for the foot, so I won't know whether or not the foot has healed, once he starts using it again. Ah well, I suppose it's only one sparrow and there are plenty more. But I don't like seeing even a sparrow in pain and discomfort . . .

Now I must go; my boss has lost some book or other and claims I must have borrowed it. As I never knew he had it, it is unlikely, especially as I have never borrowed any sort of book from him in my life; but I shall have no peace until I find it.

So au revoir until next Saturday, and I hope you have recovered from your cocktail parties of Christmas and your gay New Year's Eve ditto.

Very sincerely,

Frances Woodsford
Graduate, School of Upholstery-Botchery, Inc.

BOURNEMOUTH
January 24th 1953

Dear Mr Bigelow,

. . . If this letter is more inaccurate than usual, it is so because I am typing it in the cashier's office as the duty cashier is ill and the other one went home before this one felt unwell. On Tuesday I went to my boss and said in the sweetest tone I could manage, 'Where would you like Mrs Mollison to work today, Mr Bond?' and when he glared and asked what I was talking about, I said innocently, 'Oh, she's the only person who's turned up today.' That'll teach him to shout at me for trying to arrange for a spare body about the place just in case yet another one went off sick. It's this wretched flu epidemic, which is really hitting us hard. I do hope you're not being fashionable. The World Influenza Centre or something is getting very upset because, though they say they usually can plot an epidemic, they don't know whether this one started on the Continent and spread to England or vice versa. As the patients feel just as badly one way as they do t'other, and as any plot they like to make only shows the facts after the events, I don't feel that it matters a great deal.

Did I tell you last week I was reluctantly going on a picnic on Sunday? Well, I was and I did and it was lovely. We went, as we so often do, over the Purbeck Hills in Dorset. It was misty when we started, on the 10.40 bus from the centre of Bournemouth, but the sun came out in odd moments when it wasn't doing anything else, and the mist wrapped the horizon around in a pretty little fuzz and comfortably hid the scars of war as the bus went across the moors. To reach the village at the foot of the Purbecks – Studland – the bus runs through Bournemouth and Parkstone and Canford Cliffs, all very la-di-da districts, then dives down to the flat Sandbank that is so called, crosses the mouth of the Poole Harbour by the bus ferry, and goes on for about three miles over wild and deserted moorland, with the long line of hills edging it to the south, and the arms of the harbour to the north. This moor is slightly undulating, and has a vivid blue piece of water called 'Little Sea' set in its brown and purple scrub on the left of the road – with the sea beyond the blue lake, and the white cliffs of the Purbecks in the distance. Hill after hill rises in the mist in pale grey, like so many scenes on a stage. And then we reach Studland and have to get out and walk on our own flat feet.

There was a cold little breeze from the north-east which chased itself around our back hair in most unfriendly fashion, but the climb to the top of the cliffs, and then up the long slope of the hill to the highest point, warmed us up quite satisfactorily. Gave us a good appetite for our lunch. I had brought a flask of hot soup, sandwiches and an apple and tomatoes. The soup was delicious, and so much better for a winter picnic than tea or coffee. We ate sitting in the sun under a broken-down bit of wall we discovered. It didn't keep off the wind (if it had, we would have been sitting in shadow) but it shut out 50% of the view, which was unkind. Immediately after eating, we went on, meaning to find a path which ran along the south slope of the hill, as we knew from experience that to go down into the Corfe valley meant drowning in mud in the only pathway open, and walking along the very ridge of the hill was chilly. We slid down the hill a few yards, and found ourselves in the warmest, cosiest, sunniest and most sheltered position you could wish for. So we spread our raincoats on the grass and went to sleep in the sun for nearly two hours! How's that for England in January?

Somebody I know, who is coming to England in March for his first visit to this country, asked me what sort of weather he could expect. I replied, 'Everything.' But even I didn't really anticipate getting freckled on a hillside in January, between two days when the frost was heavy and white and the fog came down in a blanket night and morning. Incidentally, I have never known so much fog as we have had in Bournemouth this year. Normally we get a damp sort of seamist, which drives in from the beach and disappears in the morning. But this month we have had really thick fogs (twice the bus services have been stopped for some hours, it has been so bad) and they smell like wet washing hanging about a house . . .

My brother has been very worried recently over a big decision he has had to take. He has discussed it with me, and with one or two friends, and we feel we have had to fail him just when he needed us, as none of us felt we could advise him one way or the other – it was a decision for himself alone. Most of us have felt rather strongly on one side of the question, that it is better to work where you are happy than to tie yourself to a better-paid job that you don't like. I know from bitter experience how miserable it is working with one man with nobody at work with whom to associate other than the boss! However, my brother has taken his decision – for more money – and, although I have been able to do nothing, his other friends have pulled strings to see to it that he is given a month in which to try out the new job before committing himself to it irrevocably. So they at least have been able to help when it was needed. After working about fifteen years (except for the war) in one department, in very happy conditions, it's an awful jolt having to leave in one day, which is all the time the Town Clerk has given

Mac to clear up his outstanding work and move over to the other office. We are very proud of him – there were 150 applicants for the job, but the Committee decided not to consider any as they wanted my brother. Now it remains to be seen whether or not he can get along with his new boss, who is notoriously difficult when she's not being downright impossible. That is all very hush-hush and secret, so don't say a word to nobody, no how.

Now it is high time my missing cashier felt better. I must go and investigate.

Bye for now.

More next Saturday,

Fran

BOURNEMOUTH
February 7th 1953

Dear Mr Bigelow,

. . . Poor little Holland; it was only last week, I believe, that she said thank you very much but we don't want any more dollar-aid, America. And so few hours later, she is devastated and drowned. Our own floods are bad enough, goodness knows – I know Canvey Island as well as I know Bournemouth, and can imagine how awful a flood would be, for the whole island is like a flat saucer, with the rim only a few feet above the surrounding sea and a causeway usable at low-tide the only way off to the mainland. But Holland! One sixth of her land flooded, and such a little land, at that.

It was on Thursday last week that we celebrated the flight of that Canberra 'plane which took 22 hours to go from England to Australia. On Friday it was announced we were building two more passenger-carrying jet 'planes capable of transporting 150 passengers, 550 miles an hour. And on Saturday Nature decided we were getting cocky, I suppose, and sent a ferryboat, on a 25-mile trip from Scotland to Ireland, to the bottom, then went on around the coasts and brought devastation all down the East Coast, before hurling her waters point-blank into Holland. We are such little people, when it comes to a hand-to-hand fight with nature, aren't we? In spite of Assam Dams, and Tennessee River Valley schemes and Golden Gate Bridges, and Atom Bombs . . .

I've not heard even a whisper of a rumour from Rosalind about the possibility of coming over to England and/or Europe this year. Is the matter shelved or cancelled, do you know, or is she waiting for exact dates before telling me? Or, it occurs to me as I write, are the Akins going only to Europe and missing out England altogether and Rosalind doesn't like to say so for fear of hurting my feelings? You might tip me off if you know. You see, if they *are* coming to England, and Rosalind will have time to spare to stay with us (with or without Mr Akin) and their visit will coincide with our water show at the Baths, I must start working on the Boss quite early to advise him of the situation so that he will know what's coming! . . . He's awfully difficult about time off at the best of times, but early in the summer it's nearly impossible, for then we are trying to get settled with new staff and there are always the most ghastly muddles for me to sort out. *He* can be spared, but has no intention of sparing me at that point; so if he's got to have his mind changed I shall need time to work the miracle.

Last week I sent you a sarcastic cutting from the newspaper about the 'bonus' of margarine and sugar in honour of the Coronation. The next day a letter appeared in the paper which said:

> To the Editor, *Daily Telegraph*.
> Dear Sir, I am appalled by the sarcasm and ingratitude
> shown by people over the announced bonus of four ounces of
> margarine to celebrate the crowning of our gracious Queen.
> Surely, anybody, even of the meanest intelligence, can see that
> the quarter-of-a-pound of margarine has been given to us so that
> we can baste the ox.
> I am, Sir, yours etc.,

Whereupon the subject has been dropped, it being really shooting sitting birds to take pot shots at the Min. of Food over this point. I will give them credit for one thing – they have taken sweets off ration this week, high time too, instead of waiting (as I suspect the Socialists would have done) to release them for the Coronation, with a big splash. And now that I can eat chocolate until I feel sick, I feel too sick (dentist) even to start. What a world!

Yours in a deep depression,

Frances Woodsford

BOURNEMOUTH
February 14th 1953

Dear Mr Bigelow,

Hurrah! I got two fillings done for the price of one bilious-attack. Not being able to bear standing around the house doing nothing but think for one moment longer, I accidentally caught an earlier bus than usual, and arrived in the Town Square at 8.30 a.m., with half an hour to waste and a five-minute walk to waste it in.

So I walked through the Pleasure Gardens, and never were so many shrubs so thoroughly examined as they were on Monday morning. In spite of this, and despite talking to every cat I met on its morning parade, I still arrived at the dentist's at six minutes to nine. His nurse was still struggling into her white coat, but at least the waiting room was warm and there were magazines to look at. But no, Mr Samson has returned to live in the lovely flat over his offices, and hearing I was already there, he popped down on the instant and got to work, so that by 9.15 when the next patient was due, two teeth had been drilled, filled and declared saved for the time being. After that, it shouldn't be so bad . . .

Last night I attended, in an icy hall in an icy evening, my first lecture on Civil Defence, and now I have no worry at all about the future. The day war breaks out I shall just simply die of fright. All my little problems will be solved, just like that. Actually, the lecturer made everything seem quite simple. Nobody asked any questions except, of

course, me. I said, 'You have described how to deal with an ordinary fire-bomb on an upstairs floor; you smother it with a wet sack and spray water on the edges of the sack – not directly onto the bomb. Well, how do you stop it burning its way through the floorboards into the room beneath?' The lecturer said, 'You don't.' Easy as all that. Of course, we gathered that that was just a little ordinary fire-bomb
without any explosive gadgets, and not a phosphorous one or an oil bomb nor an atomic bomb (nobody mentioned hydrogen) . . .

Yesterday I went to buy some more turpentine for my painting, and as I came away one of the attendants in the shop rushed up and said, 'How's it going?' He's rather sweet – every time I go in he comes up to ask what progress I am making, and when this time I told him I had finished 'six masterpieces' I'm sure he was as pleased as me! Then I went to the post office to send Rosalind a cable for her birthday, and found to my dismay that the old cheap night-letter-rate no longer applies, and the cable was a very expensive mode of communication. I wouldn't have sent it at all but for the dock strike in New York which might have delayed the present I had sent, so I wanted at least something to arrive for the day . . .

Hope you remain well and happy.

Sincerely,

Frances W.

BOURNEMOUTH
February 21st 1953

Dear Mr Bigelow,

. . . Today – it's Friday today – a letter came from Rosalind which at last disclosed her plans for a trip to Europe this year. She just couldn't have chosen better dates, so far as I'm concerned, for she arrives at Southampton on a Saturday, which I intend taking off in order to meet her and escort her to London. And she leaves on a Friday, and if the ship sails after midday I shall be able to rush up to Southampton (taking Friday as a half day because I would be working all Saturday that week) and wave a damp pocket handkerchief from the dock. She says she is coming to Bournemouth 'for a night and a day', so already I am trying to organise a month's sightseeing and entertainment into one day and one night. You hustling Yanks!

Just like the English – to say 'No, it can't be done'. I decided to escort Rosalind up to London on the boat train, and telephoned a local travel agent to ask how I got a ticket. They were highly amused, and horrified, in about equal parts, that anybody should even consider such a thing permissible. So I stuck out my lower lip and got to work, determined to go on that boat train if I had to ride the rails on it. Eventually, I got on to some department or other at Southampton Railway, and they said of course I could go, just buy a ticket in the Dock Shed. Oh, they said as an afterthought – I'd have to get a permit to go into the docks in the first place, did I know? I said yes I did know but that the last time I had met somebody I'd got into the docks on the strength of a beaming smile only. 'Oh yes, that helps; but bring a Pass as well,' said the man the other end. So now I am all set, and there is only a little matter of several weeks to get through before the Great Day . . .

Well, my brother has at last made up his mind. He will take the new job offered him. The glint of money was too much for him, poor soul . . . He is now Deputy Children's Officer, which is quite a step up from being a Committee Clerk, putting him second-in-command of a Department as it does. Of course, come to think of it, I suppose I'm sec-ond-in-command of the Baths Department, but nobody thinks anything of *that*, as it isn't official and it's only in the salary line that it shows up. And, being female, I have to be so very, very careful not to tread on the corns of sundry Engineers, Foremen and suchlike temperamental creatures . . .

I am deep in another biography, this one of Whistler. At this distance, and safely out of reach of his acid tongue, I find Whistler's rudenesses most amusing. Especially did I laugh at the account of his being asked by a very rich man to go around his picture gallery and give his opinion on the collection. Whistler accordingly was taken around the gallery, and at each picture he said, 'Amazing!' all the way round. At the end, he added to his terseness by saying, 'Amazing – and not even an *excuse* for it, either!'

I'm very sorry, but I can't write any more this morning. For some reason or other I feel most depressed, and my thoughts keep flying to troubles and worries and miseries. Perhaps it is a combination of staff troubles . . . and the misery of Civil Defence lectures, during which the students laugh now and then but merely as a form of nervous release. And the weather is enough to depress the Empire State Building – you may have had a fine, mild winter, and I believe Scotland has, too. But what you've left over in the way of horror has been heaped upon England with a vengeance, ever since the bathing belles got frostbite at the end of last August.

Pah! I shall go out and buy a bunch of daffodils on my way home, just to pretend spring is here and make us all feel better . . .

Very sincerely,

Frances Woodsford

BOURNEMOUTH
March 7th 1953

Dear Mr Bigelow,

. . . Two extracts from my collection of Mother Woodsford Whimsies this week; first, I asked her how her new teeth were getting along, and Mother answered, 'Oh, they're just fine, I wear them all the time except for eating.' Second, when I heard dimly this morning the radio announcement of Stalin's successor, and sleepily thought the name began with a B (I was thinking Beria, head of the police) and called out, 'Who was that Mother?' 'Oh, Vishinksky, dear, I expect,' said Mother cheerfully. Presumably that was the only Russian name she could remember offhand, but I must say it doesn't sound very much like Malenkov, even to Mother's ears.

I don't know about you, Mr Bigelow, but I felt a sudden feeling of gladness when the first radio announcement of Stalin's stroke was heard, followed a little later by a smaller feeling of self-revulsion that I should feel glad about anybody else's misfortune, even somebody as evil as Stalin. There's no need for me to be horrible merely because he was. I wonder what will happen if there is another world, and it is one in which we are cognisant of our life on this one, and recognise our faults and mistakes? Won't Stalin be taken aback? I wish we could always keep the faith we have so strongly as children. Mother likes telling of the time I was reprimanded for kicking my way delightedly through piles of autumn leaves (slightly wet and probably muddy) and said cheerfully, 'It's a good job the Lord Jesus isn't here today. He *would* think it a mucky place.'

The latest copy of *Holiday* arrived this morning, just as I was getting out of bed. So I only had time to turn to Toni Robins's page on 'Lingerie for Travelling' and gape at the slips and nightwear. There was one – no doubt you turned over the page hurriedly, so you won't remember it and I shall therefore insist on describing it – very fitting underslip, with an enormous frill around the bottom of embroidered nylon, which looked good enough to wear *outside* the dress. Either that, or one should become a Wicked Woman in order to give other people the benefit of looking at such pretty things. So I sighed and put the book down, moved the cat sufficiently to crawl out of bed, and the day had started. As I put on my slip I stepped over and looked at it in the mirror, and I looked something like this:

I will admit it was a gift some two Christmases ago and I thought the other day I really ought to wear it a bit before it falls to pieces with old age and lack of use. Besides, this way I am giving my nylon slips (very plain, but very serviceable) a much-needed rest. If ever you see a blue banana, you can give a small gasp and walk up to it and say, 'Why, Miss Woodsford, I wouldn't have recognised you!'

. . . Civil Defence lectures progress from bad to worse. Last week we were given a horrific booklet on Atomic Warfare, and this week, before I'd got over that, we had 'Chemical Warfare', and next week I am warned we get 'Bacteriological Warfare'. Perhaps they will finish up with the Technique of Mass-Grave Digging. Life promises to be most complicated; last night we were told what to do in a gas attack. The main things are, put on the victim's gas mask (or your own), get out of the contaminated area pronto, strip off all clothes, hose-pipe down, put on fresh clothes and Bob's your Uncle. Can you see us all going around with a fresh set of clothes in a gas-proof bag, a wet pocket-handkerchief (for dabbing gas off odd people found around and about) a hose-pipe and stirrup pump for hosing-down, and a bucket of water in which to push victims' heads so that their eyes get washed out. Oh yes – we should also have a feather for tickling their throats to make them sick if they've inhaled or swallowed any, and our instructor said they'd tried that on him and it didn't work so he recommended salt and water or castor-oil instead. That means a packet of salt and a bottle of castor-oil to add to the rest of our equipment. I still think my idea of dying on the day war is declared is by far the best way out. I don't mean to be flippant, but these things are so unbelievably ghastly that they really cannot be considered seriously.

Looking at the programme Rosalind appears to have mapped out for her all-too-few days in England, I can quite understand why Mr Akin feels no need for culture (being Harvard). Rosalind will be here in Bournemouth one evening and the main part of the next day. She wants a) what she calls 'a bath' and I suspect means a bathe in the sea, b) to buy an antique sideboard, c) to see some famous gardens, d) to have lunch in an English pub. I am saving up to buy a stop-watch. Am also panicking slightly at the notion I might not pass my driving test in time to take her around. Daresay all will be well, though.

Hope all is well with you, too,

Yours sincerely,

Frances Woodsford

BOURNEMOUTH
March 21st 1953

Dear Mr Bigelow,

If ever you get a warm fire burning in Casa Bigelow – one that is not authorised, I mean – just let me know and I'll come over right away with my little stirrup pump, and my even littler hatchet, and put it out for you. Me, thoroughly experienced putter-out-of-fires. Since Civil Defence class last Saturday.

Eleven years ago, or thereabouts, I reluctantly bought myself a pair of slacks for fire-watching and air-raids in general. I dislike women in trousers, and myself especially, but they have their uses in such troublesome times. Since 1945, however, mine have reposed with moth balls in the rag-box. Two weeks ago I fished them out, cleaned and pressed them, and to my joy discovered they still fit! I think they must fit a little more closely than when they were new, for I know my weight is up 15 pounds or more over wartime years; but they fitted well enough.

So I clad myself in them on Saturday and rushed headlong after luncheon, full of good food and peppermint, to the place where the local Corporation people burn our refuse, and where a shed is placed at the disposal of the Civil Defence crowd for training such as me. I was the only one (apart from two men) to arrive wearing trousers, but we all finished up wearing navy blue boiler suits (men for the use of) so I was practically the only comfortable woman present. Especially as I have such large feet they *almost* fitted the rubber gumboots we were also made to wear. Two of the women have tiny little feet, and in spite of stuffing the toes of the gumboots with their gloves, they could only proceed by shuffling along. When it was their turn to be No. 4 in the team (the water fetcher) we had to hold up the fire until they had shuffled the fifty yards or more to the water faucet and back.

Being silly-like, and nobody else showing any signs of volunteering, I went first. There was a small tin shed, with a corridor at the back and a door opening from this into the main room. This latter was fitted up with a furnishing scheme I don't think Park Avenue would approve of. There was a large armchair, sort of greeny black in colour and circa 1900 in years; there was a sofa of completely indeterminate shade and no pedigree whatsoever; there was a little table, and there was a pile of wood shavings. In one corner was a small incendiary bomb which the instructors lit, as they did also the piles of wood shavings. When they thought it was nice and warm and smoky one of them yelled 'Fire!' and this was my cue. I dashed (at least two yards) to the door in the corridor. Opened this a trifle, reeled a bit, recollected myself and shouted 'Water on'. Remembered I was English, and hastily added 'please'.

This is the opening scene. If you would like time out now for a drink or a smoke, please do so. The three-piece orchestra will play (probably 'In a Monastery Garden') during the interval. If your appetite is now sufficiently wetted, we will return to the scene of the conflagration.

In Scene 1, Act 1, we left the gallant team (No. 1 to put out the fire, No. 2 to pump the water, No. 3 to keep dashing up to No. 1 to ask if she is alright and get her thoroughly annoyed at so much interruption, and No. 4 to be water-boy and slop gallons over No. 2's feet. Hence, possibly, the gumboots) battling with the fire.

After poking the end of the rubber hose through a crack in the door, which I had opened a trifle and propped open by one foot, the incendiary went off. We knew it was going off, having been warned that the Germans, finding we treated their little toys with disdain, soon started fitting small explosive charges to the bombs, which put paid to the fire fighters if they were too close. Just the same, the harmless 'bang' which was put in *our* bombs, still made quite enough noise for me. It was my second cue; this time I flung open the door and myself onto the floor inside, narrowly escaping a gory death by falling on my little hatchet. This I was carrying in my breast pocket, as the boiler suit was made for a man and the ordinary pocket opening didn't coincide with my own slacks' pockets by at least six inches. As the boiler suit had no belt, the breast pocket was the only place to put it, and very uncomfortable it is, too, I can tell you, dashing about horizontally with a hatchet missing one's nose by millimetres.

Once on the floor, I was kept busy playing the hose on a) the bomb, b) the pile of shavings, c) the sofa, and d) the chair. The bomb got most; we only shot a few vicious squirts at the furniture, which wasn't difficult to put out; though the chair did start up again after I had finished, which was a Black Mark to me. The bomb spurted and glared and fizzed and generally behaved like a firework. I had time to appreciate its icy blue flame, and to think how beautifully it turned to vermilion on the edges. Once I even managed to score a bullseye with my little shoot of water, getting right around the bomb and down its throat. It spluttered most indignantly. Presumably that's not playing fair. Of course, I don't suppose I really did it much harm – you can't stop an incendiary once it's burning, you can only hope to stop it lighting the surroundings, which of course we all did quite satisfactorily.

Finally, the bomb having exhausted itself, and my demands on the water supply having exhausted the pump-operator, we declared it a day. 'Water *on*' as a small flame spurted up, putting its tongue out at me. Then, 'Water off again, please!' and I trotted out, slightly dirty and smoked like a haddock, to say 'Knock off and make up' in approved style, and give way to the next victim.

It was all surprising fun, once the first few seconds of natural flummox were over and one discovered that the bomb didn't come at you, or throw flames all over the place. We all got thoroughly wet (leaky pumps, of course, and sloppy carrying of over-full buckets) and we all feel now confident of coping with anything this side of Hades. Of course, if another large liner goes up in flames, I don't think I'll volunteer to be the first to go and put it out, but any time you have, as I said at the beginning, a nice cosy woman-sized fire, send me a letter. Better send it airmail, in case the fire gets too big in the interim.

I am enclosing a few sketches from life which possibly you could sell for millions of dollars to some foreign power interested in knowing exactly the sort of people they would be up against, in the event of you-know-what.

Probably my sketches would be the cause of lasting peace, if properly shown around and about. I give them to you with that in mind.

Last night, Friday that is, I went through the Gas Chamber. That in itself was nothing – just a small bare room with tiled floor and walls, crowded with seven people and one instructor all looking like things from Mars. But the after-effects were most unpleasant, for we came out with the gas impregnated on our thick coats, and as we sat in the lecture

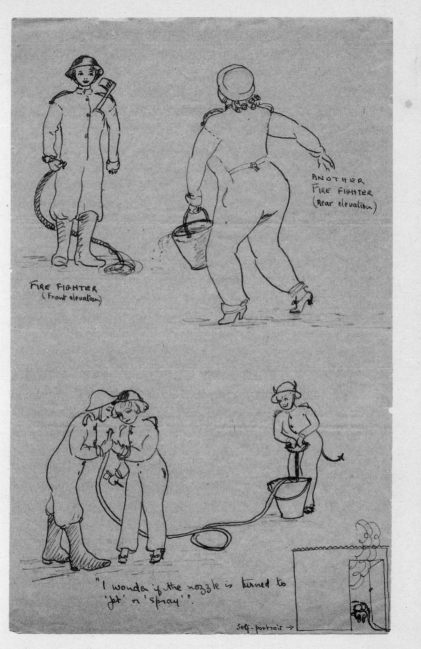

FIRE FIGHTER
(Front elevation)

ANOTHER
FIRE FIGHTER
(Rear elevation)

"I wonder if the nozzle is turned to
'jet' or 'spray'."

Self-portrait →

room afterwards we were all, instructor and all, weeping like servant girls at a sob-stuff film. Only, we had more cause!

While I came to the conclusion last week that tin helmets were most becoming, having caught a glimpse of myself in a mirror as I filled buckets of water in a room, I didn't need a mirror yesterday to tell me that gas masks are *not* the thing to buy in the spring when one needs a morale tonic. The instructor said to me, 'Have you had your mask fitted?' and I answered bitterly, 'Yes, don't I look like it?' knowing full well that my freshly washed hair was not lying flat or smoothly fitting like the novelist's cap.

Ah well, that really *is* all for now. More next week. Best wishes, and I hope you are well and happy,

Yours sincerely,

Frances Woodsford

BOURNEMOUTH
April 4th 1953

Dear Mr Bigelow,

In the days of the Tudors, women wore (so I am told) iron stays with which to restrain their figures. Today, April 4th 1953 as ever it was, I am using metaphysical mental iron stays with which to restrain my remarks, and I hope and believe you will appreciate and applaud the care with which I tell you the following tale.

Last Sunday, about five minutes before luncheon was to be ready, I was called to the telephone in a neighbour's house, to find my brother on the other end. 'I'm at the Queen's Park Garage' he said (I'd never heard of it) 'and there's a 1934 Ford 8 car here I'm thinking of buying. What do you think?' I asked if he had Dez with him (Dez is a departmental manager at one of the big motor firms in the town). No. I asked if he had Vic Hill with him. (Vic Hill is a skilled amateur motor mechanic and driver.) No. I asked if he had anybody with him. No, but he'd looked under the bonnet and the motor was a reconditioned one and had only done 100 miles. The tyres were fair. The bodywork poor. Somebody was coming back in ten minutes to make a decision. What did I think? Not much, I said, so he went off rather disconsolately saying he'd do nothing about it. And half an hour late for lunch he turned up, having bought the motor car!!!

It was delivered on Tuesday, and now reposes in a garage along with half a dozen other cars, for all the neighbourhood to see our shame. Mother and I have inspected it, and I have named it (privately, Mac doesn't know for the sake of his self-respect) Hesperus.* Hesperus is black. More or less. Under the black, where the old paintwork has not been properly rubbed down, it is a sort of petrol-blue colour. And under that again, is a grey undercoat, patched here and there with a bright shade of rust. Mac says gaily that the speedometer cable seems to be broken (did the garage proprietor recognise the pigeon by its bright green colour when it wandered in that Sunday, I wonder?) and that nothing but the anometer works on the dashboard, and that the trafficators don't work. He hasn't tried the windscreen wiper, but would you place a small bet?

. . . We all went to the theatre last night (the first time Mother and I had had an opportunity to look at Hesperus) and Mac was the last of the party to arrive. He whispered to the friend sitting next to him, 'Are they annoyed? What do they think of it? Are they disappointed?' so apparently, in spite of a sphinx-like face on the matter, he *is* a trifle worried. To pacify possible sisterly remarks, he came out with two paper bags containing loose covers for the two front seats, saying blandly *he* was paying for them. That leaves us with two maroon-covered seats, and a navy blue back bench and a strong hint that Sister might like to provide maroon loose covers for the rear, I suppose. As the rear seat covers, I see from the catalogue, cost exactly the same as two front seat covers, Mac's generosity in paying for the latter wanes a trifle, don't you think so?

There is, I suppose, just a possibility that when we clean the thing up, and have the dashboard instruments put right and the windscreen renewed (broken) and buy three new tyres and new mats for the floor

---

* *Editor's note*: a name inspired by Longfellow's poem, 'The Wreck of the Hesperus'.

and paint for the paintwork and polish for the rest, the car *may* look presentable. I sincerely hope so, because it is already taking all my spare money and leaving me with about £15, £10 of which is earmarked to pay for Mother's teeth work. Money doesn't worry me, and I don't really mind if the car falls to pieces tomorrow, but if it does I know Mac will feel terrible about it, and it would be depressing to have to start saving for a car all over again.

I have warned Rosalind that we have bought a 1934 Ford 8, but at that time I hadn't seen Hesperus. Could you break it gently to her when she visits you next month? Tell her to pack, say, a suit of dungarees with her Minks when she comes over, so as to be more in keeping with Hesperus.

Later. Well, I think I know the worst now, having spent Good Friday afternoon cleaning Hesperus. You cannot lock the car. You cannot open the nearside front window as the winder is broken off. For the same reason, you cannot altogether shut the off-side rear window. The back seat is held to the frame of the car by one very rusty hook; I suppose the passenger in the rear holds it in place normally, but any passenger who sits on those springs more than a hundred yards has my admiration and my sympathy. The front off-side headlamp doesn't work . . . The rear light is suspended by a single wire, waiting for the first bump in the road. Mac says there is an electrical short as the battery is discharging all the time. This, presumably, means re-wiring the junk heap or always starting up with the starter handle and hard work . . .

Apart from that, I find I have no friends near enough to ask them to come out with me when I practise, and as in England a learner driver is not permitted on the roads without a licensed driver alongside, the problem is becoming acute as to how to learn to drive before Rosalind arrives. I have quite given up all idea of ever getting any money for the junk heap when we save up enough to buy something a little better, but the state of the thing in itself is very depressing. And I know that friends of his must have told my brother a few facts of life, for he goes around in a mist of misery and seems to have no interest in the car whatsoever, all of a sudden. Ah well, never mind, never mind . . .

There was a great deal I wanted to put in this letter, but matters are crowding in on me which require immediate attention. I'm not working this afternoon (at least, I think not) so hope to go out and buy a bright yellow hat, to cheer myself up in contrast to yesterday's mournful cleaning of Hesperus.

I hope you are having a pleasant Easter. I was getting quite worried about you, it was so long since your last letter; but the very day I wrote Rosalind and said I hoped you weren't ill, a letter arrived, proving you were full of zest, knocking women down in grocery stores (by frightening them, touching them with the finger of scorn or something!) writing long letters, reading many books, and generally being a very busy man.

Happy Easter (bit late, but never mind, never mind).

Very sincerely,

Frances Woodsford

BOURNEMOUTH
April 14th 1953

Dear Mr Bigelow,

From many years past, the parcel postman and I have been on very friendly terms. Whenever I see him up the road I call out – 'When're you coming to see me again?' This morning he called next door as I was finishing my morning face, and I sang out of the open window 'Come along down-a-my-house!' in a cheerful way, and he answered 'Just a moment!' And lo, he *did* come along-a-my house (or whatever are the words of the song) and delivered a parcel from you to Mother. On being opened, it looked as if the parcel which arrived the day before Good Friday was the entrée, and this package contained dessert, the sweet, or 'afters', depending on the class of household. We were particularly delighted with the cake, which we know (you sent one at Xmas, remember?) is mouth-wateringly filled with fruit; but M. and I were also very, very pleased with the tinned and dried fruit and the shortening, which seems so much fatter than that we normally see over here.

But honestly, Mr Bigelow, *please* don't do it again. I know Rosalind, when she arrives, is going to be very surprised to see how healthy we all are, and how well fed. And I would hate her to feel – and so would you, I know – that we had been taking your food parcels under false pretences. After all, we can buy nearly everything we want now: we are rationed only by money; and luxury goods are just as expensive to you as to us, so why should you continue to pay high prices for things we don't or can't buy for their cost? Please, I do want to feel a little bit independent and not all on the receiving end all the time. Will you help me? At the same time graciously accepting (!) our most sincere thanks for both entrée and afters! How about dropping in one day for a coffee?

Very sincerely,

Frances Woodsford

BOURNEMOUTH
May 16th 1953

Dear Mr Bigelow,

. . . The day of the test dawned. I know that quotation usually runs 'the day of the test dawned clear and bright', but my day jolly well didn't. It was raining bucketsful at seven o'clock, and deteriorated rapidly, so that by lunchtime it was blowing three parts of a gale and the rain was horizontal. There was not a vestige of a hope of its clearing by 2.15 (zero hour) and I set off with my instructor for a last trial test at 1.30 with what little courage I had oozing rapidly out of the soles of my shoes. I did the trial run almost without fault, but that was no help to the Examiner, a dour and silent man, probably put that way by all the impossible drivers he has had to sit beside and suffer with all these years. The test run proper was never taken, I should imagine, by two more miserable creatures than the Examiner and myself. He because he was that type (my instructor said, 'You've got Poppa to examine you, but don't take any notice of his pig-like face, he's really quite a nice chap underneath') and I because of the butterflies having an orgy in me and because I got soaking wet through the open window. And the window was open so that I could make manual signs whenever told so to do. Actually, the instructor at one time said only to use the automatic traffic signals; then he said only hand signs, and lastly he said use what I like. I did all the way through, anyway, having been taught to use very definite hand signs backed up, at the last minute, by the trafficators to leave both my hands free to use on the steering wheel. My starts from scratch (and, going over the route this morning, I counted at least twelve in the half-hour test) were more like a jet aeroplane take-off than a smooth-running car. I twice stalled the motor, due to the fact that the gale was making such a din I couldn't hear the engine and know when I needed more gas. I touched the kerbstone in reversing. And, of course, with my years of cycling still strong in my mind, I wove my usual way along the roads, rushing back to the gutter as soon as I passed any standing or moving vehicles . . . However, I believe my work in traffic was good; at least I never had to brake suddenly because I had got myself into a traffic jam I didn't see approaching. The gale kept a lot (chiefly cyclists and pedestrians) off the road, so my good traffic work was more the result of luck than any cleverness on my part. We returned to whence we came, still with two completely miserable creatures in the car.

And there, while I sat in misery and wetness the Examiner cross-questioned me on the Highway Code, which I know backwards, and I believe I got full marks for that. At least, try though I might to answer quietly and slowly, my answers just rushed out because I knew them all so well. It was rather disconcerting to have an Examiner, who obviously knows all the answers himself, saying in a mildly interested tone, 'I see' to all my answers. On asking my instructor later, he said all the Examiners do the same – they are taught never to say 'Right', or 'No, that's not the answer' because that might lead to arguments, and they Never Argue With The Driving Applicant.

Eventually, after weighing me up and my answers and all my faults, the Examiner said he was giving me the benefit of the doubt, and I PASSED! For my own part, I would have failed myself thoroughly and absolutely, so awful was the co-ordination between clutch and accelerator on the test run. However, when he pointed out that there was considerable doubt, I did murmur something about being ashamed of my roughness, which was worse than I had ever put up before, and perhaps, as I hadn't offered any excuses before hearing the verdict, the Examiner felt that his judgement was not misplaced. Provided now that I never let my driving licence lapse, nor hit too many pedestrians in any one year, I can now drive for the rest of my natural life.

And, of course, another good thing is that I can now fasten all my waist-belts two notches farther back than a couple of months ago . . .

Yours very sincerely, and licensed car driver,

Frances Woodsford

BOURNEMOUTH
May 23rd 1953

Dear Mr Bigelow,

As they say, the Devil looks after his own. And on Saturday morning, when I had finished my letter to you and gone home, what should I find but a cash refund of three shillings awaiting me from the Transport Dept (I had returned an unused bus season ticket some weeks before, and had almost given up expecting them to do anything but frame it) which successfully swelled my purse to finance my travel and eating until Wednesday, when my Savings Book came back and I was able to withdraw a pound or two from the Savings Bank. One nice thing about living down on my low financial level; the least little uplift and you begin to feel like shaking hands with the Whitneys and the Du Ponts and the Rockefellers on equal terms.

On Saturday afternoon my brother said would I accompany him (as a fully fledged test-passed car driver) to the War Memorial Homes (of which he is honorary secretary) where he was attending the opening of a hall. So we climbed into Hesperus, we climbed out again and wound her up, and off we set. And oh, Mr Bigelow, I now know why Mac failed his test!! He is a two-wheeler where corners are concerned, and when Mother said one day this week he had worn out the sole of one of his shoes and Mac said, 'Oh, I expect it's the clutch or the brake pedal,' I was able to call out, 'It's the accelerator and well you know it, m'boy!' We tore along at the top speed Hesperus can produce, and when we arrived at the driveway to the Homes, it was to find two cars containing Aldermen just turning in. So we politely waited. And when Mac got into bottom gear to move off in turn, he kangaroo-hopped, and hopped, and hopped. At the sixth hop we were bang slap in the middle of the entrance, and there was a nice little queue of cars behind us in the main road, waiting to get out of the way of the Saturday afternoon traffic. Mac thereupon opened his door, hopped out with his little black briefcase, and said gaily to me, 'Well, you can have the car for an hour. Call for me at 3.30 will you?' and went off. Nice boy, my brother.

I pottered around back streets and country lanes until the hour was up – I left the 'L' plates on to encourage other traffic to be kind to me – when I got back to the War Memorial group of houses. The drive was by now chocked up with bigwigs' cars, and not liking to do a kangaroo hop myself in the strain of the moment, I reversed Hesperus into a side turning off the main road, up a little incline, and in a good position to see over the hedge and across the grounds to the doors of the hall. After a while the bigwigs started coming out, and eventually I saw the Mayor and the Mayoress and the Mace Bearer and the Borough Architect and Mac, all in a little clump. Mac stood at the top of the steps, looked haughtily to the right down the line of cars; looked haughtily down the left row; raised his left arm, bent at the elbow, and looked very hard indeed at his watch. My goodness, here it was half past three and his chauffeur hadn't obeyed his orders. Tut! Tut! This required looking into. All this as plain as dumb show from my seat. I waved vigorously, and at long last His Majesty noticed me, gave a curt nod of the head, turned on his heel and strode manfully back into the hall. And kept me waiting half an hour!! He said there were reporters who wished to ask him some questions.

If, in your long and no doubt ill-spent life, you have come across a fool-proof recipe for taking people down a peg, Mr Bigelow, you might like to pass it on to one who is in bad need of the secret sometimes . . .

Yours very sincerely,

Frances Woodsford

BOURNEMOUTH
May 30th 1953

Dear Mr Bigelow,

. . . This week has suddenly appeared on the hoardings the wittiest poster I have seen for years. I must tell you that Guinness – the brewers of a sort of beer – run two series of posters. One depicts great feats of strength – a road worker in a hole in the road lifting a steam-roller off the hole in order to reach his free hand out for his glass of beer – and the caption is always 'Guinness Gives You Strength'. The other series shows a chubby little zoo keeper and an animal (an ostrich, lion, toucan etc. the toucan caption was 'If a Guinness is Good For You, Just Think what Toucan Do') and the animal is, or has, swallowed his beer. The caption here is 'My Goodness! My Guinness!' Well, this poster I was describing has nothing on it whatsoever to show what product it is advertising. At the bottom of the poster is a mass of cheerful faces in a crowd. Standing slightly above the crowd is the little zoo keeper, who is holding a bench on his uplifted hands. On the bench are all the animals which appeared in their series of advertisements, and they are all waving little Union Jacks. Everybody, animals and humans, are looking in the same direction. Coming as it has done, the week before the Coronation, I think it the most delectable mixture of the series and the occasion that could possibly be thought of.

We are all decorated and bedecked for Tuesday: the town gardeners have been rushing around taking the dead tulips and wallflowers out of the beds, and yesterday night we bloomed in the dark, for this morning everywhere you look you see great masses of hydrangeas – brilliant pink, bright blue, and white. Or, alternating with them, purple and mauve lupins and pink geraniums. There are baskets of flowers hanging from the lampposts, urns of them along the edges of the pavements; and, of course, the public gardens and the traffic roundabouts are planted and brilliant with them. I bought a little flag to put on Hesperus, but it clicked off in the wind the first time we went out with it, and although we turned the car at the first available side road and went back to look for it, all we found was a group of innocent little children playing on the grass. No flag. Even the most sedate and grand houses, which normally are so sedate and grand and respectable they give an impression of slate-putty colour throughout, have, as it were, undone their stays and burst out of their respectability by putting little blue plaques in windows, reading 'God Save the Queen'. Any stray Americans who may, accidentally on purpose, be in England this week will be very hard put to it indeed to reconcile the goings-on with their previous ideas of the phlegmatic British . . .

Very sincerely,

Frances Woodsford

(reproduced by kind permission of Guinness & Co)

BOURNEMOUTH
June 6th 1953

Dear Mr Bigelow,

. . . Tuesday, Monday, and Wednesday this week have between them broken all records ever kept in England for coldness in the month of June. Trust Dame Nature to put her spoke in at such a time. Anyway, I suppose it was a good thing in one way – people didn't pass out with the heat. Instead, they went to hospital suffering from exposure! I read in the papers that about three hundred went, mostly people who had been sitting and lying on cold, wet stone pavements for upwards of forty or fifty hours. Apart from that, there were 'a few' punctures or scratches from bayonets, caused when the marching columns turned sharp corners. I couldn't help wondering whether the punctures or scratched Guard of Honour let out a squeal, or whether they remained stoically 'At Attention' while being punctured. And, on top of that, one man had his foot crushed by a horse and one other man had a leg broken in the crush of the people. Not bad, for so busy and crowded a day. I was alright; I sat in a room about twenty-five feet long by fifteen feet wide, with eleven other people, watching a four inch television screen and nobody got crushed though we all got headaches.

On Monday Mother and I are going to a cinema to see the coloured film of the event, for I believe colour will make all the difference in the world to the scenes. It was difficult, watching the ceremony on a T.V. screen, to realise that it was actually taking place; it seemed more like a film going on slightly shaky but unreal, as a film usually is to me. The Queen's gown did, indeed, look unreal – like soft light shimmering on water, and it made one realise how much is missed in a static photograph of the flashing and scintillation of the embroidery Royalty have on their gowns. I was sure the Queen, poor dear, was over-come when her husband paid homage, for I caught a glimpse, as he backed down the steps, of something white which she was holding to the corner of her eye, and hurriedly put down and tucked in her waistband.

Towards the climax of the Communion, I began to feel most

embarrassed, as though I were eavesdropping, or looking through a key-hole. This was due to the fact that all the people at my friends' house were getting hungry, and had started eating their lunches, so the solemn ceremony was accompanied around me by a sort of running commen-tary of 'Pass the Mustard', or 'Like some more coffee, Connie?' So I was quite glad that the B.B.C. did not televise the height of the service, but showed us, instead, a hanging tapestry in silence for a few minutes, until the service had reached a less intimate point once more.

Of course, Sir Winston Churchill took a plum for himself; he was suitably solemn and emotionally overwhelmed, I thought, in the Abbey, and like a schoolboy on half-holiday in the procession afterwards. As we watched the procession going through Hyde Park, along came nine black coaches, each containing Prime Ministers of parts of the Empire and Commonwealth, and then we heard extra loud cheers and laughter and knew that the tenth contained Sir Winnie. It didn't contain him altogether, for he was hanging half out of the window, his plumed hat tossed aside, making the V-sign for all he was worth and having the time of his young life. London also took the Queen of Tonga, all six foot three of her, to their hearts, and she took us to hers. She refused to have the carriage roof up, in spite of the rain, and went the five miles beam-ing and waving an arm big enough for Samson of Carnero, and wiping her wet face with an outsize in handkerchiefs.

All in all, it was a memorable day. I did find television non-stop from 10 a.m. until 4 p.m., when I had to leave to come to work, far too long, and I never did find the marching of batches of troops, batch after batch, all that enthralling. But on the whole, it was a magnificent spectacle and we all had a whale of a time.

This is being written on Friday afternoon: I am incarcerated in the Cashier's office. No. 1 Cashier didn't turn up at nine this morning, and No. 2 didn't come in at ten either. In one instance we had a message that her husband was ill (interesting, but not much help to me) in the other we have had grim silence all day. I could *spit*! To crown it all, my boss couldn't get his figures right in working out the amount of the cheque for the water show producer, and came to me in the cash desk to sort it out. When I gave it back to him I said mildly, 'You and seaside landladies! Try it *without* adding in the date.' 'What date?' 'You've taken the "y" of

Coronation Day as a seven and included it.' He was so mad, and I don't blame him. And now I must stop and get some more work done.

Hope you are well and happy,

Very sincerely,

Frances W.

BOURNEMOUTH
June 13th 1953
(The Day Before The Great Arrival Day)

Dear Mr Bigelow,

Rosalind's travelling companion wrote me last month, asking me to look for some things she wants to buy (to save time, she says). Their 28 hours in Bournemouth now include; a bathe in the sea; buy an antique sideboard; visit some famous gardens; have luncheon in an old English inn; buy a china animal; buy a 'Scotch golf cap' (whatever that is) and buy a navy cashmere jumper. If we can get a look at Salisbury Cathedral, Corfe Castle, Buckler's Hard and Winchester, all well and good.

Please don't expect anything lucid in today's letter; my mind is chock-a-block with the sizes and shapes of Sheraton sideboards or alternative pieces of furniture; with the whereabouts of that rarity in England, a *real* cashmere sweater (as opposed to the things we send abroad to people who don't know real cashmere when they see it) or china dogs and horses; and a veritable turmoil of restaurant addresses and possibilities in cases of rain, fog, snow or other seasonable weather changes.

. . . A letter arrived yesterday for Rosalind from, I assume, Mr Akin. There is a pencilled note on the back 'mailed such and such a time'. Does Mr Akin not trust the postal authorities and want Rosalind to compare the postmark with his own information to make sure the letter didn't go sculling around the post office for days before they got down to franking it? It will make a pleasant welcome for Rosalind, though (unless maybe she took the front door key with her and the letter is a plaintive plea to return it in a hurry!!!) and I am looking forward to waving it at her from the docks.

I am glad you saw and enjoyed the television of the Coronation. Do try to see the coloured film as well, if it comes anywhere near Bellport, for it is *wonderful*. It is not very long – about an hour or just over – and it is a joy from one end to the other. My one complaint is that I don't like Sir Laurence Olivier, and therefore felt irritated at his stagey shouting of the commentary, particularly right at the beginning where the royal coach is coming out of the Palace, and he says, in a rising crescendo, '. . . . . . comes to a rising noise of cheers,' whereas the only cheers you can hear then are very feeble and by no means rising. But the colours are so lovely; the people in Hyde Park look like massed pink hydrangeas against soft and misty trees . . . And that unbelievable cloth-of-gold coat which the Queen wears, and the square robe over it for the homage, make the richness of the Bishops and Archbishops look really dowdy, if you can imagine anything doing that.

Seeing the film, I found I was wrong in thinking the Queen wiped her eye as her husband made his homage. The camera in television was behind the Duke, and it did look like a furtive wipe. The cinema camera, however, was on the Queen's right-hand and you distinctly saw the hand push the crown back into position after the clumsy clot of a husband had knocked it skew-whiff!

. . . All for now; I must get my office work finished quickly as I want to get out to lunch early and book my seat on the coach* and collect some shoes from the menders and buy a bright lipstick to rival my yellow jacket.

Expect a jubilant letter next week.

Very sincerely,

Frances Woodsford

* *Editor's note*: Frances was travelling to meet Rosalind at Southampton.

BOURNEMOUTH
June 20th 1953

Dear Mr Bigelow,

No rose without a thorn, sang the Victorians. The thorn these last two days has been in the form of a 1934 Ford 8 saloon otherwise known as Hesperus. The rose has been your daughter Rosalind, the loveliest and most delightful heroine Shakespeare wrote of, and so graceful in spirit. And now she has gone on to France and Italy and Mac and I are feeling low and drab. We had so little time to get acquainted and the weather was AWFUL. GHASTLY. DESPERATELY DISMAL. DREARY. WET. VERY WET. COLD. VERY COLD. A colleague, knowing of my plans to pass through as pretty a stretch of country basking in the sun as I could manage (to impress the visitors, of course) said this morning: 'Bit difficult to explain away, wasn't it?' And indeed it was.

Thursday, now, was a very fine day with a brisk breeze and warm sun. We (Hesperus and I that is) picked Rosalind and Mrs Beall up at their hotel and took them home to meet Mother and have a cup of tea. There Mac joined us and we motored through Lyndhurst (where the original Alice in Wonderland lived) and the New Forest to Beaulieu and, we hoped, Buckler's Hard for dinner at the Master Shipbuilder's Hotel. The road from Lyndhurst to Beaulieu reminded Rosalind of the easternmost point of Long Island; rolling land covered in gorse and heather and grass. In Beaulieu we had a puncture and had to prevail upon a farmer (who had been working with only a five-minute break for tea since seven that morning, bless him) who helped him change the wheel. A passing motorist kindly stopped and lent us his brace and bit which fitted. Then they found that the spare wheel valve was leaking, and the Good Samaritan motorist took that one off his own spare and gave it to Mac.

Arriving at Buckler's Hard we found that, being over an hour late, Mine Host had given us up and sold our dinners to four hungry yachtsmen who had sailed up Beaulieu river with sea-size appetites. On our saying we didn't in the least mind a cold dinner, he stepped back and allowed us to pass into a very old and charming dining room. The waiter brought, in turn, deep bowls of soup with cream crackers and fresh bread; cold veal and tongue, new potatoes, tiny little carrots steeped in butter, fresh broad beans, crisp lettuce and home-made mayonnaise. To follow we had bottled apricots, ice cream and whipped cream, which he named Manhattan Melba in honour of our guests' accents. After that we retreated to a sort of ante-room to the lounge, where we had coffee and watched the evening descend on the river and reeds at the foot of the garden. It was quite enchanting, and I must say I thought it wasn't bad for a scratch meal!

Yesterday I awoke to find the whole world whipped in flying rain. I called for the ladies at their hotel (and a fine waste of a room looking over the sea it was, too, with weather like that) and when they had finished writing mountains of postcards we went shopping. Rosalind we let loose in an antique shop where she had no end of fun until it was time to rush home for luncheon.

Rosalind herself will no doubt describe the pleasures of Wilton House where the tour was so intimate we felt we had met the Earl and Countess of Pembroke themselves . . . . . . ('Don't fall over the dogs' bowl!' said our guide.) All rooms were filled with family photographs and sweet with the scent of climbing roses. Then we tore back to Salisbury where, alas, we couldn't go in the Cathedral because a service was in progress and there wasn't, anyway, time. Dinner followed in a 1500 inn in Romsey and so, still, in rain, to Southampton where we drove in and out of various docks until we found the right one, and Rosalind and Mrs Beall were hustled hurriedly through Customs, Passport Inspection and all too quickly onto the boat for France.

Mac and I returned, dismally, to home and bed, and today to dreary normality again.

And on that depressing note I will leave you.

Very sincerely,

Frances Woodsford

BOURNEMOUTH
September 5th 1953

Dear Mr Bigelow,

At last, at last, my brother has passed his driving test. When told the good news, he asked the Examiner if it was 'all right' to drive the car away, and of course, the man said 'No', because the little chit they give you is not a driving certificate, but merely a note authorising the Licensing Department at the Town Hall to issue a driving licence (on payment of the appropriate fee). Mac said he waited until the Examiner had tootled off, and then, to the great interest of a passing policeman, he removed his 'L' plates and drove off to the Town Hall. He there obtained his licence and drove back to his office in the most legal and law-abiding manner, as though he has been keeping within the law all these months!

On Monday morning Mac said to me, 'If you'll go and get the car out, I'll take you down to the office.' . . . As I got into Hesperus's driving seat I touched the steering wheel, and the horn started blowing again non-stop. Mac, frowning like thunder, strolled over and said coldly (it was his bad day, obviously), 'I don't see how you can do it; the car never does that with me!' I pointed out that there was a first time for everything.

But, in truth, it wasn't the first time. It was the third, and all three times had been when I was, alas, driving the thing.

On Sunday I took Mother out for a run, and as I was turning the car on top of a hill the klaxon started blowing. As I hadn't touched it my conscience, pricking slightly, told me that there must be some part of its mechanism at the rear of the car, and I had bumped it in bumping into the grass verge as I reversed. When I went forward again, the horn stopped. We got to within a mile from home quite happily, and were bowling along the main road when the darn thing started again – right bang outside a garage. I swung the car into the garage yard; thought a moment of my financial state (it was the day before payday) and the nine pence which was all I had, and swung her out again. So we sailed along the main road going full blast, with people bellowing at us, staring at us, shouting at us, blowing *their* horns at us, and laughing at us. Mother was hysterical with laughter, and I was hard put to it to continue driving when we came across a very old man sitting on a bench waiting, I thought, for a bus. As we rounded the corner there he was, leaning forward onto his knees, one hand cupped around his ear. Ah, I said to myself, you'll *hear* us, alright, Sir, even if you don't hear the bus when it comes. His face was a study as we passed him on our strident way.

On driving into the garage, still klaxing, I discovered – quite accidentally – that when I turned the steering rod to the left, the noise stopped. So I had left it turned that way on the Sunday evening, and on the Monday it was merely the touch of my coat which brought the wrath down on my ears again. Mac very kindly tinkered with it until he got a wire off, so we have run for two days without a horn. Never a dull moment, eh?

. . . Now I must off and away for my lunch. Tomorrow I am taking some friends out in Hesperus for an all-day picnic. If you don't hear from me next week you'll know that something worse than the horn went wrong this time . . .

Very sincerely,

Frances Woodsford

BOURNEMOUTH
September 26th 1953

Dear Mr Bigelow,

On Monday I was bitten by a dog for the first time in my life, and I don't mind if it is also the last time. A nasty, snappy little Peke with which I was only being sympathetic as it obviously was upset at the rain and the wind. And the wretch bit me. Three fingers of my left hand it got, too. Wait until later in this letter to see if I get rabies, as I am beginning the letter on Tuesday evening, and by Saturday it's bound to show. If you can't wait until the end of the letter, you may peep at the postscript . . .

My heart tells me it is I who am obliged to *you*, since you
appreciate so kindly the letters I am sending you. And don't you
realise that I find some consolation in writing to you? I assure you
I find much, and I have at least as much pleasure in talking to
you as you have in reading what I say.

I quoted that from the book I am currently reading, with the alteration
of only one word: it seemed to me to be most apt for our correspondence; you for ever being appreciative, and me for ever trying to say the
debt is mutual. Can you guess who wrote the quoted paragraph? None
other than Mme de Sévigné, that Princess of letter writers. And aren't
they magic – they almost make me wish to speak and read French, that
I might enjoy them in the original.

My mother and her grocer get into mutual difficulties with their
respective handwriting; usually, I am called upon by one side or the
other, to give a judgement. This week there was some muddle about
Mother's order book – she had been given somebody else's by mistake,
and couldn't find her own. It was eventually found, and to prove her
point that she had never taken it to the grocer, Mother (who couldn't
find her spectacles either) asked me to read the last items entered.

Surprisingly, they were fairly clearly written. I read,

'Zulu, Flu, All Set.'

'Yes,' said Mother triumphantly. 'And I haven't had any of them yet!'

As Zulu is the name given to the small black poodle next door, Mac and
I are being very careful to investigate all our meat dishes this week. The
items, when correctly interpreted (and we went to the grocer to find out,
in the end) were: Izal (a disinfectant), Flour, and a box of Liquorice All
Sorts. How dismally disappointing is the truth at times!

. . . On Sunday last week I sawed, clawed, tore, broke, or cut about
nine inches off the top of our garden hedge, and some six or seven
inches off the side of it. This entailed standing on the kitchen stool,
which in turn usually means falling face first into the hedge from time
to time when the stool hits a soft piece of earth and sinks to one side
under my weight. The hedge, now cut down, is still about six feet high
and it is very, very hard on the arms and hands to cut the far side of a six
foot hedge, standing on a small and inadequate stool. I may say that due

to the presence of sundry hen-houses on the far side the top of the hedge *has* to be cut from our own garden. I didn't count the scratches, but somebody who saw me on Monday thought I had scarlet fever . . . And I thought I was dying, for I hadn't the strength left in my hands to wring out my face flannel on Monday morning! However, I am able to grasp things again by now, which is just as well because Wednesday is payday and wouldn't it be ghastly if I went to the bank and was physically incapable of grasping all that nice new money? . . .

Now if I write any more, the letter will be too heavy for its single stamp, so I won't burden you further until next Saturday.

Very sincerely,

Frances W.

PS Indeed, Sir, and what do you mean – 'Don't miss a mail!' I would have you know, Sir, that I have a secret store of letters in case I fall down and break both arms and can't write for a couple of Saturdays. Fie on you for your lack of faith Mr B.

PPS Was it not fortunate that the dog had many years and no teeth!!

BOURNEMOUTH
November 14th 1953

Dear Mr Bigelow,

What I want to know is, who decided I was to be the Belle of the Ball? Not by public acclaim, I am sure; nor was it by private demand that I was awarded the role. No. I am beginning to believe I Have Enemies At Work. And when you have read to the end of this sad story, I think you will agree with me; and, perhaps, you may be able to put your finger on the culprit.

The Ball was officially known as 'Exercise Flash', and was a thing got up by the local Civil Defence crowd in order to make use of a Mobile

Column of air-raid defence workers. This Mobile Column is the Home Office's favourite baby at present, and wanders around the countryside demonstrating how efficiently air-raid casualties and troubles can be coped with. The idea is that a certain town (Bournemouth, this week) has been badly bombed and the existing Civil Defence groups in that town cannot adequately cope, so they call on the nearest Mobile Column for help. So everybody works in with everybody else; police, fire-brigade, medical people, air-raid wardens, and the folk who look after what are technically known as 'Enquiring Public' and who feed the homeless and so on. Helped by the Column.

Of course, to make the thing realistic they use smoke bombs and thunderflashes and Very lights and so on. And, to add the final touch, they have 'casualties' for everybody to practise on. I was asked to be a casualty.

That last, simple little sentence, innocuous if ever there was one, was the cause of all the trouble. True, when the person on the telephone asked me he did remark – sort of as an aside, or afterthought – that everybody taking part was insured. That should have told me. That should have stopped me. And if that didn't do as it should, then I should have stopped, backed out, and retired to my safe little home when he added, 'Wear your oldest clothes, tie your head in a bag, and come pre-pared to be dropped.'

Dropped? When that sank in my little mind I decided, optimistically, that it meant I might be dropped by some ham-fisted Home Guard who was holding one handle of the stretcher. Was I worried? No.
Well, not much, anyway.

My first appointment was in the Make-Up Room. Here we were togged out in large navy blue dungarees – mine went over a pair of slacks, and a jacket which I was wearing over a warm woollen jumper. You see, I expected to be told to go and lie in a corner out of doors, and it is November and cold and damp, so I had prepared accordingly. Not, it turned out, accurately. We were identified, and given labels to tie on ourselves. I was representing Miss Ponsonby, Matron in charge of the Madeira Road Nursing Home (the police station represented the Nursing Home, and a more depressing and unhygienic nursing home I have never seen) and was said, on the card, to be 21. I have a feeling that the Unknown Enemy put that down as a sop, to soothe me when I Discovered All. The doctor in the First Aid Post, reading my label, remarked that I was very young to be a Matron, but of course he was not to know how brilliantly clever I am.

Anyway, I was Miss Ponsonby and I was suffering from a right arm having been blown off at the elbow, and deep shock.

I was given a small – too small – tweed jacket to put on top of my over-alls and jacket and jumper. The right arm of this jacket had been torn off halfway and was stuffed, with a bit of white and some red sticking out at the end. When, wearing this, I went to the Make-up Table, the officer in charge there seized my false arm and just literally poured something out of a bottle all over it. I dripped 'blood' for nearly half an hour, and can only hope it didn't stain anybody's good clothes. My face was creamed powdered white, and large black rings were put around my eyes (shades of Joan Crawford!) and black was smeared on the lobes of my ears, and replaced my cheerful red lipstick. This was a shock, and a sight of myself in a mirror practically made the make-up unnecessary. The 'best' casualty was a woman who, apart from 'badly gashed forehead, bruised and cut face' was said to have a compound fracture of the arm. To get this, a piece of bone was stuck onto her skin with invisible tape . . . When she came over to the little huddle of 'casualties' who had been made up there were, I must confess, many shudders. Somebody asking what the bone was made of, I carelessly said, 'Oh, I expect it's a bit left over from the last war,' and we nearly had a couple of *real* casualties on the spot.

Eventually there was a loud 'bang' as somebody let off a thunder-flash, and that was the signal to get us in our positions. I was taken into the police station and into a warren of passages. We twice came up against a barred corridor and felt almost felonious. Eventually we reached a staircase, and went up and up and along and up again and into a large room containing about thirty chairs, some small tables, a piano (flat) and a desk on a dais under the police badge. My guide left me here with instructions to wait until I heard something happening, when I was to switch off the light, barricade the door, and put myself in a suitable position for somebody who had had her arm blown off.

When he had gone, I went around and looked about me, and found that the door was labelled 'blocked by debris, not to be used', and nearly all the windows were marked 'stuck fast by blast, not available'. One window, slightly open, looked onto a small well; and another window, also open, looked out onto the drill-yard where there was a small grandstand for onlookers, reporters, visiting bigwigs and so on. This, I decided glumly, must be the only possible means of exit.

So I chose a spot on the floor which might be less hard than the rest – but wasn't – and I flung myself gently down. After half an hour or eternity, I couldn't tell you which, my left hip went to sleep in great agony. So I got up and prowled about and put my head out of the window to see what was happening. Now Mr Bigelow, a joke's a joke, but what sort of sense of humour can a person have who, immediately on seeing my poor forlorn head, lets off a thunderflash and smoke bomb immediately underneath?

I went back in with such a jerk I nearly gave myself concussion on the window frame. Back, then, to the floor. My third arm – well, half-arm – kept getting in the way, as the jacket was so small the blown-off stump was somewhere near my right back shoulder blade. From time to time the roof of the room was illuminated by blood-red flares, and in their light I could see the smoke curling in and around. Besides, I could smell it; taste it; practically spit it out, it was so thick.

After about an hour and a half, the sound of motorcycles heralded the arrival of the Mobile Column, and the top of a ladder started appearing at different windows and then going away again. People started calling for 'Jock'. Where Jock was I have no idea, but he did eventually appear in my open window and flash a torch on my unconscious body. Rescue! At last – just as the last drop of my blood was about to seep out of my stump. He came over, followed by other smoky figures, and read my label. This was convenient, I must say; and it was so dark I'm sure he couldn't see my beautiful shock make-up. In a moment of lucidity in my state of unconsciousness I murmured 'Tell me, are you an amateur or professional?' and a broad Scots accent said, 'Dinna you worry, lassie, you'll be alright – we've been doing this since January the first.' I allowed myself to sink back into unconsciousness, only coming round to murmur to the doctor who came in, 'Apart from my arm I feel fine, thank you' in the Brave Tradition of the Blitz.

To the accompaniment of grunts and complaints, 'You *are* a weight,

Miss,' I was moved onto a stretcher and wrapped in blankets. By this time, in spite of all my swaddling clothes, I was shivering with cold (and fright) and my teeth were chattering so hard I had trouble keeping my mouth shut to keep in the noise, so the blankets were more than welcome. Jock then strapped me to the stretcher with ropes – quite loose, they are – and finished up tying the ends of the ropes around and around my feet and looping them over hooks at the side of the stretcher. This, I gathered, was to stop me sliding out of the ropes and off the end of the stretcher. At last I was ready, and the stretcher was lifted up and moved across to the window and balanced on my rear end, on the sill. The Sergeant or whoever it was in charge of the rescue party then wandered around in the smoke, and came back carrying a triangular bandage. 'What's that for?' I asked. 'Oh, a bandage to put over your eyes,' he said. I assume that sometimes they get trouble with nervous females who squeal as they see what is being done with their helpless bodies. 'Oh, don't bother – I'll die brave,'I said, with bravado and hardly a tremor. So off I went, with a shove, into space.

We will now draw a veil over the few succeeding moments, as my point of view was such that I can't tell you how they got me down. All I know is that there were four ropes, attached one to each handle of the stretcher, and the motion was gradual. When the voices from the ground came up and passed me, I knew I had arrived, but I wasn't prepared for the feeling as somebody said 'put her right down on the ground' and my head came down and down and down and my feet went up and up and up. So it felt, in reaching the horizontal; so I can only guess that I actually came down from that window more or less feet first, even though it did feel as though I was travelling on an even keel.

Once down, and the ropes taken off, I was whisked off to the First Aid Post, and whilst I can (faintly) recommend coming out of third-storey windows on a stretcher as a reasonably comfortable way of getting down, I cannot recommend a stretcher as a means of loco-motion. If ever anybody puts you on one, Mr Bigelow, see to it that you are given seasick pills first.

In the First Aid Post they gave very bad shock treatment indeed. I was lying there looking at the tin roofing, when suddenly this apparition came into view:

Somebody to whom I telephoned last week said, 'Did you see the uplift Nurse?' See her? I was right in the shadow! Never have I seen such a sight, and I should recommend to the Powers in Charge that if ever we do get a real need, she be kept well out of sight. Otherwise, there will be self-inflicted casualties to deal with as well as the ordinary ones.

Anyway, this apparition leaned over and, putting her arms around herself – which was the only way she could reach, she scribbled M (for Morphia) and T (for Tourniquet) on my already smeared forehead, called loudly for an ambulance, priority, and I was whisked swiftly into it. A St John's Ambulance girl crawled in with me and sat down. She told me she was there 'to cheer you up'. We shot out of the police station yard, turned left, left, and left again and stopped, with a screech, in the Law Courts parking yard. At least ten yards, as one could walk, from the First Air Post we had just left. Here the St J.A. girl said, 'This is where it gets silly – you have to walk now.'

And walk I did, back to the make-up room, where everybody admired the manner in which Jock had bandaged my stump, and where most of my shock make-up was removed and I was told 'Oh, you can go home now.' Nobody told me I should have gone to the mobile kitchen canteen, where hot soup was being ladled out to everybody concerned and faces were being scanned to see if they looked any better cleaned up. So I came home, and it wasn't until then I discovered my ear lobes were still black, and so was one eye. Daresay the bus conductor thought I'd been fighting again.

Next time, I am firmly resolved on playing a more active role, so that somebody else can shoot out of third-storey windows for a change. I discovered later that my friend Dorothy Smith, who is chief administration officer to the Mayor, was 'Miss D. Ponsonby' a member of the

Enquiring Public, and she spent the evening looking for her sister, the matron of the bombed nursing home. This made me more certain than ever that my role was a deliberately cooked-up bit of business, done by somebody who knew that I *am* matron of the Baths in real life, that Dorothy Smith is an old friend of mine, and that I have no head for heights.

What's your guess, Mr B?

And that's all for now, from your rescued, and shaken correspondent,

Frances Woodsford

BOURNEMOUTH
November 21st 1953

Dear Mr Bigelow,

. . . Last Saturday afternoon I was to have 'Hesperus' and my brother said, 'Shall I get the car out for you?' and, slightly overwhelmed, I said, 'Yes, please.' When he had gone, I turned to Mother and asked if she'd like a lift to the library, and M. dashed off to get ready. Ten minutes later we emerged on the pavement – no car. We thought Hesperus was play-ing us up again, and wouldn't go through the garage door, so Mother and I walked across to the garage. No car there, either. We stood like lemons on the pavement for nearly half an hour, and as no sign of a car or Mac had appeared by then, we got on a passing bus. Mother very worried, because Mac doesn't usually bother to take a door key with him (somebody is usually at home to let him in, so he doesn't worry). *I* was delighted, hoping he would come home and not be able to get in . . . . . . I was so cross. I was even more cross when I discovered it was the very afternoon 'Father Christmas' arrives in the town, and that it took the bus over an hour to do a journey which normally takes 20 minutes, and which can be done in seven in a car. When I was flouncing out of a shop in Westbourne, who should appear but Mac, rather shame-faced! He'd only used the car to go and see somebody, and never thought (in a most hurt tone of voice) we'd go rushing off in a huff like that, just because we 'had to wait a few moments'. He then had the *absolute nerve* to borrow his bus fare home from me. Why brothers are allowed on earth I have yet to discover . . .

See you Saturday next.

Very sincerely,

Frances Woodsford

PS Where *would* we be without each other to write to! Don't stop.

BOURNEMOUTH
December 26th 1953

Dear Mr Bigelow,

If I cheat a little, and start this letter on Wednesday, I'm sure you won't mind, so long as you get one by the usual mailing . . .

We are all set for the holiday, except Mother, who has chosen this, of all times, to have sciatica. She was so hot and bothered with it on Monday I sent her to bed and did all the evening work myself and so missed first-aid lecture. On Tuesday she was worse than ever, so I packed her off again and missed pottery. This time, after washing the dishes and getting the cat's supper and Mother's ditto and filling the hot-water bottles and turning down the beds, and so on, I asked Mother if she'd like me to ice the Christmas cake. Mother made a bit of a fuss, but eventually said yes it *would* be a help. So, leaving her to go back to sleep, I set to work.

First of all, the icing sugar was damp and in concrete-like lumps. I ironed these out with every implement to hand. This took the best part of an hour.   Next I mixed in the beaten-up egg whites, and beat the whole mixture until both arms were cramped. A final dash – mind, now, only a drop – of colouring matter, and the icing was ready to put on the cake. But where was the cake?

It wasn't in the cake tins; it wasn't in the cupboard. It wasn't in the cupboard under the sink, nor in the oven. It wasn't in a tin under the table, nor on the table. I moved next door. It wasn't under the sideboard, in the sideboard, or on top of the sideboard. Nor under the writing desk, the bookcases, or the radio cabinet. It wasn't even in the airing cupboard, because I looked there, too. Not in Mac's room, nor in mine. I opened Mother's door and crept in on hands and knees, and although I can tell you, Mr Bigelow, exactly what Mother keeps under and on the various pieces of furniture in her bedroom – and tell you all by touch, too – the cake wasn't there.

In the end, desperate for a cake in the rapidly stiffening of my beautiful icing, I iced this week's ordinary, humdrum cake, cleared up the mess, and retired to bed.

Next morning Mother said, 'You didn't make enough icing for that cake, dear.' I replied, 'Don't worry – I'll ice the cake tonight.' Mother looked puzzled – what a silly remark to make when I had obviously iced the cake the day before. 'But please, will you first of all tell me WHERE IS THE CAKE?' It was in the meat safe. You've heard of my mother before, haven't you Mr Bigelow? But she never palls and never varies in her variety, does she?

On Christmas Day Mac is going to a football match in the morning, so I will run him over to the ground in the car, pick up our guest for the day and take her for a little ride in the New Forest to collect (no, wrong this time!) the Yule Log, returning in time to collect Mac and get us all home for Christmas Dinner. Mother always prefers to be left severely alone while she prepares a meal, so she gets the dinner and I clear it away and get tea for anybody still sufficiently unstuffed to partake of that meal. This usually means that I miss hearing the Christmas Broadcast, as I loathe and detest leaving dirty dishes around the room while I listen to the radio or do anything at all. Conscience does not give me peace until I have cleaned up. Such a prickly conscience. There is a newly dedicated church quite close to us, built only this year, and I would like very much to attend a service some time over Christmas there. Our real parish church is some distance, and we loathe the vicar and detest his sort of sermon, so we have been very, very poor parishioners. In any case, our church attendances are erratic and liberal . . . Aren't you shocked? . . .

I leave you with the wish that your New Year will be a very, particularly, happy one for you and all your family down to the last, least, and smallest grandchild.

Very sincere and affectionate greetings,

Frances W.

1954

June 12th (p. 177), 'To wish you dear Commodore, your happiest birthday yet.'

BOURNEMOUTH
January 16th 1954

Dear Mr Bigelow,

Alas, here we are once more on our annual pilgrimage to the dentist,
losing weight by the pound and sleep by the night. Usually, my 'twice
yearly visit' is so dragged out that I turn up each time just as the mimosa
tree outside the surgery window is puffed up with yellow flowers. This
year, instead of waiting until about May before I plucked up courage,
the keen North wind coming suddenly into an open mouth sent me
helter-skelter for a telephone and an appointment.

So I arrived at Mr Samson's on Thursday in my usual state of
shivers and shakes, and was furious to see a large bowl of mimosa on a
marble column in an embrasure in the surgery. I said, indignantly, 'Oh!
And I was *sure* I was early in my visit this year!' and Mr Samson looked
so smug I confess I thought he'd had the blossom picked and put there
to come fully out in the indoor warmth, just to make me feel the
usual cowardly worm I do feel. I felt that way more than ever when the
examination was over, and I found that the drilling in one large back
tooth was but a preliminary. Now I have to go and see the junior
partner on Monday morning ('and be sure and tell him you're to have
an injection,' which bodes ill) and have some more drilling on the tooth.
Then, on the following Thursday I see Mr S. once more and he'll decide
whether or not he can avoid taking out this bad tooth. Three visits
for one tooth! I shudder – especially at the idea of, perhaps, finding
it hopeless on Monday and taking it out forthwith, for my first-aid
exam is Monday evening and an aching jaw is no help at all as an aide-
mémoire . . .

We read in the papers that you have been having appalling weather
lately: I hope you have stayed snug and warm indoors, and not decided
to see just how warm the Mercury can remain in below-zero weather.
We had a pelting hailstorm, with thunder and lightning and all the stage

effects thrown in, two days ago, but since then it has been warm and muggy, though a bit ghusty. I sat and considered that last bit of spelling for some time before I noticed what was wrong with it. Don't you agree with me that a 'ghust' sounds much more windy than a plain 'gust'. After all, the aspirate sounds like a blow: let's reform spelling, shall us? . . .

Last Sunday morning the police telephoned my brother, and the upshot of it was that he had to collect two children from their home, and find them a foster-parent. As it is always awkward moving children and driving the car at the same time, he asked me if I would accompany him. The sudden necessity for moving the children had arisen because on the Saturday night their mother had eloped with the man next door. This left the deserted father with three children to look after (the baby was collected Saturday night, as it was too young for the father to cope with) and the deserted mother next door also with a family – she had four. A total of nine lives upset, and in many instances, changed and made unhappy, because of the selfishness of two adults. Ah well, I am not in a position to judge, and I must say when I met the deserted father I thought him an awful weed . . .

Now I must get this posted. I hope your cold is now quite a memory, and that your recent bad weather has not affected you except by keeping you snugly indoors with the dogs and the cat and The Tin-Opener, Television, and Telephone to keep you in touch with the outside world.

Very sincerely,

Frances W.

BOURNEMOUTH
January 23rd 1954

Dear Mr Bigelow,

The Event of the Week, apart from two trips to the dentist at which he drilled merrily through to my left eardrum on Monday, and my Adam's Apple on Thursday, has been, of course, the First Aid Examination. Listen, and you shall hear about it.

The first-aid lectures – and the examination – are held in a large old house in Bournemouth, sparsely furnished with stretchers, broken-down wooden chairs which fold up unexpectedly, a telephone switchboard and piles of red and grey blankets and grey bandages. These last were once pure snowy white, but have been subjected to long use and misuse by generations of students.

We were herded into what passes normally for the 'staff room'. Here was a small wooden table, a tin trunk, and about six leather-covered seats removed from old motor cars. Not even an out of date copy of *Punch* to make us feel we were at home, in the dentist's waiting room. Make all except me feel at home, that is, for as you know, the dentist's waiting room is never, never homelike to me. Anyway, we nearly all arrived, as per instructions, at seven o'clock, burping our hastily eaten dinners and biting our fingernails. At twenty past seven an untidy, lumpy figure was seen going down the hall – this was the examining doctor, at the sight of whom sundry groans went up from girls who had met him before. He is apparently one of the school doctors who examine all the children in our free schools (your public schools).

Four men – chosen to be the 'patients' for following students – went to our lecture room. The next four, of which I was one, waited. And waited. And waited. By half past eight our shattered nerves were lying all over the place – you never saw such a sight – and it was almost a relief to get our call. Not, I may say, for very long.

The doctor was, at a guess, Austrian. Rather flabby fleshed, with sparse pale hair turning grey, and thick fat hands to match his thick fat lips, I thought him most unprepossessing. He sorted us out alpha-betically, and as I am a 'W', I knew I'd be the last to be examined. But there we were: doctor, table, four students in a row, and behind us lying about on mats and rugs and things, the four male 'patients'. In one corner a St John's Ambulance Brigade lady – our practical instructor – sat rolling up triangular bandages and smiling to herself. No doubt to keep up her spirits.

The first question, mouthed in an effort to make the accent (and the question) completely clear, was, 'Vot are de zigns and zymptoms of a fragture of de loombar region of de zpine?' The first student hadn't the remotest idea. Helped, prodded, hinted and cajoled by the doctor, she decided that the patient would be in great pain and unable to move his *head*! More than this she could not say. When the doctor, trying hard, said 'Vot abart his legz?' she merely said 'they'd be painful', which was not really meeting the poor man halfway, was it? She had three other questions she answered just about as well. Not altogether giving up hope, the examiner then told her to go and do a 'collar and tie', and a bandage for a broken upper arm. She did the first, and part of the second, but unfortunately she did them both on the same patient. 'Ah well!' said the doctor philosophically, 'I suppose it was *my* fault – I didn't tell you to use two patients.' So she slunk out of the room, I imagine, though we were so terrified by then we none of us could have turned our heads if Christian Dior himself had been waving free frocks at us from behind our chairs.

Patiently the doctor started on No. 2. Her first question was 'You (you must imagine the accent, I can't keep it up) are going along a road and you come across a man lying in the road, unconscious, and bleeding from the left ear. What do you suspect has happened?' The girl said brightly, 'Oh, I'd suspect he'd had a blow.' A passing carthorse, no doubt – a specially trained carthorse that could kick sideways. Passing rather rapidly – well, after about five minutes hard prodding and equally hard resistance – to the next question, the doctor asked what she would do if she found a man with a broken leg lying unconscious in a room full of gas. She would give artificial respiration. Obviously very pleased with herself.

By this time it had penetrated even through my thick skull that the doctor was a man who wanted first things first. The first thing he wanted in that question was – 'Get the patient out of the gassy room.' I took heart and resolved to get my answers in their right order. After all, the doctor went out of his way to *make* us give correct answers: he was extremely kind in that way. Student No. 3 fared no better – she was beginning to get the end of the doctor's tether, and no wonder. He asked her what she would do if she came across somebody, perhaps in a war, who had had their arm blown off at the elbow. Shades of me and the Civil Defence exercise, I thought, and wished I'd had that question, knowing its answer from hard experience. Quite correctly she told him about a rubber bandage. 'And then what?' She racked her brains – you could distinctly hear them racking and said, 'Oh, I'd feel the pulse.' The doctor counted up to a few dozens or so, and I wondered whether he'd say 'Where would the pulse be, in the next building?' but he didn't, he merely sighed and said sadly, 'You would be wrong, young lady. For your future information, there should be no pulse beyond a tourniquet if you put it on correctly.' No. 3 passed out of my ken to do a bandage. That left me, shivering.

'What is shock?' was my first question, and a horrid one to answer, too. I described the zigns und zymptomz, and chattered merrily about 'primary' and 'secondary' shock, 'surgical shock' and so on. (Afterwards I looked it up and found that surgical and secondary are the same thing.) Gently prodded, I found myself bringing out a bit about the causes of shock, and suddenly the doctor and I were merrily engaged in arguing about whether or not it was possible to get into a state of shock when you didn't know what hit you. He gave me a little lecture, and I was (I hope) suitably grateful.

'You find an unconscious person in the road. What do you do?' Well, the book-answer says to start at the head and look for causes of insensibility, and then work your way down the body, both sides. So I started on the head, and five minutes later we were still on that bloomin' head, looking for causes. We had done five different types of fractures on the skull (I knew them, so if you think I didn't let the doctor know I knew them, then you too need your head examined, Mr Bigelow) and eyes and haemorrhage and blood in the skin tissues. In a hurry, I mentioned possible asphyxiation (which should have been first, to be sure, and there I was doing what I had despised the others for doing) and the doctor said sternly, 'You've done First Aid before! Where?'

I murmured something about doing a little in my job . . . Now this, Mr B., was a major error in tactics on my part. From there onwards, whenever I hesitated for a second, he snapped 'Come, come, now – the Matron of the Baths *must* know!' until I wished I'd said I was a washer-up or a time-watcher or something; anything but what I was . . .

And so thankfully I crept out. I shall pass, I'm quite sure of that, if only out of sheer relief on the doctor's part. I would dearly love to know if *all* the class gave as stupid a performance as my three fellow sufferers, but really don't think such a thing would be possible. Of the three, two were very young girls who had missed three lectures, which was an excuse for them. And the first was a middle-aged woman who knew everything, at the time of the lectures. Just goes to show – I must remember to emphasise my ignorance in future!

I rushed home intending to have a large brandy to steady what were left of my shattered nerves, and to tell my family, no doubt all agog to hear, what had transpired. The family were playing Scrabble, as to Mother and Mac, and upside down on the sofa asleep, as to Freckleface.

Nobody was a bit interested in my needs for brandy or for an audience. I almost went straight back to the office and wrote you on the spot. Only sheer laziness, and the knowledge that, if I did, I would be left high and dry today with nothing to write about, stopped me. However, now, if you feel yourself going unconscious at any time, just drop me a postcard. I rather hope to be fully qualified to discover the cause . . .

Very sincerely,

Frances Woodsford

BOURNEMOUTH
January 30th 1954

Dear Mr Bigelow,

. . . My boss is away ill, and so are three of my staff, so perhaps it's just as well the weather is bad, otherwise goodness knows what I should be doing. When Mrs Bond telephoned me to say her husband was ill, I remarked crisply, 'If you don't mind my saying so, Mrs Bond, Sir is an idiot!' When asked why, I told her the silly creature spent 40 minutes outside the Baths in the snowstorm cleaning his car. When he came in he was, of course, soaking wet (especially his shoes, for as you probably know, the English don't wear rubbers for some unknown reason) and when I attempted to whisk him down with a towel, he exploded. So I left him to go wetly back to his job, and eventually home, where he deservedly caught a bad chill and is now sitting up in bed with his usual little basin, which he fills as regularly as his wife gives him anything to drink – even water, at such times, makes the poor man sick. Men!

Talking of men, I'll tell you about my brother this week, too. Now MacPherson is, let us face it, somewhat spoiled. He *had* to be indulged in every whim, when he was ill with rheumatic fever as a child, and we've never been able to break him of the habit since. Anyway, one of his habits which infuriates his punctual sister is his inability to be ready on time. Also, his own fury if anybody happens to keep *him* waiting so much as ten seconds. *He* isn't the one to do the waiting; on the contrary, everything, and everybody, waits for him. Well, on Thursday the roads were ice, and we sagely decided not to practise skating with the help of Hesperus, and both went out to go by bus to work. I was busy filling the coal scuttles and sweeping the paths, and was a bit pushed for time, so Mother said crossly to my brother to go out to the bus stop and see that it waited for me. I tore out; no bus, no brother either. He had walked the other way to buy some cigarettes. He turned up, and walked beyond the bus stop and down to our garage. Up came the bus, and in we all piled. I dawdled as much as I could, until the bus conductor asked if I was, after all, intending to catch that bus or the next one. On the platform, I caught a glimpse of Mac's face as we went past the end of the driveway to the garage . . . . . . a wonderful mixture of astonishment and fury! The bus wouldn't wait!!! Did the bus know for whom it was supposed to wait? Of course, he was born lucky; he ran to the next bus stop. Normally the bus would have left that point long before the fastest runner would have reached it, but this morning there were so many people there waiting to get on, that Mac arrived before the end of the queue had climbed aboard. Again, any ordinary person running on those icy pavements would have broken at least their spine and seven ribs; but not Mac who, as I said before, was born lucky . . .

I also had a very charming letter this week from Mrs Dall. It was so kind of her to write, wasn't it. Full of praise for somebody she called 'Commodore'. Who on earth could she mean? . . .

This morning, the sun is shining forcefully through my window and baking me as I sit at my typewriting desk. The snow – or rather, the ice – outside is still very conspicuous, but at least some of it melted in the sunshine yesterday. Freckleface was much happier this morning, for the snow on the coal-heap has melted and he was able to scratch on it instead of in the snow. When I left, he was lying upside down on my bed, with his forepaws up in the air and his rear end covered by a blanket, his flank supported by a hot-water bottle, and his little pink mouth slightly open. Ditto, one eye – that being all he feels is necessary. I called Mother and said, 'You can see where Frecks has been digging today, can't you?' He was, apparently, wearing black elbow-length gloves . . .

Thanks for your letters, as always.

Frances W.

LEFT-END OF SOFA
NEAREST THE FIRE
WINTER
February 9th 1954

Sir,

How dare you! Your letter was read to me yesterday in which you expressed surprise that I didn't like going out in the snow.

My reason for not going out when it is cold and snowy is – *I* have a *gorgeous* tail, and if anything happened to it how could I tell the family of slaves who wait upon my every whim, when they displease me? Such logical self-preservation appears beyond a certain 'Angel Face'. How she *dares* to call herself so, I do not comprehend. *Nobody* has such an angelic face as your irate correspondent.

Freckleface
Plushbottom
Beau Bully
Woodsford

BOURNEMOUTH
March 6th 1954

Dear Mr Bigelow,

. . . Well, to go from bad to worse. Cars. And brothers. And car-salesmen. And car-salesmen *and* brothers, in conjunction. I told you letters back, didn't I, that we were negotiating for another car when Hesperus incontinently let us down by collapsing? Well, the other car was a very nice-looking little Standard and the deal was originally only stopped when I, being brought along so that this time I couldn't blame my brother if we bought another pup, said innocently that I personally wouldn't dream of buying a car without so much as hearing the engine run. This pulled everybody up somewhat – it turned out later, we were told, that the car was out of petrol . . .

Isn't this situation – or series of situations – in Egypt comical? It would be, were it not tragic for so many, and serious for so many other nations. Monday everybody is denouncing Neguib* and saying how kind they were not to have him killed. Tuesday he is back, and Wednesday they are all photographed holding hands and smiling like tame gigolos into each other's eyes. Probably the hand-holding is to prevent each other using back-stabbers, but the smiles puzzle me. Unless, perhaps, they are so used to seeing crocodiles in the Nile the politicians automatically adopt the same facial expression . . . . . .

What with us in Egypt, and you in Puerto Rico, we *are* having trouble, aren't we? Isn't it horrible to realise one is so unpopular, especially when one tries so hard to do what is best for the other bloke. Couldn't someone in your country suggest that Senator McCarthy (Macarthy, Mcarthy?) is looking the wrong way and should turn his eyes away from the Army for a bit, and down to the Caribbean . . .

A miracle happened on Monday, Mr Bigelow. I was sitting reading the paper by the fire after dinner, and my brother, who was later home than me was eating his dinner, when suddenly he said, 'Norah.' I said 'Um?' and my astounded ears heard his voice saying, 'I realise it was entirely

* *Editor's note*: Mohammed Neguib, Egyptian leader, had deposed King Farouk in 1952, but was himself forced to resign in February 1954 when Colonel Abdel Nassar replaced him.

my fault, and I do appreciate your not throwing it in my face that I bought the Ford . . . . . . !!!!!' The upshot was, that he intends paying the difference between what (we hope) we get for the Ford and what another car costs, if I in turn will pay for the car tax and the insurance. As this would save me anything up to £12 or £15, you can imagine I was far from displeased! I am, however, woman-like, intrigued to discover where Mac has suddenly acquired all this money, because he was flat broke directly after Christmas and all through January, and his job certainly doesn't pay him all that much cash. However, no doubt if I sit tight and ask no questions, I shall hear in due course . . .

Advertisement in last night's local newspaper: '1933 Singer 8 for sale. Runs like its namesake. Brakes squeak more than prodded politicians. Clutch fierce as a Sergeant-Major. Better downhill than up. Got £39 to spare? Phone Wareham 54.'

And that's all for now. Be with you again next Saturday.

Very sincerely,

Frances

BOURNEMOUTH
March 20th 1954

Dear Mr Bigelow,

Short of arsenic, what can be done with my brother?

You remember my interim report on Hesperus? Well, that was sent on Wednesday morning. That evening Mac and I dolled ourselves up in overalls and old gloves and things and went to work again. We finished the first coat of cellulose, and had time to do the second coat on the bonnet (the first having been put on there a day or two earlier). About eight o'clock, not being able to see any more, we came home and scrubbed most of the skin and some of the cellulose off ourselves. Mac said he was going out – and did, by way of the back door which leads to the shed in which he keeps his bicycle.

Next morning it was wet, so I rose early and dressed in a hurry and tore over to put some wax polish on the finished bonnet of the car, so that it would not suffer in the rain. To find that the paint was spotted all over with wet drops and that, as fast as I wiped the paintwork with a dry cloth, so the paint came off along with the water. My brother had only taken it straight out – in the rain – the night before, within half an hour of the paint being put on! Now he is sulking in an injured innocence fashion because, when he asked when I was going to help finish the painting I replied that I wasn't. Sometimes I wonder why God made men; given a tiny bit of common sense I'm sure He could have so arranged matters as to make them redundant.

Oh – I collected my Civil Defence Ambulance Section uniform last night. Look absolutely smashing in it. Only thing is, I can't move.The blouse-top fits around me, and so do the trousers, but they meet only with the greatest difficulty, and at the slightest movement on my part there appears a wide strip of me around the middle. The only thing I can think of to do about it is to wear a bright cummerbund, which should cheer up the Civil Defence Unit considerably. The material is a very dark grey thick heavy stuff, and so scratchy I was advised to wear stockings under the trousers and can see myself being their first genuine casualty – a bad case of the itch!

I have been on a sort of semi-diet this week: instead of having a scrambled egg – one – for my midday meal, I am having fruit. Keeping off sugar and sweets and cakes and biscuits, but enjoying a hearty meal in the evening, as usual. The result is that my measurements seem much the same, but my weight has gone down 6lbs since the beginning of the month, when I started by cutting out sugar. Now isn't that just too bad? What's the good of losing weight if you don't lose size as well – one might as well be H. G. Wells's character, who lost weight and ended up crawling around under the ceiling, he was so light, and still looking like a bloated slug, he was so fat. So far as I can see, the only result of this careful eating is that I feel d-mn hungry!

. . . How very disappointing for you and Rosalind to drive all that way to look at the late Theodore Roosevelt's old home, and then find it closed! I know the feeling . . . . . .

Very sincerely,

Frances

BOURNEMOUTH
March 27th 1954

Dear Mr Bigelow,

. . . We, Mac and I, discussed the advertisement for Hesperus this week. Mac wanted to know whether I thought '£75 or near offer', or '£70' would be better. I said as we would be delighted with £65 I thought the latter was more likely to attract buyers. It was agreed that '£70' would appear. So Mac puts in an advertisement saying '£80. Nobody has nibbled!! . . .

Very sincerely,

Frances

BOURNEMOUTH
April 24th 1954

Dear Mr Bigelow,

. . . One afternoon over Easter weekend, when I wasn't working, Mac and I walked to Wimborne with a friend. How the friend manages it I have never discovered; she cycles to work each day, and her work is sedentary, but at weekends she thinks nothing at all of a 15-mile walk in an afternoon. Now Mac and I think nothing at all of a 15-mile walk in an afternoon, but we aren't thinking on quite the same lines. Wimborne is about eight miles from home. We had walked one mile, in single file (all there was room for) along the pavement, with a bumper-to-bumper stream of cars running alongside, when I revolted and refused to do so any more. So there we waited for a bus which took us another mile or so along the route, to a point at which we could leave the road and do the rest of the walk through green fields and pastures new – to Mac, anyway – and under lovely budding chestnuts and alongside large black and white cows. Also, alongside a river for part of the way. Very pleasant, with the sun strong and the wind blowing half a gale in our faces.

'Never mind the wind,' said the friend, 'it'll be at our backs on the way home.' I looked back at Mac's face, and what I saw made me giggle. Dorothy asked why I was laughing but if she were as stupid as all that I wouldn't be bothered to tell her!

In the end we reached Wimborne, and found there was fifty minutes or more to go before the first bus back. We sat for a while on a bench in the village square, only I was sitting next to one of the oldest inhabitants and he was making a valiant effort to win the world's spitting contest, so I soon gave up the unequal struggle between my tiredness and my nausea, and went and stood at the bus stop, first on one leg and then on t'other. Dorothy, apart from being cross at losing half her walk, was also annoyed because both Mac and I complained our backs were broken in the lumbar region! According to her, a little eight-mile stroll would put all that right.

And now, of course, you are waiting to hear about The Pippin. This friend asked, while we were walking, whether I had thought of a name for the new car, and on my saying yes, I had, Mac put on a long face and said pompously, 'It was all very well naming Hesperus, and I realise that it was a suitable name, but there is no need to give a nickname to a car which is *not* a wreck.' I said meekly that I thought of calling it 'The Pippin', and the little face lighted up like a Christmas tree candle!

Anyway, as I expected, he came motoring round to my office yesterday – yes, we only finally got the thing on Friday, and even now it has to go back for two lines to be painted on the body – at midday, unable to wait until five to show me the car. I went out to see it, Mac's face being all screwed up with anxiety until he noticed how pleased I was with the Austin. It really is a very nice little car indeed, and looks as though it's just come, not off the assembly line, but off the workbench where it has been made by hand. When I tell you that the clock goes, you will realise it must have been very carefully looked after in its life. As we walked around it admiring and exclaiming Mac suddenly exclaimed a bit louder than usual, and ran back to the other side of the car. He then clapped one hand to his forehead and said a few rude words. Apparently he had taken somebody out before he came to me, and while they were bowling along there was a loud noise, which obviously *couldn't* have been the car after its long and arduous going-over by the car dealers. But it was! And we are now minus one chromium-plated wheel hub . . . . . . typical of our motoring experience, what?

Now to finish off: I hope this reaches you before Thursday, so that you won't think I've gone down the drain. Never think that – if I were flat on my back with double pneumonia and three broken arms, I'd drop you a postcard with the pen held between my toes, whenever Saturday came round . . .

Very sincerely,

Frances

BOURNEMOUTH
May 1st 1954

Dear Mr Bigelow,

When patience runs out, manners are a very thin veneer indeed. Or so I have found this week, under somewhat trying circumstances, and goodness knows how soon (it's Wednesday now) it will be that the veneer will crack.

For on Tuesday, as I ushered a traveller out of my office, from around the corner came another figure – it was Dr Russell from Canada, who announced that he had arrived and was come to live permanently in England. Well, so long as he lives well away from Bournemouth, I don't mind where he lives for, as I hinted above, I long ago ran out of patience with him.

In the meantime, he has been hanging around either at the office or at home, and behaving in his usual manner, with, as I said, a resultant strain on my politeness. After all, if within a space of four hours you were to say eight times to me, 'Were you surprised to see me?' – and that remark was usually pushed bang in the middle of a sentence somebody else was saying, wouldn't you rather expect the person of whom the question was asked to start giving you variations of answers, just to make a change? After a silence lasting five years, Dr Russell cannot realistically expect me to take up exactly where I left off (and I'm sure he would not like it, for I remember being very angry with him last time he was over here) but, just the same, the minute he manoeuvres me alone, he starts looking soulful and saying 'Nori, what's wrong? What's the matter?' Well, Mr Bigelow, my private opinions and my soul are my own, and I will not discuss them at the whim or the insistence of any questioner in the world, if I don't feel so inclined . . .

Anyway, finally we had a sort of a row, which I thought did little good at the time, but apparently it was borne in on that man that his presence was not as overwhelmingly welcome as he imagined it would be, and on Friday he rang up and said he thought it a good idea to push off to London. I said I thought it was a good idea, too, and goodbye and there we were. He also telephoned Mother and asked what was wrong with me. Mother, flying to the defence of her chick, said there was nothing wrong with me. So Russ said well, what had he done? And Mother, being quite his equal, retorted it was less what he had done and more what he had not done, and wasn't it time he realised one had to work to earn people's friendships, or to deserve them.

He is now out of my hair, off my conscience – except that I don't like to think of him going off all hurt and huffy – and once more I am breathing normally and looking normal, too! On Wednesday, knowing I was faced with a tête-à-tête all evening I was so sick with apprehension that the staff started asking what was wrong. It's no good trying to continue a broken friendship with somebody who affects one so heavily, and I don't believe anybody has the right to inflict his emotionalism on other people to the extent that Dr Russell tries it. He wears out everybody around him, and then sails on to wear out somebody else. Well, he can sail as far on as he wishes . . .

Now I must get back to work: my boss is away this weekend so naturally everything has gone wrong, and I've even had the police in and out of my hair these last two days over an unpleasant event I reported which *would* have to happen when the boss is away. Eight years I've been here, but it waits for his absence! Just like events.

So au revoir until next Saturday.

Very sincerely,

Frances W.

Blue Bigelow   *Better Bigelow*

BOURNEMOUTH
May 5th 1954
Bonus Day

Dear Mr Bigelow,

How very unlike yourself you sounded in the letter I had yesterday: I hurry to send you an 'extra' to tell you to cheer up. *All sorts of things* are worth doing, so you get that negative idea out of your noodle. It's well worth sitting in an easy chair with a cat on your knee; it's well worth watching birds; it's well worth eating a good meal; it's well worth watching the seasons change. It's well worth writing to me. It is well worth looking forward to Rosalind's visits, and then looking back at them until it is time for forward-looking again.

Really, Mr B. I am surprised at you! Kindly refrain from such pessimistic perambulations in future.

Anyway, on its way to you, and due to arrive in a few days after this letter, is a funny book I thought you would like to read. Called *Doctor in the House* it has recently been made into a very amusing film, though that isn't as funny (in my view) as the book. Perhaps, if it arrives before Rosalind, you can chuckle over it together.

I was trying, as tactfully as I know, to suggest to my apprentice-boy that he should take lessons in English, the other day. Or, failing evening classes, he should read and read and read – *good* books – in order that his written English might become improved by precept. Reading will do it, but it is a long way round. Anyway, he affirmed that he did read, 'Honest, Miss Woodsford, I get a book out of the library every week, and I read everything that Kipling writes.' I was delighted to hear it, and asked which book he liked best – *Soldiers Three*, or *Plain Tales from the Hills*, or perhaps *Stalky & Co*. By this time it became obvious from the blank face a foot or so above mine, that Peter didn't have the slightest inkling what I was talking about. So I stopped my catalogue, and said, 'You *did* say Kipling, didn't you?' 'Yes, Kipling – you know, the man who does the butterfly stroke.' Education, where is your aim? In the meantime I get little notes from Peter, 'Mr Brown wonts for towle. Can he hav them?'

You didn't mention in your letter exactly when Rosalind was likely to visit you . . . I may write Rosalind myself tomorrow or Friday if there is time but anyway I hope you both enjoy yourselves terrifically, and don't you start worrying because you 'can't do much for her'. I'm quite, quite sure Rosalind is absolutely content to stay Chez Bigelow when she visits you, and am certain she doesn't always want to go dashing around here and there, having parties in all directions, and fetes and fireworks and so on. A nice cuppa tea and me feet up, is some people's idea of Heaven, and I'm positive that at times it is equally Rosalind's ideal, and one you can easily supply. Cheer up. And stay cheered. Them's orders, Sir.

Frances W.

PS Thanks for the sketch of Angel Face. I would know her anywhere!

BOURNEMOUTH
May 22nd 1954

Dear Mr Bigelow,

. . . What a lot of fuss everybody has made over Roger Bannister! Personally, I had never heard of the mile-in-four-minutes before he did it in less . . .

Sir Bertrand telephoned me last night: I was just about to go out, so didn't hang on talking long and got him off the line when the three-pips (to indicate three minutes) came along. He giggled a good bit, but apart from telling me his new address, and where he had been staying and what doing ('Have you got over your dismay, Nori?' was every other sentence but I ignored that and merely answered the alternate ones) he wasn't too much of a nuisance. I had an idea he rang when he did to get invited down for the weekend, but I didn't bite, having things to do. As he has been staying in an hotel, and is moving to another soon, I imagine he hasn't got invited to stay or live with any of his London friends. Poor Sir Bertrand! Shouldn't be such a bore, should he? . . .

In the paper this week, reported from Australia: The Queen and the Duke watched a log-chopping contest, and afterwards the Queen said to the winner, 'You must be *so* fit!' 'My oath,' replied the burly Aussie, 'I could lift a bl—dy ton!' 'Here,' protested the Duke, 'tone it down a bit.' 'Well,' said the Australian, 'I could lift a bl—dy half-ton, then.'

And that's all for now. I hope you have had Rosalind to visit you, and enjoyed every minute (as I know you would) and are now counting days to the next visit.

Very sincerely,

Frances

BOURNEMOUTH
May 29th 1954

Dear Mr Bigelow,

. . . On Thursday this week, as it was a more or less fine evening, the Civil Defence class was held out of doors. More or less out of doors. The two instructors put the casualties in a specially built 'bombed house' in a field, and then the three competing teams had in turn to rescue and attend to them. The house has two downstairs rooms, one of which has the ceiling down, and half a staircase with newel post and other posts in the most awkward positions, as we found to our cost. There is no roof or upper storey, and the sky appears in unexpected quarters. It was a very heavy evening, with millions of flies and gnats about, and we made 'phewing' noises at the smell of pigs nearby until somebody remarked that it wasn't pigs, but that the town's Sewage

Disposal Farm was just across the hedge. After *that*, we all dashed into the long grass and picked clover to hold under our noses, in spite of the remark a Town Hall man made that there is less sickness in the Farm staff than at the Town Hall.

Now after Thursday, Mr Bigelow, I am of the firm opinion that dragging 'unconscious' bodies about on stretchers, over and under and around bomb-damaged houses, is no job for women. Next Thursday I shall either be a victim myself, or sit on a chair and look on, for I am quite certain my muscles will not, by next Thursday, have grown back onto the bones from which they were wrenched *last* Thursday.

I don't know which team won, but we didn't do very well from all I could see – I was Ambulance Attendant, which meant I was sent with the driver to fetch the ambulance, run it up to the nearest point to the house; prepare the stretchers with blankets, bring them into the building, load the patients on, take them out, put them in the ambulance, and drive them off to the 'hospital' ten yards down the lane. When I got into the room with the first stretcher, my team were milling around the first patient who was *sitting* with a complicated fracture of the ribs. I consoled myself later, when I saw Team B tip her off the stretcher into the road (accidentally) and Team C with the fracture on the left side and the bandages on the right side.

On Wednesday, I had a refresher lesson on the ambulance, driving up and down side roads at enormous speeds (for me) and reversing into gravel pits by use of rearview mirrors only.

At that, I was extremely bad, but hope to be better next week. I was surprised to find how easy a large and powerful vehicle is to drive: it could be turned in a normally wide road in three goes, quite easily – a lot more easily than the Austin which is only half the size of an ambulance. By now, my motoring experience consists of:

1 ancient Ford 8 hp. wreck
1 fairly ancient Singer 9 hp. car
1 fairly new Hillman Minx, 10 hp.
1 oldish Austin 10
1 32 hp. Buick ambulance
1 32 hp. Packard   ''

Next lesson, a double-decker bus, yes?

At work, we are in the throes of rehearsals for the summer show, due to open on Friday next. The consumption of indigestion tablets is reaching wholesale figures. I am getting new frowns of worry, trying to decide whether to ask the Mayoress to have a drink before I ask the Mayor, as she is the lady: or whether the Mayor comes first, as the Head Man in the town for the year. My boss stays well behind the scenes, seeing that the chorus girls are on time and so on, and leaves the gracious hostess work to me, all dolled up in black satin, new shoes, and a harassed look. I shall no doubt moan about this next week . . .

I will say 'au revoir' until next Saturday, and I hope you had a lovely visit from Rosalind, who was looking forward to it as much as you, and as equally sorry it had to be so short.

Very sincerely,

Frances

BOURNEMOUTH
June 12th 1954

Dear Mr Bigelow,

. . . Friday, worked until 10 p.m., rushed home and did my week's washing, so that today, Saturday, I can set off for my summer holiday with a clear conscience. As the 'holiday' consists of three and a half days during which I have to do all the car-driving and Dorothy, who is going with me, is likely to refuse to do anything to help (such as paying the bills and seeing to tips, reading the maps and so on) I can imagine my return Tuesday night will see me rather tired . . . Today, Saturday, the skies are lead and about ten feet overhead, letting out gallons of water in a solid sheet. Just the weather for motoring or walking. Just my luck.

And talking of my luck, I'm beginning to feel confirmed in my belief that I have a jinx. You remember in my last letter I said I was bewildered, bothered, and very, very depressed, and if *you* were right and Rosalind wrong, I would be even more so. This morning, on top of the weather, was a letter from Rosalind, in which she quite calmly confirmed the newspaper cutting Mrs Dall sent me last week, wherein you were reported as saying proudly that you were '91, just getting going'. Now I wouldn't mind if you were 101, personally, but for one thing. In two letters I had from Rosalind in 1948 (December) and 1949 (Jan.) she mentioned her father (84) whom she was about to visit, or had just returned from visiting. After I had written to you for some time I looked up these early letters, to confirm whether it really was possible that anybody as spry in his writing could really be 84 or 85, or whatever it was by then. I made a note in my diary, and each year since have brought it forward so that I would know, well in advance, when you were due to be 90. According to Rosalind's early information, this great day was to be in 1954, in September. Since early January I have been preparing for the event. Since early January I have been taking trips to the Reference Library, and spending my lunch hours in my office with scratch pad, drawing paper, pen ink paint and brushes. All those elaborate questions I asked you were only to one end – to discover the difference in cost of a letter being sent locally, and being sent to England, so that I could send Mrs Dall enough money to pay her for the stamps she was to use. For she, poor dear, was to be dragged in, as the 'surprise' was to be in nine parts, and each part was to be posted separately, so that the first came ten days before your birthday, and the final one on the day itself. That was why I wanted to know if you had a mail delivery on a Sunday, remember? I even spent an hour or so looking up an impossible word in a rhyming dictionary, knowing your fondness for long and unusual terms . . . . . . you try to find easy rhymes for Ninety.

And now it turns out you are 91. Or, anyway, will be on your next birthday. I might just as well send you theatre tickets for a show which closed last week, as to send you my 'surprise' now. But in order not to waste entirely the time and trouble, I have done the whole wretched lot up in a bundle, and posted it off to you today, and will you please just imagine you are celebrating your ninetieth birthday last September and I'm just a day or two late, due to circumstances over which I have no control. If Mrs Dall hadn't been kind and sent me that newspaper cutting I might never have known I was too late. As usual, my good intentions go wildly astray. Do you think I should decide just to be selfish and let everybody else go hang, so that perhaps, by my usual contrary luck, I might hit the bullseye by accident? A thing I have, of late, never, never managed to do by design. Do you mind letting me know in plenty of time – say at least ten months beforehand – when you intend being a hundred? I am determined to be on time one year or another, but 91 is such an in-between age, it fails to inspire me one little bit. Oh, *damn* my bad luck!

On which heartfelt note I will leave you and go dashing out in the downpour (matching my mood) to post this. I hope to sound a little more cheerful by next Saturday, even if tired.

Very sincerely and down-in-the-dumps,

Frances W.

BOURNEMOUTH
July 10th 1954

Dear Mr Bigelow,

Oh dear, I *am* sorry about the Adventures of A. Marsh. The *Telegraph* critic referred to it as a full-blooded masterpiece, but I didn't have any idea it was bl—dy as well! Writers these days seem to think that as so much has already been written, there is only left for them those subjects hither to be discussed only in medical books. Anyway, I am awfully sorry to have inflicted this one on you. I hope it hasn't irredeemably damaged your gay innocence!

And oh dear, again, that Sir Bertrand is here once more. Fortunately, this time he only came down for the day, so as I refused to take time off work (not having known he was coming) I had him only from 5 p.m. until his train left at eight. Now he has progressed to the stage where he remarks lugubriously that he has 'had time to have a look at himself, and doesn't like what he sees' but perks up to say there is 'always Seconal'. Or whatever the thing is called – a sleeping drug people are apt to commit suicide with, I believe. I told the silly thing to stop crying in his beer; if, as he said, he was of so little importance, then he was too unimportant to ruin good beer. I think Dr Russell should have been born Dr Russelsky, with his Russian love of misery and emotion, don't you?

Admittedly I do feel sorry for the poor man, for he's been in England only about a month, and already his bad lung is giving him trouble, so he has to go back to America. He is aiming at California, which is the sensible thing for him to do and the thing I've been advocating ever since 1946 . . .

What with Sir Bertrand threatening suicide on Wednesday; a woman customer considering herself 'insulted' because the bath-attendant put her in a bathroom on the right-hand side of the corridor instead of the left-hand side which she preferred; and a man complaining bitterly that he didn't like the way a male attendant looked at him – *and* my boss shouting abuse at me because I hadn't told either customer I thought they were cranks, well, not in so many words! – *and* Mother ringing up in the middle of all this to complain that the expensive Hoover I had bought her the day before wouldn't work, I am back in my old slough of despond with a vengeance. So I was rather silent with my miseries in the car this morning, and Mac was as funny as Danny Kaye, trying to get the normal chatter out of me. And Mother at lunchtime was going around with her 'sorry I spoke' attitude. How we do affect one another with our moods! I can quite understand why Russ rushes to me when he can, for a good blowing up, or advice or sympathy, for my own family do just the same. Never mind what calamity overcomes them – they'll just 'ring Norah and tell her; she'll do something about it!' Oh yes – on top of all those horrors I described at such heart-rending length in this paragraph, I finished up my Awful Yesterday having a lady pass out with (query) heart trouble during the water show, and I had to get an ambulance for her. Afterwards, I had to rinse out the towels and blankets I had wrapped her in, because by the time I had run downstairs, across the hall, up the other side, into the café, around the counter, to the sink, and run back all that way with a basin for the patient to be sick in – it was too late! I didn't dare let them stay overnight, for the boss might have found out, and as his idea of First Aid is to get the victim out of the building and his jurisdiction as quickly as possible, he would have been furious at having our towels and blankets used for such a purpose.

With such sharply divergent outlooks, it is odd that Mr Bond and I have managed to work alongside each other for so many years, isn't it? . . .

Very sincerely,

Frances W.

BOURNEMOUTH
August 14th 1954

Dear Mr Bigelow,

. . . My favourite police inspector came in this morning with a reasonable excuse for his visit and a bit of grit in his eye! I think he went out a very disappointed man. No little-womanly gesture with a bit of lace-trimmed hankie was forthcoming. No lace. Instead, I handed him an eye bath and a towel to weep into, neither of which can reasonably be said to come under the heading 'the woman's touch'. I never indulge in little-womanly gestures unless I am quite sure they'll come off, and as I know grit is extremely difficult to get out of an eye, the poor man was forced to roll his around on his own. My own eyes, today, feel as though the lids were literally lined with emery paper, due to a series of bad nights. Why don't people sleep? One of life's major mysteries; along with my favourite, Why Do Acorns Grow into Oak Trees and not Poplars, and the one about who started the common cold . . .

On Sunday afternoon last weekend I took Mother to Durdle Door in Dorset. This is an enormous block of rock jutting out from the main edge of the coast, in the last bit of which is a natural arch of rock – the Door – famous in this part of the world for its beauty. Of course, this being our first visit we must needs find the beaches strewn with hundreds of people from a nearby camp – as if I didn't have enough people at work! There were four or five perfect curved beaches, and as we sat halfway down the cliffs we could look down at their waters and watch the changing colours as the sun came and went. When it was out, the water was purple and deep emerald and peacock blue; when the sun went behind a cloud, then the water was blue-grey and brown. The cliffs here are white, grey, or sometimes streaked with vivid red, and we could see them stretching their heads towards the south for miles in both directions. To the west, we could see Portland Bill – the dark prison on its heights looking quite pleasant in the sun – and three aircraft carriers at anchor in Weymouth Harbour. To the east, the sun shone on the Needles at the western end of the Isle of Wight. I suppose this would mean a stretch of view extending some fifty miles with us in the middle. It was an unusually clear day (portending more rain, of course) and we don't usually get so long a view, but we enjoyed it while we did.

As a contrast to this noisy scene of people enjoying themselves, we stopped the car for tea on the topmost point of the Heath which is used by the Army for training tank crews. And if you don't know what tanks do to countryside, don't try to find out for it's too depressing. Miles and miles of black and brown earth, with here and there a stunted, scarred little tree or a bit of heather. Talk about blasted heaths! It is part of that heath made famous by Hardy under the name 'Egdon Heath', and it explains amply and without words why his books are so depressing. They merely reflect their surroundings. Parts of Dorset are extremely lovely – the hills towards Devon, and the northern part of the county where it nears Wiltshire or Somerset; but that small area which Hardy wrote about is almost without exception an indifferent countryside. Many people have written of this facet of its character: it is a country age-old – long, long before the Romans or even the Druids, and it is filled to overflowing with burial grounds and ancient earthworks and so on. The earth has been lived on so long it has become quite indifferent to what human beings care to do to it; it just goes on and they don't. It gives me the shivers.

This appalling summer is making us break all records for attendances in every department at work. A side-result of this is that people keep walking in and out of my office smoking big cigars, and as today (Saturday) I have a smashing headache, they are not being very well received. Neither have I the self-control left, what with headaches and sick feelings from too many aspirins and more nausea from cigar smoke, to polish a nice final paragraph for you. Will you please rest content, this week, with my felicitations,

Frances Woodsford

BOURNEMOUTH
September 25th 1954

Dear Mr Bigelow,

It was just as well the police held their annual swimming gala here this week because they always give me a large drink during the course of it and this week I *needed* it, having just returned from mailing your birthday card at the post office. Talk about profiteering! Why, for another seven or eightpence I could have bought you the Brooklyn Bridge for a present, and on that there would have been no extortionate postage, as it is already there, in place, ready for you to cross next time you go into New York to do some town-painting. Anyway, flummoxes notwithstanding, I hope the card arrived on the right day, and hope the birthday went off very well indeed, with Rosalind's presence in spirit adding to the occasion . . .

It was just as well, to repeat my opening sentence, that the police were holding their gala here this week, when they gave me that large drink, because it was such a very large one I felt relieved, as I motored home directly afterwards, that most of the cops in the town weren't out looking for weaving motorists. And all I asked for was an orange-and-soda, as I was *thirsty*! They pooh-poohed the idea, and insisted I should have gin with it. Now, I hate gin, so I refused indignantly, and we compromised on 'a drop of whisky'. I suppose a drop can mean many things, from a single globule of water to being hanged by the neck, but this drop of whisky was about halfway between the two. Fortunately, the full effect did not hit me until I climbed out of the car in the garage, but it took most of the night before I could get to sleep for flashing lights in front of my shut eyes. Liver? No, no, of course not – what a nasty mind you have, Commodore. It was over-tiredness, and over-excitement that did it. If only I had seven pairs of hands and three sets of brains, I could work the front-of-house part of the police gala with ease. One pair of hands could be counting out money for the stewards to use as change; the second could be making a note of where I'd borrowed the money from; the third could be opening drawers looking for last-minute requirements such as chalk, string, paper and pins. Pair No. 4 could be counting out programmes, chocolates, cigarettes, ice creams and matches, for the usherettes to take around, while No. 5 could be making unhurried notes of the value of all these issued. No. 6 could be using the telephone to ring up various expected parties who hadn't arrived, but whose seats were being held in the teeth of great competition from the general public. And No. 7 could be articulating graciously to the Important Guests who *will* always arrive when I am tying up somebody who has just fallen downstairs, coping with a man complaining that he can't get his favourite brand of cigarettes, sudden requests for 'change for a £5 note, please' and trying to stop my stocking from laddering where I caught it on the door as I rushed through just now. I *think* three brains could properly co-ordinate and control seven sets of hands, and if Mr Bond had only complied with my request, the Police Gala-before-the-last-one, and given me roller skates for Christmas instead of bath towels, then the seven sets of hands could get to their various jobs so much quicker than my flat feet take them . . .

Very sincerely yours,

Frances W.

BOURNEMOUTH
October 9th 1954

Dear Mr Bigelow,

. . . Something very nice happened to me yesterday. A letter came by hand for my boss; he opened and read it, then handed it to me to read the last paragraph. I will quote it:

> I am enclosing a cheque for two guineas made payable to you and I would be obliged if you will share it among your staff after one guinea has been given to Miss Woodsford with our special thanks for the help she gave us. I know for a fact that paints are expensive and that she will find it useful.

Now, wasn't that kind? I felt a bit conscience-stricken, and it took some persuading on the part of Mr Bond to get me to take the money, because I had scolded the man who sent it, when he told me he was going to send that amount for the staff. I told him – it was my favourite police inspector of course, he's the only one running a gala here who ever bothers to say thank you — that he always overpaid the staff. That we were always glad to help the police, partly because they ran their gala so efficiently, and partly because they always took the trouble to say ta ever so, and we all appreciated that no end. And the only result of my lecture is, as you will see, that I get half the swag myself! I didn't scold him with that end in view at all, so perhaps as I am enjoying the fruits it is only right and proper that my conscience should prick as I eat. Anyway, having the money (a guinea is a very polite £1. You pay a tradesman in pounds, a gentleman in guineas. Don't ask me why) I went out straight away and spent it on oil-paints and a lovely big palette before my conscience could think of another excuse (shoe repairs) for pricking . . .

Very sincerely,

Frances W.

BOURNEMOUTH
November 11th 1954

Dear Mr Bigelow,

For somebody who didn't 'know the date' you have done remarkably well, I must say. Today, the postman arrived with two boxes of chocolate liqueurs! And today we are having a specially good dinner, which will follow up with chocolate liqueurs all round (my choice will be the Grand Marnier) and a sip of Drambuie to make us all feel very content with the goodness of life . . .

Phyllis Murray and I came back from holiday a day earlier than arranged. On Phyl's part, she had run out of money. On mine, I didn't like to suggest staying longer and paying for us both, as she is most independent (I'd got away with twice filling the petrol tank) and the car wasn't going very well . . . By a mistaken interest in a place charmingly called 'Wellcome' we went down a 1 in 4 incline on our last day, and I was wondering who was going to push us up, but we managed it. We had a very fine day for the run home, and to my horror I discovered when I reached Bournemouth that I had driven 170 miles practically non-stop. Anyway, it was a good thing to do, for now I know that the maximum day (140-odd) planned for Rosalind's tour next June will be easy. Mother was desperately worried all day, for we were motoring over Dartmoor and a very dangerous criminal escaped from the Prison on the Moor and was at large all day. We came blissfully over, ignorant as anything, not having seen a newspaper for three days, and we couldn't imagine why the police stopped us in Honiton and looked in the car . . .

Now back at work, and it's still pouring with rain but at least we can change wet clothes. Coming home from Devonshire, I wore my brother's ancient coat normally used to cover the car bonnet on cold nights, and Phyllis wore all the jumpers and skirts she had plus my plastic raincoat. Never mind, it was a pleasant change and we came home revived mentally and spiritually if not physically.

Once again, thank you very much indeed for the lovely liqueurs, and for being so exceedingly clever over the date. Did you cheat and ask Rosalind, by any chance?

Very sincerely,

Frances W.

1955

Bournemouth Pleasure Gardens
(*copyright* Daïly Echo, *Bournemouth*)

BOURNEMOUTH
January 6th 1955

Dear Mr Bigelow,

. . . The first customer in the Baths this morning was a large gentleman accompanied by a small boy. They walked up to the pay-desk and the man said, 'One martyr and one enthusiast, please.' It quite made the cashier's morning! The enthusiast went scooting across the hall to the dressing room, followed by his father proceeding more on the lines of Shakespeare's schoolboy . . .

I had thought, until I looked up your first letter to me, that we had been corresponding far longer than is actually the case. Your first letter, without either salutation or closing address, is undated, but in my own writing on the top is written 'April 1949'. In the spring, therefore, we shall celebrate our sixth anniversary, though what in, I do not know.

I looked up this date because I remember so clearly how it was we started writing. I had sent Rosalind a newspaper cutting which I thought would amuse her, and she in turn, thinking it would tickle your fancy, had sent it on to you. That was the first time I had heard that Rosalind had a father. And then, one day this week, I could hardly believe my eyes because there, in the staid *Daily Telegraph*, was a long paragraph on the same subject as our opening topic – toads. True, the first cutting was about the use of frogs in some out-of-the-way village in Cornwall as units of money, and this is about toads, but I cut this one out and am sending it to you, to repeat history. Do you remember that first cutting? One man was suing another for the balance of payment for a motor-cycle, the second man having given him £10 and the rest in frogs, and he hadn't delivered the frogs. The poor creatures were gathered in sacks and sold to London hospitals, and I remember the judge in the case remarking that he'd never heard of quite such an awkward coinage in his life . . .

How is your weather? Continuing fine, or have you had the rough edge of the tongue of ice which swept over the Middle States? Over here we have had blizzards and gales of ice and drifts on high ground in Devonshire up to twelve feet in depth. All the roads I went over in November on holiday were impassible. We had a little snow in Bournemouth, but missed the worst of everything, although judging by the cat's behaviour, it was sub-zero weather and we utter brutes to expect him to go out for penny-spending. We sit by the fire all evening and push for front place for our feet, and play Scrabble and eat nuts and enjoy ourselves. A real life of sloth . . .

Now to do some filing, awful thought. I hope you are keeping well, warm and contented.

Yours very sincerely,

Frances Woodsford

BOURNEMOUTH
January 22nd 1955

Dear Mr Bigelow,

. . . Have you read *Venture to the Interior* by Laurens van der Post? It is the account of his three journeys into the heart of Africa during the last war; is exceedingly well done, I remember, and a most sensible and interesting book. If you have not read it and will let me know, I will send it across. We are almost at the point of instigating a Cross-Ocean Library Service to each other, aren't we!

Whilst still on the subject of books: did the Giles books of cartoons arrive your end? You never mentioned it, which is so unusual I thought about it the other day and wondered whether it had gone astray or been in the mail on that 'plane which burnt out on Christmas Day. If you haven't had it, please let me know and I'll get you another copy before the printers run out.

I daresay your newspapers reported the peculiar phenomenon in London the other day, when a sort of midday blackout passed slowly

over the whole city. Some of the Italian newspapers, according to the
Daily Telegraph, published vivid accounts of people panicking in the
streets, and knocking on strangers' doors for refuge; streets thronged
with hysterical people, and so on . . . Anyway, one odd result did occur
– all the London sparrows put themselves to bed, in the Blackwall
Tunnel! I can't make out whether they thought it had been a short day,
or whether they eventually decided it had been a very short night.
Which do you prefer?

Blackwall Tunnel runs under the Thames, rather as your tunnels do
between New York and the New Jersey shore. Incidentally, just a
moment while I try something out, will you? Tunnel. Tunell. Tunnell.
Tunnel. They all look a bit peculiar, don't you think so? The more
alternatives, the worse they look . . .

One evening this week Mac was, as usual, late in picking me up at my
office, and his excuse was that he had a case of eviction and, as usual
again, the children were not turned over to him until teatime, which
makes an awful rush for everybody to get the children vetted by a doctor, and settled into some temporary home, before five o'clock. This
time Mac took the three children to a Miss Ashby, who already looks
after four. In England, I must explain, adoptions by unmarried women
are either illegal or very, very rarely permitted, but this lady, who owns
a many-bedroomed house, seems to be so fond of children she takes
them in as a foster-parent. She can't do it for money, for the most the
town ever pays a foster-parent is 35s.od. a week, and out of that the child
must be fed, housed, and clothed. Anyway, Mac turns up with these
three infants, and Miss Ashby takes them in, saying, 'About time, too – I
wondered when you were going to bring me some more.' 'She doesn't
work,' said Mac calmly. I gulped for a few moments, and then asked
indignantly whether my dear moronic brother considered looking
after seven children single-handed came under the category of 'work' or
not . . .

He will shortly be going away, probably to London, to do his
practical work in the studying he is now starting for a Diploma in Social
Science through the London University. He will do field-work either in
an old people's hostel, hospital almoner's office, or with the Red Cross.
I suggested the second might have the most interesting and varied cases

for him, but at the moment he is busily engaged going through the book of charities still working (you'd be surprised how many, from Society of Cat-Lovers and Tail-Wavers, to the Society for the Abrogation of Laws Penalising or Favouring Religious Bodies) to choose one he thinks best suited to his particular talents. I feel sorry for him; it must be hard starting studying a new line of work at the age of 37 or 38 or whatever he is, especially as it isn't long since he finished studying for his Associateship of the Chartered Institute of Secretaries. Wish I had the energy to do likewise, but I couldn't cope with C.I. of S. and you, and I think I prefer you!

Very sincerely,

Frances W.

BOURNEMOUTH
April 9th 1955

Dear Mr Bigelow,

History, common sense, and my own inclination insists that the first paragraph of this letter should be concerned with the news of the week – the resignation as Prime Minister of our very much beloved Sir Winston Churchill . . .

I am quite without a really concrete idea as to the reason for this drastic step. Whether Sir Winston thought it time, and high time, to give Sir Anthony Eden a chance. Whether he just felt his health was failing and he could no longer enter into the strenuous days with his full vigour. Whether Lady Churchill put her foot finally down and insisted she had her husband to herself for a bit. Or whether the *Daily Herald* was right – which I greatly doubt, as disapproval from his own party has never worried Churchill in 80 years and I don't see why it should now. Or whether, perhaps, remembering his promise to remain at the head of the Government until he could give us a reasonably safe peace, and realising that this would take decades, if not miracles, he has decided to give up the struggle. I just do not know. I am very sad and forlorn at his going. Something dependable and stable and brilliant, all at the same time, seems suddenly to have gone, and I feel a little lonely and unprotected and frightened.

This week I have been reading the second half of Lord David Cecil's biography of Lord Melbourne, and at the moment am just approaching the end of the part called 'The Queen, First Phase'. It seems to me that Queen Victoria must have felt rather as I feel now, when the change of Government first removed her beloved Lord Melbourne from her side, where he had given advice and help and knowledge and devotion and affection to such great result. Still, the world gets on, with or without its great men, and I would not begrudge Sir Winston a few quiet years with a seat on the back benches of the House of Commons, and a fresh supply of brilliant colours and new paintbrushes and canvasses . . .

There was a letter this morning from Rosalind's travelling companion, Mrs Beall, in which she said both Bill Akin and her own husband had put their respective feet down in insisting that the planned trip to Europe this summer be cancelled if war breaks out in the Far East. Being without newspapers for over a fortnight now, I had no idea things were so serious. Or is it just the usual pessimistic thinking going around? . . .

This morning Mother trotted over to the little half-shop our butcher maintains in R— Drive. It is seven houses away from our flats, and on the other side of the road. Some customers were in the shop as Mother arrived, and one was saying, 'I wonder who it is singing.' The butcher looked up and remarked, 'Oh, I can tell you that – it's Mr Woodsford.' My brother likes singing as he washes in the morning . . . . . . I leave you to imagine the volume of sound to us poor things in the same building!

Bowls and baskets of daffodils from the garden, and primroses and blue periwinkles from the countryside, are in every room of the flat this weekend. Spring has suddenly burst out in every direction, bless it. Today it is warm and sunny and you can positively feel the delight of the crowds. I hope you are enjoying equally lovely holiday weather. I am determined not to take the car on the roads again this weekend, as they are a solid mass of motors and very uncomfortable. Instead, I will brave the wrath of the birds, and spend my spare time in the garden.

Goodbye for this week, then, Mr Bigelow, and I hope you are well and happy.

Yours very sincerely,

Frances W.

BOURNEMOUTH
April 30th 1955

Dear Mr Bigelow,

Now that was a very kind gesture, to send me the *New York Herald Tribune* with the articles on Churchill's resignation, and I appreciate the gesture immensely, just as I enjoyed reading the paper. We did not get the text of Sir Winston's speech to the Queen at his farewell dinner, even when the English papers did get back into circulation, so I was particularly pleased to be able to read it in your paper. It started in true Churchillian style, and finished with an epithet to add to his collection of unusual, but beautifully tailored adjectives – 'the way of life of which Your Majesty is the young, gleaming champion'. Just perfect – not as cheap as 'glittering' would be, nor as ordinary as 'shining'.

The newspaper arrived on rather an awkward day, for I had overnight painted the front stairs leading down to our hall. There was the paper, halfway through the letter box, and there was I, at the top of the stairs. However, it was done quite easily by temporarily dismissing my upright stance (to match my character, of course) and walking down on the unpainted sides of the stairs. Something like this.

And in case you wondered, no, I was not drunk. Especially at that hour in the morning, 7.30 a.m.

. . . It looks as if the end of this page is about due to arrive, so I will just wish you well until next Saturday, and say thank you again for the newspaper. I hope you are well, even if you aren't writing letters!!

Very sincerely,

Frances W.

BOURNEMOUTH
May 14th 1955

Dear Mr Bigelow,

. . . On Thursday of this week I was a Presiding Officer at a Polling Station – a nice little 15-hour day. It was in a rather poor district, but the people who came to vote were so very friendly it was quite pleasant. On another Station, not far away, but as you would possibly describe it, 'on the other side of the railroad tracks', it is like digging in cement to get a 'Good Day' out of the voters; but here, nearly everybody beamed when I greeted them . . .

The policeman on duty at the election told me of his experiences on duty in London during the Coronation. They were on duty from 12 midnight the night before, to 7 p.m. after the procession had passed, but from midnight until 2 p.m. the police were relieved every two hours and marched to canteens set up nearby, where they could buy whatever they wanted. It was very cold weather, you will remember, and the police all wore their capes. This copper told me that they never once went off for their 15-minute break without having at least a dozen thermos vacuum flasks under their cape, to be filled with hot coffee or tea for the crowds along their part of the route. When they got back, flasks clanking like so many medals, they would get back to their post, back to the crowd, and mutter over their shoulder, 'Here – take this; pass it back.' Then, from 2 p.m. onwards until the procession arrived, he said they were on duty non-stop, and during that period the crowds repaid their kindness. A small child would sidle up to the policeman and say 'Hey, Mister, put out your hand,' and in would come a ham sandwich, or a slightly melted chocolate biscuit.

The reason I got all these tales from the policeman was that I asked innocently where I'd heard his name before – had it, perhaps, been in the newspapers? It had; he had rescued somebody from drowning and been awarded the Royal Society's medal, and he told me all about this with great gusto and obviously decided I was wonderful, to remember his name, and worthy of some more tales of How Wonderful he was . . .

No doubt you have heard about Mr Beall's heart attack and Rosalind's altered plans. We are all most sad about it. Last night when I got home there were letters both from Rosalind and from Harriet Beall, and I knew that this morning I would have to write and offer to cancel the whole Tour because it was so silly and selfish to expect Rosalind to come all this way just for a week's car touring. But this morning she seems to have obtained a replacement travelling companion in the person of Mrs Florence Olsen who will, I daresay, not prove nearly as entertaining for Rosalind as Mrs Beall would have been. Poor Mrs Beall, she must be out of her mind with worry, and disappointment. Still, she has seen some part of Europe, and if she never manages to get back again, she can always conjure up the scenes she remembers, and enjoy them; just as I shall always be able to picture parts of America and thus enjoy, at second-hand, another trip around that continent.

Thank you very much for your letters: I do not know what I should do without the stimulation of the Saturday Special in my mind all week; it spurs me on to doing things when my normal lazy way would be to stay at home and not keep my eyes and ears open for things that might interest you.

Very sincerely,

Frances W.

BOURNEMOUTH
June 4th 1955

Dear Mr Bigelow,

It seems to me that in one or two expurgated novels I have read, the word 'flaming' is used in place of another word, unidentified as yet, which is common in the Navy as a swear word. Perhaps that is the real use of the word in the expression 'Flaming June'. Today, anyway, whatever it was yesterday or may be tomorrow, it is dull and wet and blustery and thoroughly disagreeable. I don't altogether mind, for if we get it nasty now, we may get it pleasanter from next Thursday. So thoroughly selfish I am being . . .

Memo: get some 'anxiety-state' pills. I really cannot go on like this – every meal sickens me, so that I eat one slice of dry toast and four peppermints for my breakfast; one potato, one mouthful of greens, two mouthfuls of meat, and a cup of coffee and four peppermints, for lunch. And so on. It's getting so expensive in peppermints. I am so worried about staff; so worried something will happen to upset The Tour; just so worried generally it isn't funny. Wouldn't it be nice to be an irresponsible type, just letting things flow along as they wish. One evening this week, following a terrible day during which I burst into tears in front of my boss, he telephoned me at home to say he'd just engaged a new cashier and thought I'd like to know, so that I could go to bed and count sheep and sleep, instead of going to bed and counting cashiers and lying awake. What a life!

. . . I don't think the rail strike will much affect Rosalind's holiday. I have a vague notion her Scotland trip is by motor-coach, which won't therefore be affected; and as our tour is by car, there will be very little difference there. Again, Rosalind is being met at the docks by a car to come to Bournemouth, so that will be alright. It is the most infuriating strike, with, as is so often the case, high tempers, heavy emotion, a disappearance of logic and so little responsibility to anybody else. For a leader of a trade union to say 'The country will break before *we* break' is sheer madness, and helps his men as little as it helps anybody else. My own opinion is that conditions for workers (I use the word the way the unions use it, in a restricted sense) gradually improve over the years by weight of public opinion, and economics. In other words, the firm that offers the best conditions gets the best workers and can compete favourably with other firms. So the other firms start offering better conditions to their workers, and so on, everybody starts getting a little better. People won't work for bad employers any more, that's all there is about it. But everybody expects far higher services from some people than from others – for instance, there would be utter horror if doctors withdrew their services, but they are just as much public servants as the railways' drivers are. More sense of responsibility, that's what it boils down to I suppose.

My garden is looking enchanting this week, and so very neat now that we have cut the hedges and lawns and trimmed the edges, weeded the beds and generally cut off or out the untidy bits. True, we are not often allowed to go in the garden because the birds object so noisily to our presence, but when we do, it is a joy to look at . . . The rhododendrons are at their loveliest, and the rain this week has heightened the greenness of all the new leaves, so that if the weather is good next week, Rosalind should see the English countryside at its loveliest.

Very sincerely,

Frances W.

PS Yes I can think of something – your Natural History book arrived yesterday, so I tried reading it at breakfast this morning to take my mind off food. And what were the articles about, pray, Sir? Praying Mantis eating Mate; and Attempts to Cure Screw-worm in Cattle, with full and juicy illustrations. Don't think I'm blaming you: I merely think Natural History might have been more tactful this month!!!! Took six peppermints instead of four, it did.

THE ANGEL INN
LUDLOW
SHROPSHIRE
Sunday, 12th June 1955

Dear Mr Bigelow,

Here we are – not at Ludlow, where I got no farther than the address – but in Port Meirion in Wales, where a small (artificial) waterfall clatters down outside our balcony, and beyond is a green lawn (real) and golden sands and clear water and a little green island and, far off, green mountains. It is so cutey crafty it is funny, and I think it was built by a man with his tongue in his cheek. In one small cottage there is a small bricked-up window painted to show a wicked old satyr peering out as a novel change for a wicked old satyr's normal habits at windows.

Today it was fine and very sunny: cold, too, but at least fine. Due to my planning, about which you have heard much, I daresay, the Castle (Powis) we were going over wasn't open until the afternoon, but we did go around Harlech Castle, an ancient coastal fortress, and shivered in the sunshine under the influence of the antique ghosts.

Rosalind and I are having *such* fun: at least I am and I hope she is, too. We found (almost by accident) the most gorgeous gardens yesterday and I removed (almost by accident, too) several interesting seeds with which I intend turning R— Drive into a garden fit, like Hidcote, to be given to the nation eventually.

We had a most luxurious suite at Ludlow, including Jacobean style beds and red velvet covers, but nowhere to dry our smalls. I do think for the charge made they might have included at least a launderette, don't you?

Now to use some of the hotel notepaper for a change. Au revoir until Saturday.

Very sincerely,

Frances W.

VICTORIAN MAUSOLEUM
MINEHEAD
SOMERSET
16th June 1955

Dear Mr Bigelow,

It is raining tonight and it rained this morning. When it isn't raining big, heavy, palsied drops it is being suffocatingly stuffy. When the hotels *I* picked out so carefully (should have used a pin) are clean and comfortable they are cold; and when they are warm they are terrible! Altogether not the success I would wish for and I'm sure Florence Olsen is more unhappy about it than her chest cold explains. Rosalind is being very, very gay and pretending like mad, bless her. And perhaps in a way it is good for me to make such a failure, for I'd be insufferable, were I always right and 100% efficient.

Anyway, we *have* seen two lovely gardens, really beautiful, which exceeded our expectations, and they offset some of the others which were either too sad and run-down or too park-like. We have seen an awful lot of everything and are beginning to suffer the melancholy of mental and visual indigestion. R. and I have climbed spiral staircases till we stagger. But we have met many people who have all been so kind to us – we arrive too late practically everywhere but get allowed in just the same, and are treated with the greatest kindness by everybody. All this, of course, I will tell you when I get home and digest it all. When, too, I shall be able to view the week as a whole and not as a series of failures, semi-failures and successes. Tonight is definitely one of the failures and this is, in consequence I daresay, a depressing letter. Never mind – you don't mind putting up with my vapours just this once, do you? You should be used to them by now, poor man.

This room has brown walls (pale), brown furniture (dark), brown carpet, brown bed quilt and spread, pale brown curtains a brown and black tiled mantel. Do you wonder I am feeling brown, too?

Never mind – the 'cork' will be up again next week and no doubt boasting of its prowess as a Travel Agent. Just you wait and see. Until then.

Very sincerely,

Frances W.

ROYAL CLARENCE HOTEL
EXETER
Saturday night
June 18th 1955

Dear Mr Bigelow,

It is very sad to think that tomorrow is the last day – for me – of this trip. Earlier this evening I was stupefied to hear Florence Olsen say, 'Well, the week's gone now. Now perhaps things will be better.' Stupefied, because I had not thought Florence *that* tactless, but after a pause she continued, 'The first week you have a cold you just *exist*, and after that it seems to start getting better.'

Yesterday was a really delicious day in weather, and we had a pleasant variety. First, Clovelly for quaintness. Next, the romantic ruins of King Arthur's castle perched on a cliff top over dark emerald Atlantic waters. Then the flat, high, windblown north Cornwall. Later there was a visit to Cotehele House on the steep side of the Tamar Valley, which is warm enough for azaleas, camellias and lush greenery to rival the tropics. The house (about 1300) was perfectly beautiful. Lastly, we came over Dartmoor, bleak and rocky and high and lonely, into more lush valleys and eventually Exeter. There we were not exactly lulled by the bell-ringing practice! This may be very fine indeed, but a little distance lends enchantment to the finest church bells in the world, and we here are in the Cathedral Yard . . .

Now I must dart out into the corridor and see if I can catch the bathroom empty. Up to now it has produced loud sounds of splashing but never a peaceful silence!

Next week, back to normal. Well – nearly normal, as I shall have to do extra late duties to 'pay' for having this week off. Never mind. There's always 1957.

Very sincerely,

Frances W.

BOURNEMOUTH
July 2nd 1955

Dear Mr Bigelow,

Now, where was I? Ah yes – in Shrewsbury, shivering in a miserable com-mercial-travellers' hotel with brown wallpaper and a hideous structure outside our room window with tower, chiming clock, and 'Floreat Salop' in stone letters around its dome.

However, we were there only one night and the clock only chimed during one night's rest, but neither of us felt inclined to spend much time exploring Shrewsbury in the morning. We paid our bill – Rosalind used a travellers' cheque to do so and I'm almost certain the cashier gave us £1 too much for it, which should balance the sixpence she was diddled out of later on at Tintern Abbey – and then we were off again.

So from Shrewsbury we went down the Wye Valley and had a lovely time going over the ferry from Beachley to Aust, getting lost in the Cotswolds again, and eventually arriving at Bath, to find Florence already there. I had been having little bets with myself, whether or not she'd make it on account of the railway strike and having a good time with her friends. The friends were stoic and the country cottage very, very cold, with outdoor sanitation and a pump for water. This, knowing Florence, may have had something to do with her arrival in Bath, complete with bronchial cold. She was terribly upset to discover that the English Kleenex tissues were not only larger than the American ones, but of better quality! Rosalind capped this by saying so was the English toilet-paper, which didn't tear in one's fingers. A quality I had not expected anybody to praise in this article. We sat and thought about Kleenex and toilet-paper and felt very strongly about it all, one way and another.

Then from Bath we had a ball-and-chain with us, in the shape of Florence. Rosalind dislikes driving over 30 miles an hour; this threw our programme out of schedule a little, but when you added Florence doing a snail-crawl some way to our rear, the whole thing became ridiculous. I felt a strong rubber elastic chain would have been a good idea. Fastened one end to the car, and the other to Mrs Olsen. Then, when

Rosalind and I reached the car, we could give a good strong yank on the rope and up would bounce our laggard. She did her best, poor Florence, but she just isn't geared to other people's rate of progress. She also had – you know about it, no doubt – a most amusing way of making the most ridiculous statements in a deadly serious way, never realising for one moment how wrong she was in her facts. Rosalind and I had a nice catty time exchanging delighted grins behind her unsuspecting back. Don't know who Rosalind has been smiling at since they went off to Sweden . . .

. . . However, chacun à son goût or whatever it is. And Florence was a very kind person; very simple, and it was really bad taste on my part to laugh at her, however kindly. She was a sitting bird for a joke made with a straight face. At our last lunch, in Salisbury, where Mother and Mac were joining us, there was a little struggle between Florence and Mac over the bill, and I leaned over the table and said 'Oh, please Florence, let him pay it. If you insist, poor Mac will lose face and have to resign his job and leave town and everything.' Florence blushed scarlet at her appalling breach of English social custom (!) and gave up the bill forthwith, poor soul. Poor me, too – I had to reimburse our Willie when we got outside . . . . . . Don't tell Rosalind, *please*!

This week I have had nothing but bad news from all directions (not from Sweden), so that I hope most sincerely the next letter from you will tell me the *Pauline** has won all the races in Long Island Sound, under the skippership of your son, and that you have discovered oil in your back-yard. Or made a score of 756 at Scrabble. Or acquired a new dog or cat. Or something delightful, and pleasant, for a change.

All for now: more next Saturday, and aren't you glad to be back at the old typewriter-game again, after my handwriting!

Very sincerely,

Frances Woodsford

* *Editor's note*: Mr Bigelow's boat was named after his late wife.

BOURNEMOUTH
August 13th 1955

Dear Mr Bigelow,

If ever – which is extremely unlikely – I had enough money to retire on before reaching the age of 65, I would like to take a full page of the local newspaper and on it put, in large letters, my opinion of the Great British Public as I have experienced it during my nine and a half years as a Corporation employee. Trouble is, if all these 'ifs' came to pass, I don't suppose for one moment any newspaper in the world would accept my advertisement because of libel laws.

My outburst is caused through an experience this week, when a 'lady' came into my office and, within thirty seconds, told me I was lazy, inefficient, and grossly overpaid. The reason? The elevator was not working. After her first thirty seconds, she added that I was rude, and by that time there was some basis for her accusation. When the electricians got here this morning (the earliest they could arrive) I told the man in charge that I was lazy, inefficient and grossly overpaid because the lift wasn't working and I hoped he would quickly see to it that I became energetic, efficient and underpaid. He looked at me in astonishment. Said, 'Who said all that?' 'Oh, a lady yesterday, who was annoyed because she had to walk up one floor.' 'Well,' he said sturdily, 'I hope you held her head under water.'

This has been the most ghastly fortnight, from the point of view of difficult customers . . . I for one don't blame the staff one little bit. Anybody who didn't get irritated with the Great British Public in August would either be in an institution or in need of canonisation . . .

I had a letter from Rosalind this week, full of the joy of ownership of a new Springer puppy named (poor dog) Arthur Tintagel. Judging by our own experience of Tintagel, the puppy is going to be very, very full of wind. She, Rosalind, said you had had Paul and Nancy to stay with you and all the children had been ill. What a to-do! Did you rush off pronto and judge yacht-races? I would have done, in your position. And incidentally, talking of yachting, we are following in the newspapers the course of your hurricane 'Connie' which, at the moment of writing, is slowing down a bit off the coast of Carolina. Now I know a Connie, and she's a very devil, so I hope for all your sakes this namesake keeps well out to sea. We had a small thunderstorm last night; nothing much, but enough rain to beat down a few flowers and make the hard-baked turf soggy underfoot. The cat was terrified – it is so long since he heard the rain beating on the windowpane he put on quite a panic, silly creature, and spent the rest of the evening crouching under the sideboard among empty wine bottles and bits of fluff.

In my few spare moments during the last fortnight I have been making myself a new winter frock in tweed. It is now at the stage where only the finishing-off, hem turning up and buttonholing and so on, remains to be done. I look like a putty and brown banana in it, as it is in the new sheath-like style. Kindly remind me from time to time, Sir, next winter, not to eat another helping of that nice batter pudding, will you? Which conjures up a problem. What does a banana do when it gets too fat for its skin?

My brother is still on holiday, with exclusive use of the car and I shall be downright glad when he's not, because every time I am on late duty I miss the bus home and that means I leave in the morning at 8.15 a.m. and get back in the evening at 10.15 p.m., and it's too long a day for any-body, let alone a fragile little flower-like creature like ME! He politely said I could have the car yesterday morning, so I did, and discovered we were out of gas, so instead of saving a shilling bus fare to work and back, I paid out five shillings on petrol. Mac is short for Machiavelli, did you know? . . .

Yours sincerely
Indignantly
Forlornly

Frances W.

BOURNEMOUTH
October 8th 1955

Dear Mr Bigelow,

. . . Now if you want a bird's-eye view of the Conservative Conference
this year, come to me, for I am on the doorstep and can give you such a
view. A very small bird, mind you. The Conference is being held in the
large Pavilion, directly across the road from the Baths. The Conference
is the largest ever held in Bournemouth, and overflows in all directions
– right now my boss's car is parked outside my office window, smothering the sparrows who are once again pecking on my windowsill for their
winter food – and it's parked there because there just isn't room in our
driveway, which is full of the cars of the smaller delegates and officials.
There are seven B.B.C. television vans, and one Independent Television
Network van . . .

Sir Anthony and Lady Eden, and about 400 of the other delegates, are
occupying the entire Carlton Hotel up on the East Cliff, and Sir A. and
Lady are having a suite on the first floor. I wonder if it is the same one
Rosalind and Matt Beall had when they stayed there? They are making
such a to-do about the whole thing the hotel owners have been to the
trouble to have the Eden arms embroidered on new pink bed-quilts! I
wonder whether they'd sell them off cheaply afterwards, or do you
think they'll charge extra for the honour of being warmed by a bed-quilt
which has warmed the Prime Minister . . .

Willie Jackson, the Pavilion Puss, has been over twice this week – I was
astounded, for I had no idea his politics were anti-Conservative. This
morning he arrived early with a complaint that he had been turned out
because his face was dirty. Well, it was, so I cleaned it up for him and then
he decided that he might as well give me the benefit of his company for a
while, so he is curled up precariously (precariously because he is far too
wide) on the windowsill on a pile of old swimming costumes, watching
the birds and purring like a hobbed kettle.

Tomorrow Mother and I are motoring up to London with Mac to
deposit him and his belongings at an aunt's house. As he has done
practically nothing whatsoever to prepare for this 10 or 12 week visit, I

imagine tonight will be a panic plus, as I keep repeating at hourly intervals 'You realise we are starting promptly at nine o'clock on Sunday, dear?' and Mac only groans, not realising there is such an hour as nine o'clock on Sunday mornings. Well, he'll know tomorrow.

On Thursday he went to the Reception for the Conservatives, and on leaving the house about 8.30 p.m. asked me to ring up Highcliffe 313 and tell Ann Allport he had been delayed. Now I have met Ann Allport once or twice when Mac hasn't been able to avoid it, so when I got her on the telephone I said, 'Now, how long have you known my brother?' 'Oh, years.' 'Well, then, you'll realise I am ringing up at his request to tell you he has been delayed, but he has left now and by the time he gets to Highcliffe I have no doubt but that he'll have a specious excuse all ready.' 'I bet he will!' said Ann, and I haven't found out yet what it was. He finished up his last week in Bournemouth (for some time) with his boss away on holiday. On Monday he had a case of two children being kidnapped. On Tuesday a mother tried to kill her children and succeeded in half-killing herself instead. On Wednesday two teenage girls played hookey from school, and the police found them hitch-hiking to the nearest Army camp. On Thursday he had a mother having hysterics all over the office (she is a very bad creature, and the Court have denied her access to her children for a while) and on Friday he had a quiet day. Comparatively. Poor soul, he does have a nerve-racking time, as even this 'comparatively' involved one member of the staff going home with a bad haemorrhage from a tooth. The next ten weeks should be quite a holiday for him, for as he says he'll be a pupil, and have no responsibility whatsoever. As your successive Presidents know, responsibility can be a man-killer if you get it in too great a quantity.

End of paper. More next Saturday, while I am on holiday. So until then, keep well and happy.

Yours truly,

Frances W.

BOURNEMOUTH
November 11th 1955

Dear Mr Bigelow,

Here is my birthday – and, so far as the weather is concerned, you can have it! It is pouring with rain, and has been all day and all day yesterday and the day before yesterday, and it shows every signs of pouring with rain all day tomorrow and the day after tomorrow. My day is therefore surrounded, flooded, with tears. No doubt mourning my wasted youth, but depressing, nonetheless.

However, on the bright side are many remembrances from my friends, you not least of all, by any means. Mother gave me money towards the clothes wardrobe, and so did Mac. I had gift vouchers from two or three friends with a lot of sense, because it is always a good thing to give somebody, letting them have the choice of what they want or need. There were two or three lots of handkerchiefs, of which I never have enough; and a large pile of ornate and simple cards. The cat gave me a dirty look . . .

Now to wash my hair and pin it up to look glamorous in the morning, if not tonight.

Thank you again, Mr Bigelow, for your magnificent birthday-cum-Christmas gift.

Very sincerely yours,

Frances W.

1956

'Mrs Phyllis Murray and yrs truly in Cornwall.'

BOURNEMOUTH
February 4th 1956

Dear Mr Bigelow,

Solvent again! At least for a week. I got home on February 1st and said gaily to Mother, 'Only four weeks until payday, dear!' Mother, somewhat disbelieving, made a remark about it being payday that very day (which it was) so I told her that when I had paid my debts and bought flowers for a friend who was ill, and china ducks for another who is dying (to console her for the loss of her own pet ducks, taken by a fox) and paid the garage and my insurance and so on, out of a salary cheque of £45 I had exactly £3.15s.0d left!!! However, Mac gave me £1 towards the cost of the garage, so I feel reasonably solvent again, and able to face life without worrying whether I shall have to walk home in the absence of the bus fare . . . . . . What a life. However, I still haven't touched my savings, which is the main thing, and next month I shall have so much spare money I hope to put another £10 in the Bank . . .

Yours very sincerely,
Frances W.

BOURNEMOUTH
February 11th 1956

Dear Mr Bigelow,

. . . I was moaning last week about the cold weather. Somebody must have heard me, because by Saturday night the temperature had risen from 20° to 49° F, and Sunday was a really lovely day. We took Mother out for a drive in the afternoon, with Mac doing the driving, and for once I was not nervous in my seat at his side. The reason was that our brakes are binding so badly we are terrified of using the brakes at all, so Mac drives with the aid of the gears and cuts down his speed for corners and so on by taking his foot off the accelerator well in advance, and, then, if that hasn't brought our rate down enough, he will change down a gear. Very comfortable motoring indeed, it makes, and I am all for the brakes to go on binding indefinitely. The cold weather, alas, had another effect on the car – it put paid, finis, phutt, to the battery. My Resolution Not To Draw Money out of The Bank lasted until February 6th, but it was a nice resolution while it did last . . .

Last night, in my opinion, every single member of the Civil Defence who turned up for their lecture deserved the gold badge which the Government is giving those of us who complete 100% of the training programme. 80% entitles you to a silver badge, which is the highest most of us can hope for. But last night should have counted for the whole thing, for it was bitterly cold, with a violent, knife-like wind and, when we eventually reached the lecture room (ten minutes walk from *any* bus stop) we found we were having instruction in map-reading and had to sit at map-equipped tables spread around the room, and not, as we had hoped, in a tight little bunch around the only radiator in the place. However, the map-reading was interesting and maybe I learned some-thing of use, although most of the 'tips' we were given seemed to me gravely suspicious. For instance, we were being told how to find North: Compass, which we were unlikely to have. Churches, built East and West. OK. If we could find a church. Trees likely to grow close togeth-er on the S. or W. of hills. Fiddlesticks. Moss growing on the West (instructor) or South (instructor, five minutes later) or North (my own belief of many years). Not helpful. I said, 'Isn't there a way of telling North by using a watch-face?' Yes, there was, said the instructor, but he'd only discussed it at the Government School for Instructors, with the other pupils there, and they hadn't been able to work it, because they understood you pointed the hour hand at the sun and the North was where the minute hand was. Nonsense and fiddle-de-dee, said the class. North is halfway between the two hands when the hour hand is pointing to the sun. Well, I've just tried it and in fifteen minutes North has moved from one side of my office to the other. There *is* a way of doing it with a watch, but I still don't believe I know it. Do you? Of course when the sun is out it does give you a rough idea of the general direction of North and South, providing you know the approximate time of day – whether it is morning or late afternoon, for instance, and presumably most of us know that. We were also told to use telegraph poles, which always bear the cross-pieces on the side facing towards London. But what if the road isn't going towards London, but at right-angles to such a road? They certainly don't add the cross-pieces sideways just to help lost souls find their way to the North Pole. As for finding it by the North Star, that, to me, is like Mrs Beeton's recipe for Jugged Hare – 'First, catch your Hare.' However, I learned enough of map-reading to be able to complain bitterly that two of the map references given us on the blackboard in a test we took at the end, weren't on our maps at all. Neither were they. We were given seven references, which indicated places in which the road was blocked by bomb debris. Then we had to plot our route, using only first- or second-class roads, from Bournemouth Square to a rendezvous by Blandford Railway Station and give the mileage involved. All I have to do now is to remember what I learned . . . . . .

. . . I was reading this week in the paper that two gentlemen in America were suing a railroad company for half a million dollars because a train they were travelling on arrived at the race-track too late for them to place their bets on a horse which, in the event, won and would have won them $200 had their money been on. I have an idea that in England you can't sue anybody for more than you have lost by their negligence; perhaps these two American punters are the original discoverers of a new gold-mine. You might let me know if they succeed, and next time the car is (as now) out of action and the bus is late I shall sue the Corporation for, oh, say £30,000 – a nice round sum – for loss of prestige and morale.

You may keep your term 'gas' for the stuff cars run on. I prefer our 'petrol'. After all, gas is a term embracing many forms of gas, from the very air we breathe to deadly poisons and anaesthetics. To call it gas is too general. To call it petrol does at least distinguish which gas it is. I must say I am trying to be impartial, for there are many of your terms which I think preferable to ours; but gas isn't one of them. Nor is elevator. On suspenders v. braces I am biased slightly in your favour.

On drapes v. curtains I prefer curtains, because they aren't invariably draped. Slip v. petticoat leaves me undecided. I prefer petticoat from the sound, although it isn't a coat, petit or otherwise. And it shouldn't be a slip, though it sometimes does. I definitely prefer car to automobile, which is a nasty made-up sort of word; but on the other hand I am all in favour of movie instead of pictures. Incidentally, I saw Gene Kelly in *It's Always Fair Weather* this week, and, as with all his films, thought it utterly delightful; witty, kindly, colourful, beautifully danced, and in extremely good taste . . .

What a long letter – and the second this week, too! Must be the cold weather keeping me energetic. Goodbye for now while I go and feed my sparrows dotted on the windowsill, thinking, poor things, that the flakes of snow are breadcrumbs.

Yours most sincerely,

Frances W.

BOURNEMOUTH
March 17th 1956

Dear Mr Bigelow,

Do you realise – bet you didn't – that March 22nd sees the seventh anniversary of my first letter to you? There is a note in my 1949 diary against that date, 'wrote Roady's Father.' At that time, you see, you weren't an individual in your own right – you existed only in relationship to your daughter; but you have grown quite a bit since then.

Certainly I must say you have grown quite a bit more *sensible*. Your reply to my original letter started, without salutation or preamble, and date-less, address-less:

It was interesting to learn that you enjoyed eating a squirrel cooked in a bag in Central Park and also watching some old hen making off with another paper bag to stuff in an egg in her nest, at or near New Orleans. Nature *is* wonderful!

No wonder I wondered what made the American people so! Especially as you went on to say *all* Englishmen in novels were so intensely repulsive, and finished your letter by putting my name (wrongly spelled) and 'R— Drive, England, so help me'. I cannot tell you whether your opinion of England and the English has undergone a change since that date, or whether I have merely worn down your rude comments by throwing other rude ones back in exchange. However, you seem to be able to understand my letters, and do not get quite so mixed up as you appeared to have done over my account of the Central Park squirrel dragging a paper bag up a tree and into its nest.

Last Sunday, as we were clearing luncheon, I said to Mother, 'Would you like a ride this afternoon, dear, or do you prefer to have a rest?' You will notice that there are two clear questions there. One would imagine that such a question called for a reply choosing one or other of the alternatives. But anyone imagining that would not know my Mum. *She* answered, 'No thank you dear, I know you want to get out and dig the vegetable bed over.' A veritable mind reader, that dear lady is. In reverse. The last thing in the world I wanted to do was to dig the vegetable bed over. And of course, you can guess what I did. Yes – my back still aches . . .

Until next Saturday, then, thank you for your letters, all of 'em, and keep well and happy.

Very sincerely,

Frances W.

PS Have I said thank you yet for *Reader's Digest*? I got full marks in both the word exercises. Genius, of course.

BOURNEMOUTH
March 24th 1956

Dear Mr Bigelow,

. . . We had a lecture at Civil Defence this week on rescue from crashed aircraft. I thought it a waste of time, as the likelihood of any particular person being on the spot when a 'plane crashes is so remote as to be almost non-existent. However, you never know when odd knowledge might come in handy. Of course, I upset the lecturer no end by my questions – particularly as, having worked on aircraft during the war I knew more about them technically than he did – and he got quite put out. But, after all, when a man tells you the only practical way to break into a crashed civilian aircraft is over the windows, somebody with a mind like mine (like Kipling's Elephant Child, that is) is bound to ask how you are expected to get up as high as the windows. 'Well, you'd just have to use your common sense' he said to that one. And then, when I remarked that it was all very well showing us a poster of a crashed Army 'plane on which the starboard engines were on fire and the escape panels were all on the port side, but how did you get the crew out if the port side engines were on fire because there were no escape panels on the starboard side? He looked with loathing at me (poor man, who can blame him!) and was heard to mutter something about 'common sense' again. I take it he meant your common sense would tell you it was hopeless so you might just as well leave the wreck and go to the movies. Never mind: I now know how to break into a crashed aircraft provided it comes down close enough to the earth for me to get onto the wings, and providing the fire (if any) is on the starboard side of the machine, and providing I get to the scene of the crash in time . . .

Bought my brother a pale green nylon and pure silk shirt for his birthday, on Monday, at an astronomical figure and an even greater figure on the sale-ticket. I bought it at a reduced price because it was the last of the consignment and they were wanting to sell it before putting the new lot out – at even greater, astronomical prices. I do feel sorry for men: you have such dull gifts on your birthdays and so on. The only time I gave my brother anything exciting, it was an after-shave lotion and brought him out in a rash. True, he did give *me* something exciting once – a hand shower set for attachment to the bath taps, which he used fourteen times that particular weekend, but as a general rule he gets very dull bits of clothing. And please, I ask you, don't write back and suggest either emerald cufflinks or gold wristwatches because he has neither and is most unlikely ever to own them.

On Thursday evening, on my way to Civil Defence class, I dropped in at a friend's flat to deliver our family gifts to her for her own birthday. Now Dorothy lives alone in a flat, and when she is not there she tucks the front door key under a ledge at the bottom of the door. So I felt there, and got it out and opened the door. And there, on the door-mat, was a tiny bottle of milk. On the first stair (Dorothy lives in the upper flat) was a small pile of letters. On the second, a small parcel. One above that, a cardboard box containing (at a guess) groceries. One up another wrapped gift. Above that, the second delivery of mail. I put my lampshade on the sixth stair and Mother's on the seventh, with Mac's card on the eighth. This took us nearly halfway up the staircase, and I felt quite sorry for Dorothy when she came home after working for 14 hours, having to collect and carry all this stuff upstairs. It seemed to me, also, that the hiding place for the key wasn't *terribly* secret . . .

Now I must go and help in the café: I am on my own today, and the place is absolutely swarming with small children. I know washing-up isn't quite the thing for a Baths Matron and Secretary to do, but it is out of sight of the public and I don't see why I shouldn't help a very good staff when they are being run off their feet and I am not. After all, I have never laid any claims to dignity, much though I would like to be able to do so.

So, until next Saturday, au revoir, and I do hope your weather is better and won't be such a foul nuisance again for a very long time.

Yours most sincerely,

Frances W.

BOURNEMOUTH
March 28th 1956

Dear Mr Bigelow,

What a sad indictment on modern manners! A day or two ago I had notification from Barker & Dobson that a parcel of candy (your gift) had been dispatched to me, and adding coyly that they thought the sender would be pleased to be advised that the chocolates had arrived! As though I would need a hint to write and thank you! A tactful reminder not to forgo the pleasure of saying thank you, and of telling you what a very well-chosen parcel it is!! Which reminds me:

> First child: We've got a radio set and television and a washing machine and a car. You don't seem to have anything here, do you?
> Second child: Oh, we've got manners.

So now Easter is here and we shall be able to guzzle ourselves, and be large-handed to any friends who may visit us: And B & Dobson's hint or no, we all thank you most sincerely, and wish you to have as happy an Easter as you well deserve. I do hope all that snow has gone and you are no longer confined to the house by mountainous drifts; and that both you and the birds got through the bad patch satisfactorily.

Thank you again, very much indeed,

Frances W.

BOURNEMOUTH
March 31st 1956

Dear Mr Bigelow,

. . . It is only Thursday today, and I am stuck in my office waiting, as usual, for my brother to arrive and take me home. On Tuesday this week he hadn't arrived 40 minutes after I left the office, so I went home by bus in a terrific temper. And he sulked because I was angry. Said (to Mother. I wouldn't speak to him) that he became very busy a few minutes before he should have left the office, and forgot all about telephoning – or asking one of his staff to do so – me not to wait. He is always fairly sorry to keep me waiting, but always sulks if I am annoyed by it. I nearly gave him my share of the car, then and there! As my boss says, I could come to work and go home by taxi and it would still be cheaper than sharing a car with my brother! Ah well. C'est la guerre or something.

Friday, I shan't have to go to work. I know I should go to church, but as a day off is so rare a thing I am going to motor Mother down to Lyme Regis instead. Her brother living there has been rather ill lately, and I know Mother has been longing to go and see him. So we shall take her, and have a picnic lunch on the way if the weather holds – at present it is fine but not sunny. I have bought a bottle of white wine to go with a tin of chicken Rosalind sent in a parcel at Christmas. (Mother dreamed the other night how nice it would be if we could have a picnic with tinned chicken if we had a tinned chicken and we had a picnic – and in the morning she got a chair and climbed on it and looked on top of her wardrobe – where, surprisingly, she keeps such things – and there, in solitary state, was a large tin. Of chicken! So we are all set.)

And, of course, we have the chocolates and the creamy mints, and so on, from your Easter Egg. And I have bought Mother a pale green cardigan and Mac green nylon socks, so all together our outing should be perfectly Easter-ish.

I am afraid this will have to be a short letter: I can hear Mac honking away out the front – his polite way of informing me he is here, and although he has no real objection to keeping me waiting, of course it is lese-majesty to do the same thing to him. So I must away in a hurry.

Yours very sincerely,

Frances W.

BOURNEMOUTH
May 26th 1956

Dear Mr Bigelow,

This, being the first full week of our summer water show, is always one of the busiest and most headachy in the year for me. This year, opening night came and all my staff arrived – except TWO. These did not have the common decency to telephone and say they'd changed their minds about coming to work for us, and thereby left us in a complete flap five minutes before the audience came in, as we hadn't enough usherettes to show them in, nor doormen enough to take their tickets.

Since then I have written to five more, not one of whom has bothered to answer – even to say 'No', and have arranged for two girls who were friends of those already working for us – and they, bless 'em, did have the manners to telephone and say 1) that the parents wouldn't let them work in such a place as the Baths, and 2) they didn't want to work Saturdays. Ah well . . .

But to more cheerful matters. Let us start with Mother. She went down the garden on Thursday, a very warm and humid day, and got bitten by a midget. According to her. It's another one of the book of Mrs Woodsford Malapropisms, and, I think, a very good one.

It was raining a little on Thursday, so instead of giving my genius to outdoor painting class that evening, I gave my services to the good of my country, and turned up at the Civil Defence class. We were on a small exercise at the 'bombed' house, where I was given a label reading 'Fractured femur' and told to drape myself over some rubble and be a casualty. Fortunately I was also given a blanket as well as a label, as the grass was both long and wet, and the rubble was dirty and uncomfortable, being composed of bits of old iron, bricks, loose odds and ends of wood – in fact, just the sort of thing you would get around a bombed building. I lay there on my little blanket for ten or fifteen minutes, until the rescue party discovered me, and listened to a cuckoo in the next field echoing my thoughts *exactly*.

. . . I must, of a surety, be my mother's daughter. Last evening, I was working late and, on reaching home, had my supper in bed. I was a bit worried about something that had gone wrong, and was thinking of possible causes when I noticed I had taken the stopper out of the vacuum flask and poured my coffee – over my salad. As I told you of Mother's meeting with the midget in the garden (it drew blood, she said) it is only fair that I should tell you about this episode as well.

And now it is Saturday morning, and there is so much to be done I can't spend any more time writing to you – I got to work at 8.30 so, in any case, only having from 10 p.m. to 8.30 a.m. to go home, feed, and sleep, I am in no real condition to write bright letters anyway. So au revoir until next Saturday.

Yours very sincerely,

Frances W.

BOURNEMOUTH
June 22nd 1956

Dear Mr Bigelow,

You are letting your side down, Sir! Do you realise that the Bellport Grapevine (your nom-de-plume) did not let me know that Rosalind was flying to France to take a coach trip next month? I found out from Mrs Beall in London, who said Rosalind was dreading having to write and tell me she was coming to Europe without visiting England. Poor Rosalind! Does she see me as a sort of ogre-spinster, all frowns and recriminations, I wonder. I seem to remember friends being chary of giving me bad news before; it gives me deeply to think. Either they believe me to be so tender-hearted I shall be quite broken up; or they are scared stiff of my reactions. Of course I would naturally prefer the former explanation, but there is sufficient element of doubt about it, for, as I said, serious heart-searching on my part. I wrote to Rosalind within a couple of hours of hearing, giving her my complete permission to visit Europe any time she chose, and graciously forgiving her for this lapse on her part. My only reaction is a somewhat plaintive wish that I could take the tour as well; but as that is impossible from all angles, I just hope the four ladies will have a wonderful holiday. Coming from an ogre, that's pretty generous wishing, don't you agree?

I listened to Mr Truman last night on the radio, speaking at the Pilgrim Dinner given in his honour. He was an easy speaker. He told a tale of Lord Halifax – a previous speaker – who was showing a party of American ladies over the British Embassy in Washington during his Ambassadorship there. On the walls of the staircase are hung, as no doubt you know, portraits of the English monarchs. One of the ladies stopped before one, and exclaimed, 'Oh, what a handsome man – and what a kind face! Who was he?' Lord Halifax paused before the portrait of George III to collect his thoughts, and then said, 'He was one of the founders of your Country, Madam.'

. . . Now for London. I came back late Sunday night. Later than I had expected, but that's railways for you these days – they run to please themselves. In fact, the 7.30 p.m., which I was catching, wasn't even shown on the Departure Board. The first thing, the thing of paramount importance in England – the weather, was foul. However, we 'did' Westminster Abbey, which I hadn't seen before. I did go inside one day, many years ago, but whether I picked the wrong door, or what I did, I don't remember but it looked so like an old junk shop I came straight out. This time I was stronger of will, and went around like a good little tourist . . .

We went also to the Tate Gallery where I wanted Mrs Beall and Miss Henry to see the luminous Turners, and the French Impressionists. Alas, it turned out that they much preferred Watts's *Hope sitting on top of the World*, which they had seen on umpteen Christmas cards and calendars! Then Mrs Beall and I went to Windsor to go over the Castle, only to find a) it was Sunday and the State Apartments aren't open, and b) St George's Chapel was also closed as there was a service going on, and it was to be shut, anyway, until Tuesday, when the ceremony of installing a new Knight of the Order of the Garter took place. So we were blown from the ramparts by the wind (I noticed in the paper, the Queen was dealt with in the same way at the Tuesday ceremony, nearly being blown overboard in her heavy cloak, and almost losing her plumed hat, to the great amusement of her two children, watching nearby) and had lunch in a very old hotel in the town . . .

And then, of course, we went three times to the theatre. We saw *The Boyfriend* which is a delicate take-off of the 1920s and quite enchanting. Mrs Beall wasn't impressed. She is a very unimaginative person, and kept saying, 'I'm sure we weren't as silly in the 1920s, quite sure.' I don't suppose they were – the whole thing was a delicate exaggeration of the manner in which musical comedies were presented *on the stage* then. The girls wore knickers with elastic just above the knees; their swimming suits had legs almost to the knees, and brightly coloured bands around the hips. They wore bandeaux around their eyebrows, and they were so sweet and so utterly refined it was difficult for them to get the words out of their plum-like mouths. We also saw Edith Evans and Peggy Ashcroft in *The Chalk Garden*, which was exquisitely acted and we all loved it. . . Finally – only we saw it first, which was a mistake: it should have been the final item on our programme – we saw Alec Guinness in *Hotel Paradiso*. This is a French farce, some 80 years ago and still, like some people, going very strong indeed. It was a joy, a wonder, a jaw-acher, from beginning to end – and the timing, Mr Bigelow, must have been done with a stop-watch timing the stop-watch. The scene was a gloriously run-down hotel interior, absolutely perfect of its kind. And every time I think of it, I laugh – especially the bit where Alec Guinness (M. Boniface) has explained his presence in the hotel to a neighbour, who is staying overnight, by saying his wife always said to him 'Any time you are passing the Hotel Paradiso, do run in and give my regards to Madame Cot' (she was the friend's wife, with whom Boniface was hoping to spend the night). Next time he was confronted by his awkward neighbour, Alec Guinness was hugging an old-fashioned stone hot-water bottle (he was feeling ill from the effects of too much wine) and the best he could do on the spur of the moment was to say his wife told him they did a very good line in hot-water bottles at the Hotel Paradiso, and any time he happened to be passing, to be sure and pop in and get her one. Probably that doesn't sound very funny; it needs the genius of Alec Guinness to brighten it, and I can still see him and you probably never have.

Now it's half past five and I must get going with the evening work. It's quite nice to be peacefully back at work: I must say trying to keep two very different characters (and different from one's own) happy over

four days in bad weather, is quite a strain. And so, au revoir until next
Saturday.

Very sincerely,

Frances W.

BOURNEMOUTH
July 31st – in readiness for Saturday August 4th 1956

Dear Mr Bigelow,

. . . We went to Horsham last weekend and passed a side-lane with the
post saying STEEP, and, under that, SLEET. I asked Mother whether she
would prefer to live in Steep or Sleet, and (being Mother and therefore
practical before all else) she said it would depend on what they looked
like. I gave up. Next we came to a turning leading to WOOLBEDING.
Take the slightest pinch of poetic licence over that, and what a delightful place to have for your home address. And then on Sunday, when the
Observer came, there was an article all ready for me to cut out and send
to you, based, as this letter had intended to be, on place-names. Every
single one of these names is the name of town or village: the author has
merely put them in a list, removed their capital letters, and played with
the idea that there are so many words in a dictionary. We loved his idea
of the meaning of Bovey Tracey (Bovey is pronounced Buvvy) – but
most of them are good and some are excellent, so I will leave you to
enjoy them for yourself. What can you do with Long Island name-
places? Or place-names? Quiogue – a form of rheumatism accompanied
by shaking; the palsy. Mastic Beach – putty used in sticking wooden
houses together. Rampasture – an aggressive attitude, a posture. Speonk
– a rude noise. I am sure you can find many if you delve into the old
original names, and avoid the made-up ones like Holtsville and
Port Jefferson. I see Hauppauge, and Nesconset, Ronkonkoma and
Sweyze (Hay Fever) and there is Aquebogue (the normal number of
strokes taken at the water hole on the golf links?) and Peconic Bay.

You could get up a sort of parlour game with this for the long winter evenings . . .

Yours most sincerely,

Frances W.

Dear Mr Bigelow,

Before I go any farther, let me breathe a deep sigh of relief that the last show of the 1956 Aquashow has been on the calendar. If this place were a proper theatre, there would be arrangements made for adequate working conditions and hours; but as it is, a swimming pool by day and a theatre by night and the staff working the lot, I find 19 weeks non-stop is too long. In a few weeks, when the galas are over as well, I shall be able to relax and perhaps dye a few million white hairs and regain my lost youth, ha ha.

This has been a week, to be sure. The town has been full of Baths Superintendents, Managers, Deputies, and their Chairmen and Vice-Chairmen. My boss has been flitting from office to Conference Hall and back again; and then, quite suddenly, and without any warning whatsoever, the whole lot descended upon us on Thursday afternoon, in the middle of a downpour of rain and a right hearty gale. They had decided, apparently, to come and spend the afternoon going around the Baths.

By half-past the last visitor had gone, and by 5.45 p.m. we had washed up everything we could find, cleaned ourselves, counted programmes and money, and organised everything ready for the evening performances of the water show. We were, I may add, noticeably shorter, being worn down to the knees . . .

One of my less brilliant cashiers came to my office while I was at lunch the other day and said, 'Oh, Miss Woodsford, where are they to

put the goat?' I said 'Goat, Mrs Allen? What goat?' 'Oh – the goat the
Pavilion have sent over for the Baths to stable for them.' I swallowed
hard, and then after counting ten remarked fairly mildly that if the goat
was too much for the Pavilion to stable I hardly thought the Baths
Department was likely to accommodate it for them, and why didn't she
tell the goat (and attendant) to try the little hut on the other side of the
road where, in previous years, they stabled the donkeys the children
rode on the beach. My cashier thought this was a wonderful idea, and
was overcome at my brilliance in thinking of it. Adding to my own great
knowledge her own wish to be helpful, she told the goat (and goatherd)
to go to the shipping office and ask there, where no doubt they would
tell them where to go. I am quite sure the shipping office manager,
confronted by a goat, would do so. The goat is appearing in *Teahouse of
the August Moon* at the Pavilion, and it is not (I repeat, NOT) being
stabled in the Baths, which remain reasonably hygienic.

We have been dashing around at weekends with my brother, retriev-
ing runaway or just lost little boys on his list of children. Sunday before
last it was Adrian; last Sunday, Malcolm. Adrian is a maladjusted child,
age about ten or eleven, and he goes to a school for such children miles
and miles into the heart of Dorset. He was in the Children's Home in
Bournemouth for the school holidays. On Sunday, then, he got up about
six o'clock, packed his pathetic belongings in his one suitcase, and
set off, stealing a bicycle as he went and pushing the suitcase along,
balanced on the saddle. This he found a bit tiring, so he hid the case
under a bush and went on, pushing his bicycle, until apparently he
noticed another bike he liked better, when he did a swap. When he was
eventually found, he was pushing yet another bicycle – it was about the
sixth he'd had – and following along behind the Salvation Army Band.

We had to hurry with this one because he had, about three hours
previously, been given travel pills which were expected to wear off any
moment now. So we kept a wary eye on his colour and general disposition on behalf of the upholstery. When we arrived at the school,
it was a really ancient place – it was in Domesday, we were told –
practically falling to pieces, and smelling of moth balls, must and
mildew in equal parts. After sitting in the car for an hour or so, waiting,
Mother and I were invited in for a cup of tea or, at least, a warm by the

fire. The little boy played host and did it very well indeed, all his apparent shyness and awkwardness in the car disappearing as he discovered he was not, it seemed, in dire disgrace for his behaviour. He had 'laid the table' – he had brought in a large tray with a big brown teapot on it, four glasses (yes) four white plates, two or three enormous knives, a plate with some pieces of bread, pieces of cake, and lumps of 'I-hope-it-is-butter' on the edge.

The lay sister who was then in charge – the school is normally run by an Anglican Order of St Francis, the monks wearing the usual long brown habit and sandals on their feet – told us a bit about these maladjusted children, the trouble being, in her view, that none of them get enough loving when they are very small. She believed that babies need to be loved for a very long time before they are capable of loving on their own – they can react to affection and love quite early on, but remove that affection and they are lost, as it takes years and years for the habit of out-giving to be formed in them. And these poor little boys all lack that individual love of parents in their lives. She said they had a farm attached to the school, and when they reached the age of 14 all the boys gave good help on the farm. 'You see,' she said, 'it's so much easier to have a relationship with an animal than it is with a human being, so they tend to take the easy way out of their difficulties in getting adjusted to living with other people.'

One thing I disagreed with her over: I did think the child was losing something if he was not told off or punished, or at least lectured, on the naughtiness of stealing bicycles and wandering off without telling people, and giving so much trouble to everybody. If the children are not treated as normal children, how can they get a normal outlook on what is right and what is wrong? . . .

Now to get this off to the post, if I can reach the pillar-box through the gale now blowing. One walks in a horizontal position in order to keep even remotely upright, the wind is so howling-strong.

Yours very sincerely,

Frances W.

BOURNEMOUTH
October 6th 1956

Dear Mr Bigelow,

. . . Yes, thank you, I not only did read the Dorothy Parker poem about various reasons for not committing suicide – I still have it, in the book of her work you sent me for Christmas some years ago. It seems a very poor collection of reasons, in a negative way, but I daresay if it works, it's sufficient. I did myself have a distant cousin who walked into a river with the intent of killing herself, and when the water reached her armpits she was suddenly struck by the awful thought that she'd probably catch pneumonia, doing things like that. So she walked out again . . .

On Sunday last it was a lovely day, clear, sunny, and with small white puffs of cumulous clouds dotted high in the sky. I suggested a picnic, which the family thought an excellent notion, so we had lunch early and set off about two o'clock. Our objective, Bulbarrow. Barrow is the name for an Ancient Burial Ground, and I don't know where the Bull comes in because, as you know, that is something I never *indulge* in. Anyway, Bulbarrow is a sort of horseshoe shaped hill, and on the outer side – as it were – you look down a long narrow valley, with forests on each slope, to one of the Stately Homes of England (ex, now a boys' school). A dozen paces or so brings you across the spur to the inner side of the horseshoe, and there you look outwards over the Blackmore Vale, a wide and fertile valley in Dorset and Somerset which is a famous dairy area . . .

Well, we reached Bulbarrow and found the best spot for parking the car, where you get both views at once (if equipped with eyes both sides of your head, of course) was occupied by about a dozen cars. We were cross, but not too put out, and turned along one arm of the crescent, to park by the side of the road. Unfortunately, as we progressed, we found the place was stiff with cars and motorcycles, perambulators, caravans, religious placards, and thousands and thousands of people, drat 'em. We had arrived right bang in the middle of the last big motorcycle 'scramble' races which take place up and down the side of the hill. When we eventually found room enough to put the car off the road, and had our picnic on the high bank on the opposite side, we were some two miles from the very top of the hill, but still within easy listening of the loudspeakers and eternal buzz-buzz of the cycle engines, as they fell down the hill or pushed themselves up. We had sandwiches and tea, very crumbly cream cake (Mother said it was a nice cake for an alfresco meal, because you could just drop the crumbs anywhere and it didn't matter) and more tea to the accompaniment of appeals for doctors, people who'd lost children, and children who'd lost their parents.

. . . Yes, you may well have read about some Russian woman lifting some small hats in a London shop. It is still simmering; a regular storm in a samovar. Apparently this woman – she was one of the Russian athletes visiting England officially a few weeks ago – went shopping in a big, cheap London store and collected half a dozen out-of-date, and cheap hats. Nobody knows whether she just didn't know how you went about paying for hats in England. Nobody, apparently, knew what language she was speaking for a long time, which cannot have helped anybody. The store has a strict rule about charging pilferers, and they took the same line with her. Once they had discovered who she was, I think they might have given her the benefit of the doubt, but they didn't, and that was that. The charge was made; the Russians exploded. The rest of the team went off home in a huff, and everybody said rude things about the British Government for not stepping in and quashing the whole thing. Now the whole point of the Brit. Gov.'s answer is this: in England, the Government has no say whatsoever about the judiciary. By this time the big store had got a bit scared of all the hullabaloo, and it was suggested (by whom I do not know) that the Public Prosecutor should take the case over, which has been done.

And now, the silly woman – who, we all realise, has only to appear in Court and, through an interpreter, tell the Court what she was up to, to have them say 'Well, we're sorry there has been a misunderstanding, and goodbye' – she is still being held incommunicado in the Russian Embassy; she won't come out for fear of being arrested, and until she does come out, she can't get home to Russia . . . It's all too silly for words and the amount of hot air that has been circulated should keep us warm for the rest of the winter.

Last week I entered in the Football Pools competitions, and one of my three lines got 20 points, only one point less than was necessary to win a prize. I told Mac this, and he was extremely interested and suggested I should use some system or other, by which you calculate the mathematical chances of the teams drawing their matches. I said coolly, 'How else do you think I did them?' Mac was terribly impressed, so you won't tell him, will you, that my mathematical calculations netted 14 and 17 points respectively, and the 20-point solution was based on my initials, plus my age, plus my lucky number? This week I am almost certain to win astronomical sums, as I have done the solutions with a pin. If I win, oh say £70,000 I might even send you a cable to tell you. If not, you'll just have to wait until next Saturday to hear my excuse . . .

Only two weeks to go, now, before my holiday . . .

Yours very sincerely,

Frances W.

BOURNEMOUTH
October 13th 1956

Dear Mr Bigelow,

It is a fine, chilly, sunny week, this week, and people are still swimming hardily in the sea. Others are sitting about on deckchairs on the beach and Promenade, and every wooden bench in the Gardens is filled with people. My boss is on holiday, no doubt revelling in the fine weather and putting off his return as long as possible. As it remains fine the longer, so the odds lengthen against its continuing that way for *my* holiday, so my heart is going down and down into my boots. But it may be kind yet; we shall see.

The joke of this week is the appearance of Miss Marilyn Monroe with her husband Henry Miller at the first night of his play *View from The Bridge* in London. Miss Monroe gave it out that she intended wearing something simple, in order not to steal the limelight from her new husband . . . So last evening she dressed in something simple for this opening performance, and today the newspapers are full of

photographs of Miss Monroe's dress, which in turn is full to overflowing of Miss Monroe . . .

I have read *Under Milk Wood*, and one or two other books by Dylan
Thomas, and I must say I agree with the critics that he is a wonder of
the century. Do you think, when he began to get well known and, in a
tiny way, lionised, he found his emotions got a bit dragged out – or worn
out, perhaps – and getting a good strong drink in him made him *feel*
more sensitively – or made him think he was feeling more sensitively.
And that was the beginning. Next day there was the horrid hangover,
and a drink put that right. And more people trying to dig a little
memento out of his personality, so that he had to drink a bit more in
order to avoid feeing he was being torn, little by little, to bits. It seems
an expensive, and terribly unpleasant way to commit suicide. Towards
the end of his life, Dylan Thomas used to complain of the awful feeling
of dread he had always, and of a tight band of iron around his head. I
often get that, too . . . . . . do you think I'm going to break out into
matchless poetry any moment now? I am sure it doesn't come of drink,
in my case, unless you count six bottles (each containing three wine-
glassfuls) of ghastly wine Mr Markson gave me a month ago, and which
Mac and I have shared with the sink . . .

All for now, I hope you are well, too,

Yours very sincerely,

Frances W.

BOURNEMOUTH
December 22nd 1956

Dear Mr Bigelow,

Your letter of December 13th was waiting for me at home yesterday
when I reached there, together with a small pile of Christmas cards. On
my brother's dinner-mat was one single, solitary envelope! He was so
mad!! Gets furious because I have so many more cards and gifts at
Christmas, and gets even more furious when we try to get him to

acknowledge those he does get. He seems to imagine friendships, at a
distance anyway, grow naturally, like little apples, without any help on
his part. Perhaps his memory is to be so strongly in his friends' minds
that no letter-writing is needed to remind them he is still about the
world . . .

No, no! You mustn't look or feel like Sir Anthony Eden, with your
new walking stick. You look and feel like Sir Winston Churchill, instead.
Much more satisfactory. I believe the right thing to do with a stick these
days (for of course fashions change) is to put one hand over the other on
the handle, and holding the stick centrally in front of one, to lean somewhat on it and look down over it at whatever small boy one wishes to
impress, with lowering look and beetling brows . . .

As a sort of holiday-task I have started on another of those patchwork
pictures, of which you have a sample at Casa Bigelow. This one is for
Rosalind (if I get it finished). Not realising how ambitious I was, I drew
a sketch of the street at Clovelly, the little Devonshire village we all
stayed in one night in 1955. Then there is Rosalind, Mrs Olsen, and me
(pushing Mrs O.) climbing up the street in the morning, watched by an
amused donkey looking over a wall. Well, that sounds alright, but there
are thousands of tiny bits of material to be cut out and fitted together,
and until I started, I never realised quite how many! Would you tell me,
when you write, if you are expecting Rosalind to come and visit you say
around her birthday date. If she is, when it is finished I will send the
picture to you and ask you to give it to her when she comes. That way
you'll both get to see it. Otherwise, if I send it straight to Alton
you might never have the opportunity to say how clever I am, and I
should hate that. Don't forget, then, to let me know when you next
expect her . . .

Tonight when I get home there will be the lovely vision of nothing to
do. No chores, that is. All my parcels are packed and ready for
delivery by hand, or have been posted. All my household jobs have been
finished (for the decorating of the living room I shall leave until January)
and my hair is washed, as well. So I can sit by the fire and get on with
my embroidery, which, now that I am started, is fascinating me. I sewed
it so often to my skirt last night I finished by kneeling on the floor, with
the embroidery spread out on the carpet, tacking the tiny bits of mosa-

ic materials on. I have even gone so far as to have two shades of grey for the cobblestones; one in the sunshine, and the darker shade in the shadow from the houses!

. . . Even if you don't go to your son's home for Christmas, I hope you have a very comfortable, warm, cosy one in Bellport, with half the town popping in from time to time to wish you joy and smother you with mufflers, cigars, bottles of hooch (or whatever you drink: might even be methelated spirits, for all I know) and their neighbourly affection. Anyway, have a wonderful Christmas, and a very happy, healthy, New Year full of interesting happenings and good books and pleasant sights and deep sleep.

And thank you for all your entertaining letters this year; *and* your many kindnesses.

Yours most gratefully,

Frances W.

BOURNEMOUTH
December 29th 1956

Dear Mr Bigelow,

. . . Christmas is over, and we are (more or less) back to normal, although I am still having belated cards arrive, and those we have had and pinned up are still giving us heart attacks. You see, one year we hung them over strings, and they looked like so much wet washing hanging about we loathed it. And for years we pinned them to an old screen only that has now collapsed with old age so another place had to be found for them this year, and some bright person told me to stick the first card with Scotch tape to the picture-rail, and then stick each succeeding card to the one above it, until you were able to fasten the lowest one to the skirting board. This we have done, and they look very gay, if a bit untidy, all along one wall. About once every seven and a half minutes the weight of one or another is too much for the top bit of Scotch tape, and the whole thing slips off the varnished wood and collapses with extraordinary loud noises, considering that it is only a dozen or so cards falling down. Usually, at least one card depicts the flight into Egypt, and features a donkey. But this year, because I am frantic for details about donkeys for my Clovelly 'picture', there is not one in sight!

. . . Everybody in America this year sent me something edible! On Christmas morning the last parcel arrived, and Mother, who was looking at the label, said, 'It's for you, dear, from a Jane Henry, and it says "Cake Mixes" but I expect it's more than that.' But it wasn't – it was two packets of cake mixtures, to our huge amusement and delight. Amusement because I just couldn't imagine sending such a thing to anybody, and delight because one of the mixtures was of an Angel cake with the equivalent of 13 egg whites in it, and although I have for long wished to make an Angel cake I've never a) had 13 eggs to spare, or b) known what to do with 13 yolks if I had a). So now I shall know what an Angel cake tastes like, when we finish our Christmas cake, and our ordinary cake, and the rich fruit cake that was part of Rosalind's parcels. About the middle of February I will report more fully.

And now we come to the New Year once again. I know this year I am making only one resolution, NEVER AGAIN TO EMBROIDER A DONKEY! But always at this time I say thank you to you, I know, for all your kindnesses and all your letters, and for all the fun it is, knowing you. You put a postscript to your latest letter, saying something about it being a mistake to grow old; but so long as your spirit is young, what on earth does it matter? And, believe me, reading your first letter (which was more than a little eccentric, as I remember, and puzzled me a lot) and reading your latest one, one would be justified in reversing the two dates, and putting April 8th 1949, on the one I am answering today. After all, if you do have a bit of difficulty getting out of a bath – it is something I understand is regularly experienced by all young mothers-to-be, and by people like me, with the rheumatics. And it gives your agile brain something concrete to work on, to overcome the inertia in your muscles. And if you feel too tired to go out yachting, or pushing the town around, or shooting poor inoffensive ducks – you have all that much more time to spend reading about the world, or writing to me. And believe me, I regard writing to me as far more important than all the yachting in Cowes, Newport or Bellport Bay, *and* all the ducks in Bombay.

So please don't worry about age: I am going greyer every day, and every day I care less to see more white hairs. And the wrinkles in my face – they are of character, and who would wish to spend a lifetime looking exactly the same? No: if your mind is bright, agile, alert, interested, nothing else matters really. So thank you very much indeed for remaining as young as in 1949 – for the outcome of your mind is all that I see of you, you know – and I hope you will, one day, let me into the secret of your mind's eternal youth, for it is a recipe I should just love to add to my collection.

So on to 1957, and the hell with the calendar, say both of us.

Yours most affectionately,

Frances W.

1957

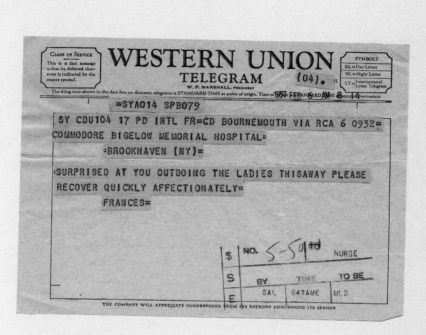

February 6th (p. 241), 'When you had written me about all the various sick females of your acquaintance, and gone on to say you didn't feel so good yourself, I thought you were cadging for sympathy.'

BOURNEMOUTH
January 9th 1957

Dear Mr Bigelow,

The other morning, as I was inching my way between the kitchen table
and the dresser, opening the door to the backstairs with my foot, holding in one hand a coal hod and a large spoon, in the other a jug of water,
and a colander full of bread for the birds topped by a piece of newspaper holding the seed and crumbled-up cheese – oh yes, and with a tin
of rat-poison clutched under one arm – as I was, I said, inching my way
along, I remarked to Mother, 'I don't see why I shouldn't brush the back
steps as I go down in the mornings, Mother.' Mother turned and looked
at me and said, in absolute gravity, 'Oh don't you bother about that, dear
– I'll do that, later.'

. . . Everybody feels sorry for Sir Anthony Eden, even me. I dislike
him as a man quite considerably, and although I think he did the right
thing in Egypt, I think he was weak once he had been strong, and
instead of going right along the canal between the Egyptians and the
Israelites and saying, 'Now we're here, and we are staying here until
U.N.O. does something positive to stop this scrapping', he just stopped
when asked to do so, and then retreated when asked to do that, too.
Leaving, as Mr Eisenhower and Mr Dulles remark, 'a vacuum'. We got
out of the Persian oil fields because America insisted, for the sake of
peace – and then, after a time, the vacuum there became too rusty and
too dangerous. So what happened? The American oil companies went
in and filled the vacuum. Now they are going (not the oil companies
particularly, but the U.S.A.) to fill the vacuum created because, by their
indignation, Eden gave orders for us to get out of the Middle East.
Which vacuum, created by the U.S.A. indirectly, do they intend to fill
next? We do so wish to know. But this is merely being catty, and
getting away from my subject, which was the retirement of Sir A.
I feel sorry for him for, having waited and worked so very long for the

position of Prime Minister, he has now to retire in the middle of such a sorry mess, and it is obvious that the U.S. Government – not the U.S. *people* – will not have anything to do with Eden, and it would therefore merely be a waste of his health, and possibly our future, if he stayed any longer in his job to try and straighten things out. It is an exceedingly sad ending to a long and selfless career, and in spite of my personal dislike, I feel he deserves better luck. And, of course, his going will leave quite a little vacuum again! Heaven help us if we have a General Election and Labour gets back, for you – and I do mean *you*, the U.S.A. will get Bevan as British P.M. then, and then we'd be in a mess, both of us. Aren't politics the absolute nadir!

Mac and I have got in an awful mess over changing our car. We went around the town, and as I believe I told you last week, narrowed the field down to two Austin A30s. One was 1955, £445 and £85 allowed for ours, and the other was 1956, £515 and £100 for ours. Well, eventually one day this week we decided on the newest car, for although it strained all our resources to the last penny, the car had done only 2,700 miles and we felt that by the time we had finished paying off our indebtedness, the car would be worth more. So Mac and I went up and signed the agreement to buy the car for £515, and paid a deposit. Then Mac signed an agreement to sell the garage our car for £100. And we went home, where Mac consulted our car's registration book – and to our horror discovered it was a year older than we had thought! I had visions of being held to the contract to buy the £515 car, with the other one just cancelled. And as buying it with £100 allowed for our car meant we had to borrow £300 from friends, we just could not possibly raise another pound. Fortunately, the garage salesman told us they would not hold us to the contract if they could not, eventually, 'do a deal' with us. After several days of waiting with churning insides and bated breaths, the garage managed to find a buyer for our car, and the deal is 'on' again. All that now remains is for Mac and me to find the cash! We are, as I said, borrowing right left and centre but hope to have paid everybody back by two years and four months, providing nobody wants anything in the way of extras, holidays, birthdays, medicine, teeth out, or suchlike extravagances for that period. My brother says he is going to stop smoking. If, and it is in capital letters, IF he does, this will save him £6 a month right off, and as I am once more to pay all the car insurance, tax and garage (Mac's share of which is normally £2 a month) that gives him £8 a month to use to pay off our indebtedness. He is aiming at paying £10, so he should not find it too hard a task. IF he stops smoking. But, of course, Muggins here is so horrified at the extent of our loans that she at once said she would pay £4 a month towards reducing them, plus the insurance, garage and so on; and as I have no smoking or other extravagances that I know of, to cut out, I am going to be £6 a month worse off from the word go. At least, for six months: after that I shall pay £4 a month altogether. It should not really be quite as awful as it feels right now, for there should be no repair bills for me to find. Mother is lucky to have the carpet and the oil radiator and new net curtains for her bedroom! The rest will just have to wait.

Now I must get back to work: it is a very cold day, but there is a lovely strong sun out and the sea is almost Mediterranean in its blueness. I hope it is as fine over on Long Island, and that the sunshine is streaming in your living-room windows and fading the colours in your hooked rugs, perhaps! No, I don't wish that: I hope it is merely brightening up any dull corners there may be.

So au revoir until next week, when I hope to write you as the part owner of the Beetle.

Yours, insolvently sincere,

Frances W.

BOURNEMOUTH
February 6th 1957

Dear Mr Bigelow,

When Rosalind's letter came this morning I was mildly surprised to read her first sentence, 'Well, here I am, as you will see, at Bellport'. But not more than mildly surprised, as I thought she had 'got to go' to New York when Mr Akin was there on steel matters, and had popped down to spend a few hours with you.

But the second sentence . . . . . . 'if you miss a letter from father for a week or two the reason is that he is in Brookhaven Memorial Hospital having had his appendix removed last Tues. night!' . . . . . . that shook me like the San Francisco earthquake. When you had written me about all the various sick females of your acquaintance, and gone on to say you didn't feel so good yourself, I thought you were just cadging for sympathy. Not that you had any deep-laid plot for doing even better than the ladies. *And* to leave matters so late before you called your doctor! I am not only surprised at you; I am ashamed of you, Sir.

Especially after all the good examples I have set you – moaning to high Heaven whenever I get lumbago or a cold or a thorn in my finger. What did you think it was, when you started having a pain in your tummy? Had you allowed The Can-Opener, perhaps, to dispense with that instrument, and eaten your meals still in their container, which had disagreed with your digestion? Or have you decided on taking up another career, say as a sword swallower, starting with tin-tacks and practising your way to better things. Or did you just decide, as many people do when they retire from business, to dispense with all unnecessary accoutrements, the appendix being one of them?

Rosalind tells me you had a local anaesthetic and that it hurt horribly. I wasn't sure whether she meant the anaesthetic, or the subsequent operation. I do remember Mac had his appendix out under a spinal anaesthetic, and said it was very nasty; and that he was furious because he had been told it was done to avoid post-operative sickness – and he was sick anyway!

Rosalind tells me you are up each day for a little while, following the newest form of therapy. I don't know how long they will keep you in hospital, and knowing your feeling for hospitals, and knowing, from Rosalind, that you are up and about, I cannot imagine you staying there very long unless they padlock you to the foot of your bed – and even then I am sure you would go into cahoots with the gentleman in the next bed and get a file smuggled in, or something. So I am sending this letter post-haste to the hospital, but I will send the next one to the usual address in the fond certainty that you will be there. I have just thought: was all this to-do a put-up job to avoid having to unpack all that ghastly sticky paper off my Clovelly picture? I am suspicious. Also, glad you are doing so well – keep it up, please, and oblige.

Frances W.

PS Your cane should be most useful for a time, now.

BOURNEMOUTH
February 16th 1957

Dear Mr Bigelow,

Well, I do hope you and Rosalind had a happy St Valentine's Day, at home in Bellport, and that the sun shone on you both and made you feel comfortable and at ease and invigorated.

I was listening to a broadcast from America one evening this week, and the speaker mentioned the tug-strike, which might have a very harsh effect on Manhattan's heating arrangements, as all your fuel for central heating had to come across one or other of the rivers, and once the tugs were not working, the position might become uncomfortable . . . You see, once I have convinced myself that you are safely home, and well on the road to recovery, then I can find something else to worry about. I must *like* lines on my face, that is the only possible explanation.

Well, Mac has passed all his examinations. He had an unofficial letter early this week, from the Tutor and Adviser in Social Studies at London University, who has been watching over him these last two years, to say she hoped he wasn't having any sleepless nights worrying about the result, because he didn't need to. The results aren't officially announced until early in March, but believe me, the letter we waved from member to member in our household, to the accompaniment of sighs of relief, cries of 'yippee', and deep felt 'Goods!' I don't think Mac could have borne it, had he failed – as you may remember he was horribly afraid he had done. Now he says he hopes to goodness he's taken the very last examination in his life.

. . . This morning I bumped into Mac unexpectedly in the hall. It was something of a surprise. He had just risen from his bed and was wearing dull blue pyjama trousers and a long, knitted, navy and white striped sort of sweat shirt with short sleeves. It was a garment he removed from somewhere or other before leaving Germany on being released from the prisoner-of-war camp. According to Mac, it was part of the uniform of a Dutch sailor. Wherever it came from, and however he got it, it has shown determination to outlive the entire Woodsford family. At first, it was worn on holiday. Then, in the garden for bonfire operations (practically the only thing Mac does) and now it is sleeping apparel. He looked like something out of the chorus of, say, *Fanny*, and in case you don't know, that is a musical play about sailors in Marseilles, fishermen, spivs, and so on. I'm not sure which category Mac would come in; perhaps a hybrid fish-sailor, say.

And so, leaving you in my mind elegantly dressed by your elegantly furnished fireplace, in your elegantly equipped room, with, I trust, your health restored to its normal, elegant ruddiness, I will depart until next Saturday. I do hope, said she coming back with an afterthought, you were so well on February 14th you gave Rosalind the happiest possible birthday for years.

Yours sincerely,

Frances W.

BOURNEMOUTH
April 13th 1957

Dear Mr Bigelow,

Very many thanks for the cheerfulness in your letter this morning (it is dated April 4th). I had wondered how you were going to retain further hold of 'Clovelly' after this visit from Rosalind and Mr Akin, and now I know! If you run out of ideas, in the early summer when they motor over, no doubt you will be able to claim that they might have a smash on the road and it would be better to leave the picture until they walk home . . . . . . !

. . . I told you last week, did I not, that I had been to see the film of *Anastasia* – yes, I am sure I did, and went on at great length about that fascinating creature, Yul Brynner. Well, in one scene in it he was making Ingrid Bergman walk about with a book balanced on her head, because the Grand Duchesses of Russia were noted for their deportment. I have always found it quite easy to balance a book on my head, but the other day I remembered this scene, and promptly stuck one on top my top-knot. And there I was, standing thinking in the window of my office (it was after hours, in case you wondered) when I suddenly realised a very surprised looking man was standing on the other side of the window, looking in. Rude creature. I took my book off to him, and he moved off hurriedly.

. . . Last night I visited some friends, and while there, they had their television set on to see the Queen attend the dinner in her honour, at the Louvre. It was rather sweet. The French Government had written to England giving a list of the best paintings in the Louvre, and asking which the Queen would like to see. She had chosen a dozen. They then built a smallish room in one of the Louvre courtyards, next to the gallery in which the dinner was to be held, and lined it with pale blue curtains, on which they hung these paintings for the Queen to see while she waited for dinner. There were enormous bowls of pink apple blossom about the place, and lovely furniture from Fountainebleau. And, being French, they added to those paintings the Queen wanted to see, a couple by Degas showing horses! The Queen, seen through the camera, seemed delighted about this. She went round the others quite sombrely, accompanied by the Minister responsible for Art in France, and coming to the end, the President, M. Coty, came up to her and, suddenly, the Queen was lit up – lively and loquacious and full of spirits. She bent toward M. Coty, who bent her way, too, and whispered something to him, then they both roared with laughter. From the camera position we could see the Queen making very Gallic gestures with her white-gloved hands and arms – including a sort of dog-paddle with her hands and arms in front of her, as though she were describing how a dog used his paws in begging – or perhaps one of the racehorses she had seen that morning, and how he pawed the ground . . .

Mother, last night, looking at my arrangement of red tulips and dark green rosemary in a shallow turquoise bowl in the living room, 'Those carnations look just like roses, dear.' . . .

I daresay this letter will reach you before Easter, so here is my good wish that it will be a very happy one for you, and now that Lent is nearly over, your haircloth shirt will leave you in unirritated peace once more.

Most sincerely,

Frances W.

BOURNEMOUTH
April 27th 1957

Dear Mr Bigelow,

. . . On Sunday Mac asked us to go for a drive, and once we were out with him it appeared he was due to take his girlfriend out too. I have more than a suspicion he is trying to disentangle himself, because she was most annoyed at seeing Mother and me in the back . . . we had to pretend an aunt was due at our house for tea, so that he had an excuse for not inviting Mary home as well! Later on in the week he said to me as he went out one evening, 'If you-know-who telephones, tell her we're going away tomorrow and won't be back until late on Saturday evening, will you?' Yes, everything points towards disentanglement. Mac's trouble is a) he will fall for a pretty face, and b) most of the girls he knows are ghastly little snobs to start with, and a) so blinds him to b) that by the time he notices it, the girl quite likes going about with him. Eligible males are as rare as purple diamonds, in Bournemouth.

Anyway, that was Sunday. On Monday we took Mother to her old honeymoon haunts in North Somerset. It was 49 years since she was there, and the dear soul kept saying, 'Oh – that's new!' as we passed cottages or shops or bus shelters. Quite likely she was right. We had a picnic lunch on top of a very high hill with glorious views, as I believe I told you before, but I don't think I mentioned the fact that we were surrounded by little skylarks nesting and darting about and singing their little heads off. Nor did I tell you that as we sat at our meal a young man came down from the peak of the hill, and swung by us on his way down the rest of the 1,700 feet into Porlock. Nothing unusual in a young man, with rucksack on back and stick in hand, walking up and down Exmoor, I daresay. But this young man had a wooden leg . . .

Friday. Friday we took Mother to Lyme Regis, and it was fine all the way, fine there, Mac played golf with a cousin and a cousin-by-marriage and somebody else, and Mother and I sat and made polite conversation indoors. Saturday it was work again. Sunday afternoon I took Mother to Blagdon Heath for a picnic and to paint, but the sun went in, and the view was so immense from the top of the hill I didn't even attempt to paint it, but went scrambling down the hillside in my stockinged feet (shoes are too slippery on steep grass) and picked stinking purple iris and golden cowslips and read Lord Chesterfield's letters to his son. And so home, to wash my hair and tease the cat and so to bed.

Monday followed all too quickly and I now no longer feel I have had any holiday at all. I really must make up my mind to have one at the end of the summer, and *not* act as chauffeuse to all and sundry most of the time.

To finish. Mac is, as perhaps you know, honorary secretary of the Bournemouth War Memorial Homes (instead of a Memorial the money was spent building special houses for disabled ex-service men).* He gave this voluntary work up while he was swotting for his exam, but this week took it up again. Reporting the Minutes to the Committee, he took the chance to say how sorry he was to learn of the death, in January, of an elderly member of the Committee. Another elderly member said, 'Ah, dear me! So that's the reason I haven't seen him at Committee meetings lately.' The Mayor, in the Chair, said dryly that it was an excellent reason . . . . . .

---

* *Editor's note:* Years later, in 1991, Frank MacPherson Woodsford received an M.B.E. for his voluntary work for the Bournemouth War Memorial Homes. Frances went with him and his wife to Buckingham Palace.

Thank you very much for your letter, which broke the long drought of letters to No. —. I was so glad to hear your penicillin troubles were leaving you, and the sooner the better.

So, au revoir until next week, and I hope you keep very well until next time I can make you that wish.

Very sincerely,

Frances W.

BOURNEMOUTH
May 18th 1957

Dear Mr Bigelow,

. . . If ever – perhaps I should put ever in capitals – If EVER I go to Heaven, Mr Bigelow, it will be mainly because I was known to have taken my mother for a car drive at least twice a week without once hitting her! I took her, and a widowed neighbour, out last evening. Mother, to my left, kept up her usual running commentary on the names on the signposts – not the places we were aiming at, but those down the roads we weren't travelling; and lots of oohs and ahs and looks! all along the route. All aimed at me, for of course when I am present no conversation can possibly be carried on unless I am the centrepiece. That is obvious. And in the back of the car Mrs Nixon, doing exactly the same sort of thing – only she doesn't call out wrong names from signposts, thank goodness. She merely talked at me non-stop, and on subjects completely different from those Mother was currently engaged in. At one point I was in such a tizzy I near as dammit stopped the car and said, 'Now let's have a cosy little chat, shall we? And then, when we've got it all out of our systems we will proceed, leaving the driver just enough peace to avoid killing the lot of us!!' But I didn't, and for that, as I said, I expect my reward hereafter. Here, they just drive me insane. My mother you probably find quite unbelievable: I know, most of my friends do, but when they meet up with her they find she is exactly as I have described . . .

Mac goes on holiday tomorrow. It is raining and dull and cold today. We are praying it will be better tomorrow, for this is his first holiday for many years. The removal of petrol rationing has come just in the nick of time.

My boss is away today, thank goodness. He is not well, and his temper terrible, and yesterday we had an overnight flood and half the building was under water in the morning, and Mr B. practically exploded! Thank Heaven I was at the dentist's and therefore missed the first full blast. Thank goodness, too, I had made such a fuss about the water cisterns in the toilets for women that the engineer had put them all in order only the day before – for the flood was caused by a ball-cock breaking off in the men's toilet on the first floor and, this building being so beeeautifully designed by a London architect who doesn't have to run it, that all our toilet overflows go, not out through a drain or even down the toilet itself, but straight onto the toilet floor. Thence, under the doors and down the stairs, across the hall, into the cash office, my boss's office, my office, down through the tiled floor and more stairs and into the basement storeroom, where they just about ruined all the tickets for our water show and three dozen brand-new bath towels which were on the top racks in the store. Oh yes, and all the nice new posters we had done specially to last us through the summer and next winter. This is the second flood due to faulty building design we've had – the other was at Christmas when I ruined my best shoes wading through for help. Yesterday I paddled about in my next-best shoes and you can guess the result!

Ah well. More next Saturday if I haven't drowned in the meantime. I hope you are well, and enjoying all these visits from your grandchildren and great-grandchildren. You should never let a great-grandchild get within reaching distance of a bottle of ketchup: it's a lethal weapon, didn't you know?

V. sincerely,

Frances W.

BOURNEMOUTH
June 15th 1957

Dear Mr Bigelow,

Thursday evening, and I daresay my brother will be very late, this being his boss's first day back after a holiday. So she will trot into his office at 5.14 p.m. (they shut at 5.15) and sigh heavily and start telling him what a terrible time she had all through her holiday, and I shall be fuming up and down the pavement outside here for nearly an hour, I daresay. So, to rest my shattered nerves a bit, I am instead, getting on with something much more useful than pavement-pounding ever could be – writing to you. I am also yawning my head off with the stupidest nerves, as this evening I am to see my doctor and have every intention of talking him out of this silly visit to the hospital next Tuesday, re appendix, which I am positive I do not have. How, my problem is, to tell the doctor he's wrong, without offending him?

. . . Since my last letter, History has Been Made. I met a young (about 25) Spanish student, a graduate in Political Economics who is studying English with a view to entering the Diplomatic Corps, and after chatting a while – mostly, this consisted of a well-chosen question from me followed by a fluid outpouring of words from him, at which I nodded sagely and hoped for the best – after chatting for a while we shook hands, and whilst mine was still in his, it was raised to his lips and kissed! My hand, Mr Bigelow! Large, square, rough, scratched, and useful. But certainly not the kissable type; nor yet the inspiration of poets or song-writers. No, definitely utilitarian. I trust that in future you will be more flowery in your letters, to suit such a romantic lady as me. None of this 'Hi – you!' business in future, please . . .

Now I must get this away. I hope you continue to keep well and avoid taking any more rides in the Dalls' new open tourer – unless you hide under the floor mat at the rear, that is.

Yrs most sincerely,

Frances W.

BOURNEMOUTH
June 22nd 1957

Dear Mr Bigelow,

First of all, to get it out of the way – I went to the hospital on Tuesday, spent all of three minutes with the specialist, and he patted me on the shoulder and told me to run away. Or words to that effect. So all is well. Apparently I have what the man described as a 'resistant tummy'. Daresay I am fossilising a bit ahead of time. Now I am taking all sorts of horrid tablets I have bought myself, to get rid of the throat trouble. I am still losing a little weight, not much, but a little, and that is a worry and until I have resolved my own mind, the loss will probably continue.

The trouble is: what job to do, and where to do it? There is this local job I have been offered. Then there is utter misery at work just now. My brother is most unhappy under *his* boss, and this morning in the car I tackled him, telling him I had heard rumours that he intended staying only another two years and then moving elsewhere – was this true? He said it was. Where would he move to? He shrugged, taking both hands off the steering wheel to gesture Gallically as he did so. Abroad, perhaps. So that's that. In two years' time I shall be left here, with a misery of a job, and Mother, and a cheap flat. Eventually, if he goes abroad, I daresay Mac will marry, and Mother will fade out of the picture one day, and that will leave me with a cheap flat and a misery of a job in a town which is clean, healthy, in pleasant country, but one which I personally dislike very much to work in.

So, today I am racking my brains as to the best for the future. It frightens and dismays me more and more. But if I am to do anything at all about it, it must be soon, while I am still young enough to be able to adapt myself to some other kind of work. Today I am toying with the idea of telephoning my uncle about that tentative job in London about which I heard second-hand rumours last autumn. London beckons me, as you know, a great deal, and I should love to work for somebody I *respected* for a change. In two years, perhaps the housing position would be a little easier and, if Mac did go abroad, I could get a flat near London and Mother could join me there. But these next two years would be very difficult, with living so much, much more expensive away from home, and home expenses to meet as well, and the car to pay for on top of the rest. But it *could* be done, and my problem is, *should* it be done? I, too, would like to go abroad – there was an advertisement for secretaries to the Government of Tanganyika in yesterday's *Telegraph*, but they are only for three-year contracts, and that might leave me high and dry at the end, if I didn't like it, or it me. And then, too, I have to think of Mother: she obviously cannot be left alone. If Mac goes away, she must either go with him, or come to me. Or I must stay here against the day when she will be too frail to look after herself. So I lose weight, and do you wonder!

Never mind: let's off to pleasanter subjects – but thank you, just the same, for your offer of a second-hand, slightly split, appendix in case I might have any use for same! Is yours pickled in alcohol or did you intend sending just the old ruin all that way by itself?

. . . We have been reading of your great heat in the papers recently, and I was just about to write to Rosalind and sympathise with her, for if it was 87° here, and 97° in New York, it would be even higher in St Louis – and then I saw a headline in the newspaper about the torrential rains and floods they had suffered in St Louis, so that was that. Do you sit at the bottom of your garden and dangle your feet in the water? Or is a) the sea too far below the level of the garden, or b) your leg too short? I don't, you will notice, put 'or c) are you too dignified?'

I want you to read the little letter I cut out from a paper first, before you read this paragraph. Ready?

Daily Telegraph Press Cutting
Bees *can* show gratitude.

Some years ago I was bathing off the Belgian coast when I came across a bee swimming in the sea. It was quite obvious it could never reach the shore 200 yards away, so I put my arm under it and it clambered on. I then walked out on to the shore and waited while my arm and the bee dried out in the sun. A dozen people stood round me watching the bee drying itself and straightening out its wings on my arm. After about 10 minutes it flew 200 yards or so away, then suddenly turned and came straight back to me with all the other people still standing round.

To everybody's astonishment it circled very closely round my head three times, then flew away.

V.W.H. Venour, Junior Army and Navy Club, Whitehall, S.W.1.

I asked you to read it because I can't now find the other letter, which appeared a day or two later. This one said, in effect,

I read the other day of a grateful bee, and to show that bees aren't the only insects to show gratitude I am telling you of an experience of mine, with ants. I found an ant one day labouring under the weight of an enormous seed. I picked the seed from the ant's back, and following the insect to its hole in the ground, returned the seed to it, whereupon it grasped it and hurried down to the nest. Imagine my surprise when, a second or two later, a long line of ants ran out of the nest, and forming up on the grass, spelled out 'Thanks, pal'.

And as I cannot think of a better line on which to leave you this week, I will do so now and stroll over in the sunshine to post it.

Yours v. sincerely,

Frances W.

BOURNEMOUTH
July 13th 1957

Dear Mr Bigelow,

. . . We had an official form from our landlord this morning, notifying us that our rent is to be increased by about 50%, under the new law just passed. Mother and I discussed it, and then, as we had agreed, Mother 'phoned the landlord and said we'd had this form and thought it was extremely fair and we were very relieved, as we'd felt awfully guilty for years at the low rent we were paying, and restricted to paying by law.

There was quite a pause at the other end, and then the landlord said, 'Mrs Woodsford! You've no idea what those words mean to me!' Poor man, I think we must have been the only tenants he has who had not either telephoned abuse, or immediately consulted a lawyer, or rushed over to shout at him in person. Far be it from me to wish that we were paying a rent as high in proportion to our joint earnings now, as we did before the war, but we haven't been paying anything like an economic proportion, and although we haven't, of course, asked the landlord for any repairs or decorations, our hearts have smote – smitten? – us quite a bit. Now we feel better, and so, apparently, does the landlord . . .

Yours v. sincerely,

Frances W.

BOURNEMOUTH
July 16th 1957

Dear Mr Bigelow,

A midweek letter to console you a little for Rosalind's so short a visit, leaving you high dry and, no doubt, handsome, ~~behind~~. + Never mind: no doubt you are getting busy for 'Race Week' and all its concomitant social occasions and busynesses. I hope you have better weather for it than is currently plaguing us, for today it is wet, wet, wet and at work we are swamped, swamped, swamped. Damp babies, damp mums, dads with everything about them damp except their language. And, of course, insufficient staff.

There is a cream-coloured flag out in the Bay, flying alongside the buoy that marks the end of the town sewer! I suppose this means Poole is having a Yachting Week, or perhaps Christchurch. Or, who knows, Bournemouth might. Bournemouth suffers from having a wide beach, perfectly safe for swimming, being all sand for its nine-mile curve, but having no anchorage whatsoever for boats or ships, which have to up

+ Second reading suggested the removal of this one word!

anchor and run for safety if any wind at all blows, for they are either blown onto the beach, or out to sea . . . Poole has an enormous land-locked harbour, second only to Rio in size, but very shallow. I haven't been around it myself, only looked at it often from the viewpoint on nearby hills, but it is an extremely beautiful harbour. Mac was there only last Saturday, taking his 'family' on their annual outing in Bolson's boats. 'Jake' Bolson is the son of a man who started off with a dinghy, and died owning a fleet of ex-Naval craft; a boatyard; a couple of shipbuilding factories, and several other worthwhile properties. But they still put all their pleasure cruisers at the disposal of the crippled children, the orphans and Mac's lot, once every year, and a high old time is had by all.

Last Saturday when he got home Mac said he was one short at the final count, but that one might have slipped behind his back while he was talking to somebody who had come up and tapped him (Mac) on the shoulder. Or, horrid thought, the missing one might still be in the lavatory! We thereupon started telephoning all Bolson's numerous telephone numbers in the book, to ask whoever answered if they had found a small boy locked in somewhere. They hadn't, luckily. Mac asked one child how many free bottles of pop he had drunk, and when it turned out to be six, Mac said he was glad the Bay was so choppy they stayed inside the harbour, and merely cruised around the islands there. He also said one child was showing off a Scout knife, and the ship rolled, and the child did likewise, and narrowly missed gouging out the next child's eye. What fun we do have in our jobs, don't we?

. . . Thank *you* for your nice letters, too. I look for the postman every morning, you may be sure.

Yours most sincerely,

Frances W.

BOURNEMOUTH
August 24th 1957

Dear Mr Bigelow,

. . . My brother has a new girlfriend – probably she's 'one over the eight' – and she lives in a very elegant part of the town, in a house just on the corner of a road we pass in the mornings, on our way to work. So Mac has an arrangement with her: she stands at a window, possibly elegant in a peignoir or other sort of frills – and waves to him, and Mac waves back. But, of course, his sister musn't know about this, so he just puts his hand out the window on his side of the car, and turns it up, and waggles his fingers over the car roof and she sees this as she stands at her upstairs window on the far side of the street from Mac!!!! I met her last weekend: she was quite pleasant, although with a rather better opinion of herself than I thought quite mete to display at first sight. She is nearer Mac's age, which is a change, and I think it quite possible that her awful situation at the moment is playing on his sympathy – she has a hole in her heart, discovered only last year, and the doctors are trying to build her up in strength to enable her to come to America next year to have a very dangerous operation: otherwise she will be a complete invalid in a few years. So apart from being reasonably pretty, and extremely well dressed (very rich father, which helps!) she has this tragic sword of Damesthenes or whoever he was, to make her even more romantic.

I trust you have made your peace with the Dalls by now, which reminds me: I have asked so many favours of Mrs Dall I would very much like to send her a little gift, to thank her for all her help in a more practical way than just by letter. Do you know of any hobbies she has? Or does she collect anything? Don't say 'Yes, Dresden China', *please*, I just couldn't bear it. Something fairly simple to find. I should be most grateful for your help in this direction.

Mother is – she says – going to win a competition in which the prize is £1,000 and a weekend flying trip to New York: just fly there Friday, and fly home Monday night. If she wins it – and she has been going to for 35 years, now, without quite managing to *do* it in the present tense – if she wins it, she will give me the trip to New York, so please have that spare room ready, as I should disdain being taken on a sightseeing trip to Radio City on the Saturday, and to Niagara on the Sunday. Waste of time: I'd go and have a look at the Long Island Railroad. Much more interesting, I am sure.

Yours v. sincerely,

Frances W.

BOURNEMOUTH
September 14th 1957

Dear Mr Bigelow,

The sea within the lee of the pier is putty-coloured, and the top surface is corrugated into small wrinkles on rather large, oily waves. But beyond the pier end, it is deep green and dark blue, in lines, with white horses tossing their proud mains + like mad. In other words, the wind is blowing and the clouds are rushing, and the fall is upon us before we have had summer – for we only had a lovely warm long spring. Summer just went down the drain.

To celebrate the end of a horrid summer, I have had my hair waved again. I went to the hairdressers, and as the man stood behind me, scissors poised, I said, 'You know, I have always wanted to have my hair up, in a bun.' He at once gave a vicious snip at my head, taking a handful of hair away with his cutters, and said firmly, 'Now you can't have one.' So, being thwarted once more (I would *love* to look fragile and ever so feminine with a big bun) I said airily very well, he could do what he liked with my hair, and I would not grumble. And now I am mutton dressed up like shorn lamb, and only the fact that I can't sing, even flat, stops me being the twin of Mary Martin in *South Pacific*.

+ well, it's *water*, isn't it?

Anyway, I wore a lovely new dress (from the usual place!) next day, and knocked the office staff cold. I was emptying something in the big rubbish box behind one of the hall counters in the morning, and the hall man was there doing something with a mop and bucket. He leaned over, and put on the electric light, and said confidingly, 'I hope you don't mind me saying so, Miss, but I do like the hair-cut.' I must say I like it myself, especially at night when it needs no setting, and in the morning, when all I have to do is to run a comb through it (plus a little of those feminine touches which are said to have such a whale of a difference on anything) and, at a pinch, I could manage by running my fingers through it. At this stage, in the blissful honeymoon as it were, I do not think about how quickly it will grow out and need waving again! Or, if I do, I quickly thrust the thought from me under the carpet like a bill . . .

You know, Mr Bigelow, I am beginning to wonder whether Mother's general daftness isn't hereditary, in which case I shiver for myself. My mother's unmarried sister has, at long, long last, been able to find a tiny two-roomed flat for herself, and has moved in, to the accompaniment of dozens of letters to all the dozens of members of the Mould family. We were invited to motor over for a flat-warming, and correspondence has been flying to and fro about the possible date. My aunt gave us a list of weekend engagements she had, the last of which is on the weekend of the 21st–22nd September, so we wrote back and said we'd go over on Sunday September 29th. In the meantime we had a postcard from some cousins who live on the way, saying how pleased they were to hear we were going over on Sunday the 15th and would we call in and see them either going or coming. We wrote them and said it was the 29th. Auntie Ethel wrote and said how surprised she was we weren't coming on the 22nd! And now she writes to say it is just as well we aren't, as the previous engagement she said she had, seemed still to be 'on', so she was looking forward to seeing us on the *27th*. (That's a Friday) and by the same post, Cousin Arthur writes to say sorry he won't be home when we call as he is going to Cheltenham on September 38th for a week. I cannot help but feel that the Mould Clan use some special kind of calendar, not related in any way to the Gregorian. The sort of calendar, indeed, that I myself use when calculating when to visit my dentist for my six-monthly attendances. However, we have now fixed the date and have plenty of time to prepare . . .

Yours most sincerely,

Frances W.

BOURNEMOUTH
October 5th 1957

Dear Mr Bigelow,

It is now Thursday, midday Thursday, and I am breathing normally again – you know, in-out, in-out and so on. Up to now, I have been going iiiiiiiiiiiinnnnnnnnnn-o't with a terrific gust, owing to a little amount of trepidation or blue funk over having to take the Committee meeting this morning, in the absence of my boss. But now all is over; the boys have scattered, nobody bit me, and I even managed to drink a cup of coffee with the others, without taking a chip out of the cup with my chattering teeth. Coffee, I may tell you, is served to the Committee before they get down to business. By the time the meeting was over, I was so cocky I asked if anybody would care to see the newly-decorated Turkish Bath – and the whole lot came. So I described the proceedings to them in my best manner, and they were suitably impressed! I got so self-confident I even invited one Councillor, afterwards, to see the plant, which he had said he wanted to see. Unfortunately for me, all set to give my little lecture on Water Filtration In One Easy Lesson, we bumped into the engineer in the first room we went into, and he took over. However, if he did spoil my limelight at least he saved me from getting into a mess, for the Councillor concerned is a B.A. and Doctor of Philosophy and kept asking awkward questions about chemistry, on which subject, as you know, my knowledge is absolutely nil or even more so.

So now I feel relaxed and definitely reduced in tension so that I can waggle my head (if I feel like it) without the top coming off. And I can concentrate for a while on writing to you . . .

Very sincerely,

Frances W.

BOURNEMOUTH
October 12th 1957

Dear Mr Bigelow,

. . . This time, quite casually, in the garden on Sunday, he said to me, 'Oh, by the way – I would appreciate it if you wouldn't talk about Audrey to Mother too much. You know I'm very fond of her; I should really like to marry her but I don't suppose anything will come of it. Her father is a sort of Mr Barrett, and won't allow a man in the house – he wants everything to go on exactly as it is.' So saying, he strolled back to the flat leaving me outwardly serene, and inwardly aghast, so that I have worried and worried ever since . . . Father is very wealthy, and judging by the look of Audrey my brother couldn't keep her in hairdresser's bills, let alone make-up or clothes. Or, Heaven help him, doctors' bills.

I have a shrewd suspicion that my brother is incurably romantic, and this early-Victorian father, coupled with the heart business and the glamorous blue eyeshadow, emphasising the invalidism, has played on his sympathies and feelings to such an extent that he sees himself as a knight errant rescuing fair maiden from wicked uncle (or Frightful Father).

My problem is this: Mac keeps talking about jobs in Rhodesia and Nyasaland and so on, presumably with the idea of marrying the gal and carrying her off on his snow-white steed. Do I help by going off to London and getting a job there and, Heaven help me, persuading Mother to come up with me if I can find anywhere within my pocket, to live? And so leave Mac on his own, with the incentive to launch out for himself. Or do I just sit pat, and await events? If I do, and nothing comes of this marriage business, I suppose I just sit pat again until I am too old to do any launching out for myself. I cannot, try how I may, visualise my brother getting up early and cleaning the grates and preparing the breakfast because his wife is an invalid. It just isn't within the realms of possibilities. Nor can I see Audrey, who is quite a pleasant sort of person, getting down to life on Mac's salary . . . but maybe I'm not being kind nor sympathetic enough. I am all mixed up.

It would obviously be impossible to live with my brother after he married (if) and certainly I would not keep a job and run a home for him if I had also to look after his semi-invalid wife. But the trouble is, that in our family we have *always* looked after each other, especially so where Mac is concerned. Another point which worries me is that if I do go away, from what she said last time the subject was broached, Mother wouldn't come with me, but would stay on in the flat by herself. This inevitably leads to the question, what would I do if she was taken ill? Oh dear, oh dear: no sooner do I pull myself out of one slough of despond than another looms before my feet. Don't think I am grumbling about all this, Mr Bigelow, for I am not: it's too important for a grouch, it really does worry me; and I know it's important because Mac is treating me as though I had to be consulted on every point and my wishes considered all the time, something which is quite abnormal for that young man . . .

Most sincerely,

Frances W.

BOURNEMOUTH
November 2nd 1957

Dear Mr Bigelow,

What, in spite of the date, a birthday gift did I get from Bellport today!!
Never have the seven floors of Beales* been so disrupted, I am sure, as
they were today in my lunch hour, when I tottered around, practically
drunk with delight, and chose my presents from you. Everybody was
most kind and helpful, and chased me all over the building as I did one
thing wrong after another, all due to the fact that, as I pointed out, I had
never had a birthday gift like this one before, and must be allowed, and
expected to mess their organisation up a trifle. So they beamed, and said
of course and how wonderful for me: in fact, they seemed to enjoy
it almost as much as I did. This is a list of the enormous variety of
presents you gave me, and how you knew exactly what I wanted, I shall
hardly ever know:

First, I had decided, as I told you, on a wristwatch. Then today I
decided against it, as it seemed to be more fun to spread the gift over
different ideas, and not keep to one thing. And it would have had to be
one thing, for while I quite liked the very cheap watches, I should not
like to waste your money; and those a step above the very cheap ones I
disliked intensely; and the step above that would have taken all the
cheque, and that, as I said, I didn't wish to do. So first of all I went to the
linen department, and hummed and ha'ed over the blankets, green and
yellow, thick and honeycombed, with and without satin bound edges.
In the end I fell for an extremely thick and fluffy pale green blanket,
with satin edge and a big bow to show it was a present. That was No. 1.
Then I picked out a feather quilt in Paisley pattern in green with peach.
Then I tottered downstairs to the jewellery counter, where you gave
me a lovely shiny black, round powder-compact, with a tiny circle of
marcasite flowers in the middle. No. 3, that was. Next I chose a
marcasite ring: I liked most of all an oval black stone with a surround of

* *Editor's note*: Mr Bigelow had sent a gift of credit to be spent at Bournemouth's
department store.

marcasite, but it only fitted my little finger and I don't like wearing rings on that one. So I picked out, instead, one all marcasite on silver, with an intricate effect of slender strands woven in and out and over and under each other. They tried to get me to buy what they said was a cocktail ring (why, I don't know: it was an eternity ring masquerading under an alias) but it was so big it would have done very nicely for a knuckle-duster, and I don't move in that sort of circle.

Next I moved over to the cosmetics counter where I frivolously bought a bottle of pale cream-coloured mud – you put this on to hide the fact that your skin is naturally putty-coloured mud – and some lip stuff and powder, and a little black and white case to hold all this neatly in my handbag.

After this, weakening slightly, I went to Gloves and chose a pair of black kid lined with wool, for the winter. And finally, after adding up all the others and doing mental sums in a sort of daze, being bumped into by the other shoppers, I went back to the blanket department and added a large flannelette blanket. This is for Mother, and I'm sure you don't mind, but I wanted her to share in my good fortune, and my brother was already accounted for as he will have my discarded quilt and a travelling rug which your green blanket replaces . . .

Yours most sincerely and overwhelmed,

Frances W.

BOURNEMOUTH
December 7th 1957

Dear Mr Bigelow,

. . . Quite casually, as we were going home on Thursday (applications *have* to be made in December or forever hold thy peace) I asked my brother if he'd applied for regrading (one way to get an increase in salary). He said no, because he wasn't at the top-rate of his present grade yet. Had I? This, because I had said I would do so, back in the summer when I was working around the clock. No, of course I hadn't, and the letter had to go before the Committee the very next morning. So I dashed something off that evening, and put it on my boss's desk. He was much taken aback, and very dismal about my prospects, but cheered up a bit when I said I would neither resign, nor sulk, if I was turned down as I fully expected to be, as I never could put my heart and soul into such a letter in the middle of winter, when I wasn't earning my salary anyhow. And, in the event, the Committee were apparently all in favour of it, and of me, and all sorts of nice things were said about yrs trly (which I am not supposed to know about, but heard in a roundabout way through friends at court) and I shall either get a £30 rise next spring, with another £20 the following year, all of which would count as salary and for pension calculations in the event of my living that long; or if the Establishment Committee – a real tough body of men – turn it down, I am to put in for over-time pay, which I know would come to more that £50 a year anyway. So either way, I shall be much better off next year. This is certainly being my year, isn't it?

First of all, I had that enormous birthday present. Then I had my aunt's fur cape, which has this week come back from the furriers made up as a stole, and looks a million dollars and quite unlike me. I just drip silver-fox like Peggy Hopkins Joyce only without so many husbands. One of these days, the occasion to wear the fur will come along, and then a few pairs of eyes will be knocked out of focus, believe me. I am not at the moment sure about hay fever, never having worn silver fox before, and getting a bit mixed up with hair in mouth, hair on tongue, twisted around back teeth, tangled with my eyelashes, and inhaled into my nostrils. However, with a bit of practice I shall grow a longer neck and that will take me out of the danger zone.

Then on top of all this, the Committee business. All I need to finish off the year, is to win a Football Pool and become, overnight, rich enough to wear the fox fur every single day, just for popping down the road for cat-fish.

And the police sent me three canvas-boards to paint on, as I still insisted on 'being stubborn and silly' (their words, not mine) about not taking money for what help I give them on the occasion of their annual swimming gala.

I can't for the moment think of anything else anybody has given me, not even a high-sign or the glad eye or the go-by, but if I do before the end of this letter, I will add it to the list. Quite a formidable list of nice things, I am sure you will agree . . .

Yours most sincerely,

Frances W.

BOURNEMOUTH
December 14th 1957

Dear Mr Bigelow,

. . . We had our first carol-singers this week. A reasonable government, some few years ago, passed a regulation forbidding the singing of carols before the first week in December. Up to that time, the trend was, go around collecting for Guy Fawkes' night, and immediately that is over, swing into your carol-singing. Anyway, I was at home after dinner, and the radio was on and Mother was banging away in the kitchen and the cat was snoring, when suddenly there came this singing from outside the front door. Loud and clear it was. It is quite difficult for carol-singers to make themselves heard in our upstairs flat, especially when our radio is going, but this lot could be heard halfway to Dorchester.

I got some money, and after a verse or two, trotted downstairs and opened the front door to give it to the singers – and there, with his little mouth almost *in* our letter box (the better for the sound to carry) was a small urchin of no more than nine years. Singing away at the top of his voice, with his little red gloveless hands in his pockets! Usually, we get so many little groups, that we make a rule to give twopence each, but I had gone down with sixpence, expecting at least three small boys. And here was one single little singer, with all that power! I gave him the sixpence, and congratulated him and said he'd do well because even without a brass band to help him, one could clearly hear his concert. He wiped his little nose with the back of his hand, tucked his sixpence in a spare pocket, put his hands back, and rushed off to try the next house. Mother was annoyed: apparently when she was young the carollers gave you some more singing when you had paid them; nowadays, what with automation and time and motion study, the minute they are paid, they're off. Could it be that most carollers have little faith in the voices they throw at one?

Thank you for your letter (Dec. 3rd) from which you sounded more cheerful, and more spry, than for months past. I was very glad to read it, but I took your remarks, about Devonshire cream making you sick, with a grain of salt which you may imagine quite spoiled the taste. However, I hardened my heart and refrained from rushing another order to Devon for cream for Christmas for you, as you will no doubt go to a dozen or so (nothing much) cocktail and other parties, and if *you* don't, at least *I* must look out for your figure, sire.

There's been a spate of writing in the newspapers this week, on the theme 'Don't be nasty to the Americans'. Nobody I know has been particularly nasty that I know of, so I can only imagine the snide remarks about the rocket were made by newspaper people being clever with words, for the sake of cleverness and without any consideration for the effect of their wit. We most of us feel that America did give too much optimistic publicity to her efforts beforehand, but that is no more than you feel yourselves; and the nasty shock to the nation as a whole is much too important to be sniggered at. So take no notice of the newspapers: they just love stirring up ill-feelings, as you know. There has, on the other hand, been a certain amount of – I won't say anger, because it wasn't heated, but dismay is perhaps better – dismay at the news, quite unexpectedly wangled out of the Prime Minister, that American 'planes are flying over England in practice, with atomic bombs in their racks. That *is* an uncomfortable feeling, for coming right now, the assurance that nothing can go wrong doesn't altogether have the reassurance it might have had, had nothing gone wrong in Florida.

And now, this week, I will indeed wish you a very happy Christmas, and a very happy New Year with no repetition of last year's hospital todo and kerfuffle. From the newspapers I fear your prophecy as to snow has been more than fulfilled, but just the same I hope it didn't handicap your visit from Rosalind, nor stop you going out and about whenever you fancied.

Very Happy Christmas, dear Mr Bigelow,

Most sincerely,

Frances W.

1958

Mother and Mrs Fagan;
Christmas decorations at the Baths

BOURNEMOUTH
February 9th 1958

Dear Mr Bigelow,

I was particularly glad to see your letter (Feb. 2nd) this morning, for as I told Rosalind in a letter I wrote her yesterday I had a horrible feeling amounting almost to certainty last week that you were ill. And lo, when Rosalind's letter arrived, and it was dated the day I had this foreboding, she put in it 'a year ago today they "dug into" Father'. So you see, I was psychic 365 days late, which I daresay is a most unusual gift although not too useful. If only I could be psychic a year ahead – know which horse would win the Derby in 1959, say – that would really be something. But alas I am only human, and when a lady came to see me one day this week to discuss having a course of Turkish Baths, and asked me what the weather would be like on Friday, as she would not wish to have a bath if it were fine out of doors, I had to admit to not knowing, and she obviously thought I was no good at my job.

Reading your letter, with the description of your full punchbowl, all I can say is that I am not surprised one guest left her hat on the floor and has not yet remembered about it – I am more surprised it wasn't left on the floor with the owner still in it, after that potent punch. What do you call your particular brand? The Joe Louis Punch? If said hat owner still hasn't remembered where she was on the Night of December 28th, by all means toss it eastwards and I will go looking for a cocktail party at which to wear it . . .

We now come to work, in the car, these days by such a circuitous route we must burn up an extra gallon or two of petrol on the way. This is to enable my brother first of all to wave at Audrey, still the Big Love of His Life. We then go down her road for two blocks, and with luck, another girlfriend (oh, way down the list, this one) will be getting break-fast in her kitchen and she too waves at us, and vice versa, as we go by. We then turn at right angles and come back into the road we first thought of, and stop bang on a bus stop (the bus gets *furious*) to pick up one or two sisters who wait there. If the sisters aren't there, we give a lift to a girl in, of all things, a parma-violet teddy-bear coat whose name we do not yet know, but whose pretty face (and coat) attracted my brother's attention some days ago. We already have one girl, usually in a bright orange coat with lipstick to match, whom we pass near our home. My brother never seems to notice any tall dark and elegant men waiting for buses; eyesight faulty, no doubt . . .

Now I must get to work: have to eat some lunch, go out and collect a repaired brooch, buy a very cheap waistcoat to embroider for my brother in the faint hope he might like to wear it, and then get back before I am snowbound again.

Yours most sincerely,

Frances W.

PS No, the yachting magazine has not yet arrived, but I will let you know immediately it does.

PPS Does not my handwriting get worse and worse?

PPPS No need to answer PPS! I *know*!

BOURNEMOUTH
February 22nd 1958

Dear Mr Bigelow,

Last week on my final visit to the dentist, I told him that on considering his argument of the week before, in which he claimed that as some interesting people of his acquaintance wrote very dully indeed, it followed that dull people wrote very interestingly, I had come to the conclusion that his logic was faulty. You may remember, I wrote to you about this last Saturday.

Mr Samson was visibly shattered; first that I should be so brash as to consider him faulty in any way, and then that I should be so rash as to say so! At least I restrained myself until all the drilling was done, knowing that on my last visit only the corners are scraped off and polished with emery powder or something like it. He was, in fact, so taken aback by all this that on Tuesday this week I received the following letter:

. . . . . . Although Aldous Huxley may be no final authority upon our recent discussion, a quotation from his 'reason and rule' at least supports my argument (Had it supported yours I probably would not have sent it to you!). Writing of the artist, Georges de La Tour, who was, he says, a 'visionary', he ends thus:
'it must be added that, as a man, this great painter of God's countenance seems to have been proud, hard, intolerably overbearing and avaricious, which goes to show, yet once more, that there is never a one-to-one correspondence between an artist's work and his character.'
Anyhow, if it doesn't 'go-to-show' you, it is just another arguing point when next you wish to delay the threatening drill.

How's that for an insult? As though I bring up all my best arguments for so low a reason, when all I need do is keep my big mouth shut and I get the same success with less wear and tear on the brain. I replied, taking two lunch hours to compile the letter so that it would simply bristle with shining logic, and from my characteristic kindness, gave him one point for honesty (as vouchsafed by his remark about not quoting Huxley, had it been in my favour) and subtracting one point for the iron mould clearly on his character from his nasty crack about delaying tactics. I must say I, in turn, was shaken, for I know that Mr Samson is a very busy man indeed, and to write even a short note by hand (and what a hand! took me hours to decipher it) must have been a chore.

We have been reading in the newspapers, and hearing over the radio, of your terrible weather. I was trying to visualise a snowdrift 15 feet high, as we came to work the other morning: it seemed to spread right over the store windows up to the next floor; and as for having a snowfall of 58 inches – words fail me. I do hope you had plenty of food in store, and are able to stay snug indoors until the weather is more amiable, and the drive is clear. What a pity Rosalind didn't visit you a week later than she did, then she might have been snowed in with you, and you would have the pleasure of her company that much longer.

I have now read, twice, the article about you in *Yachting*, and have looked with some amazement and much enjoyment at the rest of the magazine. Amazement, in this tax-ridden country, that people can still afford to run such yachts as are illustrated in its pages – although I did notice most of the larger ones advertised were suggested for 'Executives' or 'Corporations' with the hint there that they might be run on an expense account, which is a great help whichever side of the Atlantic you may be. Some of the articles might have been written in Sanscrit for all the sense they made to such a land-lubber as me, but fortunately the one about The Commodore was in clear English (for the most part) and I thoroughly enjoyed it. How you must have chuckled at that letter in the magazine suggesting you would know better, when you had had more experience of Racing Committees!! Does the young man concerned now race with red sails, to match his face?

. . . Mother has (I heard through a friend) now come to the conclusion that my brother wishes to get married, and all this refurbishing of the home is in readiness for his bride, Mother then being asked to go and live elsewhere to make room for her. How can anybody be so much a stranger to her own offspring? Mac and I were both hurt and offended when we heard; the explanation did cover Mother's careful reading aloud to me from the advertisement columns of the local paper, of all the small cottages, tiny flats, and bed-sitting rooms that appear there. I wondered at it a bit, for although Mother is very inclined to read me bits of news (usually backwards) she doesn't, as a rule, include the small ads as well!

. . . Now to go through this for the more obvious typing errors, and get it mailed to you. I do hope you are feeling well, and not doing anything silly like clearing your own driveway or scootering, while this bitter weather lasts.

Yours most sincerely,

Frances W.

BOURNEMOUTH
March 15th 1958

Dear Mr Bigelow,

Another blank month; an especially blank week, in which absolutely nothing has happened except that I have inspired 489,562 times, and expired (up to this second) 489,561 times. Even for me, that pair of facts is difficult to work up into a two thousand word letter, so I must look about for something else . . .

Oh yes, I know what *did* happen this week! Having, as perhaps you don't know, an extremely bad complexion on which I try everything from spirits of salts to handcreams, I read somewhere the other day that the best thing of all was an egg-mask, made from white of egg spread on the face extremely thinly. I always have an egg for my luncheon, so one day I whipped up the yolk in milk, and had *that* for lunch, and carried the white upstairs to a bathroom. Once undressed, I washed my face in the bath (before getting in, of course) and then, leaning over the water so as not so spill any on the floor, put my hand in the cup and scooped up a bit of egg white to slap on.

Well, I don't know whether you've ever given yourself a face-mask of egg white, Mr Bigelow (although the odds are you haven't) because the egg white doesn't come up, a bit at a time, but adheres to your hand in one horrid slippery mess, or falls off just as you are about to slap it on. In the end I just emptied the cup into my hand, and splashed the whole lot in the general direction of my face. About 87%, at an estimate, slipped off my chin and nose, eyebrows and ends of hair, and – of course – fell in the bath. Have you ever had a bath in a collection of floating meringues, Mr Bigelow? It's like trying to catch mercury. By the time I had soaked and washed and the face stuff was nicely set (talk about Mrs Frankenstein!) the egg white in the bath was almost hard-boiled, and what the attendant thought it was when she cleaned the bath out after me, I hate to think! And if you wonder, was all this kerfuffle successful, I don't know, but if I turn peaches-and-cream, or even raspberries-and-cream (that being this month's complexion colour, I understand) I will pass on the good news.

Looking for a number in the telephone book the other day, I came across this man – Reginald Pobjoy. Glorious name. Can't you see him? Not very tall – about five foot seven, plump, with a little moustache and hair parted in the centre. Spectacles, probably gold-rimmed, and a nervous habit of coughing to indicate his presence. Reginald Pobjoy. How could his parents have been so unkind as to so christen him?

Do you remember my telling you, some time last summer, about the little boy who stopped me in the Baths hall and told me he could swim two-thirds of the way across the pool? And that, when I mentioned this to his mother a little later, she told me that her son had given me this item of news because, months earlier, I had promised him sixpence when he could swim the whole width? Well, yesterday he came up to me as I was just going into my office – and claimed his prize! He was absolutely beside himself with delight when I gave it to him, and saying 'Oh, *thank* you! Thank you so much' and so on, he gave it to his even smaller brother to hold ('. . . . . and don't you drop it!') while he went in to swim. That his father was holding a wodge of swimming lesson tickets that had cost him nearly a £1, was unimportant; what was important was that he had won sixpence. I told his father the child deserved it for sheer tenacity of purpose, or for a darn good memory. Later, the instructor told me that yesterday was *really* John's Day. I had given him his sixpence and praise for, at long last, learning to swim: then I had gone upstairs and given his brother two bars of chocolate, one for him because no doubt he would get hungry applauding his brother's prowess in the water, and one for John because he would obviously be exhausted after his long swim. Not only this, but the instructor took John up to the deep end of the pool and let him swim across there, all by himself. Oh, definitely, it was John's day. How delightful, Mr Bigelow, to be so pleased with such simple things. A nicer pair of children it would be hard to find: plain little things, both of them, but so well mannered and so happy, and their little faces shine with cleanliness, like clean plate-glass windows for their sunny little dispositions to shine through.

This has been an extremely dull week for mail: nobody had had anything of interest, and only Mother has had letters – and those from our famous Aunt Ethel, noted for her interminable chatter (is it inherited I hate to wonder?) and her enormous size. Mine has consisted of one catalogue from Holland, of rose bushes, of all things, and an invitation to take part in a whist drive got up by the Civil Defence. Neither item of any interest to me whatsoever, although the roses look nice and I do have two in the garden which could be replaced.

I am currently deep in the making of a spring (or summer, if the summer is chilly) dress, made up of some of that hand-woven towel material I used for Rosalind's apron some months ago. I was going to have only a full skirt, but when the stuff was made, I got ambitious and managed to get a short-sleeved sheath sort of dress out of it, and have lined it with butter muslin. It should be delightful to 'dress up' with coloured accessories, but at the moment it is rather less than delightful as the hand-woven stuff is very loosely woven and every time I put my scissors within yards of it, masses of bits come adrift and float all over the living-room carpet and the moth-eaten bearskin rug in front of the fire that, as Mac supplied it, we cannot discard. So, Mother is hardly on speaking terms with me, the more so as she suggested an old sheet should be spread over everything while I am working, to save her carpets from getting littered, and I looked up and said mildly that I thought we used all our old sheets on our old beds! Poor Mother, she was very cross indeed, and it was some time before I got her to giggle a bit and agree. However, all is nearly finished now, and after all, what use is it to own a Hoover if you can't put a nice bit of litter on the floor before Hoovering? . . .

Yours most sincerely,

Frances W.

BOURNEMOUTH
April 12th 1958

Dear Mr Bigelow,

. . . I went to my brother's girlfriend's home last evening, to see their
new car – an enormous peacock blue Jaguar, very wonderful to look at
and with every possible gadget including one for sweeping away
people they run over. Anyway, as I was saying, we went there and I
expected OF COURSE to be the star turn because of this sciatica. But oh
no, not a bit of it. 'How are you?' said Mrs Fagan politely, and equally
politely I said 'Very well, thank you: I always am', and that was that, she
went straightway into how worried she was over Wendy's weight (she's
the little sister) and from there to her husband's peculiar health, and
then Audrey piped up to say, pleasedly, 'I'm going to see Dr Lucas soon',
as though somebody was going to buy her a lollipop. Between whiles
they kept commiserating with my brother whose teeth were hurting, as
usual, and giving running commentaries on Wendy's chickenpox (three
visible spots, to date, but my dear, absolutely smothered with them on
her chest!). In face of all this opposition, I could not allow even a twinge
to cross my countenance, and in fact, I don't think I'd even try to enter
such competition. For somebody who respects and likes doctors as a
body, I do try to avoid them as practitioners, but this Fagan family seem
to keep them in the house like pet dogs, almost. Father Fagan is once
more in hospital for a check-up, and judging by the symptoms that were
tossed around with the cocktails, he needs it. Either that, or the doctors
are finding life a bit hard on the National Health Scheme and anybody
who comes along with a fat pocketbook is manna from Heaven for
them, and they aren't going to tell manna he's a fit man, not for a long,
long time. I am quite probably quite wrong, and poor Mr Fagan may
well be a very sick man, but I've never met him and am not likely to do
so, so I judge by the rest of his family to the last little hypochondriac.
Anyway, it was a beautiful Jaguar, and they gave me a big bunch of
daffodils for Mother as I came away . . .

I had a card from Rosalind this week, which had come by surface mail
and so taken rather a long time. What a romantic address her hotel had

– 'The Surfriders Hotel, On the Beach at Waikiki'. It should definitely be
set to music.

And that's the lot for this week.

Yours most sincerely,

Frances W.

PS There has recently opened a new shop in one of the suburbs of
Bournemouth, which amuses me. It is a poorish suburb, with nothing in
the least imaginative in the shopping line, and this new store is all frills
and flounces, and they have called it 'Mes petits'. What's the betting the
district immediately nickname it 'My smalls'? It *is* rather a silly name for
a store selling children's clothes in such a district.

BOURNEMOUTH
May 3rd 1958

Dear Mr Bigelow,

Did I tell you my brother went into a shop the other day and asked for
one razor blade, and when the shopkeeper (who knows us) looked a bit
surprised, Mac explained loftily that he was 'trying to cut down on
expenses and one has to start *somewhere*'. The shopkeeper's obvious dis-
belief in this explanation apparently penetrated, because this morning
Mac asked if *I* would go over to the shop, which is quite near home, and
buy him a blade, and of course I had no such nerve and bought a whole
packet! There's extravagance for you, Mr Bigelow – a whole half-dozen
at a time. Cost me all of 1s.8d. it did, too. Poor brother: he has to pay a
£20 repair bill on the car all at once, because he has claimed income tax
relief and has to produce receipted accounts to prove his expenditure! So
you see, he is busy saving tuppence here and tuppence there, and no
doubt will soon have a few shillings saved up . . .

Having been, Sunday last week, around a lovely garden alongside a
river, I thought last Sunday we would make a change, so we all went

around one of the Rothschild estates in Hampshire. Rosalind would
know the sort of terrain it was in, for the estate runs alongside the river
at Beaulieu, and she and I (and Mrs Beall) had dinner there at Buckler's
Hard many years ago, and looked across the lovely river at the wooded
slopes on the far side – the Rothschild place.

It was a very sad visit to me. Sad and pathetic, but I could not make
up my mind whether I was right in feeling this way, or whether I should
be tough and democratic and say to myself, 'Well, why *should* I feel
sorry because they can't afford to live here?' Of course, being me, I am
jumping to my own conclusions. This was what happened.

The Exbury estate of, I think, Leopold de Rothschild is famous for
rhododendrons, azaleas, camellias and orchids. We didn't see any
orchids, but that might be because the place was so vast Mother's feet
gave out before we'd gone far. The house, Edwardian, was the queerest
sort of triangle in shape and not large – probably twenty bedrooms at
the outside, plus a few attics for staff – but it was very ugly. The front,
or long side of the triangle, faced open meadows giving a long view of
the Isle of Wight across the Solent, and there was an enormous salon or
ballroom with a colonnaded terrace in front of it. There were a few
enormous scented magnolias trained up the side walls. No other
furnishing, either inside or out; no curtains, no nothing. The stables
were occupied, and a small wing had cheap curtaining at the windows,
but the main house was empty, with nasty sightless eyes staring in rows.
But the park around was sown with clouds of daffodils, here a mass
of rich gold, there a pale cream, beautifully placed around the trees.
At the edge of all this parkland was the wooded part, in which the
rhododendrons and azaleas etc. were in abundance – and very beautiful,
but not a patch on Stourhead, where the setting is ideal for them, with
the three lakes reflecting all the massed colours. Here, all the enormous
flowers were in woods, and some of them were so enormous, and
fleshy, they made one shudder and wish not to meet them on a dark
night.

The estate was beautifully kept; the bushes well fertilised, the shrubs
trimmed, the paths kept in good order. We found two disused tennis
courts (hard) with a little pavilion shrouded in roses, connecting them,
and a handful of moth-eaten tennis balls inside. The courts had been out

of use for years; one was moss grown, and the other had all the nails coming out of the metal lines. The birds were singing, the river sparkled through the trees (you did get the occasional view) and the flowers were magnificent; it was all planned, it seemed to me, for the family to live in the house, on the estate, for five or six weeks of the year – no longer, just while the flowers were out. Now perhaps I should feel that nobody should have enough money to keep an estate up merely to use it for so short a time, but I did feel it was sad that they could not. And I felt sad, too, that apparently they liked it enough to keep the grounds in good order, even if they could not afford to live in the house at all. And perhaps I am letting my (vivid) imagination run riot, and my feelings were miles wide of reality. Right or wrong, we all felt the place was a bit haunted by Edwardian ghosts of wealthy, unthinking, sophisticated has-beens.

Mac was happily engaged, on the way home, in phrasing little sentences . . . . . . 'called on the Rothschilds on Sunday but unfortunately they were away . . . . . .' . . . . . . 'oh yes, we went over the Rothschild place – y'know, the Exbury estate', which he hoped to drop casually into his conversations. As we reached Beaulieu, where there is a very nice hotel, I said, 'Well, now, we've enough money for one of us to go in and have tea while the others wait outside', which quickly put a stop to Mac's highfalutin airs. As it was the last weekend before payday and I hadn't borrowed even a penny from any of my various funds, I thought we did very well indeed to have enough money amongst us to pay for the petrol and the entrance fees, let alone for one to have tea! That's part of the fun in being poor; you can get such a delightful contrast with imagining what it must be like to be rich. I should think to be rich all the time must be awfully boring, for you would surely never put yourself into the imagined place of the poor in the reverse way. Could you, for instance, ever imagine that silly creature, Barbara Hutton, visualising such a situation as ours – going slumming over a millionaire's estate without enough money in our pockets to pay for tea! It touched my funny bone, and the others enjoyed the point, too. Incidentally, the children we met in our ramble nearly all carried little twigs or sticks, on which they were putting the dropped petals of the camellias – they are cup-shaped, and drop off in a whole piece, so that you can thread them on a string – so that they were toddling around with little wands of coloured flowers, most prettily . . .

Yours most sincerely,

Frances W.

BOURNEMOUTH
May 10th 1958

Dear Mr Bigelow,

. . . Can you see from the snapshot where some horrid person backed into our radiator grid? The car was left outside the tennis club while my brother was inside watching the English Hard Court Championships there last week, and when he came out, this was what he saw. We asked our garage, and they said they could straighten it, but as we knew it involved removing the radiator inside the bonnet, we knew also it wouldn't cost sixpence. So Jemima had a brainwave – suggested we tied a piece of rope through the grill and fastened it to something solid, perhaps the plum tree in the garage forecourt, and then very delicately backed the car away. Mac loathed the idea, so one evening when he was having his dinner and, as usual, was nearly an hour late so that I had long before finished mine, I went outside the flat and tied a bit of string on, myself, but having nothing to which to fasten it, I just pulled on the string myself. After a few long, strong pulls the string broke and I fell over on my back in the gutter, which is quite an unusual place for me to be in, I can assure you. But I had managed to get some of the 'push' removed.

A neighbour came rushing out, literally wringing his hands! An old Jonah, he said why hadn't he come out in time to stop me, for as sure as eggs is eggs I would split the soft metal of the grill. I said thank you, but I hadn't and I wasn't going to do any more because the string had broken anyway. I told Mac what I had done, and later when he looked he was so impressed he tried it himself, only with stronger string and a stronger pull – and he got the dent completely out again! Oh, we are a clever family, aren't we! Mac was furious that the dent wasn't removed when this snapshot was taken – last Monday, but it is, now, so you must just picture the car looking in its usual perfect state. The shadow sitting by the driver's seat is Mother, and I have already taken up the hem of my coat once but it appears from this, not enough. Excuse me while I get needle and thread, and to work . . .

Last night, Thursday, I went to the theatre to see a new all-negro show, *Simply Heavenly*. Rather a mixed-up sort of thing, with some attractive dancing if you like negro style, and some very lively singing and some *very* loud playing in the orchestra pit. Afterwards, I motored to the Town Hall to await the arrival of my brother, with the ballot boxes from his polling station. It was rather fun sitting there in the warm darkness, watching the cars and taxis come sweeping around the drive and up the incline to the Town Hall entrance, where police and a few interested spectators clustered around to see what had happened as each arrival put their result up on the board. Made one feel quite part of the city. I got out after a time and wandered around, just looking and listening, simply dripping with my silver foxes – or dropping, which is nearer the right description for what they do! – and feeling quite pleasantly detached from all the hullabaloo. As you know, when there's any hullabaloo I'm usually in the middle of it . . .

Yours most sincerely,

Frances W.

BOURNEMOUTH
May 24th 1958

Dear Mr Bigelow,

. . . We had a Visit Royal at home on Sunday. Mac and I had worked very hard indeed in the garden over the weekend, and it looked quite lovely, for the weather has not been warm enough, as yet, to turn the moss brown, so we still have good green lawns between the flower beds, and all the bluebells are out and some bright yellow flowers, and even the hedges are sporting blossoms. So I said why didn't Mac bring Audrey along that evening to see the garden. Mac, who was by then all dressed up to go calling on her, hummed and ha'ed and went off. A little later, I was indoors when the telephone went. It was Mac, calling from Audrey's home. Had I told Mother Audrey might be coming? No, I hadn't, did he wish me to tell her or to warn her? Well, it was a little difficult – they were just about to have dinner at the Fagans', and then Audrey would have to change, as she was wearing slacks. I said I was wearing my gardening dress and would have to apologise when Audrey arrived, as all our tiaras were in the pawnshop at the moment so she must excuse us for not being properly dressed. Mac, who was getting more and more pompous every minute, decided it was safer to ring off, and did so. Mother and I hastily had our after-dinner coffee, and were still drinking it when Audrey arrived – still in her slacks!!

Mind you, Mr Bigelow, Audrey IN slacks is the equivalent of me in Ascot high-style . . . The slacks are green tartan and the cardigan to match is the best cashmere wool, and the shoes are handmade, and there is a special rustic sort of wristwatch being sported, to be in the right key. I, of course, was still in my gardening dress. That is, I was wearing a plain green woollen dress that has been knelt in, sat in, fallen in over a period of years. It was clean – well, fairly – but hardly straight out of the band-box. My face was fairly clean, too, but only lightly dusted with powder and a swipe of lipstick. The false eyelashes I always intend to buy and try were where they always are when I want them – still in the shop. And my hands looked, I daresay, as if I had been gardening. Understandably!

When she was leaving after her Royal Tour of Inspection, Audrey said she and her family sit and think of all the things I do, and feel so terribly *lazy*. Not really, all that eyelash stuff to put on and off all day . . . I daresay you can't expect to have bits of pottery, and embroidery, and cushion covers, and upholstery, and paintings, and gardens, and garden gates *and* look like something straight out of a beauty-shop-cum-dressmaker's . . .

Now I must dash out and post this . . . I will leave you with my usual best wishes for your health and happiness, extended on this occasion to include the cats and/or kitten/s, from your most regular correspondent, the

One and Only (Original)

Cat Nori

(*and* a stray, at that!)

BOURNEMOUTH
June 14th 1958

Dear Mr Bigelow,

. . . Oh dear, Mr Bigelow – after all my scoffing at Audrey's father and his love of popping in to hospitals to have a check-over or a cardiograph – he went and died on Monday! Apparently his action (or lack of it in this case) astonished everybody including the panel of specialists who have been attending him at great expense. Having decided that the only thing wrong with him was mental, they kept him under heavy drugs for three or four days to 'give his mind a rest' and at the end of it, his heart just stopped. Nobody was expecting it; he was all alone in his London nursing home and his family here in Bournemouth. I cannot pretend to any sorrow, first as I had never met him, and second, as I did not like anything I heard of him. But no doubt it will complicate things for my brother. Whether he is pleased at this possible solution of his problem or not, I do not know, for he is a clam on the subject. It did occur to me to wonder whether one of the attractions of Audrey was her inaccessibility? For you may remember, Father was heavy-handed and refused to allow men in the house. So Mac used to sneak in when Father was away, and when he wasn't, Audrey would telephone in a hushed whisper. All very intriguing and the sort of thing I *loathe*.

Now it's six o'clock and the mail goes at that hour, so whether or not you have your full quota of miseries and moans this week, I must finish and get this away.

I had a letter from Rosalind in Lisbon; have my 'plane ticket and £20-worth of French francs ready for July 15th, so roll on the date.

Yours irritably,

Frances W.

BOURNEMOUTH
July 5th 1958

Dear Mr Bigelow,

. . . I have unwittingly, apparently, created a precedent in Bournemouth. You know I applied last December 1st (the appropriate date) for a rise? Well, the wheels of Local Government grind exceedingly slowly, and very finely, but at long last therecommendation of my Committee was considered by the Establishment Committee this week, the latter being the one that controls all staff and salaries from high up. And they came to the conclusion that my Committee hadn't recommended a high enough grade for me! Also came to the conclusion that it wouldn't really be very nice to override my Committee and give me what they thought I deserved, so they just passed the Baths Committee's recommendation. Not, perhaps, very nice for me, since it is going to cost me the difference between £40 a year extra, which I shall now get, and £115 a year extra, which I might have got! But I was told that never before in living memory had such a thing happened, so on the whole I am both pleased with the Establishment Committee, and with all my friends at court, and, to a degree, with me. My new grading won't affect me until the 1st September: nine months from the time I asked for a rise. Excuse me while I go out and water my patience, which needs all the sustenance it can get these days . . .

I must post this now. Do you notice I have had the mechanic down to put my space-bar right on the typewriter? It used to jump two spaces instead of one, between words. Now it doesn't go one at all . . . . . . If only the window were not barred, I swear I would tip the wretched thing out into the area, honestly I would. One day when I dust the desk, I will accidentally sweep it off onto the floor and hope it will be so damaged as to be irreparable.

Next week, I shall probably be so jittery about Paris I shan't be able to type more than a postcard to you, so I am warning you not to expect too much: even now, I am having a fit of the trembles and can scarcely hold a pen, and on the typewriter my fingers get a sort of St Vitus's dance and come down all over the shop.

I do hope you are well and happy, busy with racing and cats, and collecting letters from Bournemouth and cards from all over Southern Europe.

Till next week, then, look after yourself.

Yours most sincerely,

Frances W.

BOURNEMOUTH
July 12th 1958

Dear Mr Bigelow,

One day this week, when I was coming rather sadly to work, I met the postman and he handed me a letter. It was from Florence Olsen, and do you know, she said she was so envious of Rosalind, Matt Beall, and me in Paris she wanted to get in on the party and had thought of an idea – and enclosed a cheque for $25, to pay for a dinner for the three of us, with wine, in the hope that she would be able to imagine us having a good time. Wasn't that sweet of her – and won't I, too, have a good time playing at hostess on her behalf? . . .

We wangled Mother, all unsuspecting, into meeting Audrey's mother the other evening, and after we had seen their garden, we went to the country in their car – an enormous Jaguar which has done 700 miles so far. My brother drove, with excessive care which had me, used to him slewing around on two wheels in our tiny Austin, holding my sides to stop laughing and giving the game away . . . Mother was much taken with Mrs Fagan, and was soon showing her all our guilty secrets in the way of old snapshots, so that hurdle is now safely over. The pair of them – Mother and Mac – insisted on asking Audrey and Mrs Fagan in for a drink on our return, and of course I knew all the flowers were dead, as I had done them afresh on Sunday evening, Monday they were still all alive, Tuesday I worked late – and this was Wednesday, when they were dead. However, I don't suppose they noticed much. With the warm weather, the flowers need doing every second day, and that means

18 bowls of flowers a week, and that is quite a strain on me as well as on the garden.

Now I must write another letter, and start the evening rolling. I hope you are well and happy, and enjoying fine weather, bon appetit, and good nights of unbroken repose.

Most sincerely,

Frances W.

BOURNEMOUTH
July 19th 1958

Dear Mr Bigelow,

. . . Sunday evening last, I went down the garden and finished cutting the hedge – that bane of my life. I am five foot four inches tall, and so is the hedge, only the hedge is much thicker than I am, being at least three feet from one side to the other, and nobody ever managed to wrap their fingers around three foot as they might (if their fingers were long enough) around me in places. Now, I can only get at one side of the hedge, as there are garden sheds built up alongside the other side. So, in order to cut the far side of the top of the edge, I borrow the bathroom stool and plant it in the flower bed, as close to the hedge as possible, and mount it. Usually it then collapses and me with it, but now and then it only sinks a foot or so into the earth and, perched on top, I can hurl myself across the hedge and, by holding my arms outstretched, I can just reach the far side of the hedge with the tip of the shears. As you may imagine, this palls after a few seconds, and to do it every other week through the summer isn't my idea of a gay life.

About four years ago it was even taller than it is now, and one day I cut about two feet off the top of the hedge and the family wouldn't speak to me for weeks. So last Sunday when I eventually went indoors, I said innocently to Mother, 'Do you remember that terrific row we had some years ago when I cut off the top of the hedge? Well, get started, my dear, because I've done it again.' Only, this time I have cut off about three feet and the part I have sawn down is now only waist high. It is also raw and unkempt and looks ghastly. I was coming back up the garden after carrying an armful of chunks to the bonfire, when who should I see but Harry the Blackbird, having a wonderful time exploring the raw mess of hedge . . . . . . never knew such insects existed as he was finding in the morass! I knew magpies were inquisitive (acquisitive?) but now I know, blackbirds are too.

. . . By now I hope most sincerely that you will have heard about the Paris fiasco. When I went back to Les Invalides to meet Rosalind and Mrs Beall, only Mrs Beall turned up. I looked aghast, and she said there had been a message on the 'plane as it landed, that Mrs Akin's husband wanted her to stay on the 'plane and go straight on to New York'. So poor Rosalind went off for a night flight wondering what on earth catastrophe had caused this order, and wondering whether you were seriously ill, or one of her grandchildren . . . I will write you at length next week and tell you what I did and saw and where I went in my two days: the first was mostly taken up with accompanying Mrs Beall on shopping forays (you Americans!) and the next day she wanted to 'visit with' a girl she had known in Alton, one Dolly somebody or other, and I didn't feel like tagging along, so I spent the entire day on my own and quite enjoyed it, especially as the sun shone. Forgot to eat lunch! However, all that next week.

Mother would have 'phoned me, had there been any letter from America by the second delivery this morning, so I must just go on hoping that you are well and happy and enjoying fine weather and the yachting which is undoubtedly going on, and that Rosalind's miserably worried flight to New York was QUITE UNNECESSARY! When I left, Mrs Beall was working herself up into quite a nice panic (she's the type) so I daresay the plans I have made to see her twice while she is in England will, like all my others this summer, come to grief. A veritable jinx, that's me. I had thought of cabling you, but it's a bit silly to wire 'Are you well?' because if you weren't, you couldn't answer and that might worry you. So I did not bother you in the hope of a letter, or some explanation from Rosalind which will, in any case, probably turn up early next week.

Yours most sincerely
and   "   worried,

Frances W.

PS Shop sign: 'MEUBLES,
                          PAYSAN et BOURGEOIS'.
My translation: Common & Middle-class Marbles.
NO?

BOURNEMOUTH
July 24th 1958

Dear Mr Bigelow,

Tuesday morning a letter came from Rosalind saying everybody at home was well, and it was Mr Akin's worry about the Near East situation that made him cable her to go straight home from Rome and not stop off in Paris to spend two days with me. This letter was a great relief to me, as you may imagine, for I had been waiting from midnight the previous Tuesday to hear you were alright. As I don't know him and cannot therefore have any knowledge of his good points to offset his others, it will be a long time before I forgive Mr Akin. Don't tell Rosalind this, please: it was bad enough for her to be so worried on the flight home.

    I am so glad you weren't the cause of Rosalind's unhappy rush back to America.

Most sincerely,

Frances W.

PS Thank you for another *Reader's Digest*, and for the Yacht book – nice, cheerful photo of you.

BOURNEMOUTH
August 9th 1958

Dear Mr Bigelow,

. . . Well, I spent Saturday evening, and most of Sunday, with Mrs Beall in London, and we went to the theatre (very bad, acting poor enough to have been outdone, easily, by the Upper Tooting Bec Amateur Dramatic Club in an off-season) and ate at Rules, an Edwardian restaurant off the Strand. We saw the tail-end of the changing of the guard, and went out to Hatfield, where all three of Henry VIII's children were 'kept' when young, and both Mary and, in her turn, Elizabeth were more or less exiled later in their young lives. It was a glorious house, full of many lovely things – a most delicious, carefully written letter from Henry VIII's young son to his royal father: just like any other little boy writing, in his very best hand, to show Poppa how he is progressing under his teacher. There were several pairs of enormous Chinese vases, but the only one I liked, the guide didn't mention. They were celadon green, pale and unearthly, with raised white swags of flowers on them. Now used as lamp bases. And in the great Library, I suddenly turned and looked out of one of the windows, and there below me was the most gorgeous garden you could imagine, spread out one storey below. Very lovely, and all the nicer for being so unexpected.

I also decided that Mrs Beall is a dear, but better taken in small doses for me! She fusses so it eventually gets me irritated and I'm hard put to it not to snap at her when, for the seventh time, she asks if I am quite sure a No. 9 bus will take her to Harrods. As she is inclined, unless restrained, to take the first bus that comes along, for fear she will miss the right one if she waits another second, perhaps she feels that information given her is only given to deceive, and not to help. She also talks – non-stop – in a staccato manner which eventually becomes rather tiresome to my ears – I don't mind the Middle-West accent, and after all, I have an English accent of my own so why should I object to somebody else's, but to have every word made quite separate, and fired out like peas from a peashooter, is something less than musical . . .

It is Friday now, and another sopping wet day. When this goes on for long, and the turmoil and noise all day and all evening in the building never ceases, my poor boss gets almost into a breakdown. Today is his day off, thank goodness, so we can rush around without the certain knowledge that any minute the Heavens may descend on us (or on a hapless customer, it depends who happens to be in the way when the explosion occurs!). I have been issuing tickets for agencies, paying wages, doing returns of takings and cash, washing up, making beds, serving teas, showing Councillors around the building, discussing parties coming to the water show with Aldermen . . . . . . just as I reached that word, a knock on my door heralded in a policeman with a request to see one of the show people. He knew the man was here because his car was outside. So I had to fetch the man concerned, and of course the policeman wanted to interview him in my office, so I shot off to lunch a bit before I had intended to – although it was already my lunchtime, anyway. Then I came back, rushed in to finish your letter, and got called away to attend to somebody who had cut her foot, and then to attend to somebody else who was making an outcry because she couldn't take her itsy-bitsy little dog into the bathroom with her. And finally, at long last, back to say au revoir to you until next week, when please pray for finer weather for us before we all die of duck-feet, nervous breakdowns and plain drowning in depressed holidaymakers!

Hope you, anyway, are redressing the balance by enjoying yourself and fine weather, too.

Yours sincerely,

Frances W.

BOURNEMOUTH
August 16th 1958

Dear Mr Bigelow,

Oh dear! Please don't go getting the wrong idea – I didn't send you that marmalade jar minus lid; it was a gift Rosalind bought for you in Italy, I believe, and left behind in the turmoil of the French Farce. So I brought it home with me intending to give it to Mrs Beall to carry back, and then Rosalind wrote and said could I post it to you, so I did. I understand Rosalind has the lid . . .

The other day I wandered around the Sales in my lunch hour, and bought a length of pale brown wool cloth for my mother, with the intention of making her a dress for her birthday. On reaching home and showing it to her, M. tossed her head and would have none of it, saying it was so thick she'd never be able to stop wearing it, for fear of catching colds, and she didn't need a new dress and for Heaven's sake why did I keep spending my money on her . . . . . . about here, I went out, a bit depressed, and Mac followed to say I didn't have much luck with the things I bought for Mother did I! Quite brotherly, he was, all of a sudden. Well, next morning M. had evidently had a change of mind, because she was all smiles and said she still didn't want a dress, but did I think I could make a coat for her – a summer coat?

So obligingly I went out and bought a pattern for a coat. Saturday evening I cut it out, and all day Sunday, morning, afternoon, and early evening, I made it. Finished up by making a beret in the same material, and Mother went off to dinner in the evening wearing her new coat and beret-hat and looking delightful! She is like a cat with two tails – or was it a dog? I forget . . .

Thank you, in turn, for your nice letters of August 6th and 11th. I see from the latter that you say at the recent Race Meetings you felt, compared with the other committee members, 'dead and buried'. Now Mr Bigelow, a lecture is coming up, so duck if you wish or take your punishment like a man, if you prefer. So old, indeed, as to feel that way? Really, Mr B. you know full well you may be old, but you are not *elderly*, and years are but man-made means of telling time. You may be buried in Bellport and its surrounding towns, but your mind ranges over the whole globe, via books and letters and interests: you continue to be old, if you will (and please do!) but so long as you don't act elderly, there will be no complaints from this direction. When Mrs Beall complains because her private bathroom is ten feet from her bedroom, and pays insurance so that every winter when she gets a bad chest cold she may go into hospital and be coddled; when she won't eat any toast except that actually made at the table so that it's piping hot and soggy with butter; when she doses herself with pills to keep her weight down, and overeats excessively because she has reached the age where she feels she ought to indulge herself (!) . . . . . . then you might say *she* was elderly . . . End of lecture from somebody currently feeling 110.

. . . And now, from one young soul to another (whatever our respective years) in slightly shop-worn cases,

Au revoir until next Saturday,

Most sincerely,

Frances W.

BOURNEMOUTH
September 27th 1958

Dear Mr Bigelow,

Now, if I break out into French from time to time, you will know it's all baloney and swollen-headedness, because I got on so very well indeed at the first lesson. I fear it's after, say, the third lesson my speed will reduce to normal, at which (in learning a foreign tongue, anyway) a snail in throes of rigor mortis could beat me with ease. However, we shall see. The teacher has, to my surprise, a particularly elegant French accent. To my surprise, because his English is covered with a patina of Cockney, or some local accent very similar. As a Cockney myself (though I hope to Heaven not with a Cockney accent!) I always thought it was especially difficult for us to get our tongues around French. Perhaps, as time goes on, we shall discover this teacher spent his early years in French seminaries . . .

Something I forgot to tell you about my holiday: it made me chuckle, and perhaps will have a small effect on you. As you will remember, I took the car. You probably won't remember because I've never told you, but we garage our car in a small lock-up garage behind a house on the other side of the road. While I was away, Mac needed a car for business, so Audrey insisted he took the Jaguar, and you know what they are – once around the gasometer – twice around the Jag. Well, Mac fussed and fiddled, turned and reversed, turned again – and eventually got the Jaguar pointing in a dead straight line with the open doors of our lock-up. From there, it was easy, and he got into the garage with an inch to spare on one side, and an inch-and-a-half on the other. He sat and rested on his laurels for a few minutes, then with a sign of relief started to get out. Ah – you've guessed it, you horrid thing – he was more than an inch-and-a-half thick, so couldn't get through the open door. A bit of brain-searching, and he decided to get out through the sunshine roof. He told me he had even gone so far as to remove his shoes, so that he wouldn't scratch the paintwork, when it occurred to him to wonder how he would get back in the morning. In the end, he left the huge thing outside all night, and when Mother remonstrated with him, said calmly, 'I hid it behind a large lorry.'

Quick News Flash! I went downstairs on Thursday to pick up the mail, lying on the doormat, and came up saying it wasn't much – a reminder to Mac that his driving licence was due to be renewed, and a bill, and a typewritten envelope for Mother. This I gave to her in the kitchen, and came out to harry my brother a bit, it being a trifle late. Suddenly the kitchen exploded!! Out burst Mother, waving her letter in her hand, and crying, 'I've won! I've won!' When we calmed her down a trifle it appeared she had won first prize in a local competition for a recipe for tomato soup. I remember typing it out for her about five weeks ago, and a covering letter explaining that it was a recipe she had used, as a new bride, over half a century ago, to cheer her mother-in-law up when she was feeling ill or out of sorts. Then the newspaper printed items saying they had had so many entries, the result was being postponed a week. Then we forgot all about it, it was so long ago. And now our dear clever little mum has won it! She is to get a complete set of aluminium saucepans with coloured lids, to be presented at home next Monday. As we left, she was flying to the telephone a) to tell her sister, and b) to make a hair appointment. Mac said to me, 'We'd better get cracking over the weekend, wiping a bit of dirt off the kitchen'. I remarked, sadly, 'and to think Mother has had that recipe in her memory all these years, and *we've* never even tasted the soup at all.' True, soups are Mother's strong cooking point, but here we are, after all these years, discovering hidden depths in our Mrs Malaprop . . .

Currently I am engaged in reading Stendhal's *Rouge et Noir* and loathing it. Perhaps it is a work of genius; perhaps it is the best French psychological novel ever written, I wouldn't know. I know only that the characters exasperate me, they are *so stupid*. Do you notice, I even punch the keys of the typewriter extra hard, I get so mad when I think of them. I keep it beside my bed, and read a little each night to make sure I do my daily stint. Honestly, I'd *almost* rather learn French irregular verbs . . .

Now to rush home, change into something dirty, and rush back for painting class. Nice; nobody will ask me to use my brain or my memory.

Yours most sincerely,

Frances W.

BOURNEMOUTH
November 1st 1958

Dear Mr Bigelow,

When we were very small children, on Boxing Day we all used to go to the pantomime at Wimbledon Theatre, taking practically the whole of the front row of the dress circle for the family, visiting kin, and our special chums. One year, Mac was ill and had to stay at home with the maid, and as a special compensatory 'treat', when he was better, Mother and Father took him up to town to see the pantomime at Drury Lane – *the* theatre in the whole of the British Isles for a Christmas pantomime at that time. Now, of course, *My Fair Lady* is there so pantomime will be ousted. However, this was back in the twenties, and the pantomime, from all accounts, was something specially out of this world and Peggy and I never heard the end of it. Very fed up with the Drury Lane pantomime we got over the succeeding years, I can tell you.

And now, all those years later, the same thing is being repeated on a smaller scale, and Mother is the culprit, if that is the right word. Mrs Fagan (mother of Audrey, Mac's girlfriend) is buying a new television set, and was furious when she discovered the firm would allow her only £5 or £10 on her old one, depending on the price she paid for the new one. Mac, thinking the deal had been closed, said, 'Well, if they will give you £10 for the set against this new one, I'll give you £11.' And Mrs F., discovering that Mac wanted a set for Mother, was delighted and immediately said she'd give it to Mother for Christmas!!! So now we have a television set in the living room on top of everything else, and if we buy so much as another ashtray there will be only one thing for it – we'll have to move to a bigger place.

To continue with my tale. The television set isn't yet connected (this afternoon the firm is due to come and do the work) but on Tuesday morning, leaving for the office, I heard Mac tell Mother when it was going to be fixed up, and remarked that it was a pity, because had it been put in on Tuesday Mother could have seen the historic occasion of the Queen opening Parliament. So Mother promptly goes to the grocer for her daily shopping, and moans a bit, and discovers that the grocer has had a television set himself for the past week – so he invited Mother in to see the programme. She does, and believe me, we shall go a long time before Mother lets us forget *she* saw the Queen, and we didn't. She has now adopted a most delightful air of proprietorship over the television programmes, purely on the strength of having seen that one, and goes around making gracious comments on the planning, arrangements, photography, comments, and everything else about it. Mac and I are hugging ourselves for glee! What she will be like when she can sit and watch the darn thing all afternoon every afternoon, before I get home, I fear to imagine. I think she will have a lovely time, though, and am so happy for it. For my own part, I have always been sorry not to be able to see such historic events – or sporting events, perhaps – on the television screen, but it has always gone against my Scottish grain to spend £60 (which I haven't got, anyway) just to see something for perhaps an hour a week, with the possibility of wasting many more hours a week looking at third-rate stuff just because the wretched thing is there, and one feels one must watch it to get a better return for the outlay . . .

Now for the post: I have watched the postman for days but there has been no letter from you; perhaps there will be one this evening when I get home, or perhaps I shall, after all, have to change postmen. The last one gave much better service.

Yours most sincerely,

Frances W.

BOURNEMOUTH
December 13th 1958

Dear Mr Bigelow,

What to write about this week? The probable fiasco of my talk to the 40 Thieves' Wives. In other words, the Bank Managers' Wives Club. When I said yes, I would give them this talk, the date was so far ahead it was like the millennium, interesting but unlikely in our time. But now it has arrived like a dental appointment . . .

The Talk went off, I thought, quite well. True, I got hardly any laughs, but that might have been either because, in my nervousness, I went full speed ahead and all ears had to be bent in my direction to keep pace with me at all, so that nobody had any time to spare for a giggle; or, it might have been that my little jokes weren't as funny as I thought they were. The only real guffaw I got was when I told the assembled 46 females (ough, what a collection!) that in 1862 Turkish Baths were recommended for, amongst other ailments, 'enfeeblement of the mind', and told them that if any of them felt they came in that category, to come along for a Turkish Bath and we could find them *plenty* of company. Still, they were very attentive, most complimentary after-wards, and by the Grace of God I knew one woman there – worked with her for three years during the war, but never knew her husband had gone so far ahead as to be a Bank Manager, even of a very little branch of a small bank! However, I think half the staff must have dropped down dead, and he got the job, so his wife rushed from a Literary Lunch to a Turkish Bath Tea merely in order to hear me, bless her little heart. Oh yes – they nearly stung me 2s.6d. to come in! All the women were paying a shilling, so I queued up, not seeing anybody who looked like the couple who shanghai'd me into doing the talk, and when my turn came, said to the woman at the desk, 'I'm this afternoon's victim.' 'Well, that'll be 2s.6d.,' she said. I looked a little blank, so she kindly repeated it for me, saying, 'Visitors always pay 2s.6d.' I was getting my money out, but thought I'd better put her right, and of course on my announcing, as perhaps I should have done at first, that I was the Invited Lecturer, followed Collapse of Secretary. They gave me a pound box of chocolates in the end, which was very nice and will come in handy to give to somebody else for Christmas!!!

. . . The rain is simply tippling down, and a good part of it is tippling through my office window, where an old ragged towel is fighting a losing battle to stop it running over the tiled sill, down the wall, and onto the parquet floor where it leaves a little white rivulet of stain in the morning. And, of course, I must needs make an appointment to have my hair done tonight, so that it will be all out of wave by the time I get, damply, home afterwards. Had to get it done now, in readiness for the party at the Fagans next Friday . . . I think I've been asked a) to help wash glasses, and b) to keep Mrs Fagan company while Mac looks after Audrey, and her young sister Wendy looks after the 30 other guests. I refuse point-blank to buy an evening dress for the occasion, so shall probably feel horribly out of everything, and having taken my stand on that, am being equally firm (and broke) and not buying evening or even afternoon shoes, but wearing a pair of beige summer sandals. The heck with them – I shall do the washing up in the kitchen where nobody will see me, and for the rest, will curl up on the settee with my feet under me, or as much of them as will go under me, my feet being somewhat on the large size. English understatement, classic example of.

Now, au revoir until next week, and in case next Saturday's letter doesn't arrive in time, here is another wish that Christmas will be, if not gay and merry, happy and contented for you, which is a much, much better wish than any hilarity might be.

Yours most sincerely,

Frances W.

BOURNEMOUTH
December 20th 1958

Dear Mr Bigelow,

. . . Monday evening this week . . . rather in fear and trembling, Mac suddenly announced to me privately that he was getting engaged on Friday. In fact, that he was engaged, but the announcement was being made at that party to which I had been invited 'to help with washing the glasses'. So there you are; I have been happily taking it for granted the status quo would continue indefinitely, and all the while other people have been equally happily, no doubt, engaged in planning otherwise. Audrey is to undergo an operation early next year, or never, for she will not much longer have the strength to survive it, and even now it is a matter of 50/50 odds, poor soul. Mac says they have become engaged because Audrey needs all the support she can get in this time, and he feels he must give it her . . . 'if it should come to marriage,' he went on grimly, while I held my breath to stop myself from laughing. Engagements usually come to marriage, don't they? I thought that was the whole idea. But from the way Mac said it, it sounded very much as though he were saying . . . 'if it comes to the worst, we can always have the bad tooth out.' He also told me what he could manage (he hopes) in the way of a financial help for Mother, and what he had planned about the car, and said, casually, '. . . and I would live there.' What, not live with us, and commute to and fro his wife's home? I am astounded! After all, he could spend 3 days with us and 4 with her, and alternate each week . . . I can only imagine he was so terrified of my reaction he didn't really know what he was saying. Poor man, I had no idea my opinion mattered so much to him, and I am afraid I was so shocked – not shocked, but it was such a shock – that I wasn't as sisterly and affectionate as I should have been. Never mind, I'll ask him to stop at the Fagans' on the way home this evening, and pop my head around the door and say 'Hallo, Sis' to Audrey, and all will be well.

Later: it wasn't really quite as easy as the last paragraph suggested! We stopped at the Fagans', I rang the bell, Audrey came rushing to answer, and I said, 'Hallo, Sis, nice to have you coming into the family,' and gave her a hug. I then thought I'd go even further, and apologised for not having telephoned my felicitations the night before, when Mac told me, but said I was so surprised I couldn't even move! Audrey looked a bit chilly, and remarked that she didn't see why anybody should be surprised, as she and Mac had known each other for eighteen months. I didn't make any further comment, thinking I had done enough harm even by being surprised!

To be honest, I can imagine people being surprised for two reasons. First my brother has been a very gay butterfly and his girls have changed with the seasons because, perhaps as a result of being a prisoner all those war years, at the slightest suggestion that anyone is trying to pin him down, attain a position from which to have any control over him, he shies off like an unbroken colt. The other reason is Audrey's health: for a girl with a hole in her heart, tragically destined to a life of invalidism, to get married, might be thought surprising by some people. By me, for instance. However, I don't know the whole story and it may well be, as my brother says, that they are getting engaged now so that he can give her support in her coming operation, rather than wait to see how she gets on and then announce their engagement. Certainly Audrey seems to be able to order my brother about with a good deal of success already. He told Mother yesterday morning, and I believe she was very pleased about it all, although today she is a little nearer earth as she has apparently been thinking things over. I gave her some money last night for a new dress for the engagement party, and this morning she returned it (all that means is that I shall go out and buy a dress for her today, instead of leaving the choice to her) and she also said, à propos of (apparently) nothing whatsoever, that she didn't think it was at all necessary to buy her a refrigerator, because they were so expensive and she didn't really need one . . . . . . bless her, we aren't going to be as poor as all that.

So, a very Happy New Year to you dear Mr Bigelow, and don't *you* go and get engaged: I couldn't stand it.

Yours most sincerely,

Frances W.

BOURNEMOUTH
December 27th 1958

Dear Mr Bigelow,

. . . Well, we can put it off no longer: the engagement party. You may remember in last week's letter I told you Audrey has asked me to go and keep her mother company and help wash glasses? Well, although I have seen forty summers and a few, I must still be as naive as when I was sixteen, because I thought she was joking . . . . . . By one o'clock I was very, very tired of collecting dirty glasses and washing them and bringing them back clean and collecting dirty glasses and washing and bringing them back . . . . . . was quite giddy with such a dizzy round, so I said I was tired and made my brother take me home. He was furious, as well as not being in a fit state to drive, really. However, we met nothing on the way, and he promptly turned around and went back and got home in the end about 3.30 and woke me up with his noise. The cat woke me up about 4.30 wanting to go out, and Mother dropped something heavy like the flatirons about 6.30 a.m., so whoever may have thought the party a success, it was not me. At least, not after, say 11 p.m. when the glamour of all those crystal glasses began to pall.

Audrey was very prettily overdressed, as usual, in a pale blue satin Empire line evening dress, heavily embroidered with pearls and diamanté and silver-thread. She sported a pair of earrings five rows of diamonds thick and about three inches long. Fortunately her dress was topless, so there were no shoulder-straps to get caught up in the earrings, and no monkeys to swing from them, either. As if all this glitter wasn't enough, she had a pink and gold embroidered chiffon stole in clouds around her. She also wore the engagement ring, quite a pretty thing and not, I should imagine expensive, poor Mac. I wouldn't expect or wish it to be otherwise, but cattily I did wish she hadn't worn three enormous rings set with at least fourteen stones, on the third finger of her other hand! Just for that one evening, anyway. As you may imagine, I am not terribly enthusiastic about Audrey, being rather averse to being so prettily ordered about.

Mac's friends were there in force, and the general opinion seemed to be it was about time he got engaged. He has two groups of friends: the West Hants Club group – they were the ones at the party – and the other group, who were acquired through his work and his family. This latter group is, I think, a bit dismayed by the engagement, whereas the former think it an ideal arrangement. To my horror, I cannot get much enthusiasm worked up, nor show great happiness. With my mind I wish them happiness; with the rest of me I am selfishly watching my own dismal future and feeling very, very glum about it and, possibly as a result, blaming that on Audrey, which I quite realise is terribly unfair of me . . .

Now I will finish this and get it posted. I do hope you will have had a happy, merry Christmas, with plenty of good cheer and visits from all your friends, and a letter from Rosalind bang on the right day; and of course I do hope you have a very Happy New Year, with good health and a sufficiency of sleep to keep you well and happy and full of ideas with which to prod me into a rude reply.

Bless you, and thank you for everything,

Affectionately,

Frances W.

1959

'The sun on one's tummy is *so* delightful.'

BOURNEMOUTH
January 3rd 1959

Dear Mr Bigelow,

Here we are again, in yet another New Year. I was sitting up watching television on New Year's Eve, and someone on the B.B.C. staff said he wished his viewers the old wish 'that you may live every day of your life'. And that's about the best thing I can wish you, I think; and I have a shrewd suspicion that you, of all people, may more nearly live up to that exciting, interesting, and desirable method of going from day to day, than most of us do.

As for me, I have started off very nicely with a bad cold and sciatica, in spite of making an interim resolution in the middle of September, when I had it last, never, never again to get sciatica. That's my trouble – I never take my own good advice. I am still in the throes of painting the kitchen . . .

Rosalind's whereabouts get more and more complicated. I had a letter from Florence Olsen this week in which she said she had hoped Rosalind might have spent Christmas with them in Antigua, but Mr Akin won't fly anywhere, so now she is hoping perhaps Rosalind might stay with them in March. And you say, '? Montego Bay', but Montego Bay is quite a big place, and according to last year's letters it is getting jam-packed with enormous Hilton-like hotels. Anyway, don't you worry: I'll get a letter from her sooner or later, and then I'll know. In the meantime she will just have to go on thinking me rather remiss, I daresay, although actually I have sent two letters and a card to the Hotel Casa Blanca with my fingers crossed.

From the material point of view I had an absolutely bumper, or vintage year. You remember that old song about the Twelve Days of Christmas and what 'my true love gave to me'?

Similarly, my Christmas was full to overflowing with gifts on the same bountiful scale. I had

seven bottles hooch,
 six pounds chocolate,
   five dollars, pairs stockings, pounds nuts,
    four pocket handkerchiefs,
      three tins talcum, bottles hand-lotion,
        two parcels food, hanging-baskets for flowers,
          one fountain pen, box writing paper, lipstick,
            rouge, foundation lotion, face-powder,
              cold cream, and £1 note.

It was grey all over Christmas, but warm enough to sit in the garden, had it been a little more cheerful. Of course, after three days of this greyness it had to break into a chill rain, and it has been wet ever since. I don't mind, so long as it isn't too cold: you and your nice bright cold clear days, they give me chilblains even to think of them. And you needn't tell me the climate is dry and therefore it doesn't feel cold – I spent four days in New York when it was cold, and I froze to death from the soles of my feet upwards, and this is only my ghost writing to you now, so there . . .

I have been rereading Robert Benchley, who always seemed such a pet . . . That, and another Gerald Durrell book about animals, made up most of my Christmas reading, because what with the painting and not being able to sit down very long (the back) to read anyway, and having this ghastly knitting still on the go, my reading has been very poor of late. I am still delving in the Philosophies + of Bertrand Russell, but my enthusiasm lags in the most surprising way after the first thousand pages.

Well, now, this being the first letter of my New Year, I must resolve not to pour out my selfish miseries into your ear, which is probably all too stuffed up with such vapourings already; and of course my usual

+
Philosyphy X
Philosophy
Phylosophy??
Well – take your pick. FW

New Year resolution, to be properly grateful to you for all your kindnesses and your bright letters and for always being there when I want you. That's one resolution, anyway, that I have kept faithfully for the last – oh, it must be ten years at least. Who would have thought, back in 1949 when you wrote me such a rude letter in answer to my first one (and I have it still, so don't contradict me, you!) that when 1959 came around we would still be at it, mellowed by time perhaps, but still dashing off letters at high speed and tossing them at each other with gusto.

As I have said before, bless you for your end of the gust,

Frances W.

BOURNEMOUTH
January 17th 1959

Dear Mr Bigelow,

. . . I loved your story of the dignified collie visiting your neighbours. How angry the cats must have been, to be so ignored. The tenant of the flat below ours, has a little corgi puppy, and you know how pugnacious they are. This one hates Freckleface with a penetrating hatred, and we are forever opening the back door because of the din, and finding Freckles sitting nonchalantly on a step washing his face, with Roger (what a name – I call him Podge) two steps lower, barking and snarling his head off, but not coming *too* close. Well, last night he apparently pulled all his courage together and came right up – and of course, Frecks just slapped him one, and the puppy went howling and screaming down to his own back door. Awful Fact of Life for a puppy to discover – Cats May be Teased, or Played With, but They Should Not be Attacked Unless One is Wearing Chainmail.

. . . We went to the Fagans' for dinner on Sunday and Mrs Fagan forgot to light the oven so that the chicken was red and raw, and the Christmas pudding tepid. We had them home on Wednesday and of course Mother wasn't going to be outdone, so we had

1. Her prize winning tomato soup with cheese, cream and sherry.
2. Grilled lamb chops with fried apple rings, baked celery with egg sauce and creamed potatoes.
3. Peaches with meringues and cream topped with chopped nuts.
4. Biscuits and cheese, pecan nuts, coffee and chocolates.

Rosalind having sent us four half-bottles of assorted 'hooch' for Christmas, we were able to give our guests sherry before dinner, and champagne during the meal. I forgot to ask them if they wanted a liqueur afterwards, which was just as well as we don't want them to get the idea we are millionaires. Thursday night dinner reverted to normal – bangers and spuds with tinned peas. For the benefit of the uninitiated, bangers are sausages, and spuds, potatoes, and tinned peas are horrid the world over . . .

It's a very cold crisp day with lots of sunshine and what snow there is, frozen hard. As you know I don't like cold weather so you will please arrange for a warm wind to come across next week, because I go to London on the 24th and have no intention whatsoever of freezing to death. See to it, please: I am sure you can't have anything else very important to do.

Yours most sincerely,

Frances W.

BOURNEMOUTH
January 31st 1959

Dear Mr Bigelow,

First, thank you for your latest letter (January 25th) and for your helpful suggestion as to how I may win a fortune, by writing up my brother's wartime reminiscences in the style of Jane Austen. Starting, for instance, 'It is a truth universally acknowledged that a Sergeant inspecting the troops is in need of a bribe'? But how to reconcile the Jane Austen style with your advice to omit no bad words, slang or other interesting phrases? When I have overcome that snag, I will get to work . . .

But now, to London, beloved London. I took with me one Dorothy Smith, and as her personality and presence had a lot to do with my enjoyment of the weekend, I must first tell you a little about her. She has been a very good friend of ours for many, many years and is, I should guess, in her early or middle fifties. She is what you would call 'homely', although she has always had, as long as we have known her, most beautiful grey hair. She is one of the very few people living in Bournemouth who was actually born and bred here. She has a responsible and well paid job at the Town Hall acting as Secretary to the Mayoress . . . and knows everybody in the town of any importance. With all this, she is terribly 'Missyish' and provincial. I was wondering on my return on Tuesday, whether my violent reaction against the stodginess of Bournemouth is not, in itself, a symptom of the same provincialism, but oh dear, I do hope not. We saw, in a shop window, a delicious confection of a pink tulle and ribbon hat, spangled with diamonds, designed by Dior, at which I exclaimed in delight. Dorothy looked seriously, and said, seriously, 'But you couldn't wear it in Bournemouth, dear.' She was most hurt when I snapped, 'I couldn't afford it anyway, and I am quite sure that if I could, I would wear it where I pleased and let Bournemouth care what it liked.' Everything we saw, did, listened to, ate – is related to Bournemouth.

One evening as we were eating a miserable bit of egg on toast for our 'dinner' in the hotel (D's economy) and were discussing what theatre to go to on Monday, a man sitting nearby leaned over and said, 'Let me recommend *Expresso Bongo*,' and he and I got into cheerful conversation. Dorothy was horrified; just sat there all taut and unhappy: goodness knows, her expression said, what would happen to my poor friend if I weren't here to keep her on the rails. Who knows, I might have got to talk to all sorts of interesting people! Many years ago, when I was a very shy 16, I used to know a family who had two friends, and we all used to go out walking in the country sometimes, and these two and their friends (there were us and two girls, me much younger than Cora, and three young men) were so witty, and bounced the ball of fun between them so gaily, I used to be both spellbound and tongue-tied. Now that I could at least hit the ball back sometimes, I have lost touch with them all, and it breaks my heart.

On Sunday morning, in London, I wrote Mrs Lucille Williamson in Marianna, Arkansas, and told her I *knew* I should have brought a dictionary to town with me, for there I was, writing to thank her for the $5 she sent me to pay for my ticket for *M.F.L.*, and with no dictionary to help me to find adequate words with which to praise it. I had, as you know, been growing more and more depressed as everybody, and everything I read, confirmed the belief that Rex Harrison was not acting in *My Fair Lady*, but had gone skiing or sun-bathing or just off for a fit of sulks. In fact, going up to London in the train I was reading *Punch*, and there was a joke in it about the faces in the leading parts being so strange the audience had no chance 'To grow accustomed to their face' as the song had it, and the management had been asked to put a noticeboard outside Drury Lane reading 'All Star Cast Fridays'. Well, we went Saturday and there was an all-star cast that night, which made my fears groundless and my enjoyment that much greater. And great it was, indeed. Only one small thing was lacking – the wonderful shock it must have been to those seeing it for the first time, before all the publicity and ballyhoo had made it common knowledge of everybody in England. It was a play made by three things: the music, Rex Harrison, and the wonderful sets and costumes of Cecil Beaton. In his way, Stanley Holloway was better even than Rex Harrison, but his way wasn't completely and 100% suited to the play – he wasn't Doolittle, he was Stanley Holloway giving a wonderful performance on a music-hall stage. As such, he tended to divide the play into one part in which you could almost (as almost as an audience should be able to) believe you were looking in on a scene from real life; and the other part, in which somebody sang jolly songs and everybody danced and was funny, and the singer's personality came out and buffeted you as you sat in your seat in row S and wriggled because your back was hurting! Julie Andrews was very sweet and sang very nicely, and when you have said that, you come to a full-stop. She had nothing of the dignity and grace of Wendy Hiller in the film,* which led one to believe it quite possible for Eliza to be mistaken for a Hungarian Princess, at the ball. Julie Andrews was a very pretty, well-behaved little miss who could have been anybody, but was

---

* *Editor's note*: Frances is referring to the film *Pygmalion* (1938). The movie of *My Fair Lady*, starring Audrey Hepburn, was not released until 1964.

more probably nobody. However, please don't take these comments as being of the slightest importance as criticisms – the play was everything it was boosted to be.

On Monday night we went to see the 'after dinner farrago' which is called *At the Drop of a Hat*. This is an intimate show in a very small theatre, and the props, as a pretty contrast to the enormous stuff at Drury Lane, consisted of one grand piano, one piano stool, and a very cheap standard lamp, the whole surrounded by plain, plain curtains which looked as if they were made of grey flannel suiting. The cast here is two – Donald Swann, who writes the music and plays the piano, and Michael Flanders, who writes the lyrics, does the talking in between-times, and doesn't need a piano stool to sit on as, poor man, he provides his own wheelchair. Here, unfortunately, the 'shock' was again missing, for I knew well about eight out of the sixteen or seventeen songs they sang. We had chosen (well, I had) to see this as being the only possible thing, after Saturday night at *My Fair Lady*; everything else would have been anti-climax.

Now I must finish this.

Best wishes, and don't catch any of your neighbours' colds, sinus infections or just plain germs.

Very truly,

Frances W.

BOURNEMOUTH
February 7th 1959

Dear Mr Bigelow,

. . . In London this week there is an exhibition of paintings done by stars of stage, screen, and radio. Amongst them was one which I did consider buying as a present for the Olsens, but changed my mind on seeing the price. Spike Milligan is the author of *The Goon Show* on radio, which I believe was very successful in the States. It is one of those mad non-sequitur programmes that I enjoy for about ten minutes and then feel surfeited. I should like to see his painting entitled *Semi-mortgaged Property in the Cotswolds*, though.

On my return from London it was a little disconcerting to be taken to task for going away because, in my absence, neither Mother nor Mac slept a wink for fear the cat should die in the night (he had a terrific fight) and then, when he seemed a little better, for fear he would want to go out, and squeak to that end, and they wouldn't hear him and the consequences would be unpleasant. Also, a new ash pan for the kitchen boiler had arrived and neither of them could fit it to the old fitment. They are now sleeping like small babes because I get up and let the cat out, and the ash pan is fitted and in place. Just like that . . .

A most horrid suspicion is creeping into my mind that Mac's fiancée is going to back out of her operation. She said last Sunday, in telling us all about her visit to the London specialist, that it was an easy job because the hole in her heart is situated on the outer wall, and that she would be only three weeks in hospital. Later on, she said, 'Oh, I couldn't *bear* to be away from home when the daffodils are in bloom', which, had I not heard it with both my ears, I would not really have believed as an excuse for putting off, or cancelling, an essential operation. Later, my brother announced that she was going to try to find out how much it would cost, because she feared it was going to be too expensive. I had asked her why she didn't have it done under the National Health Scheme, and she had been quite snappy and said she couldn't because she'd have to go in at the surgeon's convenience, and might even have to go into a public ward with other people! Now Mac says she is trying to get another appointment in London, and this time she won't take him with her, but her mother. If, having got Mac engaged to her because, as it was then, she was going to have the thing done and had only a fifty-fifty chance of survival and needed all the love and support she could get, she is now calling the whole thing off, I am afraid I shall be so angry I shall have to say nothing whatsoever, for fear of saying something I might later regret. After all, both her doctors have told her she must have it done before the emotional upset and excitement of a wedding, and that it should be done at once because of her age, *and* that if it isn't, with care, in about five years' time she'll find she won't be able to get up and down stairs. If Audrey thinks she can hold my brother and have him at home every night reading a good book because he has an invalid wife who can't go out with him, she just doesn't know my brother. Probably she doesn't. Having got over the initial shock and unhappiness the engagement gave me, and brought myself to a state of resignation, if nothing better, this comes as quite a setback. Audrey is, I think, working herself up into a state over this thing – she was describing luridly on Sunday what they were going to do to her. I said, 'But surely you'll be under an anaesthetic?' 'Oh yes, of course I shall.' 'Well then, you won't know a thing about it, so why worry?' Anyway, I was so annoyed with the silly creature on Sunday, believing that in her heart of hearts she is finding excuses because she's scared, I went straight to the telephone and made an appointment to visit the dentist, just to prove to myself that although I, too, might be scared, I could *make* myself do unpleasant things.

Now to pop this in the pillar-box. Last week it was foggy and as I left the Baths I saw the postman just emptying the box, so I ran like the wind and caught him with your letter, and said, 'Don't know why I rush like this, for undoubtedly the poor letter will only sit in London Airport for a week waiting for the weather to clear.' However, I do hope it didn't, and that you got it on time, and that this too will arrive on Tuesday.

Look after yourself.

Most sincerely,
Frances W.

BOURNEMOUTH
February 21st 1959

Dear Mr Bigelow,

. . . Since writing most of the above, I have developed – to go with the sciatica, which I have had so long now I've almost got accustomed to it – a nice little boil or abscess at the side of one eye, and you can guess what happened to *that*. I went to the dentist this morning, wearing a black eye patch and a jaunty expression, and when Mr Samson said 'What the!' I remarked primly that I hadn't liked the expression on his

receptionist's face over the telephone last week when I rang up to
cancel my appointment because a cashier was ill, so I didn't intend
to give her another chance to say 'Oh, she'll seize any opportunity to
cancel an appointment', so there I was. When I left, Mr Samson
suggested he would prefer to see me next week wearing my usual rose-
coloured spectacles, because I really wasn't the pirate type, and naturally
I practically screamed with delight at his suggestion, and kicked myself
for not thinking of it before . . .

  What ghastly bad luck Mr Dulles is having. As you probably know, his
policies are generally, in Europe, regarded with horror and loathing, and
as the man whose ideas they are, he is, to put it mildly, not popular. But
now that he is so ill, none of the papers I have seen has mentioned a
single word against him, and they have all gone out of their way to praise
the tenacity and integrity of his character, and the way he has fought
against this ill health for so long. I daresay it is all part and parcel of the
policy of not hitting an adversary when he is down, but it doesn't always
hold good these days, especially in politics and in journalism. I watched
the *Small World* interview on television the other evening, between Mr
Truman and Lord Attlee, and was reminded of it, when news of Mr
Dulles came through, for Lord Attlee remarked that in American politics
you never knew who was going to be the next Head of the State, and
therefore it was never possible to train somebody for the job. For, of
course, Mr Dulles doesn't seem to have anybody trained to do his job –
nor has he ever given any signs of intending anybody else *could* do it; but
in the long run surely this is a short-sighted policy, because we all pop off
in the end and it's very bad management to leave a vacuum behind us
that is too large for Nature to fill without indigestion. I was disappointed
in this *Small World* interview: I had expected more devastating frankness
from Mr Truman, and had not expected so wide a grin, nor so squeaky a
voice and so obvious an intention of 'being pally' as was displayed by
Lord Attlee. I am told his voice was not previously so high, and had probably been affected by the slight stroke he had suffered some time ago, but
I still feel that, of the two, Mr Truman had more natural dignity. And
again, Truman had his study as a background; Ed Murrow had well-filled
bookshelves – and poor Attlee had a large bit of plain curtaining, and a
tray of tea-things! We *did* look poverty-struck, I must say!

. . . I told Mr Samson, who knows the family, that Audrey Fagan had asked me to tell him she was engaged, when I was there this morning . . . When, quite casually, I said something about my brother, Mr Samson could not hide his surprise, and said *he* thought Audrey could not make up her mind which of two men she knew, to marry. I said he was certainly thinking of two other men, probably in Audrey's pre-Frank experience, but it gives furiously to think, doesn't it! How wonderful to have two at a time anxious to marry one, and not being able to make up one's mind one way or another. Apparently she made it up a third way, in the end. Anyway, Audrey rang me at the office today to ask how my face was, and to tell me she was, after all, having the heart op. Now due to go to hospital the first week in March, and to stay about five weeks; so that's that, and I, like poor Audrey, will be glad when, say, the second week in March is over, and she has had the preliminaries and the main bout and has then only to get well again.

Oh – great news, the sun has twice appeared this morning, for the first time for nearly three weeks. It's amazing what a difference it makes to one's cheerfulness, and as it is just this second shining again, I will finish this letter off and post it while, like the sun, I feel cheerful, and hope when you read this you will wear a matching cheerfulness.

Yours most sincerely,

Frances W.

BOURNEMOUTH
March 14th 1959

Dear Mr Bigelow,

. . . This week, Mac has gone up to London (4 a.m. and if you think he didn't see that the whole household was awake to see him off, you don't know my brother) to be there and sit chewing his fingernails for eight hours while they deep-freeze, operate on, and unfreeze Audrey. What good he thinks he will do, I haven't a clue. However, he has taken with him a tiny basket, made in purple and yellow and green, and filled with a little polythene beaker. I cut all around the beaker, down to a depth of about one and a half inches, and then turned all this down, so that as the frills I had made tried to bend back, they came into the edge of the basket and were held firm. This held water, as the basket did not. Next, remembering that tiny black cat I sent you, I bought another one and sewed him to the edge of the basket, sitting at one side where the handle came up. Then, about thirty little silver horseshoes were sewn around the edge and up and down the handle, or hanging like catkins on tiny twigs. Once again, I filled the container with moss, and into this stuck short mauve and yellow freesias. I tried to get white heather but there wasn't any, and as it took me two whole lunch hours to get the other ingredients, I gave up and bought freesias because they look lovely, and smell delicious, and when Audrey comes around she won't feel like looking at anything, but she will still be able to smell.

He rang us about half past six, to say the operation had been successful and essential, as Audrey had a hole about two inches long in her heart. Now the 48 hours immediately after the surgery will be the crucial ones, but we all hope that Audrey will realise that if she can but stick the pain, the future is bright for her. Mac sounded as though he was about ready for a hospital bed himself! That's the trouble with men: they are so brave in battle when there are no women about, and go so to pieces when some female person is handy to take the responsibility! Mac's usual method of dealing with a crisis is to drink too much, which may help him temporarily, but is never a solution to anything, really. He picked me up at the Murrays' Saturday evening, very solemn and dignified and not speaking to his sister (nothing unusual) but it wasn't until he got in the car and tried to start it a) by turning off the heater, and b) by pulling out the choke, that I realised anything was wrong . . .

All for now: I shall go up and see Audrey myself on Sunday the 22nd, and stay until Tuesday to visit Lucia Watson, from Alton, who will be there for a couple of days on her way around the world.

I hope you are well and hale and hearty, also duly optimistic in this fine spring weather we are having.

Yours most sincerely,

Frances W.

BOURNEMOUTH
March 21st 1959

Dear Mr Bigelow,

. . . Last Monday at French class, before we finished the lesson, the teacher read out the results of the end-of-the-year test we had taken, the week before. The marks ranged from 45, to 66, gained by the woman with the photographic memory; 72, the little coloured woman who sits in front of me and is a wizard at grammar and parts of speech; to 81, a man who has a good knowledge of French but comes to the beginners' class because his wife is starting there. This having been done, and everybody having congratulated Mr Boothe, we go on with something else. Suddenly, one of the other students said, 'Mr Watts – you haven't told us how many marks Miss Woodsford got.' Mr Watts looked up and remarked mildly that he'd had several very poor papers. This coming home to roost, I suggested that he'd said enough and let's get back to work. This made no difference to Mr Watts, who continued browsing through his records. Eventually he found it, and said, 'I feel sure I gave you Miss Woodsford's marks – she got 86 and was top.'

!!!!!!

. . . Latest newsflash. I have just come into my office after talking in the hall with a very small customer who is learning to swim. She tells me she is now learning the creep. *And*, so far as I know, she is no relation of my mother's . . .

Now, I must get back to work. I do hope your cold weather has passed, and that you will have a fine, crisp, sunny Easter; and, of course, hope that the Easter 'egg' will arrive in good shape and be acceptable as a token of my respectful esteem and good wishes.

Yours most sincerely,

Frances W.

BOURNEMOUTH
April 25th 1959

Dear Mr Bigelow,

This week I have been glancing through some of your old letters, and quite fascinating reading they have made, and I must thank you again (out of date, it is usually the one New Year resolution I do keep) for taking so much trouble over writing to me . . .

What a to-do about Dame Margot Fonteyn!* I had no idea the nation as a whole was so proud of her, and although Latin-American politics are right beyond my ken (except that vaguely I disapprove of them) I am glad the public opinion over here was strong enough to force the musical-comedy police in Panama to release her so promptly. I know we always tend to think of the nations around that part of the world as being childish, theatrical – musical-comedy, as I said – but I daresay it feels just as painful to be shot by a musical-comedy policeman as by a serious one in a more Nordic country. That horrid man, Aneurin Bevan, said in the House yesterday that 'The British public, having seen her in the role of the swan, did not appreciate seeing her in the role of a decoy duck', which I thought was very witty and quite true. I think it is very fortunate these days that a law was passed here several years ago, to ensure that when British Nationals married citizens of other countries, they did not automatically lose their British Nationality. After all, girls who married G.I.'s and found their marriages foundered, are always regarded as being English (or British, if you prefer) and looked at a little askance by Americans who may dislike my fellow countrywomen, and automatically regard the break-up of such marriages as being the Britisher's fault. And I am sure an Englishwoman married to a Spaniard or Italian or Frenchman, who got involved in police proceedings, would suffer the same way – however long she had lived in her husband's country she would still be looked upon as a foreigner. That being so, I think it is right that she should have what protection she can get

* *Editor's note*: the British ballerina had been detained in a Panama City jail following the disappearance of her husband, Dr Roberto Arias, who was suspected of planning a coup against the government of President Ernesto de la Guarda.

from the country she is regarded as belonging to. Or do I get too involved? ·

. . . And now to go out and prowl around to see that all is well, which I hope you are, and will remain so until I can so abjure you again, next week.

Yours most sincerely,

Frances W.

BOURNEMOUTH
April – no, May 2nd 1959

Dear Mr Bigelow,

There is a nasty niggling feeling in the back of my mind this week that you aren't well. I'm hoping that it is just indigestion and without any foundation in fact. Anyway, as I am starting this letter midday Tuesday, no doubt my fears will be allayed before it is time to post it.

Last weekend I went with my brother to his tennis club, where each year are played the All England Hard Court Championships. I saw the women's finals, and most of the men's finals as well, leaving at 1.15 p.m. to go home for luncheon, my brother staying behind for another hour and a half to the bitter end. You will see from this blasphemous behaviour on my part that I am not such a fan of any sort of sport that I am willing to go without my lunch for it!

. . . Anyway, I was confirmed once more in my firmly held belief that sport is sport and should be enjoyed, and never confused with war, national pride, face-saving, or a spirit of I-hate-you-let-me-do-you-down-ishness. If you lost a race in your yachting career, I daresay that private-ly you were disappointed, but it wasn't the end of the world, and I doubt very much whether you went into training, spent long hours studying your opponents' tactics in order to circumvent them – in short, you did not rearrange your whole life merely in order to beat them. I am, I fear, very rude when people come to me and ask for subscriptions to start some sort of body or another to train more and more youngsters to top standard, so that we may win another couple of bronze medals at the next Olympic Games and so come that much nearer the records held by your nation and Russia. I couldn't care less, as the saying goes, who owns the medals, or holds the records . . .

Last weekend I sprayed my rose bushes once more. It is a task which is done regularly, like winding clocks or changing babies. I was finishing the last bit of fluid by spraying it over a large, thick, bush of veronica which is soon to be smothered with pink and white roses which for years have used it as a prop. Suddenly there was a terrific bit of hysteria and beating of wings, and out of the bush flew a blackbird. On looking closely inside the bush, I found a nest with two nice warm eggs in it. Well, since then I have been most careful, and each morning when I go down the garden to put food out for the birds, I go three sides of a square to reach the lawn without passing close to this bush – and in spite of such kindness on my part, the silly bird flies off in a tizzy every morning. Mother says she doesn't, when she goes down. And certainly she doesn't turn a feather when the cat goes and sits bang underneath the nest. But me, I remain the villain of the piece, come what may. I hope the eggs hatch out satisfactorily, after such sudden spells of chill.

Our cuckoo is back. I heard him in our garden – wretch, I hope the blackbird was safely in position – on Wednesday morning, as I went down the steps, and called out to ask Mother if she had heard him. And she hadn't! First time for years I've beaten her to it, and she was much put out.

While I remember, don't feel hurt when Rosalind rushes out and gets herself fitted behind the steering-wheel of your car. She hated it when I drove, when we went on that touring holiday together years ago. You should just sit there at her side and bow graciously to the public as you pass, for it isn't often enough these days you have so charming a chauffeuse, and you should make the most of the chances when you get them . . .

Which is the end for this week. I sincerely hope that by next week I shan't still be labouring under a 'hunch'.

Yours most sincerely,

Frances W.

BOURNEMOUTH
June 27th 1959

Dear Mr Bigelow,

. . . The How-Harassed-Can-One-Get Dept. On Wednesday evening, my brother asked me if I could possibly mend a shirt of his. The shirt had a sort of strip of knitted ribbing around the waist, and the elasticity of this had long since departed. So on Thursday I bought a length of very wide elastic used for edging lumber jackets and things like that. Immediately after dinner on Thursday, Mac took off the offending shirt, draped it negligently over the back of his armchair, and went to sleep in the chair in his undervest (unlike his sister, who always drinks her tea with her little finger cocked, my brother was brought up in a gutter!!) as, I took it, a delicate hint that he was waiting for his shirt to be mended before going out to the club . . .

We had dinner, or supper if you prefer it, with the Fagans on Sunday. Mother remarked later, 'Wasn't Audrey painful?' and I must admit, I quite agreed with her. Poor Audrey, she has been an invalid for so long, and the household revolved around her health, that she is more than a little bit of a – oh dear, I've forgotten the word. It isn't kleptomaniac, nor is it – perhaps it is hypochondriac? – anyway, she is so centred on her health and appearance that nothing else interests her. At intervals of about five minutes she would butt in on any casual conversation going on to ask if we were quite sure we thought she looked better, or hadn't we admired the way she had cut up the radishes, or didn't we think she'd done the flowers well, or were we sure we thought her colour was better, and how worried she was getting because she had regained all the weight she had lost through the operation period, and was now wondering whether she was going to get fat. As she currently weighs 103lbs and is my height, her legs and arms look like well dieted matchsticks at the moment, and I told Mac privately to stop her being so silly as to even think of dieting until she has put on another twenty pounds or so. Oh, I get more and more worried about the whole thing, for from my own observations and knowledge of my brother, I think he is getting very restive and bored but hasn't the courage to say so or make a break for it.

It's horrid of me to be so critical of Audrey, I know, and when I look inwardly I see so many facets of my own character that I just loathe – my boastfulness, for instance; and my inability to keep quiet about something that may hurt somebody else's feelings; my habit of riding over other people's wishes with the blissful belief that I am doing it for their good – that I do realise I am in no position to be critical of Audrey or anybody else. And I suppose there is always the doubt whether my knowledge of my own character is as accurate as I feel; whether my deep belief that I do almost everything just a little better than average but not well enough to be good at it, is a true belief or not; perhaps I am just being falsely modest? Oh, I don't know, and if you have got this far through this paragraph I don't suppose you can sort it out for me, either! What I feel is this, I have a reasonably good idea, deep down, of my abilities as such and of my faults. Has Audrey any idea of hers? Does she ask for admiration all the time because she really feels insecure and wants reassuring?

. . . I do hope your cold is quite gone by now, or if not gone, then suitably reduced from king to pin size. Summer colds are the very devil, aren't they – I had one about four weeks ago and was delighted that it lasted only three days. Only, it didn't. It left a cough behind it which I have yet; so please take my advice, and if I am too late to exhort you not to have a cold at all, don't have a Bournemouth-type cold.

Yours most sincerely,

Frances W.

BOURNEMOUTH
July 18th 1959

Dear Mr Bigelow,

Well, well; you leave me breathless, even after knowing you so well all these years. I must try your excuse on my dentist next time I go there, and say airily that I didn't come when the six months was up because, after all, I might cross the Styx any moment and it hardly seemed worth the bother and I only turned up in the end because the pain was just too awful to bear any longer . . . You have been coming that old gag about 'not being here next year', I may remind you, Sir, since the early summer of 1949, and although I admit that on the basis of pure logic, you are bound to be right in the end, I am hoping that I shall be too old to enjoy the joke when you send me a spirit message saying 'See, I *was* right, after all'. Anyway, haven't you a set of store teeth lying around the house somewhere you can make use of? I ask such a horrid question because I was recently reading a book about Elizabethan England, and it was quite the thing in those days to keep a set or two in the great houses, so that they could be loaned to any guests visiting you who would otherwise have found it hard to tear the joint apart with their gums. Awful thoughts that conjures up, doesn't it?

. . . Well, my brother and his fiancée and her mum are all back from Devonshire, with Mac's back a mass of bright pink peeling blisters from the sun. He had a touch of sunstroke, and could neither eat nor sleep from Monday night until Friday morning. When a friend of ours heard this, she was furious and said you would have thought with two women there, they would have looked after him a bit better. Poor Dorothy, she has been so fond of my brother for so many years, without the slightest hope, for she is plain, white-haired, and as prim as could be. I hadn't the heart to tell her the case is slightly reversed when Mac is at Audrey's home – there, *he* has to look after the women-folk. Chez-moi, we look after him. I will admit I haven't mentioned to anybody (not even Mac) that Audrey told me rather smugly that as there was no lift in the hotel Mac used to carry her upstairs whenever she wished to go up . . . . . . Do you think MacPherson imagines himself to be a twentieth-century Rbt Browning? After all, Audrey had a big operation to put her heart *right* – who needs to carry her upstairs???? Mother, too, had had a dicky heart for the last ten or twelve years, but does Mac go down the stairs to fetch the morning paper when it comes bouncing through the letter box, to save Mother's heart? Does he heck! And don't say it's Lurve or I shall puke, Sir . . .

The Fagans told me that when Mac had more or less recovered from his sunstroke – by the Friday, that is – he felt it was necessary to liven things up a bit in the hotel, and to that end he astonished the staff who had worked there for years and never once seen them, by persuading somebody to switch on the lights on the terrace, and organising a flood-lit tennis match (four torches, held at each corner by giggling guests) to amuse those who were not dancing . . . . . . He also behaved exactly as if he was at home – went off and played golf and came back at 2.15 p.m. for lunch, and just calmly talked the head waiter into serving him! That, I may tell you spoiled Yankee, is practically unheard of in England, where the hotel guests do as the staff say, or else . . . . . . Altogether, when he felt well enough, Mac behaved just like his father, who always organised hotels whenever he had to stay in one of the hated places, and in spite of it all, always managed to be extremely popular with the staff as well as with the guests, so that the whole hotel would be en fête during his stay.

We have a woodpecker just arrived in our garden. Not last year's Green Woodpecker, but an ordinary one with a red topknot. He is a bit shy at the moment, but we'll tame him, you see. I couldn't agree more with you over the way this spraying of crops is ruining bird and animal and insect life, and, believe fully that eventually it will ruin the crops as well. Ah me, nothing like the good old days, is there Mr B?

And on that nostalgic note I will leave you until next Saturday, and hope that you will not repeat your cold, nor your recent fit of the dumps. Isn't there a yachting week coming along soon to take your mind off miserable thoughts?

Yours most sincerely,

Frances W.

BOURNEMOUTH
July 24th 1959

Dear Mr Bigelow,

Do you remember, some weeks ago, I lost the first page of one of my letters to you? And thought, finally, I must have packed it in error with that drawing of the monks?

Well, all this week I have been doing your weekly letter in bits and pieces, and last evening – Thursday – it was almost finished. For some reason I cannot account for, I folded it ready for putting in an envelope, and put it back into my desk drawer, so that it did not lie openly to the gaze of anybody who happened to pull the drawer out. As I said, it was folded in three, with only the plain back of the outer sheet visible. And this morning, Friday, it has gone.

Gone completely and absolutely. I have turned my office inside out and upside down, and it is nowhere. I looked in my boss's wastepaper basket, and it is not there. In mine, neither, nor in the large rubbish bin we keep in the hall and into which we empty our baskets.

Tomorrow I shall have to ask my boss if he went to that drawer. I do not for a minute think that, if he had done so, he would go so far as to open a letter and, seeing my address and 'Dear Mr Bigelow' at the top, read it. I *know* he would not. My only hope is that, having opened it and seen it was a letter of mine, he has put it away somewhere and is going to blow me up for leaving personal correspondence about. The only thing other than that is that one of the staff is going through my things when I am not here, and that is a horrible suspicion, and upsets me so thoroughly that, sorry though I am, you will have to go without your usual letter this week, as I just cannot concentrate on rewriting the whole thing. Even if this is right – and somebody is reading my letters – why take it away? True, in it I have, as usual, mentioned things that happened at work and have even told you of an incident in which my boss was concerned, but why take the whole thing away and, by so doing, warn me of what is going on? Oh, I feel sick and shivery at the whole horrid business.

I am sorry, I will write you twice next week if I can. But I just can't right now.

Yours sincerely,

Frances W.

BOURNEMOUTH
August 4th 1959

Dear Mr Bigelow,

Oh dear – I had hoped to have good news for you today, but alas, Friday got worse and worse as the day progressed.

When I found your letter had disappeared completely you may imagine I fairly panicked at the thought of unauthorised persons reading what is always a very private letter – I don't care a hoot who reads it your end for nobody in Bellport knows anybody in Bournemouth, so no harm is likely to come of their knowledge of little bits and pieces out of my life. But for the staff to read what I say about them, and about my boss and his family! That made me feel so sick I didn't eat for 24 hours, and even now, four days later, can get food down only with difficulty. For, in that particular letter, although there was nothing I have not already said to him in person, there were things about my boss and, especially, about his daughter-in-law, that I would give my eyeteeth not to have read by any other interested parties.

But the letter, although that is by far the worst, is only one of many things. You must know that Thursday morning it looked as if it might rain, so I picked my umbrella out of the stand as I left home for the office, and as it was unfurled, I rolled it up as I walked to the garage. When I got to work, I hung it on a hook on my office door, and left it there overnight as it was fine when I finished work, and I remember thinking it might be as well to leave it in town and use it at midday on Friday, when I go home for lunch. So there it was, Thursday night, in my office. Friday evening, when I was morosely getting ready to go home about 9.30, I went to pick the umbrella off the hook, and thought, 'That's funny – I didn't remember seeing it had rotted, when I rolled it up yesterday.' And I unfurled it, and opened it, and oh Mr Bigelow, somebody must hate me to the point of mania, for the whole thing had been ripped to bits with a nail or a screwdriver, or something pointed, which had been pulled hard down each of the folds, towards the ferrule. When I showed it to my boss on Saturday morning, he – he hadn't altogether believed me before – in turn opened it, and dropped it as if it were hot, saying, 'This is the work of a madman!' as he did so. Even at second hand, you see, he felt some of the cold horror I got at this anonymous hatred.

Now that I look back, that first disappearance of a letter does not seem to be my carelessness in packing it up with your tie, or the monk drawing, as I decided at the time I had. Nor does it seem possible any longer to kid myself that the piercing of the gramophone diaphragm in a dozen places was done naturally, by the pitch of the noise when I played a record. I know when I found it, the engineer said it could not have been done naturally but must have been deliberate, but so naive was I, I refused to believe anybody would do such a thing. In my own mind I believe I know who it is: it may be that in my distress I am look- ing only at those straws which are blowing in the same direction, but I still feel I am right. Apart from never leaving anything personal about in future, I am in terror of what this warped mind may think to do with the two letters he has – blackmail of me is impossible and in any case I should go at once to the police; but he *could* send the last one to my boss's daughter-in-law if he wanted to be really cruel, for it would make all friendly relationships between them (very strained at the moment) quite impossible. When I can, I am trying to make a systematic search of the building, but there are thousands of places where a man could hide something, even if he didn't take it home, or keep it in his pocket. I have told my boss, and although I didn't tell him what was in my letter, gave him a hint that it concerned him personally; he was very upset but did not upbraid me.

Of course, he then said he thought somebody had been going through his office a long time ago, that was why he had a special lock on the door to which only he and I have keys – in my office, nothing locks, not even my desk.

Never mind: I'll send you a more cheerful letter on Friday, probably padlocked. But aren't people foul?

Yours distressed,

Frances W.

BOURNEMOUTH
September 5th 1959

Dear Mr Bigelow,

Don't tell me the postal authorities have taken to using pigeons instead of aeroplanes for their transatlantic mail? You should have received my last letter before Friday. We must claim a refund . . .

On Wednesday afternoon, while the audience was coming in for the water show matinée performance, as I was working with my office door open, I heard the hall man say, 'Does anybody own this?' When I went out, he had been referring to a tiny baby, not more than eighteen or nineteen months, who was rushing about the hall and up and down the entrance steps. The baby was wearing a crew-cut and a pair of stamp-size pants. After looking at him sideways, I said dubiously that I thought I had seen him before, only on the previous occasion he had been on the seafront and his tummy was fatter, too . . .

Anyway, eventually the infant wandered off and tried to push Mr Markson's enormous red Jaguar off the road, and as he – the infant – was then heading straight for the traffic on the main road I dashed out and stopped him, and asked where his mother was. He pointed vaguely in the direction of the beach and France, so holding one hand in mine, we set off to look for her. We had a long and vivid conversation, only one half of which meant anything at all to me, but he apparently enjoyed it for he kept bubbling over with laughter . . . When we reached a stall selling sweets, under the pier, I looked in and saw a young ticket-collector (deckchair tickets) and said, 'Please, do you know where this one belongs?' The man raised his hands in mock horror, and saying resignedly, 'What, again! Every day, that one. Every day. Come on, Buster, back to the Office.' So he hoisted the small baby onto his shoulders, and set off to the Beach Office where lost property of all sorts is kept, merely turning his head over his shoulder and saying to me, 'Really should have a strong chain on, this one.' To be such a well-known character by the time you aren't two, something to be quite proud of. And such a happy baby, too. I only hope its mother was equally happy; obviously she wasn't the worrying kind of parent.

My brother took his 16 assorted children from one of the Homes to the zoo at Bristol for the day on Monday. I asked him when he got home if he had managed to lose any of them, and he giggled and said no, but almost. Apparently when the coach-driver had arrived to collect them, Mac told him they would be 20 minutes late as there was such a long queue for rides on the elephant some of his kids wouldn't get one at all if they didn't have this extra time. Finally he said, he got the lot together, and was busy counting them for the second time when they were all safely inside the coach, when, presto, there were only 15. 'It didn't matter much,' said Mac, 'as I just went back to the elephant, and there was little Eric waiting for another ride.'

Incidentally, said brother is off on holiday again at the end of the month – to Scotland this time. He's done very well this year. A week at home while the national Hard Court Tennis Championships were being played at his club ground. Fine weather. A week at Salcombe. Very fine weather. A week for the Hampshire Tennis Championships at the club. Fine weather again, and now ten days for Scotland. He'll get home the day I start off on my holiday, so I daresay the odds are the weather will break the same day or am I being unduly pessimistic? Never mind, even if it rains in France I intend to enjoy myself, and can always buy a raincoat for the occasion anyway. Having taken the plunge, I am quite looking forward to it, and on consultation with my post office savings book, don't think I shall arrive home broke after all, which is a pleasant surprise . . .

Ah well. That's all for now . . . Don't become a recluse, now – you'll hurt half Bellport, if you do, for I am sure your many friends love to see you in their homes, if only to add a comfortable atmosphere, sitting sipping your punch by their fireside.

See you next Saturday,

Yours most sincerely,

Frances W.

BOURNEMOUTH
September 26th 1959

Dear Mr Bigelow,

Well, yesterday has been and went, as it were, and I hope that way out at Bellport it went well, with everybody highly satisfied, especially the leading actor of the day . . .

I sat up late the other evening to watch our wonderful Dame Margot Fonteyn dance on television. She, with Michael Soames, did a pas de deux from *Ondine*, which was a revelation. It was incredible how a mature woman in her early forties could, merely by dance movements and mime, portray the coy, skipping soul of a young girl. She was just wonderful. To follow her in the programme some brilliant mind got Richard Hearne to do his famous 'Lancers' dance, as a sort of contrast! I had not seen him do this before, so nearly rocked off the settee as he progressed. First of all, he sits at the side of the ballroom watching a set of dancers doing the Lancers. When they finish, he decides he'll take part, but when he reaches the dance floor everybody has vanished. So he dances a set by himself, peopling the floor merely by means of his eyes, watching the other pairs doing their steps as it is his turn, with his partner, to stand still for a few moments. The music gets quicker and quicker, with the inevitable consequence at last. I understand it is almost a classic of the theatre, this dance of his, and well it might be.

My brother's wedding date now seems to be fixed for August 6th 1960, that being the Saturday nearest to the day they met, says Audrey coyly. Her mother is busy giving them bits and pieces of furniture with which to equip a sitting room, Audrey's bedroom and a small bedroom-cum-'den' for Mac. In a way I suppose Mac is fortunate, for he won't have much to provide in the way of equipping a home. I am still giving advice, and never in my life has any of mine been accepted so quickly! Last week, I said I didn't like green curtains in their new sitting room, which is a cold room, and thought the curtains at that time in the dining room would look better, and the dining room, in turn, would look vastly improved if it had light chintz. 'The very idea!' said Mrs Fagan, so down come the curtains and she pops out the next morning to order new ones, expense no object.

I have not liked to bother Rosalind, who must surely have had enough on her hands with Mr Akin's nervous disposition and that threatened steel strike at Leclades, but perhaps now that she has visited you, you can pass on any news there is – whether the strike did start, or whether at the last moment it was averted. From your remarks about strikes and M. Kruschov [sic] I fear it is 'on', but hope I misread your mind.

Winter must be well on its way, for my sciatica and other bits and pieces of rheumatics have returned, and sent me scurrying back to my tin of ghastly salts. If only the pain wasn't in the right leg, I would have the darn thing off. Trouble is, it is my left foot which is the larger, so to have the right one (complete with leg) removed would not make me take any smaller size in shoes, and I can't right now think of any other good reason for doing away with the smaller leg . . .

I am late with this letter already, so will waste no more time except to send you my very best wishes, and hope you had (of course you did!) a very happy time with Rosalind.

Yours most sincerely,

Frances W.

BOURNEMOUTH
October 3rd 1959

Dear Mr Bigelow,

. . . As I was wending my miserable way to the dentist this morning, I came across a very ancient parked motor car. It had screwed to the bonnet a neat plastic sign which read:

THIS CONVEYANCE (CIRCA 25BC) WAS REPUTEDLY COMMANDEERED BY HENRY V AT AGINCOURT TO REPLACE HIS FAILING HORSE. PLEASE DO NOT TOUCH OR DESPOIL THIS HISTORIC RELIC.

It quite reconciled me to my visit!

He gave an injection for the filling, which was nice, but didn't stop me having to go out from home on an empty stomach. He – the dentist – was also a bit taken aback when, expecting nothing but gratitude for his pain-free drilling, he found me complaining bitterly of the noise. 'Might as well live on the boundary of London Airport,' I reported sourly, on coming up for air and a nice spit. So then we had a long and heated argument about politics and ethics, which was entertaining and hard work, as he is so much cleverer than I, I am hard put to it to stay even two rounds.

Oh yes, Freckleface has a new bed. Queen Elizabeth 1 didn't do better. I got rather fed up with my sleepless nights with this fat cat lying all over my shin bones; so I folded in three an old quilt, and placed it on the lower half of the tea-trolley which I use instead of a bedside table. On top of the quilt I put each night his little silk (artificial, in case you think I am quite mad) cover, and when he comes stalking in, he gets popped there, in his own little four-poster bed. The first night he objected strongly, and for nearly an hour after I had put out the light, whenever his purrs stopped suddenly, I would put down my hand and there would be his little face, just creeping out and up onto my bed. The second night he thought he was a bit of alright, and now he pops in with alacrity, and sometimes if I am awake in the night and I can hear him washing or turning over, at my side, I can hear also a little contented purr come up, before he sinks back into sleep.

On Sunday I took Mother, Dorothy Smith, and an elderly cousin of Dorothy's, to Kimmeridge for a picnic tea. It was so hot you wouldn't believe it. We went for a short walk along the top of the cliffs, until stopped by arriving at a barbed-wire enclosure where they were drilling for oil (Yes, oil in England and finding it too). We couldn't get any further because the cliff went straight up to the sky, or down into the sea, and we, not being spiders, could not follow suit in either direction. It was magnificent scenery, though, and well worth being polite to the guards on our biggest oil-well yet. We were glad to see they weren't making a terrible mess of the beauty. Yet.

Now I must get this off and back to work. Next week I shall be in Worthing without much time for writing. Never mind, I shan't be so brief as not to be able to wish you well, as I do now.

Yours most sincerely,

Frances W.

BOURNEMOUTH
October 10th 1959

Dear Mr Bigelow,

If I can get a page of this letter done before I go away on Wednesday (Wednesday last, according to the date at the top, of course) then you won't feel you are being neglected . . .

Many thanks for your last letter, in which you ask for the impossible – my views on whether women prefer to be envied by other women, or desired by men. Do most women *have* to make the choice? It seems to me that by the time women have reached adulthood, their natures and character have formed, and they probably are no longer in a position to choose. Besides, are the two things alternatives? I think it is rather unhappily phrased anyway – you make it sound as though we are either cats or nymphomaniacs! Then again, your question suggests a woman is either immediately attractive to men, or not at all. So far as I know any desire I may arouse in men is something that grows gradually – that is guesswork: I don't go around asking Thomas, Richard or Harold 'Am I desirable?' Might have awkward repercussions. But I do think I might be envied by other women – a guess. I don't know. But as a reasonably happy person I can imagine myself the object of envy of women who, perhaps, think themselves less happy. Oh dear! Let's get out of this. I'll ask you one, 'Have you stopped kicking your cats?'

Last night I stopped up late (for me) to see which way the Election was running, and went to bed about 1 a.m. secure in the belief that Conservatives would be 'in'. As they are. The whole thing was shown on T.V. from 9.30 p.m. to about 4 a.m. And again today from 6 a.m. to 4 p.m.! The Socialist bigwigs, interviewed in the early stages of the count, were as confident as heavyweight boxers; and so looked silly in the end. The Conservatives were not interviewed at all (no reason was given us: they may well have refused, wily-birds) and so, today, nobody can say 'Oh, pride goes before a fall!' or 'Don't count chickens!' etc.

As you can see, I am at long, long last separated from my old typewriter; sitting in Worthing (halfway along the bottom edge of England) in the sun; and shortly stopping to get tea.

Au revoir until next week, and look after yourself.

Yours most sincerely,

Frances W.

AT HOTEL OF MY SAINTED FATHERS
PARIS
v. LEFT BANK
Samedi, le vingt-quatre October 1959

Cher M. Bigelow,

See how my environment affects me! Any minute now I shall burst out again in fluent, but fluent comme la Seine, French, and then you'll be sorry. Sorry you neglected your schoolboy languages the better to appreciate mine.

Still, yesterday I went out by myself, Mrs Bendle being a latish riser, and went into a small shop and asked for a little butter, and some bread, and please, that bottle of Chablis – was it sweet or dry? Having got so far, I plunged on and asked where I found the bus for Versailles. This was the end! All the customers were brought into the discussion, and the head of the house. There was gesticulation and jabbering and in the end I understood that I caught a bus from around the corner to Porte de Versailles, and from there to the Palace it was everybody for himself. So we took the train!

After trailing around Versailles, to find the Petit Trianon was shut for repair, we got lost (a little) and asked somebody the way. As somebody had already asked me (!) the way, it was poetic justice that this woman also was 'a stranger in these parts'. She in turn asked another passer-by who, but of course, was a stranger, so by the time we met up with a native of Versailles we had half the street blocked. I asked, so carefully, 'Pardon, monsieur – voulez-vous me dire où est la gare?' and he said 'Quelle gare? Il y a trois' [sic]. Not fair for two reasons. One, we had no idea there was more than one, and, two, we had no idea which of the three we had arrived at. So this meant thinking up some more French – 'the station for Les Invalides, please'. In the end, we got there, finally asking the way of a handsome young St Cyr cadet. Unhappily, nothing exciting happened – he just *told* us.

Yesterday, the Flea Market. It was not, to me, disappointing for there were a great many beautiful things to see. But everything we dared ask about was *so* expensive. I bought (for me, from you for last Easter, merci beaucoup, très beaucoup) a lovely alabaster powder bowl, which looks like a milky sky faintly touched with darker drifts of clouds. You may remember, a powder bowl has been on my 'wants' list for several years, and now I have it, and from time to time I take it out of its paper and stroke its lovely soft surface. Thank you very much indeed. My only other purchase was an old oval picture made of hair (human, one hopes) in an ebony and gilt frame. Probably they won't like the hair, so before I give it to the Fagans I shall have to replace the flower arrangement – all in hair, very clever, if a little macabre – with something more ordinary.

We have eaten splendidly and quite cheaply, really for none of our daily meals has cost us more than about 14s. or $2, and the helpings have been so large it has even been hard to get an appetite up for our second meal of the day, which is a picnic in our hotel room of bread and butter, cheese and grapes, wine and nuts and a little chocolate. Lummy! That makes us sound as though we were really stuffed!

Today we see the Louvre. I don't want to, but my companion is a woman of iron self-will, and what Lulu wants, Lulu gets. It is easier to go with a steamroller than against it and I don't really mind. When I do, then I stick to my wishes and get them usually by some devious means.

Paris is as lovely as always. At night the enormous plane trees on both banks of the river, rustling in the breeze, send up a harmonious accompaniment to the sudden rushing noise that is made by the traffic, held in leash by the red lights, suddenly being released and leaping forward like a corporate body, in one fighting, fierce surge. I have amused myself trying to picture Paris traffic rushing, six, seven, or even eight abreast, up the narrow, congested streets at home. To see two French drivers simultaneously flash around a corner into a narrow side street is, at once, an awe-inspiring sight because of their skill, and terrifying because of their lack of care for the safety of each other.

Today – Tuesday – Mrs B. had a cable saying her son was arriving in Scotland on Saturday, so we are going home on Thursday instead of Saturday. I don't really mind as she is rather overpowering, being immensely kind, but at the same time she *must* always be right, and she knows what's best for you. Right or wrong, she's still right, which can be a trifle wearing on her companion . . .

Today we saw, as all the museums were closed, an exhibition of young modern painters and sculptors. Mr and Mrs Olsen would have *loved* it! The American room had one 'painting' of which the top half was filled by a flattened-out acid drum still bearing the words 'Dangerous – the contents must be kept dry' and the rest of the canvas contained, under several layers of paint for varnish, the painter's old woollen pullover (unwashed where it was not covered by paint) some photographs of a ship at sea, a piece of wood, possibly the skirting board he had *not* used for firewood. In case you want to send an offer for this masterpiece, the artist responsible (? could one call him 'responsible'?) is Robert Rauschenberg.

Last-minute rush: we have seen another exhibit of modern paintings; the Impressionists, and the Louvre. Also went very expensively to the theatre and it turned out be to a French adaptation of one of Cornelia Otis Skinner's plays! As it was all a comedy of words, I was lost, utterly and throughout the whole thing – at top speed – got scanty words only and two whole sentences – 'Do sit down' and 'Who is this girl Frances?' Never mind, the Pierre Balmain dresses were *wonderful*.

All for now, back to work now.

All my best wishes,

Françoise W.

BOURNEMOUTH
November 7th 1959

Dear Mr Bigelow,

. . . There has been on television a series of interviews to find out the English Woman's opinions on a poll recently taken in your country. I am not quite certain about the exact words, but they were either 'What do you think is the innovation which has made the greatest difference to your standard of living in the last ten years?' or '. . . . . . the innovation which has most greatly altered your way of living . . . . . . ?' The poll in the U.S.A. revealed that your ladies think a) barbecue cooking, b) polythene hairsprays, and c) power brakes, have had the greatest effect. I was fairly speechless at this, and looked up to see what the English housewife and business girl thought. Here were their choices:

1. Artificial flowers with electric lights inside, instead of the old-fashioned type of light which was a light, period.
2. Tinned cat food.
3. Composition soles for shoes.
4. Childbirth (the interviewer could not refrain from suggesting this had been going on for longer than ten years, but the young woman insisted she meant what she said – that today it is quite painless!). I am not going to try to prove her right or wrong.

5. Plastic mirrors for budgerigars. Yes, that *is* what the woman said.
6. Electrical gadgets, in particular, spin dryers. (Bless this one for an I.Q. way up, by sheer contrast, in the genius class.)
7. Special paper coated with sand, to use in the bottom of bird-cages and stop the chore of having to put fresh sand in every day.
8. Chinese restaurants, because one can eat good food, cheaply, there.
9. Television. (I thought this had been going on for longer.)
10. Artificial flowers to put in the garden in the winter, and so make the garden look blooming all the year around.

I give up. I bow the head in shame. I splutter. I laugh. I cry. I just plain don't believe it. The commentator, after these eleven interviews, looked at the camera with a dead-straight face and said dryly, 'I never cease to be surprised by the people I meet.' British understatement . . .

More next week; until then keep well and don't throw anything through the television screen.

And now, really au revoir,

Yours most sincerely,

Frances W.

BOURNEMOUTH
December 5th 1959

Dear Mr Bigelow,

. . . This last week has been full of event and excitement for me, even though the events were but small stirrings in a teacup, and the excitement a mere leavening of my spirits from the dull doldrums they had sunk into by last Saturday.

After as many 'will' and 'won't' announcements as there are petals on a daisy, at the end of last week it was finally (and tardily) decided that I should have some central heating in my office. Joy and huggings (self-huggings, have no fear, we are a highly respectable staff, alas) and I bounced home to tell the family my good news, and started tossing padded quilted overcoats out the window.

Then I must tell you about Mother's legacy. It hasn't come yet, and won't for some months yet, but we know how much. The cousin, true to her lifetime habits, was too mean to go to a lawyer to draw up her will, so she went to a neighbour and he did it for nothing, and did it with so many inaccuracies that it will mean a great deal of work and worry for the executors to get it probated and sorted out. One of the executors is a brother of Mother's. She has left him £200, which he says he will more than earn with all the work he will have to put in clearing up the will: besides, he has always looked after her financial affairs, and only last year (he told us) he put through a property deal for her which netted her £2,600 profit, so poor Uncle more than deserves his £200. Then she left the same amount to Mother!!!!!! And a few pounds here and there to the rest of her cousins. And the remainder to charity. A matter of some *seventeen thousand pounds*!! When I tell you that Mother remembered staying with this cousin and her mother when my mother was a little girl, and they served the batter pudding and gravy before the meat and vegetables 'because it takes the edge off the appetite and you save money on the meat, my dear' you may imagine how the cousin managed to save all this money . . .

Mother has already worked out what she is going to do with her fortune, and I have worked it out another way so already, you see, the money is bringing dissension to the family! Mother, bless her, suggested a fourway split; one quarter to each of us, and the last quarter to me as well to pay for the refrigerator, as every time she looks at it Mother apparently thinks, 'There is Norah's fare to America!' My idea is that Mother should give Mac £50 for a wedding present; put the same amount in my bank account, put £20 aside for television repairs, spend that sum on a wedding-outfit for herself; have a really good holiday, and if there is anything left after that, well, she could let me have £10, perhaps, towards the refrigerator, which would make me more than happy as I was glad to be able to buy it anyway, and have long since forgotten the money was ever in my account. Mac has produced no good suggestions, merely offering his post office savings account as a 'safe' (his word) place in which to put the money.

I remarked somewhat forlornly that I was already saving to get the fare to and from America for your Special Birthday in – what is it? 1963 – but at the rate I am going (I didn't mention this bit) you had best postpone 1963 until, say, 1969 if you will, please . . .

Now to say au revoir until next Saturday,

Yours most sincerely,

Frances W.

1960

August 6th (p. 357). Frank MacPherson Woodsford marries Audrey
Fagan. Miss Frances Woodsford, third from left.

BOURNEMOUTH
January 2nd 1960

Dear Mr Bigelow,

. . . At this time of year I always keep one Resolution, as you should know by now. In fact, it is no longer even necessary to make it, because I automatically write you about New Year to thank you for all your kindnesses of the year just ended, and to tell you how very much indeed I appreciate your letters, and having my little open window
onto your life and doings. You remember that awful time when some member of the staff stole one of my letters to you? I told my boss at the time that you were my Father Confessor, my confidant, the friend to whom I could tell anything and everything and invariably did, without the least fear of repercussions for my indiscretions. So I really am telling the truth when I say you are about the most important friend I have, and I just don't know what I should do without that basic purpose in my life – the Saturday Special. Some people might say I could always pour out my feelings in a letter, it would not matter to whom it was addressed; but that would be completely untrue. I sort out my feelings most carefully, and my letters are always tailored as well as I can manage it, to fit the person who will read them. You seem to have fitted yourself into them so well there has been no need for tailoring my end; you are just ready-made for them, and thank God for it.

So, a very Happy New Year to you dear Mr Bigelow, and look after yourself.

Your affectionate correspondent,

Frances W.

BOURNEMOUTH
March 5th 1960

Dear Mr Bigelow,

. . . We over here were all fairly breathless last week, what with the Royal Family just bursting out with births and engagements and despatches. We were very, very sorry that Lady Mountbatten should have died so young, for she was a very wonderful woman and I've never met anybody who ever came in contact with her, who thought differently. Then of course we were very pleased with the new royal baby. And on top of that, Princess Margaret goes and gets herself a fiancé – and a Mr, at that. The awful pun 'It'll be hard work now, keeping up with the Joneses' has gone round and round Britain. He looks as though he has a sense of humour, and strength of character, both of which will no doubt be of incalculable assistance to him in his marriage. The only thing that worries me is – what is he going to *do* when they are married? I cannot see the Princess ever allowing anybody to treat her as other than Royal. And I cannot altogether see a man of character, not brought up in royal traditions (as Prince Philip was), just giving up an all-absorbing career to be a hanger-on to the Royal Family. They wouldn't even want him to open bazaars! I would say, myself, that the young lady was a handful enough for one man, without having all the Royal Family tacked on as well. Still, we are all glad she is marrying, and delighted it isn't Peter Townsend, that rather boring prig; or Billy Wallace, that chinless wonder . . .

Friday midday now, so will say au revoir here and now, and get this posted in time to reach you on the usual day. I hope you are well, and blooming like the weather.

Yours very sincerely,

Frances W.

BOURNEMOUTH
April 9th 1960

Dear Mr Bigelow,

. . . I have a sad little story about yet another member of the staff. She recently won £22 in a competition, which bucked her up no end for, as she told me, her husband had walked out of his job some time before Christmas, and had not worked since. Apparently, when they got the cheque for this amount, the man said, 'It's a pity it isn't one of the big prizes, but never mind dear, we shall just have to go on working, won't we?' When she tries to suggest he should go out and look for a job, he gets all sulky and nervy and says, 'Well, we're managing, aren't we?' Sometimes, Mr Bigelow, I am very sad not to be married, for I should dearly like to feel that I meant that much to somebody. And sometimes, Mr Bigelow, I am very glad not to be married and this is one of those times. Next time this particular woman gets a bit testy and difficult at work, I will remember that she is probably still keeping her husband and her mother-in-law, and overlook her tantrums, poor woman.

. . . I will tell you a secret. Mr Watts says I can hardly help passing the French exam in June; but I am not going to pass it. I am going to get Honours, so there! This will mean a lot of work, hard work, so if I sound a bit distrait in my letters between now and mid-June, pray put it down to the fact that I am probably writing you and saying irregular verbs to myself at one and the same time. Don't tell anybody about this, please, in case I miss the target.

And now I will get this in the post before I go out for a bit of shopping, and eat my egg, apple and orange lunch. I hope you are well and happy, and that the spring has sprung in Bellport, as it has here. The cat is moulting, and his fur is already disappearing from the bushes on which I place it, to line more bird nests.

Yours most sincerely,

Frances W.

BOURNEMOUTH
April 23rd 1960

Dear Mr Bigelow,

. . . It seems to me that I ought to start a Society for the Protection of Audrey Fagan, who looks like having a poor time of it once she marries my brother. Not that I shall believe she'll pull it off until about teatime on August 6th, for I am quite sure my brother is getting more and more reluctant, and more and more miserable as he sees no way out. His temper at home is very bad, which is always a sign he is worried or unhappy, but there is just nothing I can do about it. Of course, when he snarls at me I snarl back, but I don't count that as 'doing' anything about it! That's purely destructive doing, that is, and an automatic reflex of mine, alas, which I often deplore, and which has become automatic since the early days of my youth when, recognising myself to be a coward, I resolved not to behave like one, and when somebody shouted at me to frighten me, to shout back so that they wouldn't know I was a coward. Anyway, as usual we have come back to me, and I was talking about Audrey. On Easter Sunday afternoon Mac took Mother and me for a ride to Bullbarrow, where he and I picked little wild violets and white wood anemones and pale yellow primroses, and I gathered some lichen-covered hawthorn that had tiny pale green buds showing through the silver moss, and some peculiar stones that looked as if they had been nibbled by the moth. On reaching home I spent over half an hour arranging my share of these flowers in a shallow turquoise bowl standing on a straw tray (you sent it to me years ago with preserved fruits in it) with the odd stones tucked under the dish. They looked very fetching. Well, Mac saw them on Monday and grinned sourly and said, 'You should see what Audrey did with her flowers – they got stuck in one of those awful glass vases and half of them died immediately.'

He also comes home and moans because the cooking at 'Fitzharris' (what a name for a house!) is poor, uninspired, and sometimes downright ghastly. Well, if he thinks that by marrying a very pretty, spoiled, invalid daughter of a rich man he is going to find a wife who cooks like his mother, and arranges flowers like his sister, he is going to get disillusioned pretty quickly, and I don't really think it's fair on Audrey that she should be expected to come to these levels. True, I might feel sorrier for her if she didn't have such a high opinion of her abilities, but that probably goes with the prettiness and the money. Oh, those two . . .

It's when I come up against moneyed women that I appreciate Rosalind all the more, for I know it is an unhappy fact that money corrupts (especially women) and the more money, the more they are corrupted. I don't mean they are morally bad just that they expect their money to buy service and civility and deafness to their increasing rude-ness, in direct proportion to their wealth and their age. But not Rosalind, thank God, not Rosalind, who always seems to me to be the most under-standing person I know. I think she must practise for ten minutes every day, putting herself in the place of some underprivileged person, so that when she does happen to meet them, she will know how they feel and treat them as human beings, with feelings and dignity of their own.

Lecture over; that's all for this week except that I do hope you will, from now on, with the sunshine and all, start feeling younger and younger every day through the long summer to come.

Yours most sincerely,

Frances W.

BOURNEMOUTH

May – no, June 4th 1960

Dear Mr Bigelow,

By the time you are reading this, you will have seen Rosalind and heard of her holiday directly from her. I telephoned her at Kew last night, to wish them Godspeed and safe landing and to say au revoir, and Rosalind said the weather here had been absolutely wonderful – sun, sun, and more sun but quite cool. Just, in fact, what I ordered, but so rarely get.

In London last week, anyway, it was both sunny and hot, and I was quite sorry to have my fur tippet to drag around. It looked luxurious, though, even if a bit hot. Rosalind and your daughter-in-law had a pleasant room in a rather unpleasant hotel (all the corridors were wet, as somebody apparently was washing all the carpets, and they smelled a bit of soap and disinfectant) and I had an enormous room with a double bed and four huge, fat square pillows and 14 cupboards and eight drawers. I decided 14 cupboards was quite adequate for an overnight stay, and spread my other frock over as many of them as possible. There was also, oh delight, an enormous bunch of flowers and a jug to put them in, so when I had finished, with my silver-fox draped negligently (took me five minutes to get real negligent) over a chair, I looked the height of a luxurious lady visiting the haut monde . . .

We had tea together, and chatted for a little, then changed as I said, and with a nice long drink under our belts, off to the theatre. (I was so thirsty, for some reason, I ordered gin and bitter lemon, emptied all the bitter lemon into the gin, and just gulped it down as if it were lemonade. With, I may say, about as much effect!) The play, if that is the right word for it, was *Ross*, and was all about T. E. Lawrence of Arabia, during the short time he was in the Air Force after the war, under the name of Ross. It was a series of scenes from the desert warfare, and although it failed, for me, to explain why Lawrence wanted to go into the Forces, it was a most moving dramatic piece, and I thoroughly enjoyed it.

And, of course, the acting of Sir Alec Guinness was amazing. And dear Lady Churchill was sitting in the row immediately in front of us, which added to my pleasure. Afterwards, we went to Veeraswamy's Indian Restaurant and had very second-rate curry and third-rate wine (first-rate charge, of course) and so back to the hotel and to bed and, in the morning, sadly to see the others off to Kent. Your d-in-law had a formidable programme of gardens and houses to see, and I only hope they didn't wear themselves out looking for them, and at them.

Last night I telephoned Rosalind, as I said. The telephone number was engaged at first, and the operator said he would call me back. Just as the 'phone rang, and I ran to answer, there was a loud 'bang' from the kitchen and a sharp exclamation from Mother. I could either see what she was up to, or answer the telephone, and I'm afraid I did the latter: she sounded exasperated rather than in real trouble.

When I had had our short three minutes, I dashed to the kitchen, to find Mother had been lighting the boiler and blown the door off with the gas poker. And a baby blue-tit had flown in through an open window into our living room and that was too much for Freckles, who was all agog. For a little while there was pandemonium, but in the end all was well, and the indignant little bird flew off with his mum, and an indignant cat went stalking out, all ruffled, and Mother and I sat down to a cup of much-needed coffee . . .

No doubt by now Rosalind has come and gone like a passing glint of sun through the clouds. Wasn't it kind of Lady Harold Nicolson to give them flowers when they left her garden at Sissinghurst? The Nicolson son, Nigel, has been our member of parliament in Bournemouth (East) for some years, but is in process of being thrown out by the local diehard Tories because he voted against the party over the Suez question . . .

Pandemonium is reigning right now; our water show starts tomorrow so by now tempers are worn thin and everybody on our staff is rushing to telephone the nearest lunatic asylum to book a suite for themselves. Ah well, in another eight weeks we shall be halfway to the end of the season. In another nine Mac will be getting married; my heart fails me more and more, and I just cannot even make a semblance of happiness about it, but I must, if only to keep Mother unaware of my growing misgivings. I had a ghastly thought the other day, when Mac said not to give our list of wedding guests to the Fagans as he 'wanted to alter it' and I thought he was going to cross off a very old friend of ours – Dorothy Smith. So one day I asked him point-blank, and after a tiny pause he said no, of course he wasn't doing any such thing. But the pause made me wonder. And this morning he said, out of the blue, that he had spoken to Dorothy and she didn't wish to be invited. Now I don't know whether he is telling the truth or not; whether Dorothy really has said she prefers not to be invited, and if so, whether she feels too upset to come. And if so, whether she just doesn't think this particular marriage is a good thing (as I know she does) or whether she is too emotionally involved. We have known Dorothy since we were in our teens, and she was even then white-haired. I have no idea of her age, but it must be in the mid-fifties at least, and whereas Mac has always treated her as a sort of convenient sister, I am not so sure that Dorothy has looked upon Mac as a brother. So I can't ask her about this invitation business for fear I probe too deeply in something she would rather I didn't investigate. And I can't do nothing, because I should hate a good and well-tried friend to be hurt just because Mac is marrying some addle-headed little fool who is stupid enough to be jealous of somebody who befriended us twenty years before she even met Mac. Oh, Mr Bigelow, don't people complicate matters!

Now to post this; I was so pleased to see from your last letter that you sounded more cheerful, and hope in the next that the same happy progress will be visible.

Au revoir until next Saturday yourself, then, and look after yourself.

Yours most sincerely,

Frances W.

BOURNEMOUTH
June 18th 1960

Dear Mr Bigelow,

Oh what a tangled web we mortals spin, when once we start to deceive – or whatever it was, whoever it was, said. And what a mess I get into with tenses when I start my weekly letter to you on a Monday or a Tuesday, but date it Saturday and pretend I am writing it then – which I never do, as you know full well, since it is always posted by Friday afternoon at the latest. If in some future age some eager beaver of a historian digs around in the cliffs of Bellport, he may well find a painted box containing a mass of mildewed letters from Bournemouth; and what a trouble some clever creature will have in sorting out dates, apart from reality from fantasy. Makes quite a pleasant thought, giving all that work to some unknown nosy parker, doesn't it?

I had a letter from Rosalind this week, happy to be home but appalled by the weeds in the gardens, poor dear. She said you had seemed quite bright and cheerful when she reached Bellport and were sitting watching television when she arrived. Shame on you, Mr Bigelow! I thought you only used the television to switch it off with a huff and a puff of indignation from time to time!

My French exams took place on Monday and Tuesday. I was very elated immediately after doing the written exam, but next morning very depressed as I began to remember more and more mistakes I had made, and how many more I don't know I made: my essay – I chose to write about the book I most prefer, not wishing to describe a gentleman, nor the joys of campings – (if any). Of course, having got through the first sentence I suddenly realised my favourite book is *Pride and Prejudice* and I don't know the French for either word. So I had to be untruthful and pretend I liked *Pickwick Papers* best. And on top of this my subconscious took a hand, and when I was writing 'Les Papiers Pickwick' what do you think appeared on the paper – 'Une Conte de Deux Cities' [sic]. So there I was, saddled with a book I can scarcely remember reading!! And by an author I don't like, anyway. I was so mad, even at the time, and madder than ever in retrospect, so, to get my own back, I finished my little childish essay by saying that, in any case, my favourite book was usually the one I was currently reading and only the bell for the end of time stopped me waxing eloquent (and inaccurate) about the joys of unexpected delights that awaited one over every fresh page . . .

Looking at the whole thing as dispassionately as I can, I should hesitate to say I had higher marks than 70%, which is well over the 50% pass-mark but not, as you know, nearly good enough to meet my some-what vainglorious ambitions. Ah well, serves me right for flying too high. I will let you know what I do get, some time in August.

Now I must finish this; I will take it with us tomorrow, and post it from some outlandish corner of England (or possibly Scotland) and next week you may have to be content with a very short letter. Incidentally – thank you for *Reader's Digest* which came yesterday and leaves for Scotland tomorrow.

Yours most sincerely,

Frances W.

BOURNEMOUTH
July 23rd 1960

Dear Mr Bigelow, oh hitter-of-Telegraph-Poles,

One thing I must say, and you are in no position to stop me, I admire you for picking on something your own size. Height and width are, I should say, about equal but of course you have a moustache, which perhaps gives you just that little bit of an edge.

I am hoping that by the time this letter is posted I shall have heard again from Rosalind, to the effect that you are home and pottering around again with the mutts and going out to lunch with Rosalind and visiting Mr Dall in hospital or at his home, if he too has returned; generally your own self once more, with two beautiful black eyes fading into memory. We went back to the flat this morning because as we came out of the garage drive we noticed the postman down the road, so we motored back a little and waylaid him, but he disappointed us. We cheerfully told him to take a week's notice on the spot, and this so shook him he offered us somebody else's mail as a peace-offering, but we spurned it and went back on our route to work without a letter from America. (This is Thursday, at the moment.) I was a bit optimistic, expecting a letter as I know Rosalind said she would be visiting you on Monday, and she would have needed to write me as she opened the front door, more or less, for the letter to reach Bournemouth so soon. Oh Mr Bigelow, why do you do these things – you are deuced hard on the nerves!

. . . Now for the post and home.

Yours most sincerely,

Frances W.

BOURNEMOUTH
August 6th 1960

Dear Mr Bigelow,

Although, naturally, I shall be far too busy to write you on the date at the head of this letter. However, we must keep up the fallacy that I write you every Saturday, even though we both know I write you darn near all the week.

Well, Saturday is the great day and I am not exactly looking forward to it, nor to the future thereafter. At the moment we are having heavy cloudbursts and thunderstorms and so on (typical English summer) so it looks as if the reception will have to be held indoors and not in a marquee on the lawn. Goodness knows where everybody will go – 80 guests and me let loose with flowers, so there just won't be room for everything and as I am doing the flowers the afternoon before the wedding, I get in first. Mother is all set, and looks very elegant and beautiful all in palest pink with white blobs.

Last Sunday was Mac's last Sunday at home, and, stupid-like, I had anticipated he would at least suggest a picnic, or a run out in the car in the afternoon or even in the morning. We were due to go to the Fagans' for tea, to see the wedding gifts. I should have had my head examined. He got up late and dashed straight out to play golf. Came in for his lunch at five minutes to three, ate it, and went to bed. Absolutely fed up, for I had spent the whole morning ironing his clothes and on a last-minute piece of embroidery I was doing for them, I put on my hat and coat, got Mother ready, and we were just going downstairs to have a 15-minute ride in the car by ourselves when he heard us, and so got up and came with us. I was really mad that he should not even bother to be on time his very last weekend at home. If I tell you that he only just remembered in time, and said 'No' to one of his golf partners' suggestion that they play again next Sunday, you may guess what sort of a household it's going to be chez Fagan after he marries Audrey. I daresay though that as neither Audrey nor Mrs Fagan work (except in the house) they won't mind quite so much if their Saturday afternoons and Sundays are spent waiting for His Majesty. For me, my leisure in the summer is so rare and precious I get absolutely livid when it is spoiled. About the only piece of furniture I did not either choose, or help to choose, is Mac's new wardrobe, of which he is very proud and for which he paid a great deal of money. On looking at it, it was immediately obvious to me that it won't be large enough . . .

Mac is bearing up fairly nicely, thank you, except that he is railing at Mother and me because he doesn't know what on earth they'll do on their honeymoon if it rains! We have both, so far, refrained from any vulgarity.

Talking of honeymoons Audrey showed us her going-away outfit last weekend. Very elegant and lovely, and including a pair of slippers in bronze kid with heels at least four inches high and winkle-picker toes. She balanced these on her hands, and I said rather dryly, 'Just the thing for The Brace of Pheasants' whereupon Audrey laughed and said it wasn't really, but she had bought them for swank. Personally I *always* wear stiletto heels and three-inch pointed toes for a visit to the country, don't you, Mr Bigelow ?

Which brings me nicely back to you as a subject. I do hope you are your old self again, say circa 1958 (which was a good vintage year) and once more gadding about treating the local ladies to luncheon. You and your doleful 'Nobody ever comes to see me; never see anybody' – and then I find you so bucked with your social life you playfully hit a passing telegraph pole. I warn you, from now on I am strictly from Missouri where your plaintive moans are concerned . . .

All my good wishes that you are better, gayer, and quite completely absolutely and 100% recovered.

Yours most sincerely,

Frances W.

BOURNEMOUTH
August 13th 1960

Dear Mr Bigelow,

Who said, 'Came the Dawn'? Well, when it came to me, it brought, not the sunshine of a new day, but the blackest night. So, if you will bear with me for this week, I won't mention the wedding except to say that it took place, and went off very well, and the reception also, and I have lost my only brother . . .

Hurrah – a letter from you at last, proving that you are on the way to recovery, even if still full of aches and pains and weak at the knees. How very unpleasant of your leg to give way like that: it must take away your confidence in a most uncomfortable manner. And where was The Can-Opener when you fell over? Busy looking after her other home, no doubt . . .

Oh a dreadful week, this has been. Today it is fine, although there are a few clouds about – from the east coast of England right across the country to Cornwall, on the extreme west, it rained without stopping once, from early morning Wednesday until late at night on Thursday. Whether it rained in the nights as well I don't know: it was always pelting down whenever I woke up, but I didn't stay awake all night, so cannot say. But it rained and rained and rained all day. Thursday at work was bedlam: thousands and thousands of miserable holidaymakers trying to get out of the wet, and overwhelming the staff and the facilities and the seating and the water; and then grumbling because the place was so crowded. I finished up cleaning out drains, stopped up with the wet people brought in on their shoes and added to the hair and fluff they drop, and the papers, of course – and as the place was so packed, we couldn't wait until it cleared and get the engineer to do the job, so Muggins had to do it. Don't drains *smell*, Mr Bigelow?

On which sweet note I will leave you. Here is a photo from the local paper which doesn't do Audrey justice – she is much prettier, really, and not at all Jewish as this photo makes her look.

Yours most sincerely and dolefully,

Frances W.

BOURNEMOUTH
August 20th 1960

Dear Mr Bigelow,

This week I will really get down to business, and tell you about the wedding. You must know, first of all, that we are having an appalling winter – see, I should have typed 's' for summer, but my fingers automatically went to the more fitting 'w', so I carried on – because winter is just what we have been having, and the temperature rarely goes above 65° which, if not freezing, certainly fits no summer that I know.

The eve of the wedding it was fine and warm. This was the day I did the flowers for the reception, rushing round to 'Fitzharris' immediately after lunch and there finding, to my horror, that the dozen flower vases the caterers had provided were tiddly little glass things capable of holding, say, three roses or seven lilies of the valley, but scarcely adequate for decorating a marquee 60 x 40 feet, the garden (an acre) and four enormous reception rooms. I was forced to use empty jam jars hidden inside shopping baskets; biscuit barrels with the biscuits removed; salad bowls, soup plates, bulb bowls and even large teapots and a pair of silver candelabra!

'Never say "can't be done"' is my motto, and perhaps because of this attitude the flowers did look quite well when I had finished, although not up to my usual standard and a long, long way from satisfying me. This was finished, and the last flower tucked into place, at about 6.40 p.m. when Mac rushed me home, I had a tepid bath, changed, did my face again, and left home at 7.10 p.m. to entertain two uncles and aunts, Mother and Mac, at a dinner party at the Harbour Heights Hotel . . .

Saturday came along very heavy and overcast, and this dullness and stickiness turned into a fine thunderstorm and burst of heavy rain over lunch. Mac's best man, Desmond Pike, was all jittery and I had to sit down and do some mending for half an hour and talk softly with him about life in the Air Force (he's in it, not me) to get him a little nearer normal. Mac was full of beans, dashing here and there for last-minute bits of shopping. I gave them both a stiff whisky before lunch, and nothing else. Then we all changed and showed each other how beautiful we looked, and Mac and Dez went off in Dez's car to the church, and ten minutes later, Mother and I set off in our little car to the Fagans', where we were to transfer to a big Daimler, chauffeur-driven aren't we posh? I knocked my elegant hat off three times getting into the car, and once getting out, so possibly my hair and general appearance was a little flustered, I wouldn't know. I had to take a necktie of Mac's in, and found Audrey and two bridesmaids in the hall, along with Mrs Fagan, one or two guests, Colonel Pritchard (he was giving Audrey away) – and, on running up to the main bedroom with the tie, the last bridesmaid still being tittivated by the dressmaker! I may say this particular bridesmaid is slightly neurotic, and she plainly regarded the whole affair as being designed purely to show her off to her best advantage, so it was only characteristic of her that the bride had to look after herself, while Ruth had to be waited on.

I daresay you have been to one or two weddings in your time, so you know the gen. My brother was so overcome with the seriousness and emotion of the occasion he nearly passed out at the altar, although it was hole-in-the-heart Audrey who had arranged to have a doctor present in case she felt faint – she, I am afraid, did not quite match up to the occasion, for in telling me about it later all she could think of was that she thought her veil was not properly put back and it worried her all through the service – and, in fact, the vicar kept us waiting outside the vestry afterwards so that the newly-weds could have their first few moments alone. And when we did go in, Audrey was busy powdering an already well-powdered nose, and looking a bit cross because her bride-groom had sent the photographer out. Mac feels very strongly that inside a church is not the right place for flashlight photographs, but Audrey felt otherwise. Never mind – she didn't know until it was too late!

Mother was very pretty all in pale pink except for a coffee-coloured little hat with a veil, and coffee-coloured shoes. Her hat had a little veil, and four times during the course of the afternoon I leant over surreptiously and pulled the veil down, and each time Mother crossly pushed it back saying, 'It tickles!' I had made her a large spray of assorted pink roses and carnations, and she had seven or eight rows of pearls in all shades of pink and cream. She really did look sweet: not smart, but just sweet. Audrey looked very pretty, and Mac incredibly handsome in his morning dress – and we even got him to wear his grey topper for one photograph. I looked really elegant, for once – no untidy bits, as I usually have: just a perfectly plain dress that fitted beautifully, in peacock blue; water pearls (they are a pale soft colour, and don't gleam as they have a sort of matt, or velvet surface) with stud earrings to match; long white gloves, black patent leather handbag and black patent leather high-heeled pumps, and, of course, The Hat, which was quite the success of the afternoon, apart from the bride. If I appear in any of the photographs I will try and get a copy to send you, but it's a bit doubtful, as none of the official photographers wanted me in, and I daresay nobody bothered to take a snapshot of just another stray guest, at the reception. Never mind; perhaps I'll get dressed up again and have some-body take a snapshot on my own camera, just for you.

The bride retired at length to change, assisted by one bridesmaid; and the groom retired to change, assisted by two ushers, his best man, and two bottles of champagne. I was pleased to discover that the guests sang to Mac at the reception, and really went to town over it, with harmony and everything! It was a fairly rude song, so I won't publish it to you but it started 'Why were you born so beautiful, why were you born at all?' and perhaps you know the rest. We took elaborate precautions to prevent some of the wilder, younger guests from getting in their cars and chasing the bridal couple as they left, even having arranged to leave the Jaguar hidden in a garage that had two entrances, and Mac and I pushed all the cars concerned right bang up against each other, bumper to bumper, and then locked the two on the outsides, so that until those two were released, none of the others could move an inch. And as it happened, apart from singing again and a few rude shouts and lots of confetti, the minute the taxi pulled away, all these young bloods rushed back – to the champagne! Somebody eventually cleared them off, nobody knows quite how, and they all went around the corner to the tennis club, where they were playing the finals of the men's doubles in the Hampshire County Tournaments. One of the guests marched up to the centre court, shouted, 'Game, Set and Match – that's all folks – clear the court!', and had to be removed slightly by force. He then retired to the clubhouse where he filled his topper with soda-water, put it on, and complained bitterly because he couldn't see through his spectacles. Mrs Fagan retired in tears; Muggins organised hot tea all round for those guests overcome by emotion, and then went off, taking Mother, to wash and go out to dinner again with the uncles, only this time they paid! Very nice dinner in dull surroundings, but as the two uncles left (the others having gone off to their homes immediately after the reception) spent most of their time capping each other's funny stories, the evening went well.

Sunday wasn't too bad, for the relatives came up for coffee and sherry in the morning, and I took Mrs Fagan and the one remaining bridesmaid out for a drive and to tea in the afternoon. The worst time of all for me actually came last Saturday, when I was beginning to feel a little resigned to a solemn dull household. We took Mrs Fagan and Wendy, Audrey's kid sister, out to a little public house in Dorset, where we were meeting the returning honeymooners for a dinner. It was Audrey's birthday, so the giving and receiving of presents and cards, and hearing 'all about it' took up the evening quite well until we came to leave, and Mrs Fagan and Wendy climbed into the big Jaguar with Mac and Audrey, and left Mother and me standing in the drizzle, to come home alone in the Austin, as a sort of symbol of things to come. Mac came home alone, on Sunday, to tea with us and to wash some of his underwear (!) and said casually that he'd be home for dinner on Wednesday. Whether or not he has decided he must have a well-cooked meal now and then, or whether he's just a bit homesick, I don't know. He has been so kind and courteous to me it makes things all the worse . . .

Yours most sincerely,

Frances W.

BOURNEMOUTH
November 12th 1960

Dear Mr Bigelow,

. . . Feeling the beginnings of a monstrous cold on me, I called in at a chemist's shop last evening and asked for 'a box of those 24-hour or 48-hour cold cure capsules, please'. The chemist looked a bit puzzled; opened a drawer under the counter, and was looking, still puzzled, inside, when I put my head over the counter and looked in the drawer as well. There were lots of boxes marked 'Ten Hours Cold Cure'. I said: that was what I wanted, and the silly chemist retorted, 'But these are ten-hour cures!' 'Well, I am not prepared to be fussy, give or take an hour, sir,' said I, and went off to stuff myself with the nasty things. Trouble is, the cure is far worse than the cold, and at the time of writing this, as perhaps you can see from the typing, I don't know whether it's Michaelmas or rice pudding.

Well, it's Thursday today and you have a new President, and no doubt you are furious or depressed about it. It's an odd thing. I am Conservative myself, and that is the party nearest in feelings to your Republican; but I have always sensed a better rapport between our *two* countries when the Democrats have had 'their man' in the White House. This time I am not so pleased, as I cannot help feeling that Mr Kennedy is far too young and inexperienced – not necessarily inexperienced in world history or economics and all that lark, but inexperienced in handling clever, wily, brilliant, awkward, difficult, dangerous or just plain stubborn men, both in his own Government and those of other countries. Of course, I believe the general feeling in England is of some relief, for we were not looking forward to having Mr Cabot Lodge in high office, knowing his dislike of Great Britain. However, as you know, I have only the slightest knowledge of politics on either side of the Atlantic and cannot speak with the least authority on the subject. I like Kennedy's face better than Nixon's (feminine logic!) but dislike the youthful look he still wears. I like my men to look like men, not little boys . . .

As today is my birthday, very many thanks again for the two

delicious parcels. I have already made quite an inroad into the petits-fours, which are as delicious as I remembered them from last year.

See you next week, but look after yourself until I can so adjure you again.

Yours most sincerely,

Frances W.

BOURNEMOUTH
13th December 1960

Dear Mr Bigelow,

. . . Last night we had our end-of-term party at the French conversation class. Quite amusing but a bit childish all round. The men were bringing the wine, the ladies the food, only Mrs Hedges and I protested that two bottles wasn't enough for 16 in the party, so we brought a bottle of Chablis (well, I did) and I took along some cheese-stuffed celery, tiny canapés made with savoury biscuits and pâtés of all sorts; cocktail biscuits and so on, which were a nice change from cream buns and mince pies and sausage rolls. The man who had collected money from his colleagues, having even less knowledge of wine than me, apparently went into a shop and asked for 'three bottles of French wine'. He didn't know they made anything except white wine! He brought with him one bottle very sweet, one medium sweet, and one sweet. As I said, luckily I chose Chablis, dry, and mine came along iced, too, with its own ice lumps in a polythene bag. Somebody else, not knowing the arrangements, brought a bottle of Australian Port type liquid. This made five bottles, and was just about enough! To my horror (quite objective horror because I stuck strictly to Chablis, which I love) the men made their drinks out of all three sweet wines, mixed together! Perhaps it doesn't matter, though – I wouldn't know. I felt terribly sophisticated and blasé, watching the others and listening to absolute bursts of laughter at really childish humour – one of the men went down on his knees to me to implore me to have another glass of wine, and I said

'Now really, I haven't remained a spinster all my life without being quite used to saying No!' and this was the success of the evening, which, to me, isn't a very high standard by any criteria. However, I dislike feeling superior and sophisticated and blasé and looking down my nose, and I wished that, perhaps, I too had mixed my drinks so that the jokes would seem funnier. Never satisfied, me, am I?

. . . Now, in case this letter gets to you in time for Christmas, once again I hope it is a very happy one for you, dear Mr Bigelow, and you start off the New Year with lots of parties, and a new zest for life.

Yours most sincerely,

Frances W.

BOURNEMOUTH
December 31st 1960

Dear Mr Bigelow,

What else happened over Christmas? I read *Bonjour Tristesse* in French, in two evenings except for one or two words, which don't appear in my dictionaries and which, I suspect, would not appear except in the very fullest dictionaries – and then be marked 'Not used in polite society'. Also, started making a new hat in emerald and blue cellophane, which makes me look a bit like a Salvation Army lass only funnier, of course. And used up nearly all the writing paper given me for Christmas in writing to say thank you for my presents. Funny how the supply almost exactly coincides with the demand!

Do not have any worry in the world that my letters should be answered. Rosalind will tell me how you are, and if you get kidnapped and put in hospital again, no doubt the noise will reverberate across the Atlantic and if I don't think it's a thunderstorm, I shall know it's you 'wanting out' in your usual fashion.

And I do hope that you will look forward to, say, April. When the winter will be over and passed, and all the little boats will be hauled up having their bottoms scraped and painted in readiness for the summer.

Rosalind tells me you are always fitter and happier in the autumn, when you have been able to get out and about a bit in the fine warm weather; so please, just sit back and cross the days off the calendar until that fine warmth comes back to warm all our marrow and send us out to watch the birds at close quarters, and to smell the sea and the wind off the marshes.

I was thinking about you the other day, and it occurred to me that it was strange, how very formal we are, one with the other, and yet how deeply I value our friendship. It does not seem to be a friendship as my others are – a familiarity – there is too much distance between us for that, but it is a different kind of friendship and seems to me to be mostly from *my* side anyway, with you very tolerant and forbearing about all my girlish outpourings. Thank you, thank you, for all this understanding, anyway. I don't know, sometimes, what I should do without you.

And now, of course, I can't fill in this last piece of paper with trivialities. Only with a very sincere wish that you will find 1961 a happier year than this one just ending; with a revival of your old spirit and a whole succession of friends calling to see you and take you out when you wish to go, and making life, if a little more restricted than we could wish, fundamentally happier.

Yours most sincerely,

Frances W.

1961

'Lady Bountiful in Poole Park. I always use Yummo Face Cream:
that's how I manage to look 17 when *actually* I am 18½.'

BOURNEMOUTH
January 21st 1961

Dear Mr Bigelow,

At first sight I thought my newly decorated bedroom was going to
be a major disaster, like illegitimate twins, but in the end it turned
out not too badly. Not a success by any means and I still can't imagine
why I chose pink, a colour I detest, for my walls. Ah well. At least, I did
in the end bring about a marriage between the walls and the
ceiling . . . . . . When the walls and ceiling were done, the grey paint on
the picture rail suddenly turned from being grey to being turquoise and
looked absolutely unmentionable. I washed several gallons of pink off
myself and dashed down into town to change the second tin of dark
pink for mushroom. Painted the picture rail mushroom, and the door
pink with mushroom frame. The skirting board, too. And that was as far
as I had got in last week's letter. I left the window frame until Saturday
afternoon. My windows suffer badly from condensation, but before
starting to paint them I wiped them down with a dry rag, to remove the
last of the damp spots; took down the old curtains and the net ones,
which I washed. Painted everything mushroom. Looked quite nice.
Waited three hours, and then put up the net curtains and made and put
up the new green ones. Result – it looked like something in a shop window, and on going to bed that night in my bright pink fluffy nightgown
I felt like something in a shop window, too – say a French pastry . . .

And then Came the Dawn, as alas, it always does. I looked around
me, and thought sleepily, 'Now why can I see those black damp spots
down the centre of the window?' and, when I climbed out of bed, I
noticed that not only could I see the old damp spots, but the paint was
almost grey, and not mushroom as it had been when I went to bed.
On looking with horror, more closely, I found that my nice matt
mushroom paint had run all down the metal parts of the window;
formed little puddles of mushroom paint on the sills, whence it had

been greedily sucked up by the net curtains. Oh, comme j'étais fou! [sic]
That means I was up you in French. Mad, mad, mad. I tore down to
work, where the painters are at work in the hall using the selfsame paint,
and complained bitterly at them. The senior one laughed, the creature,
and said now I knew better than to use a waterpaint on metal work, and,
worse still, to use it while the metal was frosty. I am now waiting for the
spring, when a) we shan't always get frost, and b) we might not always
get condensation either. Whether we shall avoid both at the same time
is another matter, but in the meanwhile I have one strip of grey paint
and the others are mushroom and the curtains are permanently fringed
with brown. Why do these things happen to me, Mr Bigelow? Do you
think it is an evil spirit, a sort of personal gremlin or jinx perhaps? I feel
myself the object of a malicious vendetta, and if only I knew who was
behind it all I'd give 'im something to vend about.

Do you ever get noises in the head, Mr Bigelow? If you do, you
have my heartiest sympathy because I do, too, and a darn nuisance they
are. I remember one night early last summer jumping out of bed about
midnight and hanging out of the window to shout to Edwin Ridout and
tell him to stop revving his wretched motorbike all night outside my
home. Only to find everything was quiet, and it was me all the time.
This eventually passed, but it came back before Christmas and has been
with me, on and off, for about six weeks now. It's a thorough nuisance
at night, when it wakes me up and also prevents me getting to sleep for
a long time. I have tried warm olive oil in the ear; knocking myself on
the side of the head, shaking it, turning over, blowing down my nose
whilst pinching it at the nostrils. Oh, everything but going to see a
quack. At times it even goes on so loudly that during the day it gets
between me and my work (not that it requires anything very thick to do
that) and at home in the evening it is sometimes necessary to turn the
radio on to drown my other row. It wouldn't be so bad if the noise
wasn't so darn *monotonous* . . .

Mac took me to the social and dance that this particular Evening
Institute held last Friday, and as we came away rather before the end I
muttered 'Dit, l'oiseau noir' which is my French for 'Quoth the Raven'.
Trouble was, not enough people knew each other, and there were not
enough masters-of-ceremony to make people get to know each other.

And, of course, the refreshments being cups of tea didn't help the social atmosphere. And Mac was cross, because it was his night out with the lads and he'd given it up to escort me, bless him, and this was what he got – a couple of dances with his sister, and a cup of tea and a bun! He also got in a mix with two very small girls, ages being about seven and eight respectively, whom he drew as partners in a sort of Scottish dance where each man has two ladies as partners. To see Mac going under the arch made by his arm and that of his partner, first on one side and then on the other, was very amusing, and quite the highlight of the evening . . .

It is a glorious sunny day today, and so far, the Jonahs who predicted a cold harsh winter have been eating their words. Looking to my right, on my windowsill is a pot with a blue hyacinth in it, and a pot with red cyclamen, and then a dirty windowpane and then sunshine everywhere, reflecting back from the water and drying the pavements which got soaked, along with me, last night.

And now to say au revoir until next Saturday. I do hope you are obeying my behest, and enjoying life a little bit more. Summer is not far off, as I know from the urgent preparations now going on for our next water show, curse it. In the meantime, stay snug and warm in what I have elsewhere described as your sea-edge home.

Yours most sincerely,

Frances W.

BOURNEMOUTH
January 28th 1961

Dear Mr Bigelow,

Last evening, as I walked across a short section of public gardens, I looked around me, as I wanted some dead twigs on which to rest my artificial flowers, and thus, provide support which would enable me to extend the range of the flowers. I had asked my boss for a bundle of pea sticks, but he complained that as there were no peas in the ground as yet, there would be no pea sticks in the shops, Q.E.D. So, as I said, I kept my eyes open. I was debating whether or not to pick a few then and there and carry them back to my office in the dark, when suddenly a voice said, 'Hallo!' and I looked up about a foot and a half, and there was Tony Hutley, a policeman.

I said, 'Oh, Tony! How you did startle me – what are you doing, prowling around in mufti, it's not fair!' and Tony roared with laughter because I had jumped half a mile.

Just goes to show how careful one should be, when contemplating an illegal step, to have a solicitor handy in case you get caught! As it was, I went over again this morning with my eyelashes curled and asked the head gardener if I might have some twigs, a bundle of pea sticks, and if it was too much trouble for him I could ask one of my men to come over and pick them for me and get arrested for doing so. The head gardener chuckled and said 'Yes, that's about what usually happens. I'll have them sent across for you. Will this morning, a little later on, do?' So I thanked him profusely and went back and started sorting out my flowers. Two hours later, I had been away from my office for a few minutes, and when I opened the door to come back again, the floor was covered with enormous branches of flowering and berried shrubs! Pea sticks, I ask you! What I wanted was a lot of leafless twiggery, because it had to stand in big baskets fastened to the wall about ten foot above the floor. Certainly there is no water available. So now we have enormous bowls of greenery everywhere, and Mr Bond says we look like a dam' Palm Court. (That's what every second- rate little boarding house or hotel calls the place their clients sit in, usually entertained by a two-piece orchestra and the clatter of washing-up coming through the door from the kitchen premises.) So now I shall have to go foraging in the New Forest for my own pea sticks at the weekend, and Mr B. will just have to put up with us looking either like an institution or a Palm Court. His criticism that without the flowers on the walls we looked like the former, I took as a great compliment from him. It is only with such difficulty I can wring compliments out of my boss, so I hasten to report them when I do succeed in getting one.

Tony Hutley – we used to know him as a little boy, and he is an absolute darling of a young man – asked if we still had the Austin, and of course I said no, we had changed it. Tony looked a little odd, and said, 'Yes, I thought I saw your brother the other day driving a Jaguar.' I hastened to tell him that we weren't that mad, the Jaguar being Mrs Fagan's property. 'Well,' said Tony, 'I must say your brother looked the part.' Mac was very pleased when I recounted this, and made a mental note to continue wearing his white silk stock with the Royal Marine crest embroidered on it!

. . . Mother, bless her Jonah-like disposition, is saying each day as I get home and there are no letters for me from anybody, 'I expect Mr Bigelow's ill, dear,' which is nice of her. I prefer to believe you are just miserable and disinclined to write. Besides, you and I know – and Mother doesn't – that I told you not to write. And, as I told you at the time, I mean that. So don't you; just you stay snug and warm indoors until the better weather comes. Wish I could join you – today it is raining in buckets, and blowing a half-hurricane, with the result that the rain is being forced in all the windward windows and we are mopping up every hour on the hour, and the draughts are just whizzing around our necks.

All the moans and groans for this week . . .

Yours most sincerely,

Frances

BOURNEMOUTH
February 2nd 1961

Dear Mr Bigelow,

Although naturally I am intensely sorry that you are ill, in another way I can bring myself quite easily to envy you. All you have to do (it's enough, goodness knows!) is to lie quietly there and do what you are told, and hold fast to my promise that you'll feel much better in the spring – and that's all. You have your every want attended to when the nurses feel like doing it, and all your friends are flocking to see you, and none of them think 'Oh, he's got nothing to do all day, let *him* come and see *me*'; your room probably resembles Westminster Hall when the monthly exhibition of the Royal Horticultural Society is 'on', and that funny smell is probably the mixed outcome of daffodils, roses, violets, hyacinths, and nasty medicine.

All this attitude of mine is a part of my lifelong envy of very small babies lording it in perambulators. Or, as you so comically say, 'baby carriages'. Not entirely lifelong, for no doubt I disliked it intensely when I was stuck in one myself. But looking back at those innocent days, what a great pity it is that we cannot appreciate how coddled and 'babied' we are, when we are; for all too soon we have to start and fend for ourselves, even if it is only warding off the blows of our larger siblings, to prepare us for the battle of Wall Street, or fighting the kitchen stove or whatever forms the major cause of warfare in our adult life . . .

Tonight (it's midday Thursday at the moment) is the crucial night, when I shall know whether or not Mr Peet has corrected the French in my essay on you. If he hasn't, I have arranged a sheet anchor. Last night after the Wednesday class I helped Mrs Noble on with her coat, and she protested, so I said blandly that I wished to ask a favour of her and was just softening her up. So she said what favour? and I told her about the uncorrected essay, and please, if Mr Peet hadn't done it tonight, could I bring it around to her house over the weekend and get her help because it just had to be sent off by Tuesday, and even then, would cost a mint of money in airmail postage because it had been held up so long. She was delighted, bless her. Asked if I could come either after 10.30 a.m., on Saturday, when she would have been out and done the shopping and done her washing at the launderette and be home again cooking the Sunday dinner 'which we always have on Saturday'. Or, as she goes to the Reference Library to check up on details of lessons for the following week, on Saturday afternoon, I could come at six o'clock in the evening, and although she couldn't ask me to have tea, she could ask me to have a drink. All this when I was the one asking the favour! Poor dear – she is a widow with two now-almost-grown-up children whom she keeps by teaching languages. It's pretty hard going to earn a living and run a home at the same time, and do the shopping and the washing, let along undertake to correct 2,000 French word essays that get suddenly thrust at one!

My brother is in the doghouse again. If you went through that box of letters from me, no doubt you could tell me how many times he's been there during the past twelve years, but I can save you a lot of bother by saying it is x to the nth degree and no strange abode for him. This time he's there because the arrangement was I had the car last weekend. Well, I went around to his home at six o'clock Saturday and he wanted it, so he had it and promised to drop it off chez-moi at nine in the morning, on his way to the golf. At 10.30 a.m. on Sunday morning Audrey 'phoned and said he'd gone to golf but not bothered to stop in, as he had used his car all the way. He would come in at one o'clock on his way home and I could have it then. At 1.30 he telephoned to say he'd played golf and now he was playing snooker and would I please telephone Audrey and say he'd be home at 2.40, after leaving the car with me at 2.30 if I wanted it. I said yes, I did want it. Well, Mr B. at 4.10 p.m. I caught a bus . . . . . . Of course, I could not then do all the visits I had intended doing between nine o'clock in the morning and six at night. So into the doghouse it is for Master Frank MacPherson, and as a result I am getting the evening use of the car this week whenever I want it and sometimes when I don't, and I am to be taken next Wednesday to see Frankie Vaughan at the theatre. I cannot bear Frankie Vaughan, but who am I to say no when invited out by a penitent brother?

Oh joy! Last night I had the car to go to French class, while Mac stayed at home with Mother after having had dinner with us. I am always late home from this class, which goes on until 9.30 p.m. anyway (the other stops dead on nine) and last night I ran three other students home, and waited while some baby-sitters got ready, and then took them on my way home. So it was ten before I reached R— Drive, and Mac had been pacing up and down the sitting room, coated and ready, for half an hour, and Mother was almost in hysterics, he had been so infuriating! He didn't dare say anything to me, after the Sunday business, so I felt very pleased this morning when Mother complained at her suffering through my tardiness, and feel I have had my revenge a little bit. It made me wonder what he would be like, had he to wait from 9 a.m. until 4.30 p.m. for the car one Sunday.

Well, Mr Peet turned up complete with corrected essay on one Commodore B. last night. Whether he just didn't have anything to say, or whether the shock of reading it rendered him speechless, I don't know; but he just marched up to my desk, gave me a meaningful look (but what meaning I could not interpret) and plumped the manuscript in front of me. So by Monday it will be typed out, put into the hard covers along with the others and some illustrations, and posted to Rosalind for a birthday present. And, of course, knowing my sort of luck, she will have flown east to see you and not be there on the date. Never mind, it will be something for her when she gets back again after seeing you on your feet again.

Today there is a little wind and the sun is blazing down. As a result of a storm yesterday, the sea is still a bit 'swelly' and the great rollers are coming in as though drawn with a ruler – there is a strong line of shadow down the trough all the way from the end of the pier to Bolson's Jetty, a couple of hundred yards to the east; then, after this great clean-cut shadow has rolled shorewards a little, the breeze gently takes the tip and breaks it into a lacy foam, and then the whole thing gives up and comes crashing down in blue-white surf. I could watch it all morning. And I hope that you are able to watch your own bit of ocean, or bay, from your window and smell the salt air as your waves come rolling in.

Oh, thank you Mr Bigelow for *Reader's Digest*. It came one day this week, and I was very pleased because at first, not being able to decipher the date stamp, I thought you must be better already to have posted it on the 16th January. But then I got out a magnifying glass, and found it was the 16th December, and it had just taken a very long time to come. Never mind, I am hoping for good news from Rosalind in a few days now.

In the meantime, I shan't tire you, nor whoever is having to read this to you (if somebody does have to) but will get it under way quickly, and write to you another, shorter letter on Monday to wish you well again. And you know that if wishes were magic potions, you'd be out of doors right now tinkering with the bird table or feeder, or just shooing away some marauding squirrels. But I do hope you *are* better. Please do be.

Yours most sincerely,

Frances

BOURNEMOUTH
February 11th 1961

Dear, dear Mr Bigelow,

Today it is so warm somebody (and I could hazard a guess who it was, too) has turned off the central heating, at least in my office. And I don't need it, either; that's how warm it is.

No doubt it is warm in your room in Bellport, but possibly from central heating and not from sun, although I most sincerely hope that even if the snow is still thick on the ground, the sun is shining on it and making life a bit better looking for you all; especially for you. I am sure it looks better to you, with Rosalind round to protect you from the nurses and doctors, and I am certain that between the two of you, you will get them hang-tied, outslung and snaffled very smartly. If those expressions aren't quite correct, blame my upbringing – I was brought up on fairy stories and not on Westerns so I don't know the jargon.

At French class last night somebody read out a little essay on the art of writing letters, which gave rise to a fairly heated discussion on that art, mainly between the teacher and me. In English, naturally; I cannot yet be heated in French, and anyway, as I know from hard experience, when I speak in French only the teacher understands me and to have a private discussion in front of the whole class would have been rude. So we battled in English, and oh Mr Bigelow I felt very much in need of your support, that I did, because it would appear that I break every rule for letter-writing that has yet been invented. Or that Mr Peet feels should be obeyed. And naturally, being me and modest, I could not say that I write interesting and amusing letters, and I wanted somebody to come along and say it for me, to squash the creature for suggesting that my methods were all wrong. I think we were really arguing about the opposite sides of the same coin, but I claimed that it was the spirit that counted and not the elegance of style, or handwriting, nor the excellence of paper nor the highfalutin moral tone; it was the character and feelings of the writer which had to be put across, so that the person writing the letter came in through the letter box with his letter. And the teacher kept on that it was an insult to use a ballpoint with which to

write a letter, and silly little man-made rules of that ilk. I daresay it's
the nature of the beast – no schoolteacher can avoid having his eye so
closely glued to the bark of the tree, looking for boll- weevils, that he
cannot possibly see the copse, let alone the wood or the forest.

Anyway, we finished up probably not at all impressed by each other's
argument, but it gave me to think, and it gave me a long paragraph for
this letter, and encouraged the stubborn side of my character to try even
harder to ensure that my personality came to you with this letter. Last
time I sent you a letter I asked you to imagine it was a bunch of flowers,
with sweet perfume to sooth your distress and bring you thoughts of
spring. This time will you please try even harder, and imagine I am
visiting you. And, being modest again, I am darn good at visiting the
sick, I can assure you, so would you please oblige me by feeling much
better when this is finished and I have gone away again?

When I come in through the door, that being my usual means of
egress, I am not sure whether you will be surprised or not; whether you
have imagined me as being tall or short. And being sort of
in-between (five foot five) I daresay the clothes I am wearing at the time
will largely influence you, for we all look different at times, and sometimes I imagine myself short and stubby, and sometimes (not often, alas)
tall and willowy. I think I shall be tall and willowy on your behalf, so here
I am, wafting in through the door and giving you a No. 1 beam, and a
nasty jolt as I sit down bang on your feet.

So there we are; you propped up on your pillows in your
four-poster, looking very patriarchal and ducal (if that does not offend
your republican sensibilities) and me, all over willowy-like and having a
hard time of it, too, what with sciatica and that lot stiffening up the
spine. You know what I look like; dark and a bit hollow-cheeked, and
I know what you look like; especially now as I spent hours recently
drawing your face this way and that, over and over again, as
illustrations for the book of essays. So we need no introductions, and get
right down to talking.

Which is going to be difficult, because apparently people find it hard
to understand what I am saying. Perhaps just for the occasion I can put
on an act, and become as Dame Edith Evans, audible globally, like
Christmas bells. You don't mind if it's not really 'me'? Just that once.

Normally I talk very, very fast, and my words get jumbled up as they come out; sometimes I change my mind about what I am going to say, with the words all in my mouth on the point of coming off my tongue, and then the resulting mix-up is really awesome and people think I'm speaking Swahili. I hope they do; I should hate them to think that was the way I speak our beautiful English. But today I am talking very slowly and graciously and every word is coming off like a pearl; at least until we get going in our talk, and then I shall forget and the pace will become hotter and hotter until you cry for mercy. So then we shall stop and have a cup of coffee, or one of your punches, perhaps – only four bottles of whisky in it for me, please; I have a weak head.

And after that pause for refreshments you will get out your snapshots to show me; the ones of your wonderful dog, and those of all his successors; those of Rosalind as a little girl sans front teeth but with such an engaging grin, as all children seem to have at that particular age. I am quite sure you will do this – show me your snapshots – because it is inevitable when I visit somebody who is ill. Even when, as did once happen, I have something wrong with an eye and arrive with a black patch over it and the other watering like an English summer, in sympathy, I never *have* got out of seeing the invalid's snapshots. They are so often of the 'this is one of me, only the sun got in the camera lens' type, but I shall expect better of yours, so if you move the camera about when taking photographs, you'd better tuck those results hurriedly under your pillow, so as not to disillusion me about your skill.

Then, having gone through those, I shall get up and prowl rudely about your room, looking at your pictures and antiques and the view out of the windows. Shall probably pause by the windows to report to you on what is going on outside, so perhaps you will send word out before I arrive to have the bay full of scootering sailors careering around so that I can find something to describe to you other than the gyrations of your birds just outside the glass.

And then, of course, your nurse or your housekeeper or even Rosalind (though I would have thought better of *her*) will come in and say I am not to tire you out and it's time for you to take your pills, or have a nap or something equally tedious, and they will sweep me out along with the tray of dirty cups or glasses and let you rest again and gather strength so that when my next visit comes along, through the letter box with a faint 'plop' on the mat, you will be waiting to open and read it for yourself out of sheer curiosity as to what on earth I shall manage to think about for my next Saturday Special.

And in the hope that you will now rest and do as I pray, I bid you a fond au revoir, dear Commodore, with all my wishes for your contentment.

Yours most sincerely,

Frances

Postscript

Years after Commodore Bigelow's death I did pay another visit to America and, with his lovely daughter Rosalind, spent two nights in the Bellport House. Mr Bigelow's daughter-in-law, Stephanie, gave a cocktail party so that I could meet all his old friends and neighbours. It was the weirdest cocktail party in my life – me, 3,000 miles from home, every single guest a complete stranger to me – and they all knew me intimately! I have fondly decided that his neighbours came visiting to hear Mr Bigelow read the latest episodes in the Bournemouth Soap Opera, so perhaps I can believe that the letters did achieve their aim of relieving his loneliness.

FNW